Market Abuse and Insider Dealing

Market Abuse and Insider Dealing

2nd Edition

By

Professor Barry Rider
Counsel, Bryan Cave LLP

Dr. Kern Alexander
Director of Research in Financial Regulation
The Centre for Financial Analysis and Policy
University of Cambridge

Lisa Linklater
Barrister
Chancery House Chambers
Leeds

Stuart Bazley
General Counsel, City Equities Ltd

Tottel
publishing

Tottel Publishing Ltd
Maxwelton House
41–43 Boltro Road
Haywards Heath
West Sussex
RH16 1BJ

© Tottel Publishing Ltd 2009

British Library Cataloguing-in-Publication Data

A CIP Catalogue record for this book is available from the British Library.

ISBN 978 1 84766 135 7

Typeset by Columns Design Ltd, Reading

Printed in Great Britain by Athenaeum Press Ltd., Gateshead, Tyne & Wear

About the authors

Professor Barry Rider is Counsel to the international law firm Bryan Cave LLP. He has taught law in the University of Cambridge since 1976. He has held many senior academic appointments including Director of the Institute of Advanced Legal Studies, University of London. He holds doctorates in law from the University of Cambridge, University of London, University of the Free State in South Africa and Penn State University (Dickinson Law School) in the USA. Professor Rider has also served as a civil servant responsible for a special intelligence and mutual assistance unit within an intergovernmental organisation and has been seconded and served as a consultant to many governmental agencies around the world, including the Supreme Peoples' Procuratorate of China. He is currently a consultant to the Islamic Financial Services Board and has worked for the IMF, EU, UN and Commonwealth Secretariat. He is the author of many books and other publications on financial law, economic crime and corporate law.

Dr. Kern Alexander is Director of Research in Financial Regulation at the Centre for Financial Analysis and Policy at the University of Cambridge and is Reader in Law and Finance and Head of the Banking and Financial Law programme at the School of Law, Queen Mary College, University of London. He advises the European Parliament's Economic and Monetary Affairs Committee on banking and capital market regulation and has given oral and written evidence before the Committee on financial regulation issues that relate to the credit crisis. In 2007, he co-authored a highly regarded commissioned report by the EU Parliament on reform of European financial regulation and crisis management entitled: 'Financial Supervision and Crisis Management in the EU'. He is presently serving as a technical assistant adviser to the European Commission on the implementation of the Capital Requirements Directive and the Market Abuse Directive. He also advises the Chinese Banking Regulatory Commission on Basel II implementation and related capital market issues.

Lisa Linklater graduated with an MA in law from Jesus College, University of Cambridge. She was called to the Bar of England and Wales in 1995 and has practised as a barrister from Chancery House Chambers, Leeds since 1996; her practice includes advice and litigation on financial services. Lisa was appointed Junior Counsel to the Crown in 2000, being re-appointed to that position in 2007; she has conducted a wide variety of litigation for different Government departments in that capacity. In addition, Lisa is a CEDR accredited mediator. She lives with her family in Yorkshire.

Stuart Bazley is General Counsel at City Equities Ltd. He took both a bachelors and masters degree in law from the University of London and was called to the Bar of England and Wales in 1991. He has worked in the financial services industry for over 25 years – in business operations, as a management consultant and as an in-house lawyer. He is the former head of regulatory consulting at Momenta where he specialised in the management of compliance remediation projects. He is also the former head of the legal and compliance functions for Edward Jones in the UK and the UK business of Irish Life. Stuart has lectured and written extensively on financial services regulation and enforcement, including *Bazley and Haynes on Financial Services Authority Regulation and Risk-based Compliance* 2nd edition, published by Tottel in 2006. He is currently undertaking doctoral research into Market Abuse enforcement at the Institute of Advanced Legal Studies, University of London.

Preface

Concern about the harm to confidence in the integrity of the markets caused by those who take advantage of privileged information in their own dealings is nothing new. Indeed, it is not only in our own time that the markets and financial system has been traumatised by a crisis of confidence. Some of the earliest laws relating to trade outlaw attempts to artificially interfere with the proper function of the markets and ensure their fairness. While having better information and being better able to use it are factors which in most societies are considered not only acceptable but commendable, others come into play when the information in question could not have been obtained by the most diligent competitor or counterparty and, indeed, the information was taken in a manner or from a source that others would consider to be unfair. Those who appropriate for their own, or for that matter another's benefit, information belonging to someone else, have an unfair advantage and no matter whether as a matter of logic, let alone traditional legal analysis, this can reasonably be expected to justify remedies, it brings the fairness of the market as a whole into disrepute. It is the concern to promote and preserve public confidence in the expectation of fair dealing in the markets that has, at least in Britain, justified our attempts to control the abuse of inside information. Of course, in recent years the influence of various initiatives within the European Union has resulted in a wider concern to address the taking advantage of asymmetric access to information even where such has not been appropriated or misused.

The law that has developed to address these issues in a prohibitive and remedial manner is both complex and multi-layered. While the criminal law is most found in statute, the law relating to market abuse operates in what is to English jurisprudence a relatively new world between criminal law and the civil law. The specific laws and regulatory provisions also function within the context of the general law and other structures of regulation ranging from the Code on Takeovers and Mergers to in-firm compliance systems. The range of potential legal and regulatory responses to even a simple case of insider dealing is both complex and often uncertain. The perception that insider abuse is still a major issue in most markets and the traditional approach of the criminal law has not served as a significant deterrent and has led regulators such as the Financial Services Authority and the US Securities and Exchange Commission renewing their commitment to 'stamp out' insider dealing by whatever means are at their lawful disposal. Consequently it is important to consider the control of insider trading and related abuses in the rather wider context of financial crime and therefore in this edition we have addressed in more depth issues such as the new fraud law and money laundering.

There is another important dimension that this new edition seeks to focus upon. Earlier discussions of insider dealing law have understandably tended to concentrate on the legal and regulatory liabilities of those who engage in the abuse of inside information. However, today as in the case of money laundering, the impact of the law and especially the regulatory system is in practice rather greater for those who find themselves, innocently or otherwise, as facilitators of objectionable transactions. A serious and very real responsibility has been cast on financial intermediaries and professional advisers to assist in the maintenance of integrity in the markets. In the real world an authorised person and individuals such as those engaged in compliance, are more likely to find themselves subject to legal and regulatory sanctions than those who actually engage in the abuse of inside information or for that matter who engage in other profitable crimes. The obligations that anti-money laundering laws, anti-insider dealing regulations and increasingly anti-corruption laws impose on those who handle other people's financial transactions to conduct due diligence and operate effective controls to discourage and expose such activity are onerous and well policed. Therefore, the control of insider dealing and related abuses is a very real and topical concern for all those who operate in the financial sector. In this new edition we give particular emphasis to this and address in detail the role and responsibilities of compliance.

As we have seen only too well with the financial chaos stemming in part from the failure of banks to operate effective risk control systems, all financial markets are to a greater or lesser degree inter-dependent. Consequently, the laws and systems of one jurisdiction cannot be considered in isolation. Those engaged in objectionable or even merely facilitative activities may well be subject to the reach of other regulatory and legal systems. Most significantly in practical terms is the long arm reach of US securities law and in particular the concern of the US Securities and Exchange Commission to protect the integrity of its own national markets. Indeed, the criticism that has been made of the failure of the SEC to prevent and adequately control a series of recent scandals makes it more likely that it will adopt an even more robust enforcement stance. Therefore this edition attempts where relevant to address the legal and regulatory issues that may arise when other jurisdictions and in particular the USA seek to assert their authority.

The authors have attempted to draw upon their unique combination of expertise and practical experience in presenting in a clear and constructive manner an admittedly complex and dramatic body of law and regulation. In doing so they have had the benefit of advice from many involved in the day to day administration of the relevant law and in particular compliance systems. It would be invidious to name particular individuals who have been of such assistance, but their advice and support has always been much appreciated, albeit not always taken as gospel! The advice, however, of our publisher Mr Andy Hill, on the other hand is sacrosanct.

Professor Barry Rider

Dr. Kern Alexander

Ms Lisa Linklater

Mr Stuart Bazley

January 2009

Contents

Contents

Table of cases

S

Table of statutes

Chapter 1

The nature of insider dealing and market abuse

INSIDER DEALING IN PERSPECTIVE

1.1   The commonly held view is that insider dealing is a problem of the twentieth century and, more specifically, the last quarter of the century. It is certainly the case that, over the last 35 years, there has been considerable interest in the topic in many countries. The media and, in particular, the press regularly carry stories of those in positions of trust taking advantage of price-sensitive information to further their own interests. Most jurisdictions have in recent years enacted legislation specifically to deal with the problem of directors and officers of companies taking advantage of information that they receive by virtue of their privileged positions by dealing in their company's securities. Insider dealing is not, of course, confined to those holding office in a company and many regulatory systems impose prohibitions on anyone who acquires such information with knowledge that it is from a privileged source. On the other hand, despite the amount of law that has been created, there is considerable scepticism as to whether it does provide sufficient protection for investors and the markets.

1.2   In fact, the problem of insiders abusing information that they obtain by virtue of the special relationship that they have with their company is not a new one. It is possible to find references to insiders taking advantage of their privileged position to dump over-valued securities on the market in official reports as early as the seventeenth century.[1] Furthermore, the taking advantage of privileged information or, at least, information that the other party could not obtain, is as old as human nature. While history may not record examples of the abuse of such information on securities markets, there are countless examples from many countries of people profiting in one way or another from such information. Indeed, in many cultures, no opprobrium necessarily attached to such conduct and in some it would have been regarded inopportune, if not ungracious, not to have utilised the advantage in question. It is still the case that very few jurisdictions seek to impose constraints, let alone legal prohibitions, on the use of privileged knowledge in dealings other than in securities.

---

1   See, for example, B Rider, C Abrams and M Ashe, *Guide to Financial Services Regulation* (3rd ed, 1997, CCH) at Chapter 1; B Rider and H Ffrench, *The Regulation of Insider Trading* (1979 Macmillan) and, in particular, House of Commons Journals, 20 November 1697 and G Gilligan, *Regulating the Financial Services Sector* (1999, Kluwer) Chapter 4.

1.3   While most systems of law do, to some degree, protect the confidentiality of information, they do not necessarily interfere in transactions with third parties who have been disadvantaged by the use of information obtained in breach of a duty of confidentiality. Few legal systems go anywhere near imposing an obligation on someone in possession of superior information to disclose this to another contracting party. Even when that other party could not have obtained the same information even with the greatest diligence, in most jurisdictions there will be no duty to disclose or warn him. To require equality of information in such circumstances would undermine any incentive that a person would otherwise have to conduct research or acquire material information. Regarding decisions relating to the disposal of property and the conduct of commerce, it is necessary to have the best information that is available and therefore the acquisition of superior information should not be discouraged, let alone penalised.

1.4   Why should we, therefore, be concerned when such transactions occur in regard to intangible property and, in particular, in securities of public companies? Of course, the development of corporate enterprise has necessitated that we look at our ordinary laws and their application to new areas. While it is convenient for us to attribute a legal personality to the corporation for a variety of sensible and important reasons, this legal fiction inevitably gives rise to implications for those who deal with, or are involved in, the enterprise. For example, the corporation is interposed between the shareholders and the enterprise's property. In the vast majority of legal systems, shareholders do not own the company's property. It is only the company as a separate legal person that owns its assets. The shareholders' property is confined to their 'share' in the enterprise. The value of this 'share' will depend on many things, albeit most significantly, the value of the enterprise's assets and the productivity of their use. The important thing to note, however, is that we are not dealing with absolutes and value in this context will be determined by what another is willing to pay or exchange for the share in question. Of course, when we consider the value of other securities such as bonds and derivatives, the relationship with quantifiable and assessable property becomes even more remote. It is clear, therefore, that, in determining the value of securities, knowledge of events that are likely to affect the decision of others as to whether to acquire or dispose of ownership and upon what terms, plays a much greater role than in regard to many other forms of wealth. It is also clear that there will be persons who, by virtue of their position in or in relation to the enterprise, will be in a very privileged position in obtaining and assessing price-relevant information. Thus, quite early on in the development of the common law, obligations were cast upon those responsible for issuing new securities and, in particular, shares, to ensure fair and adequate disclosure of all material information relating to the enterprise and not to take advantage of their privileged position. In most jurisdictions today, such obligations have been placed on a statutory footing.[1]

1   See, for example, the Financial Services and Markets Act 2000, Pt VI.

1.5   Where such insiders deal in the market in the securities of the issuer with which they enjoy this privileged access to its information, it is not difficult to see why many consider they should be held to similar responsibilities. While the situation is not quite the same as when the issuer itself offers securities of unknown value to the market, in the perception of those in the market, the dissimilarity is not fundamental. Those in a position of stewardship over the company's enterprise are taking advantage of their position to derive profit that is taken at the expense of those in the market. Given the conceptual and practical difficulties in fitting this sort of conduct within the scope of traditional civil or criminal causes of action, it is hardly surprising that most countries have enacted legislation specifically prohibiting those in possession of inside information from taking advantage of it. Indeed, in most systems, the prohibitions extend somewhat further than to those who would ordinarily be considered to occupy positions of trust within a company. While the unfairness of such misconduct more than justifies the intervention of the law to discourage abuse, it does not necessarily justify the development of remedies for those who happen to transact with an insider.[1] Obviously, in practical if not legal terms, there are considerable differences between the matching of parties to a particular transaction, on or off the market.

1   For further discussion on this see B Rider 'Insider Trading – A Crime of our times?' *Current Legal Problems, Current Developments in Banking and Finance Laws* (D Kingsford Smith ed) (Stevens 1989); B Rider 'The Control of Insider Trading – Smoke and Mirrors!' 1 *International and Comprative Corporate Law Journal* (1999) 271 and B Rider 'Civilising the Law – The use of Civil and Administartive Proceedings to enforce Financial Services Law' 3 *Journal of Financial Crime* (1995) 11.

1.6   In the result, the regulation of insider dealing has and will no doubt continue to throw up a host of issues that would not ordinarily be encountered in the control of other anti-social conduct. The sophistication of the financial environment within which the law and regulatory mechanisms operate, compounds the practical and legal difficulties confronting those seeking to administer and apply the law. While the control of insider abuse has much in common with the prevention and interdiction of money laundering and even corruption, the crafting of legislation and the development of supporting regulatory mechanisms involve issues of peculiar complexity and sensitivity. Despite these problems, the efficacy of anti-insider dealing regulation has, in many countries, become almost a litmus test for the efficiency and competence of the wider regulatory structure overseeing the markets and the conduct of business in the financial sector.

1.7   Consequently, in practical and political terms, the control of insider abuse is a significant issue. While the various philosophical justifications for regulation may be argued about, it is the case that in many countries it is now recognised that the presence of such laws is required if investor confidence in the integrity of the markets is to be preserved and promoted. From perhaps a somewhat cynical perspective, it matters little if such empirical evidence as there is, is equivocal as to the extent of the problem of insider dealing and the harm it occasions. If enough people think it occurs and for whatever reason, including jealousy, consider this is unfair, confidence in the reputation and therefore the efficiency of the market will be eroded. Consequently, those who are responsible for the protection of the markets have a responsibility to act. Whether this is through the medium of the criminal law or some other mechanism, it is in the 'public good' that it be seen that insider dealing is not condoned.

WHAT IS INSIDER DEALING?

The classic case

1.8   The classic example that is often given of insider dealing is where a director of a company learns in a board meeting that his company's profit forecasts are about to be revised to a significant extent and then goes onto the stock market and trades on the basis of this information before it is made publicly available. In such circumstances, he has clearly taken advantage of his position and the information that came to him by virtue of his seat on the board. He has manifestly misused the confidential information that was entrusted to him in the proper performance of his duties as a director or, in the words of US federal law, misappropriated it. It would also be generally regarded as falling within the notion of insider dealing if he persuaded another person to deal in the securities of his company or disclosed the information to a third person knowing that he would be likely so to deal or otherwise misuse the information.

1.9   It is accepted that this notion of insider dealing would extend to the misuse of confidential information to avoid a loss as well as to make a profit. It matters not whether the director takes advantage of the information to buy more securities in his company in the expectation that their price will rise on publication of the information or whether he sells securities in the fear that the market price will decline. It should, however, be noted that the law might not always offer a remedy or sanction in the latter case. It requires a degree of sophistication that is not always found in the law, to regard a loss avoided as a profit, which should be rendered accountable to the company.

Other primary insiders

1.10   It is not, of course, only company directors that will in the ordinary course of their duties acquire price-sensitive information. Indeed, it is probably more likely that in most companies there are many other insiders who will come into possession of such information rather more regularly than the directors. Having regard to the obvious relationship that a director has to his company, it remains to be seen whether such persons would be rash enough to risk exposure to public criticism by engaging in insider dealing. Furthermore, it cannot be taken for granted that most company directors would be willing to risk their position and the financial and other benefits that arise as a result of their office by engaging in abusive deals.

1.11   The notion of insider dealing is broad enough to encompass all those who, by virtue of their position in the company or who, by their business or professional relationship with the company, are likely to have access to privileged information. For the sake of convenience, it is perhaps useful to describe such persons as primary insiders. They are all subject to the common denominator of enjoying a special relationship with the company that gives them access to the price-sensitive information in question. Indeed, in US jurisprudence, they have often been referred to as 'access insiders'. Debate has taken place as to whether those who obtain such information in breach of their duties attaching to the relationship in question should be regarded as primary insiders. For example, is it appropriate to regard an office cleaner, who, while having access to a company's premises by virtue of her employment directly or indirectly with the company, obtains price-sensitive information by rummaging in the rubbish bins, as a primary insider? Although it is arguable that all those who abuse price-sensitive information should be sanctioned, for the sake of convenience in drafting rules and laws, most jurisdictions distinguish between those who obtain such information in the proper and lawful exercise of the duties attaching to the relationship that they have with the relevant company and those who do so essentially outside the scope of those responsibilities.

1.12   In practice, it is usual to throw the net rather wider and regard primary insiders as insiders, not only of the company with whom they are in this relationship, but also issuers that are closely related to it and to other issuers, such as a potential offeree company. Thus, it will be considered to be insider dealing when a director of a company, having learnt that his company intends to make an attractive takeover offer for the shares of another company, acquires shares in that other company before the offer is announced.

Secondary insiders

1.13   It is also considered to be insider dealing when a person, while not in an access relationship to the issuer, acquires the relevant information in circumstances where he knows that it is unpublished price-sensitive information and comes from an insider source and then deals or encourages another to deal. Thus, although the office cleaner in the example referred to above might not be considered to be a primary insider, her abuse of the information obtained from what she appreciates is an 'inside source', would generally be considered to amount to insider trading. In some cases, it will even be considered objectionable for this tippee or secondary insider to pass the information on to yet another person in circumstances where they know or should appreciate that the information is likely to be misused.

Inside source

1.14   The law and, indeed, morality in most societies, therefore necessitates proof of a relationship between the source of the information and the person who is to be accused of insider dealing. The price-sensitive information must be obtained by virtue of this relationship. It is the relationship that taints it and renders improper its use for personal benefit. Of course, the notion of relationship is stretched far beyond what the law would normally consider to be relationships of a fiduciary quality or, for that matter, necessarily giving rise to a duty of confidentiality. The extent to which it is necessary to establish that the relevant information is obtained by virtue of the privileged access that the relationship gives to the person concerned is a matter for debate. Logically, if the information can be shown to have been obtained from some other and outside source, then its use by a person who is clearly in a special relationship with the company should not be considered to be insider dealing. However, in most systems of law, there will be a 'presumption' that if a primary insider is in possession of price-sensitive information in regard to the securities of the issuer with which he has an access relationship, then the 'inside information' was obtained pursuant to this relationship.

Inside information

1.15   Information is a very vague and ill-defined concept in most legal systems. However, in the context of insider dealing, it is generally not necessary to refine a definition that does more than indicate that it possesses a quality sufficient to influence the decision of the person who has access to it to deal in particular securities. In other words, the information that the person accused of insider dealing has in his possession must be such as would influence his decision to buy or sell. In the UK, as in most legal systems, it is enough if the information would influence the mind of a person who would be likely to deal in the relevant securities. Thus, materiality is objective and is determined by reference to the particular class or group of investors that would ordinarily be likely to deal in the securities in question. This gives the test of materiality sufficient flexibility to accommodate narrow and highly specialised markets. The more specific and precise the information is, the more likely it is that it will influence the mind of a reasonable person.

1.16   Some systems of regulation seek to define materiality not so much in terms of the impact on the investor, but on the market. Obviously, the more significant the impact that the information once disclosed is likely to have on the price of the securities, the more influential it will be on the mind of an investor. On the other hand, tests that focus on whether the information is likely to affect the decision of an investor encompass not only the relevance of price, but also other market factors. Generally speaking, it is enough to establish materiality of information that it would be a factor in taking a decision; it need not be the determinant or an especially significant factor.

1.17   The information must be inside information. In other words, it must have a quality which ties it to the issuer in whose securities the dealing takes place. We have already discussed this issue in terms of the relationship that the person accused of insider dealing must have, directly or indirectly, with the source of the information. Obviously, relevance will be bound up with materiality in most conceivable cases. The information need not be generated within, by or for the benefit of the issuer in whose securities the dealing takes place. For example, it would be objectionable for a director of a company which intends to make an attractive takeover offer for the securities of another company to deal in the securities of that other company on the basis of this knowledge. The information in such a case may be regarded as being inside information obtained through his insider nexus with his company, but its relevance is to the market in that other issuer's securities.

1.18   While the information involved in most cases of insider abuse will be confidential or at least obtained in a relationship that might be expected to give rise to obligations of confidentiality, it is not always that the information will be such that could be protected as 'confidential' information. Indeed, there will be cases where the information is too tentative to be protected as proprietary information, but which would still meet the test of materiality. It is also the case that there will be situations when the information is not confidential to a particular person or entity. In the result, it is clear that inside information is not always confidential information. Of course, in the United States, the courts have fashioned the so-called 'misappropriation theory' to justify liability for insider dealing. This approach sanctions the 'misappropriation' of information that belongs to another person. Dealing on the basis of such information will constitute a misappropriation, as will improperly disclosing it to another in circumstances where that other utilises it. The notion that information belongs to another person who will often obtain the same by the inside source is a difficult one for many legal systems. For example, while many legal systems are prepared to protect confidential information as if it were a form of property, not all by any means consider information capable of being a species of property.[1]

1   See, for example, *Oxford v Moss* (1978) 68 Cr App R 183, in which it was held information was not property for the purpose of the law of theft. And see **6.43**.

1.19   Inside information has sometimes been described as 'privileged' information. In the legal sense, privileged information is a concept even narrower than that of confidential information. Consequently, it is preferable to contemplate the notion of privilege, as referring to the circumstances in which it is acquired, rather than the information itself. Where a person in a special relationship or an access relationship acquires information by virtue of his position, then his access may be described as having been made possible in privileged circumstances. To describe, however, inside information as being privileged information in the traditionally accepted legal sense of the word is misleading.

1.20   The information to be inside information must not be in the public domain. Obviously, the value of the information to the person who deals upon it is that it is not publicly available. While it is not necessary for the information to be secret in the sense of being confidential, as we have seen, it must not be accessible to those who could ordinarily be expected to deal in the relevant securities. Many regulatory systems provide that the information should, at the time of its misuse, be unpublished. Much will therefore depend upon what publication means in this context. At one end of the spectrum, if information has been released into the public domain through a press announcement or a regulatory disclosure, then it ceases to be inside information. On the other hand, what if the company is prepared to make the information available only to analysts or other market professionals, possibly on a selective basis? The nature of the market and the sophistication of the financial environment within which the disclosure takes place will inevitably bear upon the question whether the information has been sufficiently published or not.

1.21   It is the case, however, that in most jurisdictions including the UK, provided that the information is freely available to those who would be likely to deal in the relevant securities, there is adequate public disclosure. It has been argued that the fact that the information is publicly available does not entitle those who had pre-publication knowledge to deal before there is an opportunity for the information to be adequately disseminated and even 'digested'.

The transaction

1.22   Insider dealing requires that the person in possession of the information does something partly, at least, in reliance on the information in question. It is not necessary that he does something that he would not have done had he not possessed the information. This would require a much too high standard of materiality and introduce difficult issues of causation. On the other hand, it is generally accepted that for insider dealing to occur the person concerned must enter into a transaction himself, procure or encourage another to enter into a transaction or disclose the information to another in circumstances where that other is likely to abuse the information. Merely desisting from trading would not, in most people's perception, amount to insider dealing. Of course, if a transaction has already been initiated, failing to complete it might well be sufficient.

1.23   The buying or selling need not necessarily relate to securities of the company with which the person concerned is in an access relationship. We have already referred to the fact that many systems of regulation would sanction the use of information pertaining to a transaction or arrangement between the insider's own company and another corporate issuer. It is also the case that dealing in the securities of related companies on the basis of relevant unpublished information would also be considered insider dealing. Dealings in securities other than equity securities that are price-affected by the information would be considered to be insider dealing in the UK and most other jurisdictions. Thus, acquiring options to acquire or dispose of underlying securities would be objectionable, as would dealing in other types of derivative securities. The question is simply whether the decision to deal in the relevant securities is influenced by the information that the person concerned has acquired and is using improperly.

1.24 The term 'insider dealing' is wide enough to encompass deals on or off an organised securities market. While a number of legal systems have effectively confined the operation of their legal rules to transactions that occur on an organised securities exchange or on or through an organised over-the-counter market, the elements of the abuse are the same whether the transaction is on a market or in a private direct transaction. One of the reasons why jurisdictions have confined the operation of their laws to public markets is the idea that the wrong indicated by insider dealing is one against the market as a whole. It saps confidence in the integrity and fairness of the market. Consequently, some have made available only their criminal justice system to sanction this essentially public wrong or, rather, crime. Off-market transactions are left to the ordinary law which governs the commercial dealings of private persons. The fallacy is to attribute the description of insider dealing to one type of transaction and not to the other. While there may be justifications for distinguishing market and off-market insider transactions in regard to the remedies that are made available and in relation to enforcement, the nature of the abuse and its elements are the same. Therefore, it is appropriate to regard insider dealing as taking place on organised markets as well as in private and even face-to-face transactions.

Unauthorised disclosures

1.25 It has already been pointed out that most systems of insider dealing regulation would regard disclosing inside information to another person, without the appropriate authority, in circumstances where that other person is likely to abuse the information, as a form of insider dealing. Of course, merely disclosing information even if there is an expectation that the recipient will himself deal, is not 'dealing' in any real sense of the word. While it is possible and common place to attribute the transactions of an agent to the principal and therefore the deals of the agent to the deals of the 'insider', it is less easy to describe procuring or encouraging the dealing of another as insider dealing. Nonetheless, the term insider dealing is often employed in such an expansive manner, as it is in the UK.

1.26 Where a person, without authority, discloses unpublished and material information in the knowledge that the recipient might well utilise the information for dealing, then it is at least arguable that the person should be held responsible for what is indirectly the exploitation of the information in question. In the UK, as in most systems of law that regard such unauthorised disclosures as tantamount to insider dealing, it matters not whether the recipient actually engages in transactions which would themselves be considered insider dealing. For example, while the informant might be culpable, the recipient who deals on the basis of the information may not be aware that the information emanates from an inside source. Of course, a failure to appreciate the status of the information might well in any case bring into issue its materiality.

1.27 Such conduct will, however, only be considered objectionable when the primary insider discloses the relevant information without proper authority. It is not always easy to decide if a particular disclosure is legitimate or not. As a general rule, if the disclosure is made with the actual or implied authority of the person concerned to make or authorise disclosure, then it will not be objectionable. There may be cases where, while the relevant officer of the company has authority to disclose information, he does so not for a proper purpose, but perhaps to facilitate improper transactions on the part of another. In most systems of law, agents have authority only to engage in actions that are properly motivated. Therefore, a disclosure that is motivated by improper considerations, such as a desire to promote a false market, would not be legitimate and justifiable even when a primary insider has no authority to disclose information. It may well be on the facts appropriate and legitimate for him to do so, for example, 'blowing the whistle' on misconduct. Provided that such is done for a purpose that would be considered proper and is not dishonest, it is hard to see that such conduct could be described as fostering insider abuse. The line between what is acceptable and what is not is not always clear. Difficulties have arisen in the case of selective disclosures to analysts and private briefings, as we shall see.

The inside nexus

1.28   While over the last two decades most jurisdictions have enacted laws specifically prohibiting insider dealing and penalising infractions of the law, outside the US and one or two other jurisdictions, such as the UK and France, prosecutions have been rare and have only occasionally resulted in convictions. The reasons why such few cases of insider abuse end in convictions are many and varied. However, it is not uncommon to find that the specific offences that have been created to address the problem of insider abuse require the prosecution to prove, to the high standard of the criminal law, a set of facts which in practice renders many cases incapable of prosecution. For example, the former offence of insider dealing in the UK required the prosecution to establish no fewer than 12 separate facts. Proof of the requisite state of mind, or mens rea, was particularly onerous. The record of successful prosecutions for fraud and economic crime involving complex factual situations and sophisticated business activities is not impressive in almost any country. On the other hand, there is the perception that insider dealing does occur at a sufficiently significant level in many markets to be a matter of concern to those who are charged with promoting and maintaining their integrity and, therefore, attempts have been made to simplify the essential elements for establishing the 'offence' of insider dealing.

1.29   Consequently, attempts have been made, most noticeably through the European Commission's company law harmonisation programme and then later as part of its initiative to ensure equivalence of protection and the creation of a level 'playing field', for the financial services industry to recast the law so as to render it more useable and effective in addressing insider abuse. In doing so, there has been, apart from in the United States, a tendency to move away from the need for an essentially fiduciary nexus and to base the prohibition on what might be described as 'fraud on the market' concepts. In doing so, the emphasis has been placed, at least as far as the law is concerned, on the misuse of privileged information from the standpoint of those in the market and not from the position of the company. Although the European directive[1] which seeks to co-ordinate anti-insider dealing laws within the EU is very much orientated to the market and ensuring the integrity of dealings in a market context, it still adheres in part to the more traditional notion that insider dealing signifies the involvement of persons who would be considered by virtue of their positions to be corporate insiders, ie directors, officers and substantial shareholders, albeit these primary insiders need not have this relationship with the issuer of the securities to which the abuse relates. Thus, in the context of this particular Directive we are still in the realm of company law and traditional issues of governance, although conceptually somewhat on the periphery. Of course, the new Market Abuse Directive[2] is a rather different creature and reflects a much wider and more market-orientated approach in line with the development of the law in the UK after the Financial Services and Markets Act 2000.

1   Directive 89/592/EC (1989) OJ L334/30.
2   Council Directive 2003/6/EC (2003) OJ L96/16; Directive 2003/124 (2003) OJ L339/70 and Directive 2004/72/EC (2004) L 162/70. See generally on the background to this R Alexander, *Insider Dealing and Money laundering in the EU: Law and Regulation* (Ashgate 2007).

1.30   Although there is a tendency, in at least some jurisdictions, to fasten upon the unfair use of all information that is not adequately disseminated, at this point in time, the notion of insider dealing involves three basic elements. First, the existence of information which is not publicly available, or at least is not available to those who would be likely to deal in the securities to which it relates, but, if it were, it would be likely to influence their decision to deal and upon what terms. In other words, there must be material, non-public information. Secondly, those in possession of the information must be aware that it emanates, directly or indirectly, from an inside source. Thirdly, they must then deal in the securities that would be affected by the information. It is also usually thought to be insider dealing when the possessor of the information encourages another to deal or improperly discloses the information to another in circumstances where it is likely that that other person will deal or encourage another to deal.

Who are insiders?

1.31   We have looked at what might be described as the constituent elements of what is ordinarily conjured up by the term 'insider dealing'. Before proceeding with our discussion, it would be useful to explore the various arguments as to who should be regarded as an insider. Of course, we have already looked at the traditional categories and raised the distinction between primary or access insiders and those who obtain the relevant information through such a person and are thus more appropriately described as secondary insiders. However, even in relation to this simplistic distinction, there are issues which would be useful to discuss in the wider context of who may properly and appropriately be considered to be an insider and thereby subjected to additional obligations. It is also important to remember that, under the laws of most jurisdictions, the determination of who and who is not to be considered an insider has serious implications for those dealing with them and, in particular, receiving and utilising information from them. A person who deals with an insider is dealing with an inside source and, consequently, any communication from that insider will be from an inside source subjecting that person to the obligations of being an insider himself.

Access insiders

1.32   The classic notion of insider dealing, as we have already indicated, involves a person closely associated with an issuer, taking advantage of material unpublished information that has come into his possession by virtue of his relationship to the company. While there are no doubt instances of persons in an access relationship to an issuer engaging in such conduct, as we have already indicated, it must surely be unlikely that corporate insiders would be prepared to risk their position and employment by engaging in such egregious conduct. Consequently, most of the cases that have come to light involving primary insiders acting in such an unsophisticated and blatant manner have involved individuals whose conduct may fairly be described as an aberration, possibly motivated by exceptional pressures or financial needs. In fact, in a high proportion of cases, the amounts of money involved have also been relatively small. Most corporate insiders would not in the ordinary course of events be able to raise very significant amounts of money to risk on insider trading within the requisite time frame. Those insiders who are prepared to violate the trust reposed in them and engage in a more systematic abuse of their position would tend to utilise nominees, sell or even barter the information in question. Obviously, the more sophisticated the attempts are to evade detection, the less likely it is that the insider will be identified or rendered amenable to sanctions. In those jurisdictions that have developed regimes for the control of insider abuse, in the case of primary insiders, it is on the whole only the relatively 'innocent' and foolish that get caught.

Those in the market

1.33   Professor Henry Manne suggested in 1966, in his book *Insider Dealing and the Stock* Market,[1] that primary insiders would, because of the risks that they face, be far more likely to exchange items of inside information rather than trade on it themselves. While this was thought somewhat fanciful, there are examples of insiders indulging in this activity or selling information. Obviously, the more disassociated the eventual dealing is from the relationship through which the information was obtained, the more difficult it is for action to be taken against the insider who has betrayed his fiduciary obligations. In countries where anti-insider dealing regulation is developed, a significant proportion of cases involve dealing on unpublished price-sensitive information by financial intermediaries. Such persons are often in a much better position to evaluate the impact of information and exploit it, as compared with the ordinary corporate executive. They are also able to organise exploitation to maximum effect through the use of derivatives and other trading devices. The relevant information in many of these cases is either obtained from a primary insider or relates to the financial activity of the issuer in question.

1   Free Press (US).

1.34   There has been debate as to the extent to which 'market information', as opposed to information that is generated from within the company, can properly be regarded as inside information. For example, the decision of a substantial shareholder to liquidate his holding, while not inside information in the conventional sense of the word, could well be highly price-sensitive. While it would generally be thought inappropriate to stigmatise the actual transaction by the substantial shareholder as objectionable, as he is possessed of nothing more than the knowledge of his own intentions, those who are privy to this might be thought to be in a rather different situation. It should be noted, however, that many systems impose disclosure obligations, primarily to the market, when a transaction would have implications for the control of a company. Of course, this is justified on much wider considerations than the abuse of what might be considered privileged information. The Department of Trade has stated 'a company, its members and the public at large should be entitled to be informed promptly of the acquisition of a significant holding in its voting shares … in order that existing members and those dealing with the company may protect their interests and that the conduct of the affairs of the company is not prejudiced by uncertainty over those who may be in a position to influence or control the company'.[1] In the United Kingdom, as we shall see in our discussion of market abuse, such opbligations are imposed primarily through the listing agreement. However, under the Companies Act 1948[2] a statutory obligation was placed on substantial shareholders to disclose and report their own holdings and those associated with them. This obligation has been transferred as a result of the intervention of EU legislation[3] from corporate law to the regulatory system ordained by the Financial Service and Markets Act 2000.[4] In addition to the disclosure of shareholdings above a certain level, most developed regulatory systems impose obligations on individuals and companies, once certain thresholds have been crossed, to announce their intentions and or make a public offer.[5] There are also provisions for the mandatory aggregation and disclosure of shareholdings in cases where persons act in concert to 'warehouse' securities if the aggregated holding exceeds the requisite 'disclosure threshold'.[6]

1   See Disclosure of Interests in Shares (1980) and generally Gower and Davies, *Principles of Modern Company Law* (8th ed Sweet and Maxwell 2008) 26–8 *et seq.*
2   See the Companies Act 1985, Pt VI which extended and renacted these provisions.
3   See Directive 88/627EC(1988) OJ L348/62 and Directive 2001/34/EC (2001) OJ L184/1.
4   See section 1266 of the Companies Act 2006 introducing new sections 89A-G Financial Services and Markets Act 2000 and Companies Act 2006 (Commencement No 1 Transitional Provisions and Savings) Order 2006/3428, Sch 3 and Implementation of the Transparency Directive and Investment Entities Listing Review, FSA CP06/4 March 2006, Ch 3 and Implementation of the Transparency Directive, FSA PS06/11, October 2006, Ch 3.
5   See General Principle 10 and Rule 2.2 of the Takeover Code.
6   See *supra* at 4.

1.35   There are a number of important considerations, however, that need to be addressed if the regulatory net is thrown over market information, that does not have some additional quality to it, other than being merely material and non-public. Mention has already been made of the important role that analysts and other intermediaries play in the financial services industry. It is important that what are widely considered to be quite proper and even beneficial operations in the market are not undermined. The position of market makers is particularly sensitive. In many markets, certain professionals will be charged with a responsibility to provide a market, either way, in a selection of securities. This facilitates liquidity and stability and assists in the maintenance of an orderly market. It is the case, however, that such dealers will, because of their specialised relationship with the issuers in whose securities they make a market, come into possession, or themselves generate, information of a price-sensitive nature. Having said this, however, it is also important to note that market makers, given their obligation to remain in the market, albeit within certain limits and be willing to trade, are particularly exposed to insider dealing and manipulative practices on the part of others. Consequently, market makers in many countries have often been at the forefront of those calling for stricter control of insider dealing. Generally speaking, the beneficial role performed by such market professionals is recognised in law by effectively exempting what they do in the ordinary and proper course of business as a market maker.

The corporate issuer

1.36   Discussion has also taken place in several jurisdictions as to whether the issuer can be regarded as an insider of itself. There is no objection, under the laws of most countries, to a company being considered an insider and to legal liability attaching to the corporation in the ordinary way. What has been said in regard to the intention of a person to act in a certain manner applies as much to a company as it would to an individual. However, where the issuer intends to act in a manner which would affect the price of its own securities or for that matter a related company's, the view in some of the more developed jurisdictions is that it is properly cast in the role of an insider. Of course, the circumstances in which a company can deal in its own capital are regulated and in many countries it is illegal for a company to deal its own securities or give any third person financial assistance to do so.[1] However, in certain circumstances, companies may be able to repurchase and cancel stock or redeem preference shares. Where this is permitted, the issuer would be bound to ensure that the holders of these securities are in no way prejudiced by the existence of unpublished information which might affect the value of the securities to be acquired or redeemed. Consequently, the company would have to make a full and fair disclosure. Of course, in such circumstances, the directors of the company would also have a duty to ensure that whatever is done by the company is done in its best interests.

1   See generally Part 18 of the Companies Act 2006 and Gower and Davies, *Principles of Modern Company Law* (8th ed Sweet and Maxwell 2008) Chapter 13.

'Scalpers' and 'gun jumpers'

1.37   From a conceptual standpoint, a somewhat related issue is that of 'scalping'. In its simplest form, 'scalping' involves what a journalist or analyst trading in securities has written up or, for that matter, expressed reservations about, in an article or report prior to its publication. Depending upon the circumstances, there is little doubt that comments of a favourable or negative character can have a profound and predictable impact on the price of the securities. The problem is that the information upon which the journalist trades has no insider nexus with the relevant issuer. It may well amount to nothing more or less than the fruits of his own work and reflections based upon widely available and verifiable facts. On the other hand, using advance knowledge that the article is likely to have an impact on the market to make a profit or, for that matter, avoid a loss, is objectionable. It has the character of betting on a certainty which is compounded by an abuse of position. Where the dealing is by an individual other than the person who wrote it, then it is often relatively easy to construct an argument that would bring that person within the reach of the ordinary theories of insider liability. It is where the journalist or analyst himself trades that the real difficulty arises.

1.38   While most systems of regulation would consider this unethical, few actually attempt to impose specific legal sanctions. In the United States, the 'misappropriation theory' has been used with effect to impose liability on anyone who uses, without proper authority, 'inside' information that belongs to another. Consequently, if the article has been prepared by the journalist in the course of his employment or under commission, then it is arguable that the information can only be used for his employer's purposes. If he seeks to take personal advantage of it by trading prior to publication, then he would be guilty of insider dealing. Of course, in many jurisdictions and in particular common law legal systems, it is probable that the ordinary law would impose liability on an employee who sought to profit in such a manner.

1.39   In the present context, the term 'gun jumping' is often applied to the same sort of conduct as 'scalping'. However, it is wider in the sense that it involves those, other than the person or persons responsible for the creation of the information or opportunity, seeking to take advantage of it before it is published. It is also applied to those who deal immediately on publication of the information before others have had an opportunity to assess it properly. Those who are privy to unpublished price-sensitive information and then, without authority, seek to exploit it, may well fall within the purview of anti-insider dealing laws. Under the European directive on insider trading, provided that the person seeking to exploit the information is aware that the source of the information is classified as a primary insider, even though they may have no relationship with the issuer of the securities in question, an offence would be committed. As we have already pointed out, the directive creates a class of primary insiders, members of which may or may not happen to be in an access relationship to the company in question. Where, however, the information is not obtained from a person who happens to be a director, officer or substantial shareholder of any company, the issue of liability is rather more problematical. Where the dealing takes place after the information has been disclosed, then, very few jurisdictions require those with advance knowledge to hold back for a period to allow dissemination, let alone digestion.

1.40 While 'jumping the gun' may be considered to be unfair, it must also be remembered that analysts do play an important role in refining information and thereby improving the quality of investment decisions. The costs of providing this service to the market needs to be met and it is important not to place those who develop such information at a competitive disadvantage in reaping the benefits of their own work. Perhaps the appropriate dividing line between what is acceptable use by the originators of such information and what is not, is the distinction between utilising the work product itself, as opposed to seeking to benefit from its market impact, once it becomes known.

Shareholders

1.41 Primary insiders are those who have a clear and defined relationship with the company to which the inside information 'belongs' or, in the case of those jurisdictions that have followed the European Directives, any company. Although, as we have seen, it can be misleading to describe this relationship as always resembling a fiduciary or confidential relationship, in the majority of cases, those in an access relationship to the relevant information will be subject to legal obligations similar to those of a fiduciary or an agent. Many jurisdictions, however, include in the class of primary insiders substantial shareholders and, in some cases, all shareholders. In the vast majority of legal systems, the relationship between a shareholder and his company is purely contractual and does not involve obligations of a fiduciary or confidential character.

1.42 In the laws of many states, shareholders have no special or privileged access to corporate information. Indeed, in many cases they have no right even to inspect the books of the company. Creditors, other than pursuant to special contractual arrangements that may be made, have even less access to the company. It is appreciated, however, that some shareholders, by virtue of the size or relevance of their holdings, may well have an influence on the management of the issuer and thereby, in some respects, be in the same position as an 'access insider'. In such cases, it may be appropriate simply to consider them to be potentially secondary insiders. Having said this, however, there is a tendency, which is not particularly logical, to expand the category of 'presumed insider' to encompass those shareholders with a substantial interest in a class of equity or to, at least in Europe, all shareholders.

1.43 The extent to which professional criminals and, in particular, organised crime have engaged in the abuse of price sensitive information as opposed to manipulative and fraudulent activity is an issue of some controversy. There are cases in the USA, Australia, Hong Kong and Japan where it is clear that organised crime has deliberately set about obtaining price sensitive information and then used it either by dealing itself or by selling it to others. Price-sensitive information has been obtained by illicit listening devices, bribery, extortion and penetration. While there has been relatively little discussion of such risks in the UK, there have been cases where criminals have attempted and occasionally succeeded in exploiting unpublished price sensitive information.[1] We will see when we discuss the substantive offences of insider dealing in the next chapter that in certain circumstances the receipt and misuse of inside information, in circumstances where it is appreciated that the information is from an inside source, would constitute a criminal offence. The market abuse provisions which are discussed in Chapters 4 and 5 are potentially more relevant. Such activity rarely, however, occurs in isolation and therefore it may well be that other offences, under the general law, will also be relevant.[2] While considerable steps have been taken in recent years in identifying the risks presented by organised crime and in responding to it,[3] to many criminals insider dealing appears as a potentially high reward and relatively low risk enterprise.

1 See generally K Hinterseer, *Criminal Finance* (Kluwer 2002); B Rider 'The enterprise of Crime' in *Money Laundering Control* (B Rider and TM Ashe eds) (1996 Sweet and Maxwell); B Rider, 'Policing the City –Combating Fraud and Other Abuses in the Corporate Securities Industry' 41 *Current Legal Problems* (1988) 47 and B Rider 'Organised Crime in the UK' Memorandum 15, *Organised Crime, Minutes of Evidence and Memoranda*, Homer Affairs Committee, House of Commons (HMSO) 16 November 1994.
2 See Chapters 6 and 7.
3 See generally A Leong, *The Disruption of International Organised Crime* (Ashgate 2007) and D Masciandaro (ed), *Global Financial Crime* (Ashgate 2004).

Chapter 2

Insider dealing: the civil law

A WRONG TO THE MARKET OR THE COMPANY?

2.1 In Chapter 1 we have discussed the reasons why insider dealing is considered wrongful and should therefore be discouraged. However, much of the discussion and analysis of the practice has focused on the relationship of the insider to the company with which he has an insider status. The very name of the concept – insider dealing – imports a relationship of proximity and privilege. Consequently, the early law in many jurisdictions has fastened on those in a close relationship with or to companies. Thus, misuse by insiders of privileged information has been regarded by many commentators as involving primarily issues of company law. Indeed, in many countries it is discussed almost as part and parcel of the law relating to directors' duties. Of course, today we recognise that the problem of insider dealing is a much wider one than directors taking advantage of information that comes into their possession while discharging the duties of their office. In fact, such empirical research as has been undertaken clearly indicates other than in the most underdeveloped markets, that abuse of inside information is not by such persons. They are too exposed and have rather too much to lose. Having said this, there are many examples of insiders manipulating corporate events to their own advantage. In those markets where there is a high incidence of owner control over the management of issuers, what takes places can often involve the misuse of unpublished price-sensitive information, albeit it often appears rather more as a matter of manipulation or self-dealing rather than insider dealing. As our attempts to regulate the abuse of privileged information have become more sophisticated, we recognise more clearly that the abuse of inside information is not merely damaging to the relationship of stewardship that insiders will often be in. It has, perhaps, serious and wide implications for the market as a whole and in particular for the confidence and trust that other investors have in the fairness and proper operation of the relevant market. Consequently, regulatory regimes today tend to concentrate more on the damage that the abuse of unpublished price-sensitive information may have on the market. It is partly for this reason that in the United Kingdom resort has been made to the criminal law. While in Chapter 3 we will see that a comprehensive system of control has been developed within the criminal law to address insider dealing, this has been significantly expanded by the market abuse provisions administered by the FSA. This we address in some detail in Chapter 4. It is important to appreciate that the law on market abuse emphases the relationship of insider dealing to manipulation and moves away from the requirement that the relevant opportunity for abuse derives from a privileged relationship. The common law and in particular the civil law still, however, has a very important role to play. Apart from the indirect impact of the specific offences of insider dealing on the civil law, largely as a result of the doctrine of illegality, the law relating to insider abuse has no real impact on the underlying common law. Indeed, failure to appreciate this in regard to the impact of fiduciary duties has occasioned difficulties and uncertainties.[1] It should also be noted that in the context of the partial codification of directors duties in Chapter 2 of the Companies Act 2006, it is provided in section 170(4) 'the general duties shall be interpreted and applied in the same way as common law rules or equitable principles, and regard shall be had to the corresponding common law rules and equitable principles in interpreting and applying the general duties'. Thus, the traditional common law remains of considerable significance in our present discussion.

1 See for example B Rider 'The Fiduciary and the Frying Pan' (1978) *Conveyancer* 114; B Rider (ed), *The Regulation of the British Securities Industry* (1979) Oyez, Chapter 5 amd C Nakajima and E Sheffield, *Conflicts of Interest and Chinese Walls* (2002, Butterworths) and inparticular Law Commission, *Fiduciary Duties and Regulatory Rules: A Consultation Paper* (1992) No 124.

CONFLICTS OF INTEREST

2.2   Directors and, in many countries, officers of corporations are properly regarded as 'stewards' of the corporate enterprise or at least the company. It is a matter for debate in each legal system as to the extent it might also be appropriate to encompass within such a concept others, such as controlling or even substantial shareholders, employees and other agents of the enterprise. Suffice to say that most systems of law, given the onerous responsibilities of stewardship, sensibly confine the notion to those who really are in a proper relationship of trust and confidence to the company.

2.3   The notion of stewardship is ancient and has changed little over time. Lord Chancellor Herschell, in the leading English case of *Bray v Ford,*[1] emphasised that it is an inflexible rule that the courts will not permit a person in a fiduciary relationship to place himself in a position where his own interests conflict with those he is bound to serve. Nor is he to be permitted to derive an unauthorised benefit – a 'secret profit' – from his position of trust. He must be loyal to his principal. Of course, with all such simple rules, their application in practice is anything but simple. For example, there is still debate as to whether Lord Herschell intended to require those in a fiduciary position to eschew all conflicts of interest and duty no matter how insubstantial or theoretical. Nor is it certain whether the rule that a fiduciary should not benefit – without express authority – from his position is a separate rule or stems from the primary obligation to avoid all conflicts of interest. It is also uncertain as to how far it is appropriate to apply these rules to the situation where a fiduciary is in a conflict of duties to different principals, as opposed to merely his own self-interest. A broad approach could create serious problems for those in several fiduciary relationships. Also, there is the real problem of financial intermediaries who engage in activities which might well produce conflicts between their different customers.[2] While Chinese Walls and similar devices may inhibit the flow of actual information from one function within the bank to another, they do not address the essential conflict of duty that the bank has placed itself in.

1   [1896] AC 44. Reference should also be made in the context of directors to sections 175 and 176 of the Companies Act 2006.
2   See Chapter 8.

2.4 While it is certain that those in a position of stewardship or a fiduciary relationship must not subordinate without a clear mandate, the interests of the person for whom they act or serve to their own, it is unclear how conflicting duties might be resolved. For example, would a trustee be under a duty to use inside information that he learnt by virtue of some other relationship for the benefit of the trust? It might be less easy for him to excuse himself when the information in his possession indicates that the trust will suffer a serious loss unless he takes action. Indeed, it has been said that a stockbroker may be under a duty to ensure that privileged information that he possesses does not work to the disadvantage of his client.[1] To what extent it could be argued that a broker may come under a duty to search out such information or act upon information of a positive quality which results in profits rather than the avoidance of an otherwise certain loss is rather more debatable. These issues are addressed in rather more detail in Chapter 8.

1   See G Cooper and B Cridlan, *The Law of Procedure of the Stock Exchange* (1971, Butterworths) p 104. But see the comment of Lord Browne-Wilkinson in *Kelly v Cooper* [1993] AC 205, 'stockbrokers ... cannot be contractually bound to disclose to their private clients inside information disclosed to the brokers in confidence by a company for which they also act'.

2.5 While the trust is a creature of the common law, other systems of law impose obligations on individuals not too dissimilar to those under discussion. For example, in civil law jurisdictions, agents and those operating under mandate might well be held to duties of good faith and care which would give rise to issues not unrelated to those discussed above.[1] The misuse of privileged information and opportunity would also be condemned by Islamic law.[2] In most common law jurisdictions, it is generally thought that liability under the fiduciary law is, in large measure, strict. Thus, if a person in a fiduciary position does take an unauthorised benefit from his position, then he should be held accountable whatever his state of mind. While such a draconian approach might be appropriate in the case of trustees in the strict sense, there are many situations involving those in a fiduciary or analogous position where the courts have considered that proof of lack of probity is a material factor.[3]

1   See C Nakajima, *Conflicts of Interest and Duty* (1999, Kluwer).
2   See B Rider and C Nakajima at Chapter 18 in *Islamic Finance*, S Archer and R Karim (eds) (2007, Wiley).
3   See, for example, *Royal Brunei Airlines Sdn Bhd v Philip Tan Kok Ming* [1995] 2 AC 378.

2.6 In the business and financial world, those in a fiduciary position will, it seems, be allowed to enter into situations where there is a possible and even, on occasion, real conflict of duties, provided they act with integrity. On the other hand, where there is a conflict between a duty to another and the self-interest of a fiduciary, the courts will be far more prepared to examine what has in fact taken place. Self-interest has been considered to be almost presumptive of abuse. The greater the degree of self-interest or benefit, the stronger will be the inference of corruption. On the other hand, it must be recognised that even in the case of conflict of duties, an intermediary will often expect to receive a benefit, be it in terms of commission or simply the retention of a business relationship. Consequently, it will rarely be the case that there is absolutely no element of self-interest in the equation.

SECRET PROFITS

2.7 Let us turn to a rule that is perhaps even more clear in its articulation than the 'no conflict rule'. Those in a fiduciary relationship must not derive from their position, or rather by virtue of the relationship, a 'secret profit'. In other words, any calculable benefit that comes into their possession that has not been expressly approved or permitted by the principal must be handed over to the principal.[1] This is an important rule of stewardship and is a core principle in any system of good governance. It strikes at the very root of self-dealing. Furthermore, it is one of the few rules that can be applied to directors and certain other corporate fiduciaries who have taken advantage of inside information.[2] Indeed, section 175 of the Companies Act 2006 specifically provides that 'a director … must avoid a situation in which he has, or can have, a direct or indirect interest that conflicts, or possibly may conflict, with the interests of the company' and 'this applies in particular to the exploitation of any … information … and it is immaterial whether the company could take advantage of the … information or …'. Section 176 of the Companies Act recognises the duty on directors not to accept benefits from third parties that might reasonably be regarded as likely to give rise to a conflict of interest. Sections 177 and 182 also impose a duty to disclose interests in a proposed or existing transaction with a director's company. Chapter 4 of Part 10 of the Act contains additional and somewhat stricter rules in regard to substantial property transations between a director and his company and certain other sensitive arrangements. There are civil, and in certain cases criminal, implications for noncompliance.

1   See *Regal (Hastings) Ltd v Gulliver* [1942] 1 All ER 378; *Industrial Development Consultants Ltd v Cooley* [1972] 2 All ER 162 and *Bhullar v Bhullar* [2003] 2 BCLC 241.
2   See, for example, *Nanus Asia Co Inc v Standard Chartered Bank* [1990] 1 HKLR 396.

2.8   The justification for the common law imposing such strict obligations on those who accept positions of trust is essentially pragmatic. The legal system cannot be expected to detect and monitor every transaction and therefore strict and pragmatic rules are required for the ordering of all dealings between the fiduciary and his principal and with third parties on matters in which the principal has a legitimate interest. The rule, therefore, requires all remuneration and benefits to be agreed and, therefore, strikes at self-dealing, abuse of position and the diversion of opportunities that in good conscience should have gone to the principal. The rule against taking unauthorised profits works reasonably well in the context of principal and agent, but when applied to the position of fiduciaries whose relationship is with a company, it gives rise to a number of difficulties. As the company is a separate legal person, this fiduciary obligation is owed directly to the company and to no other person. The statutory provisions in the Companies Act 2006 do not change this. Consequently, if a director uses information that he obtains as a director to deal in the securities of another company, his liability to account for his profit is to his own company and not to the issuer in whose securities he has traded. When the insider remains involved in the management of the company, there are serious practical and occasionally legal difficulties in bringing him to account. It is his company that has the right to sue for breach of the duty of good faith and the more specific duties, such as those set out in the Companies Act.[1] In practice, this will mean that the action is to be commenced by his colleagues on the board or in senior management. The possibilities for minority shareholders to intervene and bring an action on behalf of their company are, in reality, severely limited.

1   Section 178(2) specifically provides 'the duties in those sections …are … enforceable in the same way as any other fiduciary duty owed to a company by its directors'.

2.9   The law relating to the circumstances in which minority shareholders may maintain an action on behalf of their company in the face of opposition from the management and majority shareholders has, over the years, attracted a great deal of comment and discussion.[1] While the courts have been prepared to assist shareholders to bring derivative actions based on the company's cause of action against persons who have seemingly engaged in fraud and misappropriation of the company's property, there has been uncertainty as to what amounts to fraud and what can be regarded as corporate property. For example, some of the cases involving allegations of equitable fraud include misconduct, such as the taking of a secret profit, in circumstances where there is no dishonesty in the common law sense.[2] The courts have, in deciding whether the alleged misconduct is such as to justify permitting minority shareholders to proceed, at possibly considerable expense to all concerned, referred to indications of lack of good faith on the part of those responsible for the wrongdoing. Thus, attempts to hide what has occurred or frustrate the company itself proceeding, possibly by the wrongdoers or those associated with such using their votes as shareholders in general meeting, have been weighed in the balance by judges. The abuse of inside information presents real issues viewed purely from the standpoint of company law in this context. If the information can be considered, as it has in some instances, as belonging to the company, then it is possible a court will consider its misuse a misuse of corporate property.[3] Purely in the context of insider dealing there is little authority in point.[4] It is more probable that the courts would consider the taking advantage of such information as rather more akin to the taking of a secret profit. Whether from the stand point of the company this inevitably justified a different approach is questionable.[5] The circumstances in which a minority shareholder may now assert a derivative action have been clarified, at least to some degree, in Part 11, Chapter 1 of the Companies Act 2006.[6] While the new statutory provisions almost entirely reflect the pre-existing case law, the position of a minority shareholder is arguably made easier as a result of increased clarity and the endosement in statute, or what might be considered the more robust approach to wrongdoer influence. The practical hurdles before getting before a judge and much of the financial burden, however, remain.

1 See the so called rule in *Foss v Harbottle* (1843) 2 Hare 461.
2 See *Armitage v Nurse* [1998] Ch 241 at 252. Millett LJ stated that equitable fraud included 'breach of fiduciary duty, undue influence, abuse of confidence, unconscionable bargains and fraud in powers'. See also for an early discussion of this B Rider 'Amiable Lunatics and the Rule in Foss v Harbottle' (1978) *Cambridge Law Journal* 270. In *Item Softwear (UK) Ltd v Fassihi* [2005] 2 BCLC 91, it was held that a director is under a duty derived from his obligation of loyality to disclose to his company his own wrongdoing even if it does not amount to fraudulent misconduct. The dishonest failure to do this, might well render the law of fraud relevant. See **6.14**.
3 See **6.43** and **8.10**.
4 See *Nanus Asia Co Inc v Standard Chartered Bank* [1990] 1 HKLR 396 and **2.29** below.
5 See *Attorney General for Hong Kong v Reid* (1994) 1 AC 324 discussed at **2.30**.
6 See generally *Boyle and Birds' Company Law* (6ᵗʰ Ed 2007 Jordans) Chapter 18.

LOSS TO THE INSIDER'S COMPANY

2.10 While the cases indicate that liability to account for a 'secret profit' arises notwithstanding there is no qualifiable loss to the principal,[1] the possible 'injustice' of such a strict rule has been questioned.[2] While it is necessary to sanction breaches of good faith and the company to whom the insider owes his fiduciary duty not to make secret profits is better placed than most to enforce this obligation, it is often difficult to identify any specific loss. Even in those jurisdictions in which issuers are allowed to trade in their own securities in certain circumstances, it is hard to show that an insider's misuse of inside information has occasioned quantifiable loss to the company. The company may contend that its confidence in the fair dealing of its agent has been undermined. It might also be argued that if it becomes known that a particular company's directors engage in insider dealing, the reputation of the company for integrity will diminish. It will be seen as an 'insider's company'. This may have implications for its business, financial and employment relations.[3] While there is little, if any, empirical evidence to support this, anecdotal evidence abounds. On the other hand, in many developing markets, even quite significant enterprises are manifestly insiders' companies. It is often said that it is the very fact that their promoters remain in control which indicates to the market that the company is a good investment opportunity. Whether it is thought to be a good or bad thing for promoters to remain in control of their companies, it is hardly appropriate that this be determined by laws designed to inhibit insider dealing. It might be said that companies that allow their insiders to speculate on the basis of their inside information are permitting their management to, at best, waste time or, at worst, subordinate management to the ends of short-term market speculation. There is also a real danger that management will manipulate or at least influence the timing of corporate disclosures to facilitate their own trading. It is perhaps more sensible simply to recognise that corporate issuers do have a proper and real interest in the market for their shares and consequently allegations of abuse in this market are of concern to them. Where dealing takes place in shares other than those issued by the insider's corporation, it may be more convincing to argue that the insider is competing with his own company in the relevant market. However, in most cases, the impact that insider dealing is likely to have in such circumstances, even accounting for the use of derivatives trading, is hardly likely to result in calculable loss.

1   In *United Pan-Europe Communications NV v Deutsche Bank AG* [2000] 2 BCLC 461, the Court of Appeal emphasised '… it is not in doubt that the object of the equitable remedies of an account on the imposition of a constructive trust is to ensure that the defaulting fiduciary does not retain the profit; it is not to compensate the beneficiary for any loss' per Morritt LJ. See also *New Zealand Netherlands Society 'Oranje' v Kuys* [1973] 2 All ER 1222.

2   See, for example, G Jones, 'Unjust Enrichment and the Fiduciary's Duty of Loyalty' (1968) 84 LQR 472.

3   The new statutory obligation on directors under section 172 of the Companies Act 2006 to in good faith promote the success of the company may have relevance in this context.

2.11   While it is probable that an insider who is in a fiduciary position and makes a profit through using inside information may be accountable to his principal, it is not clear whether a fiduciary could be required to account to his principal for 'negative profits', ie that is where he uses his privileged position to avoid a loss that he would otherwise have sustained. For example, could a director be held to account for 'profit' that he makes through avoiding a loss by selling out his shareholding on the basis of unpublished, price-sensitive information that he has obtained by virtue of his fiduciary position? Although there is no English authority directly on the point and the courts have been reluctant to allow what are essentially compensatory claims for breach of a mere fiduciary duty, it is obviously desirable that someone who abuses his position by avoiding a more or less certain loss should be held accountable to the same extent as one who has benefited by making a profit. The Court of Appeal, with which the House of Lords agreed, in *A-G v Blake*, [1] while hesitating to award damages for a breach of what might in other circumstances have been regarded as a fiduciary relationship, held that, in exceptional circumstances, the court has power to award a 'restitutionary' measure of damages for breach of contract even if, according to ordinary principles, there would be no basis for a claim to compensation. Of course, where there is a viable claim based upon something other than the fiduciary taking advantage of his privileged position to avoid a loss, such as in *Coleman v Myers*,[2] since the fusion of the administration of law and equity, damages may be awarded for breach of a fiduciary obligation, at least where there is a parallel claim for negligence. We explore the issue of remedies in rather more detail below.

1 [1998] 1 All ER 833; affd [2000] 4 All ER 385.
2 [1977] 2 NZLR 225.

A NARROW OBLIGATION

2.12 When we contemplate the duty that a corporate fiduciary owes to his company not to take advantage of his position or, for that matter, information that comes to him by virtue of his privileged position, we must recognise the narrowness of the relationship within which this duty operates. Directors and other corporate fiduciaries owe their duties to the company and, as the company has a separate legal personality, only to that entity. They do not, as fiduciaries, owe duties to other, albeit related, enterprises, shareholders, creditors, employees or anyone else. Of course, if they step into another legal relationship, they might well find themselves owing duties directly to such persons as well as to their company. For example, as we shall see, there have been cases[1] where a director has stepped into a special relationship with one or more of the shareholders and by virtue of this has been held liable for taking advantage of privileged information in his dealings with them. Such cases, outside the United States, are, however, exceptional. It is important to remember that, while as a matter of good governance, directors are required to have regard to the interests of different constituencies, as a matter of law, their duties are owed to and are enforceable by their company. Thus, while members of the board both collectively and individually must act in what they consider to be the best interests of the company and in doing this they should consider the interests of all those 'represented' in the enterprise, their duties of stewardship are owed to the company.

1 See, for example, *Allen v Hyatt* (1914) 30 TLR 444; *Briess v Woolley* [1954] AC 333 and, in particular, *Peskin v Anderson* [2001] 1 BCLC 372. *Stein v Blake (No 2)* (1998) 1 All ER 724 at 727 and 729 (per Millett LJ) and *Gadsden v Bennetto* (1913) 9 DLR 719 (Man).

2.13 Consequently, the shareholders, individually or collectively as the providers of capital, have no right to sue on a claim based on an infraction of a duty owed to the company. The company's property is not theirs and it has been decided that even conduct on the part of directors which damages the share price does not give individual shareholders or the even the general body of shareholders the standing to sue.[1] The claim is that of the company's for the misconduct in question. To allow the issuer to sue and also give shareholders a right of action to recover for the diminution in the value of their investment might result in them recovering twice over for essentially the same wrong, as although a share does not represent a divisible part of the corporate assets, its value is tied, or at least should be, to the aggregated value of the enterprise, including all those assets belonging to the company. While there are examples in a number of countries where shareholders have successfully pursued directors and other corporate insiders for essentially insider dealing, their suit has been firmly based on breach of a relationship other than to the company. In all cases, liability has been based on the breach of a special relationship that has come into existence because of the special facts of the case. In other words, the insiders have come into another external relationship with the shareholders which has given the shareholders a legitimate expectation of fair dealing.

1 *Prudential Assurance Co v Newman Industries Ltd (No 2)* [1982] Ch 204.

2.14 There are other reasons why individual shareholders have not been permitted to pursue insiders with whom they happen to deal on the market. Although an insider taking advantage of unpublished, price-sensitive information in circumstances where the other party did not have or could not have had access to it may be characterised as 'unfair', the courts have, in most jurisdictions, appeared reluctant to recognise a cause of action. Their caution is based on a concern not to disrupt the proper operation of bargaining in the markets. While equality of access to information may be desirable, it is rarely, if ever, attainable. The law has long recognised that disparities or imbalances in information, let alone the ability to interpret or apply the information, cannot justify intervention in a bargain that has been completed without fraud.[1]

1   *Bell v Lever Bros* [1932] AC 161.

2.15 The mere failure to reveal information, even when it is appreciated that the other party does not have that information or could not obtain it with the exercise of reasonable diligence, does not give rise, in the ordinary course of events, to a duty to disclose or refrain from dealing. It matters not how significant or material that information might be to the decision of the other to deal and upon what terms. The notion of *caveat emptor* reflects more than a *laissez faire* approach to the market. It is based on a host of considerations that have developed over time and which lie at the very heart of how we do business. The law does, of course, make exceptions. Perhaps, apart from statutory intervention, the most significant is where there exists a pre-existing relationship between the parties in which there is an expectation on the part of at least one of the parties of fair dealing.

2.16 Where a fiduciary relationship can be found, it is probable that the obligation of fair dealing will import a duty of full disclosure and probably also a duty of care. Where such a relationship exists between an insider and the person with whom he is dealing, it is likely that the law will provide a remedy. However, the fiduciary obligation must generally arise from a pre-existing fiduciary relationship as it is far less clear that such obligations can arise, other than in the most exceptional circumstances, by virtue of the transaction in question. While it is probable that directors, the classic insider, may be in a contractual relationship with shareholders of their company, this is not a fiduciary relationship so as to give rise to the fiduciary obligation of fair dealing. It follows that a director who deals with someone who becomes a shareholder by virtue of that very transaction is in no pre-existing relationship, whether contractual or otherwise. The traditional attitude of English law, and for that matter all common law jurisdictions, is that a director owes his fiduciary duties to his company which is a separate legal person. He does not owe duties directly, or for that matter even indirectly, to the shareholders who also have no legal interest in the company's property. The rule established by Swinfen-Eady J in *Percival v Wright*[1] that directors do not owe duties as directors to members of their company either individually or collectively has been criticised, particularly in the context of insider dealing, but it remains a cornerstone of company law.

1   [1902] 2 Ch 421 and see also Lord Lowry in *Kuwait Asia Bank v National Mutual Life Nominees Ltd* [1990] BCLC 868 at 888. In *Peskin v Anderson* [2001] 1 BCLC 372 Mummery LJ observed, referring to *Percival v Wright*, that 'the apparently unqualified width of the ruling has, over the course of the last century, been subjected to increasing judicial, academic and professional critical comment; but few would doubt that, as a general rule, it is important for the well-being of a company (and of the wider commercial community) that directors are not overexposed to the risk of multiple legal actions by dissenting minority

shareholders ...' But see *Re Chex Nico (Restaurants) Ltd* [1992] BCLC 192 and *In Re A Company* [1986] BCLC 382.

2.17   On the other hand, whilst the courts are not generally receptive to arguments that they should discover new fiduciary relationships, they are prepared to reconsider the factual circumstances in which duties can arise and in particular take account of changes in social and perhaps moral views. Thus, the High Court of New South Wales in *Glandon Pty Ltd v Strata Consolidated Pty Ltd*[1] expressed the view that as attitudes to insider dealing had changed since 1902, a court faced with the issue today might not be as unwilling as Swinfen-Eady J was to discover a fiduciary obligation. In practice, what the New South Wales court was alluding to was a long-established approach, namely the recognition that in special and exceptional circumstances the facts of a particular case might well persuade the court that an unusual fiduciary relationship arises on the particular facts of the case. Although there are a number of examples of the courts being prepared to find that, for example, directors have stepped outside their normal corporate relationship into a special relationship with their shareholders, or for that matter third parties, perhaps the most dramatic illustration is *Coleman v Myers*. Although, at first instance, Mahon J was prepared to hold that *Percival v Wright* was simply *per incuriam* and should not be followed in New Zealand, the Court of Appeal, while taking the view that Swinfen-Eady J had been correct on the facts before him, held there were circumstances which could, and did in the present case, justify the court in finding that a relationship of fair dealing, involving both a duty of good faith disclosure and also one of care, arose as a legitimate expectation on the particular facts. In this case, the closely held nature of the company, the exceptional materiality of the information in question, the dishonesty of the insiders and the fact that the relevant shareholders had, over a long period, come to rely upon their probity, all served to justify the implication of a fiduciary obligation of fair dealing.

1   (1993) 11 ACSR 543.

2.18   The approach of the New Zealand Court of Appeal was in line with earlier English decisions[1] and has been followed by the Court of Appeal of New South Wales in *Brunninghausen v Glavanics*.[2] The circumstances in which an English court would be prepared to find a specific duty of disclosure to an existing shareholder, let alone a person buying into the issue for the first time, are not entirely clear. It is probable that the insider would have to be in possession of highly relevant and material information which the other party could not have obtained even with the exercise of diligence. Furthermore, the situation must, it would seem, be such as to raise on the part of the person dealing with the insider a reasonable expectation of fair dealing.[3] The comment of Newberger J in *Peskin v Anderson*[4] seeking to summarise the English law after *Brunninghausen* may well go too far.[5] The learned judge observed:

'I am satisfied, both as a matter of principle and in light of the state of the authorities [including *Brunninghausen*], that *Percival v Wright* is good law in the sense that a director of a company has no general fiduciary duty to shareholders. However, I am also satisfied that, in appropriate and specific circumstances, a director can be under a fiduciary duty to a shareholder ... So far as the authorities to which I have referred on this issue are concerned, the decisions ... in which a duty was held to arise were cases where a director with special knowledge was buying the shares ... for his own benefit from shareholders, where the director had special knowledge which he had obtained in his capacity as a director of the company, and which he did not impart to the shareholders, and where the special knowledge meant that he knew that he was paying a low price'.

1   See, for example, *Royal Brunei Airlines Sdn Bhd v Philip Tan Kok Ming* [1995] 2 AC 378.
2   (1999) 32 ACSR 294.
3   See *Platt v Platt* [1999] 2 BCLC 745, but note the reservations of the Court of Appeal [2001] 1 BCLC 698.
4   [2000] 2 BCLC 1 at 14.
5   See *Peskin v Anderson* [2001] 1 BCLC 372 and in particular Mummery LJ at 378 and 383. The Court of Appeal emphasised that the special circumstances must be such as to create essentially a 'fiduciary duty' of disclosure. Mere inequality of information cannot create a fiduciary relationship justifying fair dealing and disclosure. See also *Platt v Platt* [2001] 1 BCLC 698.

2.19   For a special relationship to develop giving rise to an obligation of fair dealing, it is most likely that the parties will be engaged in direct and personal negotiations. In the Court of Appeal in the Peskin case, it was emphasised that 'these duties may arise in special circumstances ehich replicate the salient features of well established categories of fiduciary relationships …those duties are, in general, atracted by and attached to a person who undertakes, or who, depending on all the circumstances, is treated as having assumed, responsibility to act on behalf of, or for the benefit of, another person'.[1] Even in those states in the United States that have developed the so-called 'special facts' doctrine,[2] remedies, are in practical terms, confined to non-market transactions. It is also likely that in most cases the company will be closely held. Indeed, there are cases where the company resembles a partnership in which the courts have been prepared to view the relationship between shareholders and directors as analogous to that of partners[3] bound by obligations of mutual good faith.

1   Per Mummery LJ (2001) 1 BCLC 372 at 397. See also *Stein v Blake (No 2)* [1998] 1 All ER 724 at 729.
2   See *Strong v Repide* 213 US 419 (1909).
3   For example, *Ebrahimi v Westbourne Galleries* [1973] AC 360 see generally also B Rider 'Partnership Law and its impact on Domestic Companies' (1979) *Cambridge Law Journal* 148.

2.20   It is not, however, just shareholders who might feel that they should be able to bring insiders to account either for their breach of 'duty' to the enterprise or as counterparties to an objectionable transaction. Those who invest in corporate bonds, who are not shareholders in the sense of being members of the company, may consider that they have been disadvantaged by an insider utilising privileged information in a trade with them on the market. Trading in bonds and other financial paper may be just as attractive to an insider than more conventional dealing in corporate shares and options. In most jurisdictions, the duties, if any, that the board, let alone individual directors of a company, may owe to creditors is even more underdeveloped than in regard to the position of directors to shareholders.[1] There is little chance of an insider who trades in debt securities, on the basis of privileged information, being liable to any counterparty unless exceptional circumstances give rise to a special relationship along the lines we have discussed.

1   Section 172(3) of the Companies Act 2006 imposes on directors an obligation to consider, in good faith among others and in the context of what is best for the company, the interests of creditors.

BENEFITING ANOTHER – A BREACH OF DUTY?

2.21   We must also remember in our present discussion that the remedies available for a breach of the fiduciary's duty of loyalty are rather limited. Where the fiduciary allows another to benefit in place of himself, the law has been less robust. What if a director passes on to another the relevant inside information in the expectation that the other person will use it for dealing? The person who uses the inside information, in many legal systems, will not be liable to the insider's company as he is not in a fiduciary relationship. The position of the insider who passes on the relevant information is also problematical.[1] As the profit is not his, can it be said that he has taken advantage of his position? Of course, if the person to whom he has given the information and who has profited through its use can be regarded as his agent or alter ego, the position may be different. However, the courts have been reluctant to attribute the profit made by, for example, a wife[2] or a company associated with the insider to the director. Provided the profit is that of a separate person who is not acting on behalf of the director, then it seems that the fiduciary law is powerless. In no small measure, this may well be due to the difficulty that the law has in finding a suitable remedy. There is no profit in the hands of the fiduciary that the company can call to account.

1   Note the position of the chairman in *Regal (Hastings) Ltd v Gulliver* [1942] 1 All ER 378.
2   See *Daniels v Daniels* [1978] Ch 406.

2.22   Judges have understandably been reluctant to stand by and see insiders facilitate the looting of their companies by others with whom there is often a fair suspicion that they are in cahoots. A series of recent decisions has underlined the significance of the constructive trust as a means of reaching out and imposing an essentially restitutory liability on those who receive the benefits of a breach of trust or who knowingly facilitate the breach. Whilst the principles are by no means new, the way in which the judges have applied them has been dynamic, while in the House of Lord's decision in *Westdeutsche Landesbank Girozentrale v London Borough of Islington*,[1] Lord Goff stated, 'it is not the function of your Lordships' house to write the agenda for the law of restitution, not even to identify the role of equitable proprietary claims in the part of the "law" has there been a burst of judicial activity in the area of intermeddlar liability'. In recent cases, the courts have fashioned a relatively effectively device to impose restitutory liability on those who, knowing the facts that amount to a breach of trust, knowingly participate in it or facilitate the laundering of the proceeds in circumstances where an ordinary person would consider what they have done, or perhaps not done or asked, to be dishonest. The liability in such cases is not that of a constructive trustee in the conventional sense of the word; their liability is as an accomplice and the monetary liability that they are exposed to is to make restoration as if they were a constructive trustee. It is interesting that Lord Browne-Wilkinson in the *Westdeutsche* case observed that the distinction between the concept of remedial constructive trusts, as developed in US law and the traditional approach of the English law, remains, despite judicial ingenuity and the desire of judges, to make the 'crooks' pay. He pointed out that the essentially institutional constructive trust under English law arises by operation of law and that it is for the court merely to recognise and give effect to it and it is not open to the judge simply to impose such a device to afford a remedy which would not otherwise exist.

1   [1996] AC 669.

2.23   The view has been taken that this area of the law is of little practical significance in the area of insider dealing as, before a trust can be found, it is necessary to identify property which can in the contemplation of the law be considered viable as trust property. In *Lister v Stubbs*,[1] the Court of Appeal established the rule that a bribe, in so far as such involved only a personal obligation to account, could not be the basis of a tracing claim and was not susceptible to being regarded as trust property. Of course, there has always been a substantial grey area in company law in regard to what the textbooks refer to as the 'corporate opportunity' cases. In one or two Commonwealth cases, the courts have seemingly regarded the benefit of a contract which in fairness should have gone to a company,[2] but which has been wrongfully diverted to another person, as a form of corporate property. As we have seen, this discussion has had a role in deciding whether a minority shareholder should be able to bring a derivative action. Where there has been a misappropriation of corporate property, the argument is that as the majority of shareholders cannot approve or ratify such conduct, a derivative action cannot be denied or frustrated. However, the law is rather less straightforward!

1   (1890) 45 Ch D 1.
2   *Cook v Deeks* [1916] 1 AC 554; *Canadian Aero Service Ltd v O'Malley* (1974) 40 DLR (3d) 371.

2.24   In *A-G for Hong Kong v Reid*,[1] the Privy Council, on an appeal from New Zealand, following the approach of the Court of Appeal of Singapore in *Sumitomo Bank Ltd v Kartika Ratna Thahir*,[2] opined that the rule in *Lister v Stubbs* was inappropriate today. The Privy Council considered that on the basis that equity looks as done that which should be done, there was a sufficient basis in law for tracing into the proceeds of a bribe. Furthermore, their Lordships' comments and particularly those of Lord Templeman were wide enough to include the proceeds of a 'secret profit'. If the proceeds of, for example, insider trading could be traced and be the basis of a constructive trust, the law in this area would be radically changed. For example, it would mean, as was in effect held by the High Court of Hong Kong in *Nanus Asia Inc v Standard Chartered Bank*,[3] that the proceeds of insider dealing could be traced into the hands of a recipient who took otherwise than as a bona fide purchaser without notice. It would also follow that accomplice liability could be imposed on those who facilitated the insider dealing, provided they had the requisite degree of knowledge and were, objectively speaking, dishonest. It would also be arguable that in so far as the proceeds were the 'property' of the company, the exception to the rule in *Foss v Harbottle*, placing beyond the reach of the majority of shareholders to ratify or excuse cases where there had been a misappropriation, would be available. While it has been assumed that the observations of, in particular, Lord Templeman, in all probability were unintended to be applied broadly to all breaches of fiduciary duty resulting in unjust enrichment, recent cases have shown that some judges are willing to throw the net very widely. In *United Pan Europe Communications NV v Deutsche Bank AG*,[4] the Court of Appeal had no difficulty in applying such reasoning to the misuse of confidential information obtained within a duty of loyalty and imposing a constructive trust on shares bought by the bank. With respect, however, in *Reid*, their Lordships clearly did not have these wider issues in mind when they showed so much determination in ensuring that the unsavoury Warwick Reid should not be allowed to whisk his ill gotten gains, as Lord Templeman said, 'to some Shangri-La which hides bribes and other corrupt moneys in numbered bank accounts'. Indeed, this is one of the real problems in this area of the law. The judges, once they sniff fraud, are prepared to go some way in ensuring that the crook's ill gotten gains are taken away from him. They are not always too concerned with traditional compensatory, let alone restitutory, jurisprudence. In looking at some of the decisions, particularly those relating to directors' duties, it is important to remember that to a very real degree the end has justified the means and a search for all prevailing and entirely rational principles of restitution may well be a search in vain.

1   [1994] 1 AC 498 .
2   [1993] 1 SLR 735.
3   [1990] HKLR 396.
4   [2000] 2 BCLC 461.

2.25   It is still probably the law that not all breaches of fiduciary duty are capable of giving rise to a constructive trust relationship. In *Nelson v Rye*,[1] Laddie J followed Sir Peter Millett's view expressed extra-judicially in 'Bribes and Secret Commissions' published in the Restitution Law Review.[2] Sir Peter took the view that a constructive trust is appropriate when an agent receives property himself in circumstances where it should have gone to his principal. This is a principle which has long been recognised in the company law cases. The Australian High Court in *Warman International Ltd v Dwyer*[3] also threw some light on this issue by distinguishing situations where a fiduciary benefits by use of his principal's property or an opportunity coming to him by virtue of acting for his principal where a constructive trust might be appropriate and other cases where he is merely guilty of a breach of his duty of loyalty. In the latter case, while there may well be an obligation to account for all or part of the 'secret profit', the more exacting relationship of a trustee may well be inappropriate. However, the Court of Appeal in *United Pan Europe NV* took the view that a constructive trust might be an appropriate remedy to deprive a fiduciary of his ill gotten gains when 'the conduct complained of falls within the scope of the fiduciary duty' to exhibit loyalty and it need not be shown that the profit resulted 'by virtue of his position'. Furthermore, the Court of Appeal did not accept that a constructive trust 'will only be granted where the applicant can trace into the property over which it is sought'. The remedy would depend upon the circumstances. Furthermore, in this context, it must also be remembered that the Privy Council has also shown a greater degree of flexibility in dealing with that old inflexible rule that a fiduciary should not place himself in a position where his interest and duties conflict.[4] Disclosure with assent and contractual delimination of the scope of duties and expectations[5] may well render what would otherwise be a conflict of interest, nothing objectionable to the law.

1   [1996] 2 All ER 186.
2   (1993) RLR 7.
3   (1995) 128 ALR 201.
4   See **2.3** above.
5   *New Zealand Netherlands Society 'Oranje' v Kuys* [1973] 2 All ER 1222; *Kelly v Cooper* [1993] AC 205 and *Clarke Boyce v Movat* [1994] 1 AC 428.

2.26   A further problem which has manifested itself in the law relating to insider dealing is whether inside information can be considered to be a form of property, thereby bringing in the law relating to constructive trust and all this might entail. The law is unclear as to in which circumstances the courts will protect information of a confidential nature in a manner which is analogous to property. The Divisional Court has decided that confidential information is not property for the purposes of the law of theft in England.[1] Whether such a view adequately takes account of the civil law and can in any case stand after the view expressed by the Privy Council in *Reid*[2] remains seriously open to doubt. In *Reid*, Lord Templeman certainly regarded the majority of their Lordships in *Boardman v Phipps*[3] as imposing a constructive trust on the defendants on the basis that they had misused confidential information. In *United Pan Europe NV*,[4] the Court of Appeal had no difficulty in considering a proprietary remedy, namely a constructive trust, might well be an appropriate remedy to impose on shares purchased by a fiduciary who had used confidential information. Indeed, as we have seen, Morritt LJ did not think it an issue whether the applicant could trace into the relevant property; what was at stake was depriving a fiduciary who had stepped into a conflict of interest of its 'secret profit'.

1   *Oxford v Moss* (1978) 68 Cr App R 183. See in regard to the civil law at **8.10**.
2   [1994] 1 All ER 1.
3   [1967] 2 AC 46.
4   [2000] 2 BCLC 461.

2.27   Whilst it might well be appropriate to protect confidential information as if it were a form of property in certain circumstances,[1] it would be pushing the boat out far too far to contend that most inside information is properly regarded as property for the law of trusts. In many instances, inside information may not have the qualities often associated with confidential information. On the other hand, as the Court of Appeal in *United Pan Europe NV* appears to have accepted, it would be somewhat illogical if the courts allowed one to trace the proceeds of a 'secret profit' obtained in breach of the general obligation of loyalty and yet did not allow such protection for the misuse of the actual information which gave rise to the profit in the first place. Perhaps the answer is to separate the issues of tracing into the proceeds of a profit made in breach of a fiduciary duty and the imposition of a constructive trust as an appropriate remedy to deprive a fiduciary of his illicit profit. Notwithstanding the uncertainty whether the principles relevant to the law relating to constructive trusts and the tracing remedy can be applied to all 'secret profits' and the misuse of information, it is useful to refer to a series of relatively new cases which imbue liability on those who receive the benefits or assist in the laundering of the proceeds of a breach of fiduciary duty.

1   See *Dunford and Elliot Ltd v Johnson and Firth Brown Ltd* [1977] 1 Lloyds Rep 505; *Indata Equipment Supplies Ltd v ACL Ltd* [1998] 1 BCLC 412 and *A-G v Blake* [1997] Ch 84.

2.28   The 'flood' of cases seeking to impose civil liability on those which might broadly be described as 'fiduciary facilitators' are based on a principle of law most clearly set out by Ungoed-Thomas J in *Selangor United Rubber Estates v Craddock*.[1] In this case, the learned judge referred to an established principle of equity that where a person knowingly participates in another's breach of trust, he will be regarded as standing in the same place as the trustee. While there has been much discussion in the books and cases as to the exact nature of this liability and whether it is properly considered a constructive trust relationship in all cases, suffice it to say in this context there would appear to be only two problems in fashioning this rule to become a most effective weapon against insider abuse.

1   [1968] 1 WLR 1555.

2.29   The first is simply what sort of misconduct on the part of a fiduciary will be sufficient to bring the principle into play. Most of the cases have involved either a conventional trust relationship or at least something so close as to make little practical difference. It would seem, however, that the property divided or misappropriated by the trustee must be capable of sustaining a proprietary or tracing claim. This point arose in *Nanus Asia Co Inc v Standard Chartered Bank*.[1] In this case, the Hong Kong court was required to determine whether Standard Chartered was in a position analogous to that of a constructive trustee with regard to profits from insider dealing in the United States made by a Taiwanese who, with an employee of Morgan Stanley, had misappropriated price-sensitive information from Morgan Stanley and then traded on it on the New York Stock Exchange. There was no problem with regard to the bank's state of knowledge as it had already been joined in civil enforcement proceedings in New York.

1   [1990] HKLR 396.

2.30   The Hong Kong court held that proceeds of the abuse of inside information were 'held' by Standard Chartered on trust for the US authorities and various other claimants in the United States. At the time, some thought this decision, although welcome, went somewhat further than the English law, as it was not thought that the misuse of confidential information, let alone mere inside information, was capable of sustaining a trust relationship thought to be a prerequisite for a viable tracing claim in equity. With the rather more robust approach of the Privy Council in *Attorney General of Hong Kong v Reid*[1] it is probable that an English court would today take much the same approach as the learned judge in Hong Kong.

1   *Attorney General for Hong Kong v Reid* (1994) 1 AC 324.

2.31   There has been also considerable discussion as to the requisite state of knowledge for liability. The cases have indicated two basic standards, one requiring subjective knowledge and the other a rather more objective or constructive standard. It was thought that the distinction could be justified in terms of whether the third party who facilitates the breach of trust comes into possession of the relevant property or simply facilitates its control or attention by another. In the first case, a more objective standard was considered appropriate and knowledge of facts which would put a reasonable man on notice that something dishonest was afoot would be sufficient to justify liability akin to that of a trustee. On the other hand, where the participation of the third party does not extend to possession of the property, it was thought that the requisite degree of *scienter* should be actual knowledge. In the view of recent cases, it would seem that the question of knowledge is rather more bound up with the nature of liability that is being imposed. Where the third party does not come into possession of the trust property or its proceeds, then it is difficult to conceive of him as a constructive trustee or, for that matter, as having any status which would involve a proprietary nexus. The liability of such a person for participating in the breach of trust will be personal. In *Agip (Africa) Ltd v Jackson*,[1] the Court of Appeal found no difficulty in regarding a chartered accountant who had facilitated laundering the proceeds of a fraud by incorporating companies and opening bank accounts in the names of these companies liable as if he were a constructive trustee and thereby holding him personally liable to restore the funds in question. Of course, in such cases, the liability is personal to the defendant and does not involve a propriety liability. In this case, the court found that the person concerned had acted dishonestly. He knew of facts which in the circumstances made him suspicious, but he then deliberately refrained from making the enquiries which an honest man would have made and which would easily have uncovered the fraud. Although the cases do indicate varying qualities of knowledge, it would seem the better view today is that before a third party can be held liable as a facilitator, the court will have to be shown that he knew the facts or deliberately turned a blind eye and then acted with a lack of probity. In *Royal Brunei Airlines Sdn Bhd v Philip Tan Kok Ming*,[2] the Privy Council handed down an opinion which does bring some clarity to this area of the law. The Privy Council emphasised that the liability of a person who assists or procures a breach of trust, but does not himself actually receive the property in question, is based on his dishonesty. The Privy Council considered it matters not whether the trustee has himself been dishonest. Furthermore, the probity of the facilitator is to be judged by reference to the honesty of others. The test is whether he had acted in a way otherwise than an honest man would have in the circumstances. This would invariably involve conscious impropriety on the part of the facilitator, rather than mere negligence, let alone simple inadvertence. However, a person might well be considered to be acting dishonestly for the purpose of imposing liability where he recklessly disregarded the rights of others. The Privy Council underlined that in determining whether a facilitator had acted dishonestly, his actual knowledge at the relevant time had to be considered by the court and this was a subjective issue. What might have been known by a reasonable man in the position of the facilitator might be probative, but was not conclusive. Furthermore, the personal and professional attributes of the facilitator must also be considered in determining what he did and for what reason.

1   [1991] Ch 547.
2   [1995] 2 AC 378.

2.32   The issue was further discussed in *Heinl v Jyske Bank (Gibraltar) Ltd*.[1] In this case, the judges used, as the basis of their reasoning, the judgment of Lord Nicholls in *Brunei* and concluded that it was not enough that on the whole of the information available to him he ought, as a reasonable man, to have inferred that there was a substantial probability that the funds originated from the bank in question, but that the inference had, indeed, been drawn. This clearly supports the idea that a high level of suspicion will be needed to incur liability in these cases. Another recent case bearing on the issue of liability in these circumstances is *A Bank v A Ltd (Serious Fraud Office Interested Party)*.[2] This again saw the probability of liability of those who negligently participate in money laundering reduced as the court held that banks did not become constructive trustees merely because they entertained suspicions as to the provenance of money deposited with them. The level of dishonesty needed for dishonest assistance was not satisfied by a general suspicion; there needed to be substantial suspicion pertaining to the specific transaction with which they were involved for liability to be incurred. In *Twinsectra v Yardley*[3] the House of Lords endorsed the trend away from the imposition of liability on the basis of an essentially objective determination. Instead, referring to Lord Nicholls in Brunei, their Lordships adopted what Lord Hoffmann described as a combined test, having both a subjective and an objective element. First, it must be shown that the defendant acted in a manner in which reasonably honest people would not have. Secondly, it must be shown that the defendant actually appreciated that this conduct would be considered dishonest by other people.

1   [1999] 34 LS Gaz R 33.
2   (2000) Times, 18 July.
3   [2002] 2 All ER 377.

2.33   There are situations where, to establish the requisite state of mind for liability under the civil and criminal law, it will be necessary to attribute knowledge from one person to another. Where companies are involved, as has already been pointed out, this involves a number of issues. A similar problem arises in fixing a company with a particular state of mind or knowledge. In *R v Rozeik*,[1] the Court of Appeal, referring to the earlier case of *El-Ajou v Dollar Land Holdings plc*,[2] accepted that whether a company is fixed with the knowledge acquired by an employee or officer will depend on the circumstances and it is necessary to identify whether the individual in question has the requisite status and authority in relation to the particular act or omission. Therefore, it does not follow that information in the possession of even a relatively senior official will be attributed to the company if that employee is not empowered to act in relation to the transaction in question. On the other hand, as was dramatically illustrated in the House of Lord's decision in *Re Supply of Ready Mixed Concrete (No 2)*,[3] an employee who acts for the company within the scope of his employment, even if against the express instructions of his employer, may well bind the company as he is the company for the purpose of the transaction in question. A similar view was expressed by the Privy Council in *Meridian Global Funds Management Asia Ltd v Securities Commission*.[4]

1 [1996] 1 BCLC 380.
2 [1994] 2 All ER 685.
3 [1995] 1 AC 456.
4 [1995] 2 AC 500.

2.34   As the decision of their Lordships in *Ready Mixed Concrete* clearly shows, a company may be liable to third parties or be guilty of the commission of an offence even though the relevant employee was acting dishonestly and/or in breach of his contract of service or even against the interests of the company. In that case, the House of Lords accepted that the management had gone to considerable lengths to ensure compliance with their instructions, but once a transaction had been entered into by an employee who had the power to deliver on behalf of the company, such considerations went merely to the issue of mitigation.Whilst the Privy Council recognised in *Meridian Global Funds Management* that it is a matter of interpretation as to whether a particular statute seeks to 'fashion a special rule of attribution for the particular substantive rule', both the Privy Council and the House of Lords were quite prepared to adopt this notion of 'merger' of minds in the case of restrictive trade practices law and securities regulation, given the discerned public policy in avoiding a result which might defeat the purpose of the legislature.

2.35   Where the employee in question is perpetrating a fraud against his employer, then it is obviously inappropriate to take his knowledge of the fraud as being that of the victim company. This much is clear from *Re A-G's Reference (No 2 of 1982)*.[1] In such situations, the employee cannot be both a party to the deception and represent the company for the purpose of it being deceived.

1 [1984] 2 All ER 216. See also generally Cheong-Ann Png, *Corporate Liability* (2001, Kluwer).

2.36   When the company is the victim, the person or persons who may be taken to represent its state of mind may well differ from those whose state of mind will be attributed to the company in cases where it is the company that is charged with an offence. In *Rozeik*, the Court of Appeal thought that in this latter situation such persons are more likely to represent what Viscount Haldane called 'the directing mind and will of the corporation'.[1]

1 *Lennard's Carrying Co Ltd v Asiatic Petroleum Co Ltd* [1915] AC 705.

SHADOW DIRECTORS AND OTHERS

2.37   In our discussion of the civil law we have focused on those in what is generally recognised to be a fiduciary relationship with the relevent principal or company. The courts have been prepared to hold persons who are *de facto* directors albeit they have not been properly appointed to the same obligations as a duely appointed director.[1] Persons in accordance with whose instructions the directors are accustomed to act notwithstanding that they may not be formally appointed as directors, are known as 'shadow directors'.[2] Section 170(5) of the Companies Act 2006 provides that 'the general duties apply to shadow directors where, and to the extent that, the corresponding common law rules or equitable principles apply'. In *Ultraframe (UK) Ltd v Fielding*[3] Lewison J held that shadow directors who were not formally appointed as director or who were not *de facto* directors, do not owe fiduciary duties to the company whose directors they have influence over. The Court took this view as, unlike directors, *de jure* or *de facto*, they had not assumed a fiduciary obligation to the company. While in many respects an unfortunate decision, other cases have emphasised the distinction between *de facto* directors, who are directors in all but name, and shadow directors who do not claim or purport to act as directors – indeed, they 'lurk in the shadows, sheltering behind others who (they) claim are the only directors of the company to the exclusion of ' themselves.[4] The Companies Act does, however, impose certain statutory duties on shadow directors, for example in regard to the disclosure of interests in existing transactions under section 187. However, it seems that the more interesting obligations in regard to conflicts or interest and secret profits do not extend to such persons. The same is true in regard to officers and senior employees of a company, unless they are regarded as *de facto* directors. In English law while is is clear that the duty of fidelity that an employee owes his or her employer is not a fiduciary duty as such, it is probable that the misuse of price sensitive information acquired by virtue of such employment would justify liability based on breach of the contract of employment.[5] In *Canadian Aero Services Ltd v O'Malley* the Canadian Supreme Court considered that the general duties of directors applied to officers of the company and senior employees 'who are authorised to act on the company's behalf and in particular to those acting in a senior management capacity'.[6] There is no relevant English authority on this point and the better view is that unless there are special circumstances justifying the imposition of fiduciary obligations, such persons are not within a fiduciary relationship to their employer. Finally, it is clear that fiduciary obligations are finite. Generally speaking, they start in the case of a director on appointment and terminate on relinquishing office. However, there are exceptions and these are preserved by section 170(2) of the Companies Act 2006. Generally speaking, where the opportunity to profit has arisen while in a fiduciary relationship, the obligation of fair dealing applies to the subsequent drawing down of the relevant benefit.[7]

1   See *Secretary of State for Trade and Industry v Tjolle* [1998] 1 BCLC 333 and *In Re Canadian Land Reclaiming and Colonzing Co* (1880) 14 Ch D 660.
2   Section 251 of the Companies Act 2006.
3   [2005] EWHC 1638.
4   See *In Re Hydrodam (Corby) Ltd* [1994] 2 BCLC 180, but see *Yukong Line Ltd v Rendsburg Investments Corporation of Liberia* [1998] 1 WLR 294.
5   See *Industrial Development Consultants Ltd v Cooley* [1972] 1 WLR 443.
6   (1973) 40 DLR (3d) 371.
7   See *CMS Dolphin Ltd v Simonet* [2001] 2 BCLC 704, *supra* at 5 and 6.

THE POSITION OF INVESTORS

2.38   Investors who subscribe directly or indirectly through an issuing house to a new issue of securities may suffer a loss if the securities in question are sold at a price in excess of their 'real' worth. While this is not really insider dealing in the conventional sense, the issuer and its agents are in a privileged position in that they are aware that the securities are worth less than the market thinks. In many jurisdictions, the law has long recognised that such conduct is highly damaging to the market. Indeed, a special commission appointed by the House of Commons in 1697[1] described such practices, when compounded by insiders dumping their shares on the market, as undermining the 'trade and wealth' of the country. Consequently, in cases of the new issue of securities, most legal systems, as we have seen, impose strict disclosure obligations on those involved in promoting the issue. Consequently, a failure to disclose material information would be unlawful and result in civil and possibly criminal liability. Of course, if those privy to the relevant information seek to use it in their own dealings, then this would be insider dealing. The justification for imposing onerous disclosure obligations on a company at the time it issues securities to the public is that all the facts pertaining to the nature and extent of the investment risk are exclusively in the possession of the issuer and its insiders. It has also been argued in South Africa[2] that the sale of over-priced securities in such circumstances is akin in legal terms to selling chattels that have latent defects.

1   *Commission Appointed to Inquire into the Trade of England,* House of Commons Journals, 20 November 1697.
2   *Pretorius v Natal South Sea Investment Trust Ltd* 1965 (3) SA 410 (W) 418.

2.39   On the other hand, the courts have been concerned to limit the scope and thus the extent of the issuer's liability. Consequently, in most jurisdictions, there is a reluctance to afford market purchasers' and sellers' actionable claims against those whose action might influence the price of securities already in the market. Thus, it will often only be those who have transacted directly with the relevant issuer that will be able to sue. Those who deal in the market with other parties will have no right to complain. By the same token, it has been held that auditors only owe their duty of care to the company for which they are appointed to act. They do not owe a duty in the ordinary course of events to those investors in the market who may well be influenced in their investment decisions by what the auditors say in their reports.[1] Although often expressed in terms of principle, the court's decision in such cases is clearly based on policy considerations. The need to consider the proportionality as to the possible extent of liability, when compared with the wrong in question, is recognised in other areas of the law. For example, in the United States, Congress enacted legislation limiting the exposure that insiders dealing on the market might have to contemporaneous market traders.

1   See, for example, *Caparo Industries plc v Dickman* [1990] 2 AC 605.

2.40   In the case of investors who are already in the market, the question as to whether they suffer loss or not from insider abuse is more problematic. They are not, as in the case of those who subscribe for securities in a new issue, left with over-priced securities that the market has had no opportunity to evaluate. In most organised markets, the matching of parties is essentially random and in the case of an active and relatively deep market there will be willing sellers or purchasers at whatever the market price happens to be. In the majority of situations, this price will be wholly uninfluenced by the insider's conduct. Consequently, the mere failure of an insider to 'share' his information with whoever happens to end up as his counterparty, cannot really be said to have misled that person into dealing at that price or with the insider on the terms he has. Therefore, the insider's failure to disclose has not in any real way caused that particular individual to deal on the terms he has. Thus, in market transactions, the elements that are usually required for a viable civil action are either absent or can only be found as fictions.

2.41   On most markets, the securities that are traded represent capital that was contributed to the relevant company in the past. Therefore, it is not unlikely that modern investors operating on the market will be primarily concerned with current valuations and returns rather than the longer term fortunes of the enterprise. Consequently, a relatively high proportion of trading on the markets will be dictated by the current price. With the advent of computer assisted trading programs and the development of related and derivative markets, trading will be far more responsive to price fluctuations. Therefore, it is argued that the only 'real' price is that currently on offer and thus there is no way in which an investor can logically complain that he has been harmed by the existence of information outside the market. It has also been said that it is only those investors who trade in the time lapse between the insider's transaction and the disclosure of the relevant information who have any real complaint. Longer term investors who remain in the security in question will reap the rewards or suffer the consequences of the information when it does come to the market, regardless of the insider's conduct. While derivatives may have the effect of gearing gains or losses, essentially the same considerations apply. If we cannot attribute price movements to the action of the insider, then it is difficult to claim that, whatever way the price moves, it is caused by, or is the fault of, insider dealing.

2.42   While the above discussion has centred on dealings in equity securities or rights derived from or related to equity securities, we need to consider whether loss arises when insider dealing occurs in dealings in debt securities. Those holding debt securities may be regarded as standing in the position of creditors to the relevant issuer. Of course, in most cases, this will be a somewhat indirect relationship. The attitude of holders of debt securities to the activities of management will be influenced by the extent to which the relevant borrowings are secured. A significant difference between an equity and a debt security is that the latter is likely to have a relatively determined life expectancy. Of course, given the complexity of structuring corporate finance today, this may be a distinction without a difference. However, in the case of securities with fixed maturity or, for that matter, any pre-determined right or obligation, their very sensitivity to time renders them a more attractive instrument for certain forms of insider manipulation.

2.43   The attitude of those who provide capital to a company to the conduct of management will be influenced by many other factors. The emphasis that has been placed around the world on the benefits of good governance and ethical management has no doubt had some effect on the way in which management operates and their conduct is assessed. Small investors may well be annoyed that those in positions of trust have abused inside information, but in most legal systems there is little they can do about it. In the vast majority of jurisdictions, even if they were contemporaneous traders, the chances of their being able to frame and pursue any claim for compensation or rescission are remote. Larger institutional investors may be in a rather different position. An institutional investor may not have the same degree of flexibility that a smaller private investor has. For example, an institutional investor with a significant holding in a particular company may find that it is almost 'locked in'. This may result not only from the size of its holding, but also from the knowledge that it acquires by virtue of its position. Although most systems of regulation tend to focus attention on protecting the weak rather than assisting the strong to ensure better treatment for all, institutional investors have been encouraged to take more interest in the proper management of the issuers in which they invest. Some, in furtherance of their own policies of good governance and ethical investment, have been prepared to stand up to those suspected of committing abuses. Of course, it must always be remembered that institutional investors are not spending their own money in pursuing those that they suspect of bad management practices and abuse. Therefore, it is necessary for institutional investors to consider the balance carefully between the costs and benefits of such a course of action.

2.44   While it is difficult to demonstrate the sort of loss resulting from insider dealing that legal systems would normally be willing to compensate, where the insider does more than trade on the basis of the information or encourages another to do so, the position may be very difficult. If the insider engages in acts of fraud or manipulation, then his actions may well result in quantifiable losses for which most systems of law would provide remedies. As has been pointed out, there must be some justification for allowing the investor to transfer the loss that has resulted in the movement of the market price on to the insider. In virtually every legal system, this can only be done if it can be established that the investor's loss was in some way caused by the insider's actions or default.

2.45   Much of what has been said with regard to the position of those who happen to be matched as the counterparty to an insider transaction is on the basis that the dealing takes place on a market. In the case of most developed markets, the dealing will be indirect, impersonal and anonymous. Consequently, as we have noted, the matching of counterparties will be essentially random. Where, however, the transactions take place in circumstances where the parties are known to each other and there is therefore an opportunity for negotiation, it is possible that the legal position may be somewhat different. For example, in direct and personal transactions, it is rather more likely that a court might be persuaded that the conduct of the insider amounts to a misrepresentation. Of course, in such cases, it is still necessary to impose on the insider an obligation to disclose so as to convert his failure to speak into a misrepresentation. Nonetheless, where the parties are contracting with each other directly, it is easier for a court to find an implied undertaking of fair disclosure than in the context of market transactions. Having said this, however, except in rather special circumstances, there is little, if any, jurisprudence or authority directly on the point. On the other hand, it is no doubt true that a judge may well be rather more sympathetic to a plaintiff who has been disadvantaged in dealings with an insider who has acted in a manner that most people would have no difficulty in regarding as dishonest.[1]

1   See, for example, Lord Lane CJ in *Re A-G's Reference (No 1 of 1988)* [1989] BCLC 193.

2.46   It is hard to find in the law or, for that matter, the institutional structures of modern enterprise, a concern for inhibiting insider abuse, other than on the basis that it undermines the time honoured notion of stewardship. While it is true that investors and other 'stakeholders' may deplore and feel personally aggrieved by the abuse of inside information, in the vast majority of jurisdictions, the law has not recognised this by imposing any duty on insiders that could be enforced, otherwise than through the company. However, as we have seen, even this cause of action is based not so much on logic, but the notion that those who are placed in positions of trust should not be allowed to abuse them.

ILLEGALITY AND PUBLIC POLICY

2.47   It is provided in section 62(2) of the Criminal Justice Act 1993 that 'no contract shall be void or unenforceable by reason only' that it violates section 51 which, as we shall see, renders the misuse of inside infromation a criminal offence.[1] The intention behind ther enactment of this provision was to exclude the operation of the common law doctrine of illegality and thus the prospect of attempts to unravel transactions in the market. As a general rule, where the performace of a contract involves the commission of a crime or other act that is regarded as contrary to public policy, the law will consider the contract void and unenforceable.[2] It is important to note that section 62(2) does not seek to prevent an innocent party seeking to challenge the validity of a transaction on some other basis than illegality, such as misrepresentation.[3] It may also be possible for an innocent party dealing with an insider to argue that an objectionable transaction should be considered void on the wider basis that insider dealing is against public policy. The subsection only refers to the transaction being impugned as a result of the specific offence. It is probable that without section 62(2) the courts would have no difficulty in striking down a contract which resulted from a criminal misuse of information. This is clear from the judgment of Knox J in *Chase Manhattan Equities v Goodman*.[4] In this case Knox J, while accepting that the almost identical provision to section 62(2) in the earlier statute[5] rules out the civil consequences that might otherwise arise from the commission of an insider dealing offence, refused to make available the powers of the court to enforce a transaction which was still incomplete, on the basis that to do so would be tantamount to ordering the enforcement of an objectionable transaction. The Court considered that the misuse of inside information was against public policy whether it amounted to a crime or not and therefore a transaction so tainted would not, in the discretion of the Court, be enforced.

1   See Chapter 3.
2   See generally *Euro-Diam Ltd v Bathurst* [1988] 2 All ER 23 and particularly Kerr LJ at 28.
3   See Chapter 6.
4   [1991] BCLC 897. However, in the Hong Kong case of *Innovisions Ltd v Chan Singchuk, Charles and Others* (1992) 1 HKLR 71 affirmed (1992) 1 HKLR 255, Kaplan J did not consider insider dealing would 'shock the ordinary citizen or affect the public conscience'. Nazareth JA in the Court of Appeal strongly disagreed with Kaplan J and his colleagues.
5   Section 8(3), Company Securities (Insider Dealing) Act 1985.

REMEDIES

2.48   It is important to recognise that the issue as to whether a cause of action exists is a different, albeit in practice related, issue to whether an appropriate remedy is available. The Courts do not like to find themselves in a situatiion where they are powerless to provide a remedy which will give effect to their determination as to the merits of a matter. Of course, in many ways the common law has developed around the existence of remedies and perhaps historically the courts have not focused as much as they might have on the issue of rights as opposed to remedies. As we have seen, it used to be said that damages were a common law remedy and could not be awarded for merely a breach of fiduciary duty. Of course, in many cases the breach of a fiduciary obligation will not stand alone and there may well be causes of action in tort and contract. While the award of damages is not traditionally a remedy of the Courts of Equity, Chancery Courts were prepared to make financial orders. For example, as we have seen, a fiduciary who made a secret profit or received a bribe could be ordered to account for this and hand it over to his principal. In appropriate cases, interest could be ordered or an account surcharged, and in cases of fraud this interest might be compounded. It was also possible in some situations to put the parties on terms. In other words, condition the award of an equitable remedy such as specific performance or rescission, by the undertaking of one party to make financial contribution to another. Section 50 of the Supreme Court Act 1981 provides that the English courts may award damages in addition to or in substitution for, an injunction or specific performance. It should be noted that it is only in regard to such a provision it is appropriate to speak in terms of equitable damages as opposed to equitable compensation. Equity is also able in certain cases to impose trusts, and in effect charges, on money and other property and demand that it be delivered up to those entitled to it. Consequently, it has never been the case that equity was powerless in regard to issues of financial compensation. With in many common law countries the merger of the common law and equitable jurisdictions, at least in the making of orders to facilitate the administration of justice, cases arose in which it was unclear whether an award of damages was being made by the judge wearing his common law or equitable hat. Many jurisdictions in effect allow their courts to award what passes for damages in cases of breach of fiduciary duty. In some cases this is pursuant to statutory provisions. It has been said, for example, by the Court of Appeal of New Zealand, that there is no difference in the rules of remoteness in the award of damages or compensation for breaches of, for instance, the common law duty of care or the fiduciaries obligation to exercise care and prudence.[1] This is not the case, however, in every jurisdiction and the availability of a financial order in cases of a breach of fiduciary duty standing on its own, cannot be taken for granted.

1   See *supra* at **2.11** and see B Rider 'A Special Relationship on the Special Facts' 41 *Modern Law Review* (1978) 585.

2.49   The law of restitution has developed significantly over the last thirty years. It might be claimed with some accuracy that until the 1980s, the law of restitution was a best a rag bag of specific remedies, mostly of an equitable nature, that could be used only in very specific circumstances. While other common law jurisdictions and, in particular, Australia and New Zealand, forged ahead the English courts showed rather more caution. We have already noted that there is, at least traditionally, no claim for damages in equity, albeit there is a reasonably expansive and perhaps ever expanding jurisdiction to award compensation. Where there is a trust and a misapplication of funds, whether capital or income, the beneficiary has an election to simply take over the investment into which the money has been placed or reject it. The trustee in breach is required to make good any depreciation in the value of the trust as a result of his breach. We have seen that he can be charged interest and surcharged. Where there is no trust, those to whom the fiduciary obligation is owed may seek equitable compensation. In English law it seems that the principles behind the Court's discretion to award equitable compensation, in terms of causation, remoteness and measure are the same as in damages claims.[1] The object of any award is to place the trust or beneficiaries in the position, at the day of trial, they would have been in had the breach of duty not occurred. While this approach appears to be correct where the relevant breach of duty is essentially a common law duty, such as the duty to act with diligence or care, it has been authoritatively doubted whether it is appropriate where what is in issue is the breach of a purely fiduciary obligation. In such cases the obligation to make restoration occurs at the time of breach and the common law approach to causation is irrelevant. To hold otherwise would be to undermine the special obligations of a fiduciary. Where the beneficiary rejects a misapplication of funds, what has happened after the breach is irrelevant. The fiduciary is under an obligation to make good the trust or fund as it was at the time of breach. This approach was taken in a case of equitable fraud and the directors or a company had to make full restoration to the company and could not simply pay over the difference between the value of the unlawful dividend and the value of a lawful dividend that they could and would have in fact paid.[2] In this case the Court of Appeal emphasised that they were stewards and had acted dishonestly. In another case involving an allegation of fraud in equity, the court held that the defendant 'is liable to restore the plaintiff to the situation he was in when the defendant did him wrong' much in the same way as the courts treat common law fraud.[3]

1   See Lord Browne-Wilkinson in *Target Holdings Ltd v Redferns* [1996] AC 421.
2   *Bairstow v Queen's Moat Houses plc* [2001] 2 BCLC 531
3   *Swindle v Harrison* (1997) 4 All ER 705.

2.50   It is open to debate whether the basis for awarding equitable compensation is the breach of fiduciary duty – the obligation of stewardship, or the loss that is occasioned as a result of the wrongdoing. It is interesting that in the *Swindle v Harrison* case Mummery LJ stated 'in considering the extent of liability for breach of fiduciary duty it is not always necessary to consider all the matters which may be relevant in determining' a claim based on negligence. 'Foreseeability and remoteness of damage are, in general, irrelevant to restitutionary remedies for breach of trust or breach of fiduciary duty. The liability is to make good the loss suffered by the beneficiary of the duty.'[1] He added, however, that it is necessary to consider the issue of causation.

1   [1997] 4 All ER 705.

2.51   One of the most important restitutory remedies is the imposition of a constructive trust on property or money. In so far as the imposition of a trust establishes a proprietary relationship between the relevant funds and those entitled, which can have significance in cases of insolvency, it is questionable whether at least in English law it is appropriate to regard the constrictive trusts as remedial. It is a way of holding property. In other jurisdictions, while the proprietary nature is still present, it has been seen as rather more of a remedial than proprietary device. Where there is a misappropriation or wrongful disposal of trust property, then as we have seen, the property in which the money is invested may be subjected to the original trust or the beneficiaries may reject this and petition the court for equitable compensation. If they take the property, there may still be a claim for any shortfall. Fiduciaries as we have seen may also be liable for secret profits and other unauthorised benefits that they have received by virtue of their fiduciary position. In such cases it is said that the imposition of a trust on those benefits is a constructive trust. It is a new trust, whereas in the case of a misapplication, equity reaches out and brings the property that now represents the diverted funds as the original trust. Until relatively recently, it was not clear whether all benefits obtained by virtue of a fiduciary relationship, could be subject to a constructive trust or traced. As we have seen the cases appeared to distinguish between secret profits tainted because of lack of authority and the potential for conflicts of interest and the receipt of a bribe.[1] In the case of a bribe there was merely a personal obligation to account. The Privy Council in *Attorney General for Hong Kong v Reid* disapproved of such a distinction and considered that applying one of the maxims of equity – equity looks as done that which should be done – a constructive trust could be recognised in regard to properties purchased with the proceeds of a bribe.[2] It is now the better view that any benefit obtained by virtue of a fiduciary office will be potentially traceable and subject to a constructive trust.

1   See *supra* at **2.23**.
2   (1994) 1 AC 324.

2.52   We have referred to the personal obligation of a fiduciary to account for secret profits and, indeed, any benefit that he receives in breach of his duty of loyalty to his principal. We have already seen that calling a fiduciary to account and demanding the disgorgement of profits that he has made by virtue of his fiduciary status, in no way depends upon establishing loss to the principal. It is enough that he has violated his fiduciary obligation. We have also seen in our discussion of the possible use of this restitutory remedy in cases of insider abuse that it only applies to profits and not the avoidance of losses. It is also probably limited to benefits that arise, directly or at least traceably, in the hands of the fiduciary himself. While an account for profits is properly an equitable device, recent cases have indicated that a similar liability may be invoked in common law actions. In *Attorney-General v Blake*, a former British spy profited from the publication of a book in breach of among other things his contract of employment with the British Government. The House of Lords recognised that there existed a power to call the defendant to account for his profits, as the Government 'had a legitimate interest in preventing the defendant's profit-making activity and, hence, in depriving him of his profit'.[1] While the boundaries of this remedy are unclear, it is necessary to show that the normal action for contractual damages would not be adequate or fair. It should also be noted that the English courts have allowed the award of damages and in many cases an accounting of profits where there has been a misuse of confidential information and particularly intellectual property rights.[2] Of course, it would rarely be the case that the sort of information that is relevant in cases of insider abuse would be protected in this way.[3]

1   (2001) 1 AC 268.
2   See *Seager v Copydex (No 2)* [1969] 1 WLR 809.
3   But see *Dunford and Elliot Ltd v Johnson & Firth Brown Ltd* [1977] 1 Lloyd's Rep 505.

2.53   We have also referred, in the context of liability for misrepresentation, to the remedy of rescission. While this may be asserted independently of the court, it is usual to obtain an order of rescission. Generally speaking it may be asserted in cases of equitable fraud, including where a fiduciary has made an unauthorised profit from his fiduciary position. Where there is a breach of fiduciary duty then any resulting transaction will be voidable in law. By asserting a right to rescind, the parties are placed back in the position they were before the misconduct or misrepresentation. There are, as we have seen, many other orders that can be obtained from the courts requiring restitution of property, whether these be in the form of decrees for specific performance or an injunction. It must not be forgotten that there are also powers in the criminal courts to order the return of property and restitution.[1]

1   See generally the Powers of Criminal Courts (Sentencing) Act 2000. Section 148 empowers the courts to order a convicted person to restore certain property and, possibly of more relevance, section 130 enables the court to order the payment of compensation for '... loss or damage resulting from the offence' or any other offence taken into consideration. The courts in cases of fraud have been encouraged to use this power.

Chapter 3

The main offences of insider dealing – dealing on the basis of inside information

THE LAW BEFORE 1980

3.1   In the United Kingdom, insider dealing can be defined as trading in organised securities markets by persons in possession of material non-public information and has been recognised as a widespread problem that is extremely difficult to eradicate. Some of the insider dealing is based on corporate information, ie information about a company's finances or operations. In recent years, however, most of the important dealing cases have concerned mergers and acquisitions due largely to the explosive growth in takeover activity during the past decade. The community of bankers, lawyers, public relations advisors and others who receive advance knowledge of proposed takeovers, which invariably occur at a substantial premium over the existing market price of the acquired company's shares, face a strong temptation to make a quick profit from inside information. Notwithstanding the fact that for over twenty years the abuse of this information has been a serious criminal offence, studies conducted by the FSA indicate that there is considerable evidence that such information is abused in a significant percentage of cases. This indicates that the control of insider dealing is a complex issue in regard to which the criminal justice system can only achieve so much.

3.2   The general criminal law has always sought to protect the integrity of public markets.[1] Indeed, there were very early common law offences which criminalised attempts to interfere with the proper operation of the markets. In the eighteenth century, Parliament and the City of London introduced a number of measures aimed at promoting the integrity of intermediaries and those engaged in stockjobbing.[2] While the effectiveness of many of these initiatives may be questioned, there has always been a realisation that manipulative and fraudulent conduct has far more serious and greater implications for the markets, than the direct harm that it causes to individual investors. The protection and advancement of confidence in the integrity, fairness and efficiency of the markets, particularly the financial markets, has long been accepted as a serious issue. Having said this the use of information obtained in privileged circumstances has not always been considered objectionable, let alone unfair. However, for a variety of reasons, mainly social, attitudes began to change during the 1970s in the City.

3.2 *The main offences of insider dealing*

1 See B A K Rider and M Ashe, *Insider Crime* (1993, Jordans) p 20. Reference should also be made to Chapter 6.
2 See **6.5**.
3 See **2.38** and G Gilligan, *Regulating the Financial Services Sector* (1999 Kluwer) Chapter 4.

3.3

Until 1980, the restrictions on insider dealing in the United Kingdom were extremely limited. There was no specific legislation other than the requirements in the Companies Acts for directors, members of their families and substantial shareholders to report dealings in the shares of their companies. While these disclosure obligations were justified on a number of grounds, a significant one was that this would discourage the abuse of inside information. Whether reporting such transactions does have such an effect is open to debate. In any case, these provisions were poorly policed.[1] Mention has been made elsewhere of the argument that the dishonest concealment of material information might constitute an offence under section 13 of the Prevention of Fraud (Investments) Act 1958.[2] We have also seen that the common law provided no real possibility for those who dealt with those who abused inside information to seek recovery in the civil courts. The use of inside information, absent some affirmative obligation to disclose it, did not and probably in most cases still does not, give rise to a cause of action in the civil law. The most significant element of regulation was that provided by a range of self-regulatory and professional bodies in the City of London. For example, the City Panel on Takeovers and Mergers[3] and the London Stock Exchange[4] had adopted rules and guidelines that restricted insider dealing and the 'tipping' of inside information in the early 1970s. However, there was considerable scepticism as to how effective they were in practice. The self-regulatory bodies in the City of London increasingly recognised that for effective enforcement, particularly where there was an international element in the transaction, statutory powers were required. Consequently, by 1980 many in the City recognised the need for insider dealing to be made a specific criminal offence.[5]

1 By contrast, the United States enacted anti-market manipulation legislation in 1934 in the form of the Securities and Exchange Act 1934, s 10(b).
2 [1902] 2 Ch 421.
3 City Code on Takeovers and Mergers, Rule 4.1.
4 LSE, 'Model Code for Securities Transactions by Directors of Listed Companies' (1987, 'Yellow Book') 5.43–5.48.
5 See generally B Rider and H Ffrench, *The Regulation of Insider Trading*, (1979) Macmillan.

3.4   After two unsuccessful legislative attempts to outlaw insider dealing in the 1970s,[1] in 1980 Parliament amended the Companies Act to make insider dealing a criminal offence.[2] These provisions outlawing insider dealing were consolidated in 1985 when the Companies Act was revised. The insider dealing provisions of the Companies Act 1985 became known as the Company Securities (Insider Dealing) Act 1985.[3] These provisions were supplemented the following year by new provisions in the Financial Services Act 1986 that were intended primarily to strengthen the government's enforcement powers.[4]

1 In 1973, the Conservative Government published a Companies Bill that would have outlawed insider trading, but it failed when the Government was defeated in the February 1974 General Election. The Companies Bill that was proposed by the Labour government in 1978 suffered a similar fate after that Government was defeated in the May 1979 General Election.
2 Companies Act 1980, ss 68–73.
3 Company Securities (Insider Dealing) Act 1985 (hereinafter the 'Insider Dealing Act').
4 Financial Services Act 1986, ss 173–178.

3.5   The Insider Dealing Act 1985 prohibited persons who had access to material non-public information by virtue of their position with a company (including directors, officers, employees and various kinds of agents of the company) from trading in the securities of the company while in possession of such information. These insiders were also prohibited from making selective disclosure of such information to others ('tipping') and it prohibited their tippees from trading on the basis of such inside information. The Act also prohibited persons in possession of non-public information about a proposed takeover of a company from trading in that company's stock.

3.6   The Insider Dealing Act 1985 established only criminal liability and its prohibitions applied only to individuals who acted while knowingly in possession of inside information. Although the Insider Dealing Act was an important step in outlawing the offence of insider dealing, the scope and impact of the British legislation was rather narrow. In fact, despite the fact that insider dealing had been an offence since 1980, there were no convictions under the Act's provisions (as amended by the Financial Services Act 1986) until the late 1980s.

3.7   The following sections will discuss the existing criminal legislation that makes insider dealing a criminal offence, which is contained in the Criminal Justice Act 1993, Pt V and applies only to the trading of securities. The Financial Services and Markets Act 2000 ('FSMA 2000') imposes criminal and civil liability for market abuse which includes activity which would also fall within the scope of the Criminal Justice Act. The market abuse regime is discussed in Chapter 4. Over the years responsibility for prosecuting crimes involving insider trading has proved to be something of a 'hot potato'. The police have never been particularly enthusiastic about such cases and the Serious Fraud Office has taken the view that the vast majority would not come within its statutory remit. Indeed, several years ago the SFO dismissed such offences as being of a 'technical and regulatory' nature. With the realisation that 'real' criminals may engage in the deliberate gathering and exploitation of price-sensitive information, attitudes have possibly changed and even the Serious Organised Crime Agency has exhibited some interest. However, given the FSA's exclusive responsibility for policing the market abuse regime it is sensible that the FSA is now the lead prosecutor for cases under the Criminal Justice Act. It should be remembered, however, that serious cases of insider abuse will often involve other criminal conduct and more general offences, which we address in Chapter 6. Proceeds of crime and anti-money laundering law might also be relevant and reference should also be made to Chapter 7.

THE OFFENCE OF INSIDER DEALING

3.8   The Criminal Justice Act 1993 ('CJA 1993') replaced the Company Securities Act (Insider Dealing) Act 1985 and represented an extension of the basis of liability for the insider dealing offence. The CJA 1993 contains a wider definition of 'securities' and 'insider' than the 1985 Act and the nature of the inside information necessary to impose liability has been altered.

The Criminal Justice Act 1993, Pt V

3.9   The CJA 1993, Pt V came into force on 1 March 1994 together with two ancillary statutory instruments (both reproduced in the 'Rules and Regulations'): the Insider Dealing (Securities and Regulated Markets) Order 1994 and the Traded Securities (Disclosure) Regulation 1994. The relevant provisions are in the 'ancillary Acts'.

3.10   The CJA 1993, Pt V provides for the offence of insider dealing that seeks to prevent individuals from engaging in three classes of conduct in particular circumstances. First, the Act prohibits dealing in price-affected securities on the basis of inside information.[1] Secondly, it prohibits the encouragement of another person to deal in price-affected securities on the basis of insider information and, thirdly, it prohibits knowing disclosure of insider information to another.[2] To prove an offence under s 52, it was necessary to demonstrate two elements: (a) the status of the person charged as an insider, and (b) the type of information in its possession to be inside information. Section 52 provides in the relevant part:

'(1)   An individual who has information as an insider is guilty of insider dealing if, in the circumstances mentioned in subsection (3), he deals in securities that are price- affected securities in relation to the information.

(2)   An individual who has information as an insider is also guilty of insider dealing if –

(a)   he encourages another person to deal in securities that are (whether or not that other knows it) price-affected securities in relation to the information, knowing or having reasonable cause to believe that the dealing would take place in the circumstances mentioned in subsection (3); or

(b)   he discloses information, otherwise than in proper performance of the functions of his employment, office or profession, to another person.

(3)   The circumstances referred to above are that the acquisition or disposal in question occurs on a regulated market, or that the person dealing relies on a professional intermediary or is himself acting as a professional intermediary'.

1   CJA 1993, Pt V, s 52(1).
2   CJA 1993, Pt V, s 52(1) and (2).

3.11   Criminal liability for each offence may only attach to an individual because the term 'individual' is defined to exclude corporations and other entities (eg public authorities). The definition of individual did cover, however, unincorporated partnerships or firms comprising a collection of individuals. Moreover, it should be noted that a company could be liable for insider dealing by committing the secondary offence of encouraging another person to deal.[1]

1   See an analysis of the encouragement offence at **3.55**.

Insiders

3.12   To commit the offence of insider dealing, an individual must have information 'as an insider', which is defined in the CJA 1993, s 57 as follows:

'(1)   … a person has information as an insider if and only if –
(a)   it is, and he knows that it is, inside information, and
(b)   he has it, and knows that he has it, from an inside source.

(2)   For the purposes of subsection (1), a person has information from an inside source if and only if –
(a)   he has it through   (i)being a director, employee or shareholder of an issuer of securities; or (ii)having access to the information by virtue of his employment, office or profession; or

46

(b) the direct or indirect source of his information is a person within paragraph (a)'.

3.13 The CJA 1993, s 57 created a distinction between a primary insider (a person who has direct knowledge of inside information) and a secondary insider (a person who learns inside information from an inside source).[1] The primary insider usually obtains inside information through being a director, employee or shareholder of an issuer of securities or any person who has information because of his employment or office. A secondary insider obtains inside information either directly or indirectly from a primary insider. Section 57 would impose liability on brokers or analysts as secondary insiders if they act on 'market intelligence' that comes from a primary insider.[2]

1 This terminology was first adopted in B Rider, *Insider Dealing* (1983, Jordans). See also B Rider and HL Ffrench, *The Regulation of Insider Trading* (1979, Macmillan)
2 See the discussion of 'tippee' liability at **3.58**.

3.14 The insider dealing offence could only be committed if the acquisition or disposal of securities occurs on a regulated market or if the person dealing relied on a professional intermediary or is himself a professional intermediary.[1] The CJA 1993 defines 'professional intermediary' as a person who carries on a business of acquiring or disposing of securities (whether as principal or agent) or a business of acting as an intermediary between persons taking part in any dealing in securities.[2] Individuals employed by such a person to carry out these activities are also defined as 'professional intermediaries'. The definition of professional intermediary does not include a person whose activities are merely incidental to other activities or if those activities are only conducted occasionally.[3]

1 CJA 1993, s 52(3).
2 CJA 1993, s 59(1)(a).
3 CJA 1993, s 59(3)(a)–(b).

3.15 The CJA 1993, s 59 defines professional intermediary as follows:

'(1) … a professional intermediary is a person –
  (a) who carries on a business consisting of an activity mentioned in subsection (2) and who holds himself out to the public or any section of the public (including a section of the public constituted by persons such as himself) as willing to engage in any such business; or
  (b) who is employed by a person falling within paragraph (a) to carry out any such activity.
(2) The activities referred to in subsection (1) are –
  (a) acquiring or disposing of securities (whether as principal or agent); or
  (b) acting as an intermediary between persons taking part in any dealing in securities'.

3.16 Under this definition, a person will rely on a professional intermediary only if the professional intermediary either acquires or disposes of securities (whether as principal or agent) in relation to the dealing or acts as intermediary between persons taking part in the dealing.[1] If deals in securities do occur on a regulated market (ie investment exchange), the insider dealing offence will be relevant unless the transaction is truly a private deal off the market without the intervention of a market professional.

1 CJA 1993, s 59(4).

3.17 The offence of insider dealing cannot apply to anything done by an individual acting on behalf of a public sector body in pursuit of the government's economic policies (eg managing monetary policy through the adjustment of exchange rates, interest rates or the public debt or foreign exchange reserves).[1] The purpose of these exclusions is to permit government policymakers to have sufficient discretion to manage the economy in the public interest. These exclusions, however, would not apply to the government's sale of shares in a privatisation.

1   CJA 1993, s 63(1).

The elements of the dealing offence

3.18 The two essential requirements for the dealing offence are that: (a) an individual must have information as an insider, and (b) the insider must deal in securities that are price-affected securities in relation to the information.[1] With respect to inside information, the prices of price-affected securities will likely be significantly affected if information related to such securities is made public.[2] Accordingly, if an insider has inside information, he must not deal in the securities to which that information relates. The CJA 1993 adopts a broad definition of 'dealing in securities' to cover any acquisition or disposal of a security, including an agreement to acquire or dispose of a security and the entering into a contract which creates the security or the bringing to an end of such a contract.[3] Moreover, such acquisitions or disposals are within the definition irrespective of whether they are made by an individual as principal or as agent.

1   CJA 1993, s 52(1).
2   CJA 1993, s 56(2).
3   CJA 1993, s 55(3)(b).

3.19 The securities to which the Act applies are price-affected securities, which are defined in the CJA 1993, Sch 2. They include shares and debentures in companies, as well as their derivatives. They also include gilts and local authority stock (even of foreign public bodies) and their derivatives. Contractual rights of differences (eg derivatives) are also included.[1] The list conforms to the EC Directive on Insider Dealing,[2] so that not only corporate securities and instruments based on such securities are included, but also that other contractual rights in other futures and derivatives markets are covered.

1   The list contained generally most of the investments that had been designated under the Financial Services Act 1986, Sch 1, Pt I.
2   Council Directive 89/552/EEC, art 1(2).

3.20 The relevant time at which to consider whether or not an offence has been committed would appear to be at the time of agreement to acquire or dispose of the security. At that time, if the individual had inside information about these securities, he will have committed an offence. However, if he received inside information only after making the agreement, he will probably not have violated the provision if he completes the deal and actually acquires or disposes of the securities. On the other hand, if the individual had the inside information at the time when he agreed to acquire or dispose of the security, it would seem that he will still have committed an offence, even if he does not complete the bargain.

3.21 The acquisition or disposal may be made by an individual acting either as principal or agent. Accordingly, if an agent has inside information, he will be within the scope of the offence if he deals in the relevant securities even though, in a direct sense, he will not gain from the transaction. This has special relevance to a trader who is engaged in a transaction as agent to benefit his principal. The fact that the individual deals as agent and not principal is irrelevant. However, where the agent deals on an execution basis only, such an approach hardly seems justified and is unfair to the principal who gave the instruction if the agent then feels inhibited from processing the order. Fortunately, it appears that a defence in this situation would allow the agent to act on instructions notwithstanding that, incidentally, he has inside information.[1]

1   CJA 1993, s 53(1)(c).

3.22   A person is also regarded as dealing in securities if he procures, directly or indirectly, an acquisition or disposal of the securities by another person.[1] Such procurement may occur in a number of ways, including where the person who actually acquires or disposes of the security is acting as an agent, nominee or at the direction of another in relation to the acquisition or disposal of a security.[2] This aspect of the definition of 'dealing in securities' is designed to cover transactions through an agent or nominee where the principal has relied on inside information without purchasing or selling the securities himself. Transactions are also covered that are undertaken at the direction of a sole shareholder who uses its influence over a company to deal in its shares.[3]

1   CJA 1993, s 55(1)(b).
2   CJA 1993, s 55(4).
3   See Parliamentary Debates, House of Commons, Standing Committee B, 10 June 1993, column 171 (per the Economic Secretary).

3.23   The broad scope of the procurement prohibition was recognised in debates in the House of Commons Standing Committee during passage of the Criminal Justice Bill in which the phrase 'a person who is acting at his direction' may likely result in liability for a principal who has inside information, but whose investment portfolio is handled by someone else on a discretionary basis. For example, this might occur in the case of a fund manager who had the authority to deal in a discretionary manner in securities to which his principal's insider information relates, thus resulting in liability for the principal, despite the principal's lack of knowledge of the specific transaction.

3.24   The government's Economic Secretary responded by stating that whilst it was possible for a person who had transferred its holdings of a portfolio to an investment manager to be exposed to liability as a procurer, 'it may well be that'[1] a person who gives a general direction to another to manage its affairs would not be considered to have directed and, therefore, to have procured dealings in securities which were undertaken by the person with responsibility for managing the fund. Moreover, the minister stated that in cases where there were circumstances to suggest that a person had procured a transaction, the holder of the shares would have a statutory defence if the holder had not genuinely influenced the dealing.[2]

1   See Parliamentary Debates, House of Commons, Standing Committee B, 10 June 1993, columns 171 and 172 (per Mr Peter Ainsworth MP).
2   See the CJA 1993, s 53(1)(c).

The characteristics of insider information

3.25   Each of the three offences provided for in the CJA 1993 and the FSMA 2000 require that insider information be an essential element of the offence. Commentators have acknowledged, however, that, notwithstanding the statutory definition, inside information is a difficult concept to define in practice. For example, at any one time, a substantial amount of information will be generated within a company and be available to its directors, employees and advisors. Much of this information will be confidential and may have some impact on share prices. Generally, insider dealing law should not be concerned with this type of information, but rather it should focus on information that is essentially extraordinary in nature and which is reasonably certain to have a substantial impact on the market price of securities.[1] Indeed, during debate over the original UK insider dealing law, ministers acknowledged that the kind of knowledge they were concerned with was that of dramatic events and major occurrences that would transform a company's prospects.[2]

1   See **1.15** *et seq* and in particular *SEC v Texas Gulf Sulfur Co* 401 F 2d 833, 848 (2nd Cir, 1968)).
2   Parliamentary Debates, House of Commons, Standing Committee A (debates on the Company Bill), 6 December 1979, column 394.

3.26   The CJA 1993 and the FSMA 2000 both assess the quality of information to determine whether it is inside information by use of criteria that seek to ascertain whether or not information has a 'significant effect' on the market price of the security. The CJA 1993 defines inside information by reference to four characteristics as provided in the CJA 1993, s 56:

'(1)   ... inside information means information which –
   (a)   relates to particular securities or to a particular issuer of securities or to particular issuers of securities and not to securities generally or to issuers of securities generally;
   (b)   is specific or precise;
   (c)   has not been made public; and
   (d)   if it were made public would be likely to have a significant effect on the price of any securities.
(2)   ... securities are "price-affected securities" in relation to inside information, and inside information is "price-sensitive information" in relation to securities, if and only if the information would, if made public, be likely to have a significant effect on the price of the securities'.[1]

The FSMA 2000 has also adopted this meaning of the term 'inside information'.

1   CJA 1993, s 56. Under the Company Securities (Insider Dealing) Act 1985, inside information was referred to as 'unpublished price-sensitive information' that contained the following elements:
   ●   the information was not generally to be known to those persons accustomed or likely to deal in the company's securities;
   ●   the information should be likely to affect the price of the securities; and
   ●   the information was such that it would be reasonable to expect a primary insider not to disclose it, except in the proper performance of its functions.

3.27   The characteristics and elements of inside information are such that they should cover information which relates to a specific sector as well as to a specific security, while excluding general information. General information has been defined, for example, under the FSMA 2000, as information which can be obtained by research or analysis conducted by or on behalf of users of a market.[1]

1   FSMA 2000, s 118(7).

3.28   The approach of the CJA 1993 and the FSMA 2000 conforms with that of the EC Directive on Insider Dealing[1] and even seems to accomplish the objective of promoting an efficient market through the timely disclosure of information more effectively than the Directive, which has been criticised on the grounds of obscurity.

1   Council Directive 89/592/EC, art 1(1).

Particular securities and particular issuers of securities

3.29   The first of these four characteristics as set out in the CJA 1993 makes clear that information which relates to a specific sector is included, as well as that which relates to a specific security. Accordingly, information may still be inside information, although it has nothing specifically to do with a particular company or its shares, but rather relates to the industry in which that company operates.[1] Similarly, inside information relating to an issuer will include information which comes directly from the issuer. Thus, for example, information about a substantial increase or reduction in profits of a company, which clearly has its source within the organisation, will certainly be information which relates to an issuer. The information, however, referred to in the CJA 1993 also includes information that arises from a source outside of the issuer. This may occur in a takeover bid where the proposal to acquire the company's shares emanates from the bidder. Similarly, information relating to securities may be internal, such as dividends, but may be external, such as a decision by the company to be listed on the Stock Exchange.

1   See B A K Rider and M Ashe, *Insider Crime* (1993, Jordans) p 30.

3.30   There are situations, however, when the question will not be so straightforward regarding when information relates to a particular security or particular issuer or issuers. Although it is clear that the definition does not include information which relates to securities generally or to issuers generally, there is much information which, although not of that general quality, is not related to a particular security, but may, nonetheless, have a significant effect on its price if disclosed to the public.

3.31   If, for example, an employee of Microsoft has, in the course of her employment, gained knowledge that Microsoft is about to submit a bid for the shares of another publicly-held company, this information is likely to be advantageous if she were to purchase shares in the other company. Undoubtedly, the information has its most direct relationship with Microsoft and, because the employee has the information as an insider (and assuming it to be price sensitive, negatively, in relation to Microsoft's shares) she should not deal in Microsoft's shares by selling them before the news becomes generally available with the likely result that their price will drop. Similarly, the information may also have been considered to relate to the target company. It would be curious, if not illogical, if the employee, having obtained the information as an insider, had committed an offence by selling the shares in Microsoft, but not have committed an offence by purchasing shares in the target company. In both cases, the employee was acting on the same information obtained as an insider and in both cases that information would have a significant effect on the prices of each share. Yet, it is arguable that the information did not relate to the target company, rather it only related to Microsoft. It would seem, however, that such a result would offend common sense.

3.32   The CJA 1993, s 60(4) provides clarification on this issue by stating:

'For the purposes of this Part, information shall be treated as relating to an issuer of securities which is a company not only where it is about the company but also where it may affect the company's business prospects'.

This provision appears to apply to the above example by ensuring that the information relates not only to Microsoft, but also to the target company, because it will affect the target company's prospects, ie Microsoft's proposed purchase of the shares will likely enhance the value of the target company's shares.

3.33 The statutory provision was criticised as being too broad because of its inclusion of the term 'business prospects' in the definition of insider dealing. The statute's inclusion of the term 'business prospects' was defended by the Earl of Caithness on behalf of the government in debate in the House of Lords when he said:

'It is included because the government believes that it is essential our insider dealing legislation catches as inside information, information which, while not relating directly to a company, would nonetheless be likely to have a significant effect on the price of its shares. An example of information in this category might be important regulatory decisions and information about a company's major customer or supplier'.[1]

1   Parliamentary Debates, House of Lords, 3 December 1992, column 1501 (The Earl of Caithness).

3.34 It is generally accepted that the CJA 1993 adopts a broad-based approach to the definition of inside information, together with an expanded approach to who is an insider,[1] but the exclusion from the definition of information which relates to securities generally, or to issuers of securities generally, appears to mean that, for example, confidential information of a particular government economic policy which will impact on the market generally is outside the definition of inside information. In this regard, the CJA 1993 appears to be less strict than the EC Directive on Insider Dealing, art 1(1), which places no such restriction and specifically includes such general news. The Directive, therefore, has a broad scope, as compared to the narrower approach of the CJA 1993. The FSMA 2000 seeks to address this discrepancy by adopting an approach that includes information that affects the market generally, but which may have a specific effect on the issuers of specific securities.

1   CJA 1993, s 57(2)(a)(ii).

'Specific' or 'precise'

3.35 Inside information may also be characterised by the terms 'specific' or 'precise'. The CJA 1993 includes the word 'specific' because the word 'precise', by itself, may not have covered, for example, information that there will be a huge dividend increase because the lack of details concerning the quantum increase would not amount to inside information. Information is precise when it is exact. The word 'specific' is intended to ensure that information that, for example, involves a large drop in a company's earnings would be considered inside information, while mere rumour and untargeted information cannot.[1]

1   Parliamentary Debates, House of Lords, 3 December 1992, column 1501 (The Earl of Caithness).

3.36   Moreover, the use of the word 'specific' may eliminate more than mere rumour and untargeted information. An Australian case held that the phrase 'specific information' meant not merely that the information was precisely definable, but that its entire content can be precisely and 'unequivocally expressed and discerned'.[1] The court concluded that specific information had to be specific in itself and not based on the process of deduction.[2] On this approach, a company that was prepared to purchase a large tranche of shares from several persons would not be considered specific in relation to a similar purchase from one person. Although this view may be attractive, it is often inferences drawn from facts which affect market price and, theoretically, if the facts are not made public, the insider who has them needs also to be restrained from trading on inferences made from those facts.

1   *Ryan v Triguboff* [1976] 1 NSWLR 588 at 596 (per Lee J).
2   *Ryan v Triguboff* at 597.

3.37   Whatever the correct approach for inferences, information may still be specific even though, as information, it has a vague quality. Thus, information concerning a company's financial problems has been held to be specific.[1] Moreover, information as to the possibility of a takeover may be regarded as specific information[2] and will likely rank as precise, given that it is more than a mere rumour. The House of Commons Standing Committee that was considering the Criminal Justice Bill provided some examples of what the words 'specific' and 'precise' would cover.

1   *Public Prosecutor v Choudhury* [1980] 1 MLJ 76 at 78 (Singapore).
2   See *Green v Charterhouse Group of Canada Ltd* (1976) 12 OR (2d) 280. The Ontario Court of Appeal held such information to be specific even though it may not have been worthy of credence or not have been of sufficient weight to justify any positive action by the board.

Example 1

3.38   As the chairman of a company and an analyst walked into a car park, they saw the chairman's battered BMW. The analyst said to the chairman, 'Isn't it time you got a new car?' The chairman replied that he would not buy a new car that year.

3.39   The Economic Secretary considered that these circumstances would lead neither to specific nor precise information in relation to the company, given that there could be many reasons for the statement, including the fact that the chairman may have been experiencing personal financial troubles.[1]

1   Parliamentary Debates, House of Commons, Standing Committee B, 10 June 1993, column 174.

Example 2

3.40   In contrast, if the chairman had remarked that 'Our results will be much better than the market expects or knows' it would not be precise information because there was no disclosure of the company's results, but it would likely be specific information because the chairman would have disclosed information about the company's result, whilst making it clear that the information was not public.[1]

1   See the comments of the Economic Secretary, Parliamentary Debates, House of Commons, Standing Committee B, 10 June 1993, column 175.

3.41   Some commentators have also noted that the section 56 of the CJA 1993's requirement that information be specific or precise was drafted more broadly than EC Directive 89/592, which required in art 1 that the information be of 'a precise nature' only.[1]

1   See the discussion in J Fisher and J Bewsey, *The Law of Investor Protection* (1997, Sweet & Maxwell) p 291 and generally R Alexander, *Insider Dealing and Money Laundering in the EY:Law and Regulation* (2007, Ashgate).

'Made public'

3.42   For the purposes of defining inside information under the CJA 1993, s 56, another characteristic of it is that it has not been made public.[1] Under the CJA 1993, s 58(2) and (3), inside information is made public or is to be treated as made public in the following circumstances:

- if the information is published in accordance with the rules of a regulated market for the purpose of informing investors and their professional advisors;
- if the information is contained in records which, by virtue of any enactment, are given to inspection by the public;
- if the information can be readily acquired by those likely to deal in any securities to which the information relates or of an issuer to which the information relates; or
- if the information is derived from information which has been made public.

1   The original drafts of the Criminal Justice Bill that were introduced in the House of Lords provided no guidance for defining what was meant by the phrase 'made public'. See B A K Rider and M Ashe, *Insider Crime* (1993, Jordans) at p 34.

3.43   In addition, the CJA 1993 provides five circumstances when information may be treated as having been made public, even though it has not.[1] These are where information:

- can only be acquired by persons exercising diligence or expertise;
- is communicated to a section of the public and not to the public at large;
- can only be acquired by observation;
- is only communicated on payment of a fee; or
- is only published outside the UK.[2]

1   CJA 1993, s 58(2).
2   CJA 1993, s 58(3).

3.44   The above definitions state that information may be treated as public, even though further efforts have to be made to obtain the information. This accords with the broad scope of the definition of 'made public' in EC Directive 89/592, which provides that information derived from publicly available data cannot be regarded as inside information and any transaction executed on the basis of such information would not constitute insider dealing under the broad definition of the Directive.

Information published according to the rules of a regulated market

3.45   Publication of insider information will not necessarily deprive insiders of their advantages because markets often take time to absorb information. It is generally accepted in financial markets that prices of securities do not always adjust immediately upon the release of material information. Accordingly, US securities law recognises this market reality by imposing liability on insiders for transactions undertaken before the market has assimilated the information.[1]

Similarly, before the CJA 1993, the UK Company Securities (Insider Dealing) Act 1985 would probably have prohibited insiders from immediately dealing on insider information after announcement until prices had adjusted to the information. The insiders were thus required to wait for the market to assimilate the information. The EC Directive on Insider Dealing has also been given this interpretation.[2]

1   *SEC v Texas Gulf Sulfur Co* 401 F 2d 833 (2nd Cir, 1968); and *SEC v MacDonald* 699 F 2d 47 (1st Cir, 1983).
2   See Klaus J Hopt, 'The European Insider Dealing Directive' (1990) 27 CMLR 51. The recital to the Directive states that investors should be 'placed on equal footing'.

3.46   The CJA 1993 clarifies the procedure for insiders to know when they can trade on information just released to the market. It adopts a procedure for notifying information to the Stock Exchange[1] that contains the following requirements: (a) the information which issuers wish to release to the public must be delivered in the form of an announcement to the Company Announcements Office, (b) the Stock Exchange then arranges for the prompt publication of announcements through its Regulatory News Service, and (c) at this point, for example, there could be an announcement on TOPIC that the information will be 'made public' for the purposes of the CJA 1993.

1   The Listing Rules, Chapter 9.

3.47   The FSA Listing Rules provide that no information may be released to a third party before such information is released to the Company Announcements Office. If announcements are made outside the operational hours of the Regulatory News Service,[1] however, the information must be given to two or more UK national newspapers and to two news services to ensure adequate coverage. This information must also be lodged with the Company Announcements Office no later than it is given to the other parties. In these circumstances, the information would appear to have been made public on publication of the newspapers.

The CJA 1993 definition of 'made public' provides the advantage of clarity because it avoids the uncertainty of waiting for the market to absorb the news by providing a clearer set of standards as to the time when insiders may deal.

1   In recent years, the Regulatory News Service operates between 7.30 am and 6.00 pm and announcements notified up until 5.30 pm are released on the day of receipt.

Information contained in public records

3.48   Information will be regarded as being made public if it is contained on records which, by virtue of any enactment, are open to inspection by the public. This covers registers set up under the statute, such as companies' or patents' registers or in publications such as the Official Gazette.[1]

1   Parliamentary Debates, House of Commons, Standing Committee B, 10 June 1993, column 184 (per the Economic Secretary).

Information readily acquired by people 'likely to deal' in securities

3.49   Information is considered 'public' when it can readily be acquired by those likely to deal in any securities to which or to whose issuer the information relates.[1] The phrase 'likely to deal' in securities is a term of art having its origin in the Company Securities (Insider Dealing) Act 1985, which defined it as 'unpublished price-sensitive information'.[2] Although it could be argued that the phrase only embraces the market professionals who deal in securities, such as market makers who are clearly 'likely to deal', it is also possible that it refers to the market in the shares itself. If information can readily be acquired by the market, that information is already likely to have made its price impact and is, therefore, not properly to be regarded as inside information. Thus, it is treated as having been 'made public'.

1   CJA 1993, s 58(2)(d).
2   Company Securities (Insider Dealing) Act 1985, s 10(b).

Information derived from information made public

3.50   Information is considered 'public' if it originates from information which has been 'made public'.[1] Although this may seem obvious, expert analysis of information may still have regard to many other factors, including the exposure of facts that had not been in the public domain. The CJA 1993 addresses the problem posed by an analyst who has knowledge of the company and industry and who can put together seemingly inconsequential data with public information into a mosaic which reveals material non-public information. Whenever managers, advisors and analysts meet in non-public places, there will be a risk that the analysts will take away knowledge of material information which is not publicly available. This should not be a violation of UK law so long as the mosaic, which contains inside information, is derived from information which has been made public.

1   CJA 1993, s 58(2)(d).

Price sensitivity

3.51   The final aspect of the definition of 'insider information' is the price sensitivity of the information. The test is that if the information were made public, it would be likely to have a significant effect on the securities. This is the most essential feature of the statutory definition of inside information. This criterion, rather than the issue of how qualitative the information actually is, is what really matters and which, ultimately, will be the determining factor when a jury considers whether information is inside information. Price sensitivity can only be determined at the moment of the deal when, by definition, the information is not known to the public and can have no impact on the price. In cases where the insider has dealt close to the time when the information was 'made public', the courts may rely on evidence that measures price sensitivity by the effect of the information on the market.[1] Because the CJA 1993 provides no further guidance, the UK courts may apply a 'reasonable investor' test relative to the securities in question and leave the matter to the jury. A Singapore court held that information will become price sensitive if it is information which would influence the ordinary reasonable investor to buy or sell the security in question. The UK courts will probably apply a careful analysis of the evidence supporting what is alleged to be a significant effect on any price.

1   *Chase Manhattan Equities Ltd v Goodman* [1991] BCLC 897 at 931 (per Knox J).

Territorial scope of the offence

3.52   The statute is narrowly aimed at insider dealing that takes place in the United Kingdom and will not apply if an essential element of the offence takes place outside UK territory.[1] The jurisdictional provisions of the Act are contained in the CJA 1993, s 62, which requires that some element of the offence under the CJA 1993, s 52(1) or (2) must take place in the United

Kingdom or the dealing was on a UK regulated market or the broker or investment firm was carrying on business in the UK.

1   CJA 1993, s 62(1)–(2).

3.53   The prohibitions contained in these provisions are subject to territorial restrictions, though the restriction 'regulated markets' included all of the major stock markets of the European Community and any other designated by order.[1] It is important to note, however, that purely private deals, even involving securities covered by the CJA 1993, fell outside the scope of the offence. By contrast, the FSMA 2000 market abuse regime covers both transactions by regulated persons and dealing by private persons off regulated exchanges.

1   The territorial scope of the offence is provided in the CJA 1993, s 62. A full list of proposed regulated markets appears in Appendix 2, Sch, Regulated Markets, Pt I.

3.54   Generally, an offence will be committed under the following circumstances: if the insider is in the United Kingdom when he deals, or when the dealing takes place on a UK regulated market, which operates in the United Kingdom, or if the person dealing in the price-affected securities relies on a professional intermediary on a regulated UK market, or is himself a professional intermediary.

ENCOURAGING INSIDER DEALING

3.55   The English law regards the disclosure of information to another person as a type of insider dealing when such disclosure is made without appropriate authority *and* in situations where that other person is likely to abuse the information. Indeed, UK law employs a broad definition of insider dealing to include both the attribution of insider information from agent to principal regarding a particular transaction and also an individual's procuring or encouraging the dealing of another. Most systems of law regard such unauthorised disclosures as a form of insider dealing. In the case where the recipient deals on the basis of inside information, but is not aware of the tainted source of the information, there might well be an issue regarding the materiality of the information. Under UK law, such disclosure will only be considered objectionable when the primary insider discloses the material information without proper authority. This chapter analyses recent developments in the law concerning the encouragement offence. Discussion of the relevant law under the Financial Services and Markets Act 2000 ('FSMA 2000') market abuse regime in regard to the imposition of civil liability on those who encourage or require others to commit market abuse is discussed in Chapter 4. Here our discussion will be confined to the provisions of the Criminal Justice Act 1993.

3.56   The encouragement offence provided for in section 52(2)(a) prohibits a person from encouraging another person to deal in securities based on knowing or having reasonable cause to believe that the person receiving the encouragement would deal in securities in the circumstances covered by the dealing offence.[1] It is not a requirement of the offence for the individual who has information as an insider to pass information to the other person, nor is it necessary that the other person should know that the securities it is encouraged to buy, are price-affected securities. The offence covers the classic situation where a tip is given by an insider to another, for example, 'sell as many shares of XYC plc as you can before tomorrow's profit report'. Naturally, this could occur in a number of other situations.

1   CJA 1993, s 52(2)(a).

3.57 If the insider knows or has reasonable cause to believe that the other person will deal on a regulated market or through a professional intermediary, the offence will be committed even if, in fact, the other person does not undertake a transaction. In practice, however, it is probable that a transaction will have taken place as otherwise it may be extremely difficult to identify the crime. A defence is available where no dealing was expected.[1] It is also important to appreciate, as we have seen, that if deals in securities do not occur on a recognised investment exchange, they will only be within the insider dealing legislation if the person dealing relies on a professional intermediary or is himself a professional intermediary. A person will rely on a professional intermediary only if the professional intermediary either acquires or disposes of securities (whether as principal or agent) in relation to the dealing or acts as intermediary between persons taking part in the dealing.[2]

1 CJA s 52(3).
2 CJA 1993, s 59(1)(a).

TIPPEE LIABILITY

3.58 The third type of insider liability[1] created by the Criminal Justice Act 1993 ('CJA 1993') and expanded upon and applied in the market abuse regime of the Financial Services and Markets Act 2000 ('FSMA 2000') is tippee liability.[2] Tippee liability arises when a person who has information, as an insider, derives such information, either directly or indirectly, from a person who falls within one of the other two categories of insider, namely, directors, employees or shareholders of issuers or those who have access to inside information, by virtue of their employment, office or profession. The essential elements of tippee liability are that the tippee must know that the information is inside information and that such information is derived from an inside source. In many cases, tippees and sub-tippees will not know that information is inside information. Indeed, the classic tip will involve a statement such as, for example, 'sell XYZ plc' or 'buy ABC plc'. Under these circumstances, no inside information will have been conveyed because, although the individual who gave the tip will have committed the offence of encouragement, the tippee will not have obtained the 'information as an insider' (even though the tippee knows the tip came from an inside source) and would, therefore, appear to be outside the scope of the provision's coverage.

1 CJA 1993, s 57(2)(b).
2 In fact, when the word 'tippee' was included in the Criminal Justice Bill in 1992, it drew strong opposition from their Lordships and the word was eventually withdrawn before the Bill was approved in the House of Lords; see Parliamentary Debates, House of Lords, 19 November 1992, columns 756–767 and 3 December 1992, column 1496. See the discussion in B A K Rider and M Ashe, *Insider Crime* (1993, Jordans) at p 46.

3.59 The CJA 1993 was a significant expansion of the scope of the criminal law to define 'insider' to include primary and secondary insiders, such as tippees who did not have a connection with the company whose securities were traded. Primary insiders are those individuals who have inside information through being a director, employee or shareholder of an issuer of securities or by having access to the information by virtue of their employment, office or profession.[1] The latter category of primary insider could be a person who obtained inside information and thereby became a primary insider by virtue of his or her employment, office or profession without necessarily having any direct professional, fiduciary or contractual connection with the company whose securities were traded. The category of persons having access to inside information by virtue of their employment, office or profession could be large indeed and includes professional advisers such as lawyers, merchant bankers, accountants, public relations specialists and the like. Whilst it would not be unreasonable to expect such persons to assume the responsibilities of insider status on a temporary basis, the section's language is wide enough to cover many others performing rather more peripheral services to an issuer. These types of temporary insiders might be office cleaners, temporary secretarial staff, postmen and couriers who have access to inside information by virtue of their employment. Although these groups would certainly have the opportunity to acquire inside information by engaging in the activities of their employment, it is arguable whether the scope of insider liability should be cast so widely.

1   CJA 1993, s 57(2)(a).

SECONDARY PERSONS AND TIPPEE LIABILITY

3.60   The CJA 1993 defines a person as having information as an insider if, and only if, the person subjectively knows that it is inside information and possesses such information, and subjectively knows that he has it, from an inside source. As we have seen before a person can be convicted of the offence of insider dealing, the prosecution must prove beyond all reasonable doubt that the individual concerned was fully aware that the information was 'inside information' as defined under the CJA 1993, s 56 and that the individual received the information from an inside source. The CJA 1993, s 57(2) provides the legal basis for tippee liability as a criminal offence. It describes the ways in which tippee liability may arise as follows:

'(2)   For the purposes of subsection (1), a person has information from an inside source if and only if –
(a)   he has it through – (i)being a director, employee or shareholder of an issuer of securities; or (ii)having access to the information by virtue of his employment, office or profession; or
(b)   the direct or indirect source of his information is a person within paragraph (a)'.

3.61   The CJA 1993, s 57(2)(b) thus creates tippee liability or secondary person liability for someone who receives inside information directly or indirectly from a director, employee, shareholder or other insider of the issuer. Secondary insiders are essentially persons who know that the 'direct or indirect source' of that information is a primary insider. Some uncertainty exists as to whether the recipient must know the exact identity of the source and the circumstances under which the disclosure occurred or must merely be aware that the disclosure came from a primary source. It is not necessary to show that the secondary insider or tippee actively sought the information or that the primary insider discloses the information in an unlawful manner.

3.62   A person can only be charged with the offence of being a secondary insider or tippee, if it can be proved that the person was aware that the source of the information was one of these primary insiders or someone who had access to non-public, price-sensitive information. Before the CJA 1993, the Company Securities (Insider Dealing) Act 1985, ss 1(3), (4) and 8 made it a criminal offence, subject to exceptions and conditions, where 'an individual has information which he knowingly obtained (directly or indirectly) from' a person connected with a company and then deals on the Stock Exchange with shares in that company knowing that the information is confidential and unpublished price-sensitive information in relation to those shares. The CJA 1993 differs from the Company Securities (Insider Dealing) Act 1985 by eliminating the requirement of a connection between the insider and the issuer. Moreover, the CJA 1993 made it clear that tippee liability could arise even if the recipient of the information received it passively and did not attempt actively to obtain it.[1]

1   See *Re A-G's Reference (No 1 of 1988)* [1989] AC 971 at 973–77 and 986, HL (holding that the defendant, who had been given unsought, unpublished, price-sensitive information, had 'obtained' that information within the meaning of the Company Securities (Insider Dealing) Act 1985, s 1(3) on the basis that the term 'obtained' in section 1(3) meant no more than 'received' and thereby had a wider meaning than 'acquired by purpose and effort').

3.63   The wider scope of liability is based on a philosophy that seeks to penalise the exploitation of advantages in information that arise from insider access. Discussion has taken place as to whether a journalist or analyst who deals before the release of his own recommendations will be guilty of insider dealing. Some commentators, however, argue that such dealing is not an offence under the CJA 1993 because a precondition for liability requires the relevant information to be from an inside source. For example, a director or employee may obtain inside information from an inside source if the information was received by virtue of the director's or employee's position with the issuer. Based on this analysis, information created by an employee would not be regarded as information to which the employee had access by virtue of employment. Thus, having access to information would appear to require that the information in question exists independently of the person seeking to obtain it or to access it. The recommendations of a journalist or analyst would not therefore be inside information in so far as that individual is concerned because he is not allowed to access his own information. If this is not so, then a person who dealt in the market prior to his making further and substantial acquisitions or disposals might be guilty. It is hard to see how one's own intentions can be considered 'inside information' in this context.

3.64   It should be emphasised that under UK law the establishment of tippee liability does *not necessarily* depend on the liability of the individual who tips. For example, if, in the course of negotiations, inside information is passed bona fide to another person and the recipient then deals on the basis of that information, the tippee who dealt will be likely to have committed an offence, even though the tipper passed the information in a lawful manner. Thus, for example, if a partner of a large law firm that is advising a corporation on a takeover overhears inside information during negotiations, the lawyer will possess that information as an insider if he knows it is inside information and knows that the information is derived from an inside source. Similarly, an individual who knowingly becomes aware of inside information and knows it to be from an inside source, but who is not an insider (by virtue of employment, office or profession), will incur tippee liability as well.

3.65   Where the information has passed through several hands it may have lost some of the qualities that made it inside information (ie precision and specificity) with the result that it may be difficult to establish that the tippee has inside information. Aside from proving the tippee's state of knowledge, it may be difficult to prove that the information is in fact inside information because at this stage it may have lost much of its accuracy and novelty. Moreover, even if the information, after passing through several hands, still retains these qualities it may be difficult to show that the sub-tippee knew that the inside information was from an inside source.

US INSIDER TRADING LAW

3.66   While most legal systems now have laws seeking to regulate the misuse of inside information, the US Federal law is undoubtedly the most developed and worthy of mention here. US law applies a complex test for determining the liabilities of insiders, which essentially narrows the circumstances in which persons are potentially liable for trading, disclosing or procuring insider transactions as compared with those in other jurisdictions. In cases not involving takeovers, primary insiders are prohibited from trading on the basis of material, non-public information in a company's securities if such trading breaches a duty under *either* the fiduciary or misappropriation theories. Under the fiduciary theory, the prosecution must prove that the trading constituted a breach of duty to the firm whose securities were traded and that the firm suffered injury on account of the breach. Under the misappropriation theory, an insider of firm A can be held liable for damages arising from trading in the shares of firm B if such trading breached firm A's policy prohibiting personal use of information produced or derived on behalf of firm A.[1] Insider trading, however, is allowed in fiduciary cases if the party to whom the duty is owed consents[2] and allowed in misappropriation cases if the party to whom the duty is owed has knowledge. Regarding misappropriation theory, the Supreme Court ruled in *US v O'Hagan*[3] that there can be no misappropriation if the fiduciary has fully disclosed to the principal his intention to trade.

1   *US v Carpenter* 791 F 2d 1024 (2nd Cir, 1986) (upholding a journalist's conviction of insider trading under the misappropriation theory based on trading in advance of a newspaper column, finding that he had breached the newspaper's policy prohibiting personal use of information produced or derived on behalf of the newspaper).
2   See Donald Langevoort, *Insider Trading: Regulation, Enforcement and Prevention* (West) s 6.05[3] at 6–33 to 6–35. See generally W Wang and M Steinberg, *Insider Trading* (2nd ed 2005, Practising Law Institute).
3   521 US 642 (1997).

3.67   A secondary insider trading violation only occurs if the tippee knows, or should know, that: (a) the information given to them is insider information, (b) the primary insider passed the information in breach of the primary insider's fiduciary duty[1] and (c) the primary insider derives either a direct or indirect personal benefit from making the disclosure.[2] The courts have adopted a rationale in which secondary insiders should only be liable for trading and primary insiders liable as accessories where the primary and secondary insiders have acted together to form a joint venture to exploit inside information.[3]

1   See a similar fact scenario in *SEC v Switzer* 590 F Supp 756 (WD Okla, 1984).
2   *Dirks v SEC* 463 US 646 (1983). The Supreme Court held (at 664) that there were three types of possible personal benefit: pecuniary benefit, reputational benefit and gift.
3   The joint venture has been criticised. See Langevoort, *Insider Trading: Regulation, Enforcement and Prevention*, s 6.07 at 6–39.

3.68   Regarding sub-tippees, it would be unlawful for a person who receives inside information from a secondary insider to trade only where that person is aware that the information is material and non-public and knows, or has reason to know, that the information was obtained by virtue of a breach of fiduciary duty by the primary insider. It should also be noted that because the US legislation only covers transactions in securities, secondary insiders may lawfully refrain or cancel trade orders.

3.69   The complexity of these issues was demonstrated in *US v Musella*,[1] where a word processing supervisor of a New York law firm was regularly passing inside information onto a broker, who then passed it to one Dominick Musella, who then tipped his brother, John Musella, a New York City policeman, who then recommended share purchases to two of his police colleagues, O'Neill and Martin. Neither O'Neill nor Martin knew of the original source of the inside information, nor were they aware of the specific basis of the tip. Not even Dominick Musella knew the identity or the position of the person who was the source of the information.[2] The Musella brothers and O'Neill and Martin were found guilty of the crime of insider dealing. The court noted that tippee liability would arise under anti-insider dealing laws for any person who receives suspicious information and that they would not be able to raise as a defence lack of knowledge of the identity or the position of the original source of the information. The court held that by deliberately not wanting to know, the remote tippees (defendants) had the requisite awareness of the original breach of fiduciary duty to incur liability on the basis of inside information. Most US circuits observe the rule that a person who receives suspicious information must *either* abstain from trading or establish that the information is not tainted by the original breach.

1   678 F Supp 1060 (SDNY, 1988); see also *SEC v Musella* 748 F Supp 1028 (SDNY, 1989).
2   In this case, the person, who was the source of the inside information, was known in conversations with the broker, who was the go-between, as 'the goose who laid the golden egg'.

3.70   If one were to apply the UK law on tippee liability for insider dealing to the facts discussed above in the *Musella* case, it would appear that an English court would have found Dominick Musella to have had the insider information, to have known that the information was inside information and also to have known that there was an indirect source of his information, but not to have known either the source's identity or its position. Most commentators observe that it would be unlikely for an English court to hold that knowledge of identity was necessary to prove tippee liability.[1] It would also not be necessary to show that the tippee knew the position of the original source of the information, ie whether the tippee knew it was a director, employee or shareholder of the issuer or a person having access to the information by virtue of his employment, office or profession. The court would probably not require that it be shown that the original source was an inside source and that the tippee knew it was an inside source. What would matter to the court would be whether the tippee received the inside information – either directly or indirectly – from the source that happened to be an inside source, unless it were rebutted to show that the requisite degree of knowledge was lacking. This issue will be explored further in Chapter 9.

1   But see *Re A-G's Reference (No 1 of 1988)* [1989] AC 971 (per Lord Lowry).

3.71   Although the position of John Musella would be likely to result in liability, it is submitted that neither O'Neill nor Martin knew that the information was inside information and, therefore, because the statute requires that it must be proved that they knew that the information was inside information and that a recommendation to buy shares cannot *per se* be inside information, it is submitted that O'Neill and Martin would be acquitted under the CJA 1993.

THE FSMA 2000 AND TIPPEE LIABILITY

3.72   The CJA 1993 extended the scope of tippee liability so that, unlike the Company Securities (Insider Dealing) Act 1985, the inside source need have no connection with the issuer whose securities are involved. This extension of tippee liability is also reflected under the civil liability regime for market abuse under the FSMA 2000. While this is discussed in more detail in Chapter 4 it is convenient to note here that the FSMA 2000 civil remedy for market abuse covers insider trading (traditionally prosecuted as a criminal offence under UK law) and applies to any person whose behaviour is based on inside information. Under the FSMA 2000 market abuse regime, the FSA may impose civil sanctions on any person or firm who engages in market abuse through insider trading. The FSMA 2000 makes no distinction between primary and secondary insiders, nor requires the alleged insider to be linked directly or indirectly to the company whose securities are traded. Thus, under both the CJA 1993 and the FSMA 2000, where the person disclosing the information has access to it through their employment, it is not necessary to show that the person was in a position (eg employment, office or profession) which might reasonably be expected to give him access to such inside information.

PRACTICAL APPLICATIONS OF TIPPEE LIABILITY UNDER UK LAW

Involuntary recipients

3.73   An issue related to those discussed above is the abuse of unpublished price-sensitive information by those who acquire it casually without any design on their part. For example, the proverbial taxi driver who overhears a conversation taking place in the rear of his cab. He might well appreciate that the information he overhears is very price sensitive, but he may have no idea of who his unintentional informant is and the standing of the knowledge that he has now acquired. It can be argued that if he does not appreciate that the information in question could only have come from an insider, then it is unobjectionable for him to utilise it. Of course, in practice, unless there is a relationship which is susceptible to proof between the person who seeks to exploit an informational advantage and his source, then it is highly unlikely that he would be identified or his trading impeached.

3.74   A more problematic situation arises when inside information is dumped on an individual or organisation who is also made aware or cannot but be cognisant of the fact that the information is from an insider source. It may be impossible both in legal and practical terms for that person publicly to disclose the information in question. Consequently, their possession of the information in question may well serve to prevent them from trading in the relevant securities. There have been examples where information has been strategically placed so as to prevent further acquisitions in particular securities that may have resulted in a change of control of the relevant issuer. To disable a potential offeror company in this manner is both undesirable and unfair. On the other hand, that person is in possession of price-sensitive information which, for whatever reason, cannot be brought into the market. The approach to this problem in some jurisdictions is to allow the person who has been given the information to proceed with the transactions that he had already planned or at least already initiated. Of course, the best solution in such cases is to require disclosure of the information, but, as we have already pointed out, this may not always be feasible.

Eavesdropping

3.75   Another scenario that has led to some uncertainty is where inside information is deliberately acquired by those who have no relationship with the source of the information. For example, highly price-sensitive information may be obtained through an electronic eavesdropping device or simple burglary. There can be no doubt that those who obtain the information appreciate its sensitivity and its source. On the other hand, is it appropriate to regard them as falling within the scope of anti-insider dealing laws? Of course, it may well be the case that their conduct will constitute some other criminal offence or tort. In some jurisdictions, before liability for insider dealing can be imposed, it must be proved where that person is not a primary insider, that he knows the specific identity of his informant. It is not sufficient merely to prove that the information clearly came from an inside source. In the case of electronic eavesdropping and no doubt other forms of espionage, it is quite possible that the recipients of the relevant information would not be aware of the specific source, although they would, of course, be aware that the person in question was an insider. In the UK, as we shall see, it would be sufficient for the prosecution to prove that those seeking to utilise the relevant information appreciated that it was from an inside source.

The insider's family and associates

3.76   Before leaving our discussion as to whom it may be appropriate to regard as being insiders, it is appropriate to address whether the spouses, children and associates of those in an access relationship should be presumed to hold the information in question. Indeed, it might be justifiable to regard the close associates and members of any person whose own dealing would be considered to be objectionable as subject to the same restrictions. In many jurisdictions, such as the UK, in which directors are under a legal duty to disclose their interests and dealings in the securities of their company, this obligation is extended to the director's spouse and infant children. It is also often extended to the interests of any company that the director owns or controls or, in some instances, in which he has a significant interest. In the UK, the specific prohibitions on directors engaging in practices such as option dealings in the securities of their companies are extended to those with whom the director is intimately and closely associated. In practice, in many of the cases that have come to light, the director or other insider has traded in the name of, or for the benefit of, a close relative or associate. The traditional civil law, which is based on the personal obligation of stewardship, may not extend to impose liability on the insider himself in such cases or, for that matter, the beneficiary of the abuse. A similar problem arises when the dealing is by a company with which the insider is associated because, in law, the company is an entirely separate legal person. While in many legal systems it is possible to 'lift the veil of incorporation', in certain circumstances such as where the company is incorporated for the purpose of evading the law or is an 'engine for fraud', the courts are cautious. They are aware of the importance of the 'corporate personality' principle in the commercial world and will therefore only seek to penetrate it where the public interest clearly mandates it. These issues involve a number of complex and difficult problems. It would not be acceptable to impose liability on an insider merely because a close family member or business with which he is associated happens to engage in a transaction while he is in possession of the relevant information. Indeed, in some countries, specific legislation has been introduced, or at least canvassed, to protect trustees who may find themselves, quite innocently, in a similar situation vis-à-vis unconnected dealings by those who manage the trust fund or by its beneficiaries. On the other hand, given the difficulties of proving to the satisfaction of the law that actual communications have occurred in the privacy of a bedroom, it may well be appropriate to resort to common sense inferences, if not presumptions. The attribution of knowledge between separate legal persons or within the structure of a body corporate are complex legal issues in all legal systems.

3.77   Tippee liability under the CJA 1993 has been simplified and extended under the FSMA 2000 market abuse regime to apply to a broad category of behaviour that constitutes misuse of information that is price sensitive and non-public. For example, a person who obtains inside information that was passed *bona fide* by another person during negotiations will incur civil liability under the FSMA 2000 and criminal liability under the CJA 1993 if that person deals on the basis of such inside information. Thus, a person who overhears inside information will have that information as an insider if he knows it is inside information and possesses it in the knowledge that it derives from an inside source.

DEFENCES TO ALLEGATIONS OF INSIDER DEALING

Introduction

3.78   The best defence to a charge of insider dealing is simply that one of the elements of the offence that need to be established by the prosecution is not proved beyond a reasonable doubt. However, given the complexity of the subject area, the legislation provides a number of specific defences. These defences will succeed only if, after the prosecution has proved all the ingredients of the offence, the defendant proves on a balance of probabilities that the offence was not committed.[1]

1   CJA 1993, s 53. See also *R v Cross* [1991] BCLC 125 (upholding the general principle that the burden is on the accused to raise a statutory defence).

General defences to insider dealing under the CJA 1993

3.79   A successful prosecution of the dealing[1] or encouragement[2] offences must first allege and prove all the elements of the offence of insider dealing as set out in the CJA 1993, s 52. For example, the prosecution might prove that the defendant has possessed and used price-sensitive information in relation to publicly-traded securities with a view to the making of a profit or the avoidance of a loss. The burden then shifts to the defendant to prove, on a balance of probabilities, any defence provided in the CJA 1993, s 53. For example, a successful defence might show that, at the time the agreement to deal was entered into, the defendant did not expect the dealing to result in a profit or to avoid a loss[3] which was attributable to price-sensitive information in relation to the securities. It should be emphasised that the offence is committed at the time the agreement is made and not on completion of the transaction. Thus, the statutory language does not appear to provide a defence in the situation where the transaction, on which the agreement to deal was based, does not in fact take place. Precluding a defence on this basis in respect of the encouragement offence seems to be appropriate because the encouragement will have factually occurred, whether or not a deal takes places, so the expectation of the parties at that time is clearly important. This approach, however, has raised some concern regarding its application to the dealing offence,[4] where it is argued that if the transaction does not take place, the deal itself will not have occurred so that the expectations at the contract formation stage seem less important. Prosecutions will probably be rare where completion has not taken place.

1   CJA 1993, s 53(1)(a).
2   CJA 1993, s 53(2)(a).
3   CJA 1993, s 53(2)(b).
4   See B A K Rider and M Ashe, *Insider Dealing* (1993, Jordans) p 54.

3.80   The CJA 1993, s 53(1)(c) and (2)(c) also provides defences to both the dealing offence and the encouragement offence where the defendant can show that it would have acted in the same way without the inside information. In such a case, after the prosecution has proved all the ingredients of the offence, the defendant must show that, on a balance of probabilities, its possession of inside information did not affect its decision to deal or to encourage another to deal. The policy rationale seems to be that an individual that is planning *either* to deal or to encourage someone else to deal should not be inhibited from doing so merely by being in possession of inside information. It would follow that a defence is available for an individual who has come into possession of inside information after making a decision to deal. A defence may also be available in circumstances where an investor who possesses inside information was forced to sell because of economic circumstances. For example, economic compulsion may provide a defence for a person who was forced to sell in the face of no other readily realisable property. In the above situations, some commentators note that it would seem proper and right to permit defences to prevail, but the second situation involving a defence based on economic compulsion would be more difficult to prove on a balance of probabilities.[1]

1   See Rider and Ashe, *Insider Dealing*, p 54.

3.81   Moreover, it would be more difficult to prove that possession of the inside information had had no effect on a decision to deal, in the absence of any economic pressure to sell. An important factor for maintaining a defence will be the timing of the deal, unless the defendant can show that the timing of the deal was not related to the inside information. For example, a defence may be available for a trustee who, whilst possessing inside information about securities, dealt in them on the basis of independent advice and for the benefit of the trust.

3.82   The CJA 1993, s 53(1)(b) provides a defence to the dealing offence if it can be shown that the individual, at the time of dealing, believed, on reasonable grounds, that the information had been disclosed to a wide enough audience to ensure that those taking part in the dealing were not prejudiced by not having the information.[1] This defence can be raised when two parties are in contact with each other and they are in possession of inside information that can or cannot yet be made public (eg properly conducted corporate transactions). For example, this defence would cover underwriting transactions where both parties know or are aware of the information.

1   Section 53(1)(b) states in the relevant part:
    '(1)   An individual is not guilty of insider dealing by virtue of dealing in securities if he shows –

(b)   that at the time he believed on reasonable grounds that the information had been disclosed widely enough to ensure that none of those taking part in the dealing would be prejudiced by not having the information'.

3.83   A similar defence is available for the encouragement offence where the defendant can show, on reasonable grounds, that it believed, before the dealing occurred, 'that the information had been or would be disclosed widely enough to ensure that none of those taking part in the dealing would be prejudiced by not having the information'.[1] In addition, there are two defences involving the disclosure offence that cover situations where no dealing was expected[2] or where the deal was not expected to lead to a profit or to avoid a loss on the basis of information that was price sensitive.[3] These defences need not cover the proper performance of professional, office or employment responsibilities because the definition of offence under the Act expressly omits 'the proper performance of the functions of [one's] employment, office, or profession'.[4]

1   CJA 1993, s 53(2)(b).
2   CJA 1993, s 53(3)(a).
3   CJA 1993, s 53(3)(b).
4   CJA 1993, s 52(2)(b). This provision states in the relevant part:
    '(2)   An individual who has information as an insider is also guilty of insider dealing if –
        (b)   he discloses the information, otherwise than in the proper performance of the functions of his employment, office or profession, to another person'.

Special defences under the CJA 1993

3.84   The CJA 1993 provides three special defences to the dealing and encouragement offences. These defences may be described generally as 'market defences'. Two of these defences are specific, covering market makers and those involved in price stabilisation. The third defence relates to what has become known as 'market information'.

Market maker's defence

3.85   Market makers are recognised under the rules of recognised investment exchanges ('RIEs') as performing the essential function in normal times of buying or selling securities registered with a regulated market. Market makers are ordinarily required to comply with the rules of an RIE or an approved organisation and to be willing to acquire or dispose of securities according to these rules.[1] A market maker may raise a defence where it can show that it acted in good faith in the course of its business, or in its employment, as a market maker.[2] It is important to note that in the original Criminal Justice Bill this defence would have applied to *any* employee of a market maker. This was later amended so that the defence would *only* apply to an employee of a market maker who was primarily engaged in market making activity.[3] Most experts agree that it is not clear whether this defence is available to a market maker who, after becoming aware of inside information by mistake, continues to deal in the securities in question. In such circumstances, obvious difficulties would arise for a market maker who, for example, was employed by a corporate broker with responsibility for dealings in a particular share and who would arouse suspicions amongst traders if he suddenly withdraws from the market. In this situation, the insider dealing offence would appear to cover the market maker who stayed in the market and dealt.

1   CJA 1993, Sch1, para 1(2).
2   CJA 1993, Sch1, para 1.

3   Parliamentary Debates, House of Commons, Standing Committee B, 15 June 1993, column 216.

3.86   Accordingly, the market maker's defence in the CJA 1993, Sch 1, para 1 is much narrower than the equivalent defence that had been available under the Company Securities (Insider Dealing) Act 1985. The counterpart provision of the 1985 Act prohibited the market maker from dealing whilst in the possession of inside information if the inside information on which the market maker dealt had been obtained by the market maker in the course of its business and was of a type for which it was reasonable for the market maker to have obtained in the ordinary course of that business.[1] The CJA 1993 sought to do away with these requirements in order to impose liability on a broader basis, but does provide a defence in the CJA 1993, s 53(1)(c) for a market maker who was wrongly exposed to inside information and continues to deal.[2]

1   Company Securities (Insider Dealing) Act 1985, s 3(d).
2   Section 53(1)(c) provides in the relevant part:
   '(1)   An individual is not guilty of insider dealing by virtue of dealing in securities if he shows –
      (c)   that he would have done what he did even if he had not had the information'.

Price stabilisation defence

3.87   The price stabilisation defence would be available for an individual who was dealing in securities, or encouraging another to deal in securities, on the basis of inside information if the individual can show that the dealings were in conformity with the price stabilisation rules of a recognised exchange or regulated market.[1] The price stabilisation rules are found in Pt 10 of the Conduct of Business Rules 1990 that are now enforced by the FSA.[2] The purpose of these rules is to permit a manager of an issuance of securities to enter the market (usually by purchasing shares) in order to stabilise or maintain the market price of those securities. A defence is available for price stabilisation if such activity is carried out in conformity with the rules of a regulated exchange. For example, the FSA's price stabilisation rules, adopted pursuant to the FSMA 2000, s144(1) and (3), contain safe harbour provisions to the effect that behaviour conforming to those rules will not amount to market abuse.[3] These safe harbour provisions for price stabilising activity are available to any person, whether that person is a firm or not, who can show one of the following: they acted in conformity with the price stabilisation rules for the purposes of the CJA 1993, Sch 1, para 5(1), their conduct conformed with the price stabilising rules for the purposes of the FSMA 2000, s 397(4) or (5)(b) (misleading statements and practices) or their behaviour conforms with the rules in accordance with the FSMA 2000, s118(8) (market abuse).[4]

1   CJA 1993, Sch 1, para 5.
2   These rules were originally adopted by the Securities and Investments Board in 1990 and, under the Financial Services Act 1986, s 48(7), conformity with these rules provided a defence against the offence of market manipulation under the Financial Services Act 1986, s 47(2).
3   Mar 1.7.2. Other FSA rules containing provisions to the effect that behaviour conforming to that rule does not amount to market abuse will be discussed below and include the rules relating to Chinese Walls, certain parts of the Listing Rules in MAR 1, Annex 1G and rule 15.1(b) of the Listing Rules.
4   See the *FSA Handbook*, Chapter 2, Price Stabilising Rules, MAR 2.1.2(1)(a)–(c).

3.88   The price stabilising safe harbours would cover any person concerned with an offer of securities for cash. For instance, there is no legal restriction on the appointment of stabilising managers to whom the FSMA 2000 price stabilising rules would apply. The main focus, however, is on lead managers when they are considering or undertaking an offer of securities for cash. These safe harbours could also apply to agents appointed by lead managers.[1] The safe harbours would cover both initial public offers and public offers of additional securities, along with securities already in issue.[2] The FSA observes that an offer is likely to be public in character where it is made in a prospectus.[3]

1   MAR 2.1.2(2).
2   MAR 2.1.3(R).
3   Other offers may be regarded as public when they are made to a section of the public, such as distributions and placements that are not essentially private (see MAR 2.1.4), but the requirement that there must be a public announcement means that some offers for sale of securities, for example by means of block trade, would not be covered.

Market information defence

3.89   The statutory language for this defence is general in nature and provides that an individual will not be guilty of insider dealing 'by virtue of dealing in securities or encouraging another person to deal if he shows that':

- the information which he had as an insider was market information; and
- it was reasonable for an individual in his position to have acted as he did despite having that information as an insider at the time.[1]

1   CJA 1993, Sch 1, para 2(1).

3.90   The CJA 1993 defines 'market information' in broad terms to be information which someone inevitably acquires as a consequence of the activities involved in the acquiring or disposing of securities. For information to qualify as 'market information', it must consist of one or more of the following facts:

- that securities of a particular kind have been or are to be acquired or disposed of or that their acquisition or disposal is under consideration or the subject of negotiation;
- that securities of a particular kind have not been or are not to be acquired or disposed of;
- the number of securities acquired or disposed of or to be acquired or disposed of or whose acquisition or disposal is under consideration or the subject of negotiation;
- the price (or range of prices) at which securities have been or are to be acquired or disposed of or the price (or range of prices) at which securities whose acquisition or disposal is under consideration or the subject of negotiation may be acquired or disposed of; or
- the identity of the persons involved or likely to be involved in any capacity in an acquisition or disposal.[1]

1   CJA 1993, Sch 1, para 4(a)–(e).

3.91   The second prong of the individual's defence requires a determination that the individual had acted reasonably in his position in doing any act, despite having acquired market information as an insider prior to the act. The CJA 1993, Sch1, para 2(2) provides criteria for determining whether the individual acted reasonably in doing any act, despite possessing market information as an insider. These criteria include: the type and content of the information, the circumstances and capacity in which the insider first acquired or had the information and the capacity in which the insider now acts. An investment practitioner should apply the reasonableness test in using market information in specific circumstances by making reference to the rules and principles of the Model Codes and the regulatory requirements of the FSA.[1]

1   Parliamentary Debates, House of Commons, Standing Committee B, 15 June 1993, column 217.

3.92   In addition, a market defence exists for an individual who acted in connection with an acquisition or disposal, which was under consideration or subject to negotiation, 'with a view to facilitating the accomplishment of the acquisition or disposal'.[1] This defence would also be available for an individual who acted in connection with a series of such acquisitions or disposals or had acted with a view to facilitate a series of acquisitions or disposals.

1   CJA 1993, Sch 1, para 3(a)(i)–(iii).

3.93   This market information defence is available only for individuals in possession of market information that was obtained as an insider and for which it was reasonable, under the circumstances, for the individual to have dealt, despite possessing the information as an insider at the time. An example of market information would be when an individual sells a large block of shares and the publication of this information would impact on the share price, as would the prior knowledge that someone intended to buy or sell a large block of shares.

3.94   On occasion it has been argued that there would be merit, given the uncertainty that exists given the complexuity of situations, if certain 'safe harbors' were created by law or prosecutorial policy. Governments have rejected these calls, largely from market professionals and analysts, on the basis that while the CJA does not require proof of 'dishonesty' in the sense thar we discuss in Chapter 6, in the vast majority of cases of insider dealing that would ever be seriously considered as worthy of prosecution the culpability of those involved is pretty obvious. The FSA has rejected the argument that there should be a blanket exemption for compliance with the rules of RIEs or the City Code. The FSMA 2000, s 120 confers a power upon the FSA to include provision to the effect that behaviour conforming with the City Code does not amount to market abuse, provided that the Treasury's approval has been given. Certain RIE rules and provisions of the City Code have been given safe harbour status as will be seen below, but these only apply to market manipulation.[1] The rationale given by the FSA for not applying similar safe harbours to misuse of information is that the criminal offence of insider dealing has a somewhat longer history and has been administered by a number of bodies ranging from the Stock Exchange to the Department of Trade. It is also the case, as we have pointed out, that given the nature of a criminal prosecution and the onerous obligations of proof and fairness placed on the prosecution, such additional safe-guards are unnecessary.

1   MAR 1.7.7 and 1.7.8.

Chapter 4

The market abuse regime

INTRODUCTION

4.1   The market abuse provisions of the Financial Services and Markets Act 2000 were designed to preserve the criminal and regulatory aspects of the previous market misconduct regime, but were also intended to address weaknesses in the enforcement of the civil regulatory framework and criminal law by creating a civil offence of market abuse.[1] The market abuse regime applies to all persons, whether or not authorised or approved under the FSMA 2000. The market abuse offence attracts civil liability that can take the form of unlimited fines or public censure by the Financial Services Authority or a court order for restitution to compensate investors who have suffered losses as a result of market abuse. The regime was designed to curb the misuse of information in prescribed financial markets and to combat market operators who sought to manipulate and distort those markets. The overriding policy objective was to ensure that participants in regulated markets were using and disseminating information that related to qualified investments in a way that did not undermine market confidence or the integrity and good governance of those markets.[2]

1   The market abuse regime became effective on 1 December 2001. Before the UK adopted secondary legislation implementing the EU Market Abuse Directive in 2005, section 118 (2) (a)-(c) of FSMA 2000 contained the three main categories of market abuse defined as: (1) misuse of information, (2) creating false or misleading impressions, or (3) market distortion. These three types of behaviour constituted market abuse if they satisfied a regular user test and were related to qualified investments that were traded on a UK-prescribed exchange or market.

2   The International Organisation of Securities Commissions (IOSCO) recognises market abuse and insider dealing to be a threat to the integrity and good governance of financial markets and can, in certain circumstances, undermine systemic stability in those markets. Accordingly, IOSCO has adopted international standards for the efficient regulation of securities markets that contain recommended prohibitions on market abuse and insider dealing. See IOSCO (2001) 'Objectives and Principles of Securities Regulation' (Madrid: IOSCO).

4.2   In respect of the criminal offence of insider dealing, the market abuse regime supplemented, rather than superseded, the existing provisions of the criminal law of insider dealing (Part V, CJA 1993) and replaced the crime of market manipulation under section 47 of the 1986 Financial Services Act with sections 397 (1)–(3) of FSMA that created criminal offences for misleading statements or misleading practices intended to manipulate prescribed financial markets.

4.3   The Financial Services Authority ('FSA') is under a statutory obligation to issue a Code giving guidance to those determining whether or not behaviour amounts to market abuse.[1] The FSMA empowers the FSA to punish both regulated and unregulated market participants whose market conduct falls below acceptable standards of market conduct as defined by a reasonable user of the market.[2]

1   Section 119. As discussed at **4.5**, the Code of Market Conduct was issued by the FSA in 2001 and has since been amended to take account of the implementation of the EU Market Abuse Directive. Sections 119 and 122 authorise the FSA to carry out a primary role in implementing and enforcing the regime.

2   The reasonable investor standard derives from the regular user test, which was set forth in the amended FSMA, s 130(3). The EU Market Abuse Directive, however, did not provide for a regular user test and the UK was only permitted to retain the regular user test for its original three types of market abuse – misuse of information, false or misleading impressions, and market distortions – as expressly recognised in the amended section 118(4) and (8). See the Financial Services and Markets Act 2000 (Market Abuse) Regulations 2005, SI 2005/381 as from 1 July 2005. Regulations 3(2) and 3(3) amend sections 118(9) and 118A(6) of the FSMA to change the date by which the provisions affected by those sections will cease to have effect. The regular user test of section 130(3) will now cease to have effect as of 31 December 2009.

THE EU MARKET ABUSE DIRECTIVE AND THE UK MARKET ABUSE REGIME

4.4   The FSMA 2000 market abuse regime was significantly amended with the implementation of the European Union Directive on Insider Dealing and Market Manipulation[1] ('Market Abuse Directive'). The Market Abuse Directive introduces a common EU approach for preventing and detecting market abuse and ensuring that the flow of information to the market is equally accessible to all market participants.[2] Significantly, the regular user of section 118(10) of the original FSMA does not appear in the Directive and is therefore retained only for those types of market abuse offences which pre-exist the Directive.[3]

The Market Abuse Directive significantly extends the definition of market abuse under UK law.[4] Market abuse is now defined in section 118 as:

(1)   'behaviour (whether by one person alone or by two or more persons jointly or in concert) which: (a) occurs in relation to a qualifying investment traded or admitted to trading on a prescribed market or in respect of which a request for admission to trading on such a market has been made, and (b) falls within any one or more of the types of behaviour set out in subsections (2) to (8) as follows';[5]

(2)   an insider who deals, or attempts to deal, in a qualifying investment or related investment on the basis of inside information relating to the qualifying investment, or

(3)   an insider who discloses inside information to another person other than in the proper course of his employment, profession or duties, or

(4)   behaviour not falling within subsections (2) or (3) (a) but which is based on information which is not generally available to those using the market but which, if available to a regular user of the market, would be, or would likely be, regarded by him as relevant when deciding the terms on which transactions in qualifying investments or related investments should be effected, and (b) is likely to be regarded by a regular user of the market as a failure on the part of the person concerned to observe the standard of behaviour reasonably expected of a person in his position in relation to the market,[6] or

(5)   behaviour which consists of effecting, or participating in effecting, transactions or orders to trade (other than in conformity with accepted market practices) which give a false or misleading impression as to the

supply of, or demand for, or as to the price or value of, one or more qualifying investments or related investments, or to secure the price of one or more of such investments at an abnormal or artificial level, or

(6)   behaviour which consists of effecting, or participating in effecting, transactions or orders to trade which employ fictitious devices or any other form of deception or contrivance; or

(7)   disseminating information by any means which gives, or is likely to give, a false or misleading impression as to a qualifying investment or related investment by a person who knew or could reasonably be expected to have known that the information was false or misleading, or

(8)   misleading behaviour or distortion of the market where the behaviour falls below the standard of behaviour reasonably expected by the alleged abuser.

Subsections 2 and 3 are known as the EU insider dealing prohibitions, while subsections 4 and 8 are 'super-equivalent' provisions which are not found in the Directive, but were retained from the original UK market abuse regime and represent a kind of gold-plating that contains prohibitions[7] on misuse of information and behaviour that misleads or distorts the market.[8] Moreover, the EU Market Abuse Directive eliminated the regular user test of the original FSMA market abuse regime, which had required that for market abuse liability to attach the behaviour in question had to be regarded by a regular user of the market as falling below an acceptable standard.[9]

1   The Directive of the European Parliament and of the Council of 28 January 2003 on Insider Dealing and Market Manipulation (Market Abuse) (2003/6/EC).
2   See FSA, *FSA publishes rules implementing Market Abuse Directive* (22 March 2005), FSA/PN/029/2005.
3   See Financial Services and Markets Act 2000 (Market Abuse) Regulations 2005, SI 2005/381.
4   See Financial Services and Markets Act 2000 (Market Abuse) Regulations 2005, and the Investment Recommendation (Media) Regulations 2005. See also discussion in See Freshfields Bruckhaus and Deringer (2005) *Financial Services Investigations and Enforcement* at p 625 (Tottel).
5   As noted above, section 118(2)–(8) applies to any financial instrument and also makes an offence of requiring or encouraging acts that are market abuse.
6   The regular user test was established in the original FSMA at section 118(10), but as discussed below was not incorporated in the Market Abuse Directive, and will lapse, unless contrary UK legislation is adopted, on 31 December 2009.
7   The FSA has referred to these prohibitions as 'super-equivalent' in relation to the original regime.
8   The relevant provisions before implementation of the EU Market Abuse Directive were section 118(2)(a)-(c).
9   The definition of the regular user test was set forth in the amended FSMA, s 130(3), which also mandated that it cease to have effect as of 30 June 2008, effectively abolishing the regular user test.

THE PRESCRIBED MARKETS

4.5   The market abuse offence is triggered when behaviour occurs in relation to qualifying investments or related investments that are traded on a prescribed market. The essential elements of the offence can be broken down into four categories: (1) what are the prescribed markets; (2) which investments are qualifying; (3) what are related investments; and (4) when does behaviour occur in relation to these investments.

The UK Treasury has the authority to prescribe markets to which the market abuse regime will apply.[1] The FSMA provides no limit on how many markets which the Treasury can prescribe. Generally, the Treasury has prescribed all markets that are listed under the rules of a UK recognised investment exchange and the OFEX. Moreover, the Market Abuse Directive requires the UK to prescribe all regulated markets and exchanges prescribed by the other EEA States.[2] As of 2008, the UK-prescribed markets are: the London Stock Exchange, the International Petroleum Exchange, the London Metal Exchange, Euronext-LIFFE, Virt-x, and EDX London. HM Treasury can amend this list, but the list is generally amended when the FSA recognises other recognised investment exchanges or revokes their recognition.[3] A list of the other prescribed EEA/EU markets can be obtained from the relevant EEA/EU supervisory authority.

1   FSMA 2000, s 130A(1). The Treasury has prescribed markets and specified qualifying investments by the Financial Services and Markets Act 2000 (Prescribed Markets and Qualifying Investments) Order 2001, SI 2001/996 (as amended by (Financial Services and Markets Act 2000 (Market Abuse) Regulations), Reg 10(2), SI 2005/381).
2   See the Market in Financial Instruments Directive. See the FSMA 2000 (Prescribed Markets and Qualifying Investments) Order 2001, SI 2001/996 (as amended) art 4(1)(c).
3   FSMA 2000 (Prescribed Markets and Qualifying Investments) Order 2001, SI 2001/996 (as amended).

4.6   The HM Treasury has authority to prescribe markets[1] which are located in other jurisdictions, and is now required by the Market Abuse Directive to prescribe all regulated markets that are listed by other EEA states. This raises the important issue of extraterritorial jurisdiction that has been created under the regime. Section 118(5) provides that '[b]ehaviour' may attract liability under the market abuse regime if:

'it occurs –

(a)   in the United Kingdom; or
(b)   in relation to qualifying investments traded on a market to which this section applies which is situated in the United Kingdom or which is accessible electronically in the United Kingdom.'

The test for a prescribed market is that it may either be located within the UK or be accessible electronically from within the UK. This potentially creates extraterritorial jurisdiction because it applies to behaviour whether in the UK or abroad in respect of financial instruments traded on prescribed markets based in the UK. Moreover, under the Market Abuse Directive, the scope of the regime has been expanded to include behaviour occurring in the UK in respect of financial instruments admitted to trading on regulated markets based in other EEA countries.[2] A market therefore does not necessarily need to be situated in the UK; it merely has to be accessible electronically in the UK, or be a prescribed market in a Member State of the EEA.

1   FSMA 2000, s 130A(1).
2   This means that extraterritorial application of the regime is now required within the European Union's twenty seven Member States and the three states of the European Economic Area not in the EU.

QUALIFYING INVESTMENTS

4.7   The market abuse offence may only apply to behaviour that occurs in relation to qualifying investments admitted to trading on a prescribed market and/or related investments to such qualifying investments.[1] HM Treasury is also authorised by FSMA 2000 to prescribe which investments are qualifying in relation to the prescribed markets. In doing so, the Treasury has referenced the investment instruments that are listed in article 1(3) of the Market Abuse Directive, which covers a broad number of financial instruments, which include:

- Company shares and securities equivalent to company shares.
- Bonds and other forms of securitised debt.
- Any other securities giving right to acquire shares or bonds.
- Derivatives on commodities.
- Units in collective investment undertakings.
- Money market instruments.
- Financial futures contracts.
- Forward interest rate agreements.
- Options.
- Interest rate, currency/equity swaps.

1   FSMA 2000, s 118A(3). For example, contracts for difference (CFDs) are covered by the market abuse regime. In *re Shevlin*, the FSA imposed a penalty of £85,000 on John Shevlin for trades he made in CFDs that referenced the share price of Body Shop International plc, a company whose ordinary share capital was traded at the relevant time on the London Stock Exchange. Shevlin's trades were made on the basis of inside information which he had obtained while an employee at the Body Shop. FSA, Final Notice, John Shevlin (1 July 2008).

4.8   Also covered are any other investments admitted to trading on a regulated market in an EEA state or for which a request for admission to trading has been made for such a market. The Directive effectively applies the insider trading laws to financial instruments that are traded or capable of being traded on a EEA regulated market. The Directive, however, contains important differences from the previous UK insider dealing legislation. For example, it applies not only to securities, but also to all financial instruments, including derivatives over commodities. The commentary to the Directive provides that 'the scope of financial instruments significantly affected by privileged information is not limited to those of the issuer, but enlarged to related derivative financial instruments (eg options on equity, futures and options on index)'.

4.9   The market abuse offence covers all investments for which the prescribed UK recognised investment exchanges (RIEs) are the primary traded markets (ie domestic listed securities and on exchange derivatives, and also investments only incidentally traded on these exchanges (for example, on the London Stock Exchange's international equity or fixed income markets)). In addition, it applies to conduct relating to derivatives on those 'qualifying investments' (for example, OTC derivatives on securities), and applies to conduct relating to instruments that underlie exchange traded derivatives or structured notes or warrants. These financial instruments are what the FSA calls 'relevant products'.

RELATED INVESTMENTS

4.10   As discussed above, market abuse can be classified into one of seven types of behaviour.[1] Two of these types of behaviour involve insider dealing and the improper disclosure of insider information in respect of qualifying investments, or related investments on a prescribed market.[2] Unlike the other types of market abuse, these two types of market abuse apply to related investments of qualifying investments that are traded on prescribed markets.[3] The breadth of the term 'related investments' should be emphasised: it could be any *financial instrument* admitted to trading (or where a request for admission to trading been made) on a *regulated market* situated or operating in the UK or other EEA state. It applies to all transactions concerning those instruments, whether undertaken on regulated markets or elsewhere (eg spreadbets).[4]

1   FSMA 2000 (as amended), s 118(2)–(8).
2   Section 118(2).
3   Section 118(3).
4   Insider dealing law also applies to financial instruments not admitted to trading on a regulated market, but whose value depends on a security traded on a regulated market.

4.11   The breadth of the term 'related investments' can be demonstrated by the following. Regarding misuse of information, it would not be necessary to show any nexus with the UK at all, other than the behaviour that relates to a UK traded investment in the broad sense described above. Compliance with local standards in another jurisdiction will not necessarily be a defence in a civil enforcement action for market abuse or to a criminal prosecution for misleading market conduct.

4.12   In addition, the term 'related investments' also has a potential application to behaviour which is less directly connected or indirectly related to the qualifying investments on the relevant prescribed market. Essentially, behaviour is covered which directly involves or affects the investments themselves.

PRESCRIBED MARKETS, QUALIFYING INVESTMENTS AND THE JABRE CASE

4.13   The FSA enforcement action against the hedge fund manager Phillipe Jabre and his employer GLG partners raised an important issue regarding the scope of the term 'qualifying investments'. In the *Jabre* case,[1] Jabre had entered into agreements to short sell the stock of the Japanese bank Sumitomo Mitsui Financial Group (SMFG) a few days after receiving price-sensitive information about the bank from a Goldman Sachs salesman. Jabre argued that his conduct in short selling SMFG stock was not, as a matter of law, market abuse contrary to section 118 because his trades in SMFG shares occurred on the Tokyo Stock Exchange and therefore were not qualifying investments on a prescribed market. He argued that it would violate the 'territoriality' principle for a market abuse penalty to be imposed in the exercise of the FSA's power under section 123. The FSA found, however, that Mr Jabre's behaviour did occur in relation to qualifying investments (SMFG shares) that were traded on a prescribed market. SMFG's shares were qualifying investments of a corporate body (SMFG) and, crucially, those shares were quoted at the relevant time on the London Stock Exchange's SEAQ International Trading System, which was a market to which section 118 applied.[2] Jabre contended that the actual shares he shorted were not traded by him on the London market, but rather on the Tokyo market, and that the term 'qualifying investments' applied only to the shares actually traded, and not to all the shares of the same kind. Moreover, he argued that the purpose of section 118 (prior to the Market Abuse Directive) was to regulate conduct in relation to UK markets, and not in respect of markets outside the UK which were not prescribed by the UK Treasury; and that his conduct on the Tokyo market had no effect on the shares listed on the London market and therefore could not constitute market abuse simply because the shares in question were listed on both markets.

The Tribunal rejected this argument by reasoning that the statutory phrase 'traded on a market to which this section applies' in subsection (1)(a) does not

University Centre Library
The Hub at Blackburn College

Customer ID: ******33

Title: Market abuse and insider dealing. (2nd ed.)
ID: BB49114
Due: 20120510

Total items: 1
22/03/2012 18:24

Please retain this receipt for your records
Contact Tel. 01254 292165

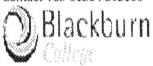

mean that the actual shares traded were the same shares that were subject to the abusive behaviour. The Tribunal held that behaviour constituting market abuse 'does not require the identification of any particular shares as being the qualifying investments to which the behaviour relates.' Indeed, the Tribunal reasoned that, if Jabre's argument were accepted, it would be nearly impossible for a regulator in market abuse cases involving, for example, disclosing inside information or disseminating false rumours, to identify any particular share or group of shares which were the subject of wrongful behaviour. Moreover, Jabre's assertion that his conduct on the Tokyo market did not have an effect on the London market was inapposite because the real issue was whether Jabre's behaviour on the Tokyo market could be reasonably expected to undermine confidence in the shares traded on the London market. The Tribunal held that Jabre's insider dealing by shorting the shares of the Japanese bank, wherever it occurred, had the effect of destroying confidence in the global market for the bank's securities and therefore constituted market abuse with respect to qualifying investments on UK prescribed markets.

1   See *Philippe Jabre and the Financial Services Authority (Decision on Market Abuse)*, The Financial Services and Markets Tribunal (10 July 2006), hearing on appeal by Mr Jabre of the Financial Service Authority's Decision Notice to Philippe Jabre and to GLG Partners (28 February 2006).

2   The Tribunal observed that SEAQ International (the Stock Exchange Automatic Quotation System for International equity market securities) is a quote-driven trading service in which securities traded on SEAQ International required at least two market makers registered with the London Stock Exchange and that two-way prices must be displayed on the LSE system for the security in question. SEAQ International was a prescribed market because of its link with the LSE and SMFG's shares, which were listed on the LSE system through SEAQ, were qualifying investments.

THE DUTY TO THE MARKET

4.14   The *Jabre case* also highlights the duty that market participants have to the market to maintain transparency and overall market confidence. An important aspect of the market abuse offence was that, unlike the criminal offence of insider dealing, it established a duty to the market for anyone whose conduct – whether on or off market – was defined as being market abuse. This meant that it was not necessary for prosecutors to prove that the defendant breached a duty to an investor or to the company or firm whose financial instruments were being traded. It was sufficient for the regulator to show on a balance of probabilities that the behaviour in question in respect of qualifying investments had impacted the market itself by undermining investor confidence and the integrity of the market as perceived by regular users of the market. In imposing liability, however, the FSA may still under certain circumstances need to show that the state of mind of the alleged abuser was relevant for committing the offence.[1]

Market abuse is therefore defined as behaviour which occurs in relation to qualifying investments admitted to trading on a prescribed market, or in respect of which a request for admission to trading has been made. It also applies to qualifying investments and to investments that are related to qualifying investments. These related investments can be traded on exchanges that are not prescribed UK exchanges. For instance, related investments could be traded on prescribed exchanges or off exchange in other EEA jurisdictions, or on or off exchange outside the EEA, if they relate to qualifying investments on a UK prescribed market. Although relevant in some circumstances, the state of mind of the market abuser is not necessarily relevant for a successful prosecution of the civil offence.

1   Although FSA is primarily concerned with the impact on the market, the purpose of behaviour
    will be relevant to regular user tests in certain circumstances. Code of Market Conduct, (the
    Code MAR) 1.2.5.

WHAT CONSTITUTES MARKET ABUSE

4.15   The statutory framework creating the market abuse offence is very
broad, covering 'behaviour' that is both on market and off market, including
trading activity and disseminating false or misleading information. The Market
Abuse Directive extended the three categories of market abuse under the
original section 118(2)(a)–(c) – misuse of information, creating false or
misleading impressions, and market distortion – to seven categories as set forth
in section 118(2)–(8):

(1)   insider dealing; or
(2)   improper disclosure of inside information; or
(3)   misuse of relevant information where the behaviour falls below the
        standard of behaviour reasonably expected by a regular user of the
        market or a person in the position of the alleged abuser; or
(4)   manipulating transactions in the relevant market unless for legitimate
        reasons and in conformity to accepted market practices on the relevant
        market; or
(5)   manipulating devices; or
(6)   information dissemination that gives or is likely to give a false or
        misleading impression; or
(7)   misleading behaviour or distortion of the market where the behaviour
        falls below the standard of behaviour reasonably expected by a regular
        user of the market or an alleged abuser;

unless such behaviour:

● conforms with a rule which expressly provides that behaviour which
  conforms with the rule will not amount to market abuse; or
● conforms with Commission Regulation 2273/2003/EC which
  implements the Market Abuse Directive in relation to exemptions for
  buy-back plans and stabilisation of financial instruments; or does not
  amount to market abuse under the Code of Market Conduct, or some
  other FSA position.

In addition, the UK regime maintains its separate civil offence of requiring or
encouraging another to commit market abuse if the act in question would have
amounted to market abuse if committed by the requirer or encourager.[1] It states
in relevant part that the requirement or encouragement offence can be
committed if 'by taking or refraining from taking any action, a person has
required or encouraged another person or persons to engage in behaviour which
if the person themselves engaged in such behaviour would amount to market
abuse'. In considering whether to bring an action for this offence or the market
abuse more generally, the FSA will take account of factors such as acceptable
market practices and level of knowledge and skill of person concerned.

1   FSMA 2000, s 123.

INSIDER AND INSIDE INFORMATION

4.16   The EU Insider Dealing and Market Manipulation Directive[1] has
defined insider dealing as a form of market abuse which can constitute both a

civil and a criminal offence. The Directive expands the scope of personal liability for primary insiders by excluding any requirement that they have 'full knowledge of the facts' in order for criminal or civil liability to be imposed. The repeal of this requirement recognises the market reality that primary insiders may have access to insider information on a daily basis and are aware of the confidential nature of the information they receive. In addition, the Directive adopts an 'information connection' requirement to the definition of secondary insider. According to this definition, a secondary insider would be any person, other than a primary insider, 'who with full knowledge of the facts possesses inside information.'[2] They would be subject to the same prohibitions on trading, disclosing and procuring as primary insiders.[3]

The UK regulations implementing the Directive replace the original section 118(2)(a)-(c) with new definitions of who are the 'insiders' and of what constitutes 'inside information'.[4] Rather than having three definitions of abusive behaviour in section 118, there are now seven categories which provide more specific definitions of prohibited or restricted behaviour.[5] This includes 'behaviour', 'where an insider deals, or attempts to deal, in a qualifying investment or related investment on the basis of inside information relating to the investment in question.' By section 118A, behaviour is taken into account only if it occurs 'in the United Kingdom'[6] or is taken outside the UK with respect to a qualifying investment (or related investment) on a prescribed UK market or a qualifying investment (or related investment) on a market prescribed by another EEA state. This provides extraterritorial jurisdiction for the FSA or other EEA authorities to enforce their market abuse legislation against parties who engage in behaviour outside their territory that amounts to market abuse if it relates to qualifying investments on prescribed markets in an EEA Member State.

Section 118B defines *insiders* as any person who has inside information, amongst other things, 'as a result of having access to the information through the exercise of his employment, profession or duties'.[7] The term *insiders* also applies to any person who has inside information as a result of his membership of the administrative, management, or supervisory bodies of an issuer of qualifying investments, or as a result of his holding in the capital of an issuer of qualifying investments, or as a result of his criminal activities, or obtained by other means and which he knows, or could reasonably expect to know, is inside information.[8]

Section 118C defines 'inside information' for the purposes of Part VII of the Act as the following:

'(2) In relation to qualifying investments, or related investments … inside information is information of a precise nature which –
(a) is not generally available;
(b) relates, directly or indirectly, to one or more issuers of the qualifying investments or to one or more of the qualifying investments; and
(c) would if generally available, be likely to have a significant effect on the price of the qualifying investments or on the price of the related investments …'

This broad definition of 'inside information' derives from the Directive's definition of inside information as 'precise, not been made public, relates directly or indirectly to issuers, and if made public, would have a significant effect on price of qualifying investments (ie financial instruments actually issued by issuer).' Information is regarded as generally available to users of the market if it can be 'obtained by research or analysis conducted' by or on their behalf.

1   Directive 2003/6/EC of the European Parliament and of the Council of 28 January 2003 on insider dealing and market manipulation (market abuse) (OJ No L 96, 12.4 2003, p 16).
2   Arts 2, 3 and section A of the Annex.
3   Art 2.
4   Under the pre-Directive UK legislation, the definition of market abuse was broadly defined in three categories: misuse of information, creating false or misleading impressions, or market distortions in relation to qualifying investments on prescribed markets. FSMA 2000, s 118(2)(a)-(c).
5   FSMA 2000, s 118(2)–(8).
6   FSMA 2000, s 118A(1)(a).
7   FSMA 2000, s 118B(c). Insiders who acquire inside information in relation to their professional and employment duties were subject to FSA enforcements in the cases of Richard Ralph (FSA Notice, 12 Nov 2008/Ralph) and Filip Boyen (FSA Notice, 12 Nov 2008/Boyen). In the action against Mr Ralph, the UK's former Ambassador to Belgium, it was proved that, at the relevant time, Mr Ralph was the executive chairman of AIM-listed, Monterrico Metals plc (Monterrico) when he asked Mr Boyen to buy £30,000 worth of shares on his behalf. At the time, it was public information that the company was in takeover talks, but Mr Ralph also knew that a takeover had been agreed in principle at a premium price that substantially exceeded the then share price. Mr Ralph was involved in the takeover discussion and knew he was not allowed to deal in the company's shares while the material information on the takeover had not been disclosed. He nevertheless directed his broker to execute trades on his behalf before the material information was disclosed. He agreed a fine with the FSA of £117,691.41, and Mr Boyen agreed a fine of £81,982.95.
8   *Ibid.*

INFORMATION THAT IS 'PRECISE' AND HAS AN 'EFFECT' ON PRICE

4.17   Section 118C(5) defines information to be precise if it:

'(a)   indicates circumstances that exist or may be reasonably expected to come into existence or an event that has occurred or may be reasonably expected to occur, and

(b)   is specific enough to enable a conclusion to be drawn as to the possible effect on the price of those qualifying investments or related investments.'

Section 118C(6) defines information as likely to have an effect on price if the '[i]nformation would be likely to have a significant effect on price if and only if it is information of a kind which a reasonable investor would be likely to use as part of the basis of his investment decisions.' Furthermore, the Code of Market Conduct provides that someone's behaviour is deemed to be on the basis of inside information 'if the inside information is the reason for, or a material influence on, the decision to deal or attempt to deal'.[1]

1   The Code MAR 1.3.4E. See FSA Final Notice to Steve Harrison (8 Sept 2008) at p 3.

BEHAVIOUR

4.18   The term 'behaviour' has been interpreted broadly by the FSA to include action and inaction,[1] and the Code of Market Conduct states the following factors shall be taken into account in determining whether inaction amounts to behaviour that is market abuse:

(1)   if the person concerned has failed to discharge a legal or regulatory

obligation (for example to make a particular disclosure) by refraining from acting; or

(2)   if the person concerned has created a reasonable expectation of him acting in a particular manner, as a result of his representations (by word or conduct), circumstances which give rise to a duty or obligation to inform those to whom he made the representations that they have ceased to be correct, and he has not done so.[2]

Moreover, behaviour can be undertaken by one person acting alone or two or more persons acting jointly or in concert.[3] Unlike the criminal offence of insider dealing which applies only to natural persons, the market abuse regime defines a person as not only an individual or natural person, but also as a business entity or non-profit organisation. The offence of market abuse therefore can be committed by a single person or any combination of natural and legal persons acting jointly or in concert.

1   FSMA 2000, s 130(3).
2   Code, MAR 1.2.6 (1) & (2).
3   FSMA 2000, s 118(1).

THE CODE OF MARKET CONDUCT

4.19   Essential to determining whether behaviour amounts to market abuse is the Code of Market Conduct (the 'Code') issued by the FSA. The Code has guided market participants in identifying practices which do or do not amount to market abuse. The Code has played an important role in determining what conduct is acceptable.[1] The FSMA recognised that the adoption of the Code was necessary given the breadth of the statutory definition of market abuse.[2] The Code provides guidance on what the statutory provisions of the market abuse regime mean and on the FSA's views regarding what behaviour or conduct is acceptable. For authorised firms, the Code has been praised for adding greater transparency in determining what does and does not amount to market abuse and therefore has clarified compliance objectives and promoted legal certainty.[3]

The main provisions of FSMA governing the Code provides as follows:

'119. –

(1)   The Authority must prepare and issue a code containing such provisions as the Authority considers will give appropriate guidance to those determining whether or not behaviour amounts to market abuse.

(2)   The code may among other things specify –

    (a)   descriptions of behaviour that, in the opinion of the Authority, amount to market abuse;

    (b)   descriptions of behaviour that, in the opinion of the Authority, do not amount to market abuse;

    (c)   factors that, in the opinion of the Authority, are to be taken into account in determining whether or not behaviour amounts to market abuse.

and

122. –

(1)   If a person behaves in a way which is described (in the code in force under section 119 at the time of the behaviour) as behaviour that, in

the Authority's opinion, does not amount to market abuse that behaviour of his is to be taken, for the purposes of this Act, as not amounting to market abuse.

(2)   Otherwise, the code in force under section 119 at the time when particular behaviour occurs may be relied on so far as it indicates whether or not that behaviour should be taken to amount to market abuse.'

1   Section 122(2) provides that the code 'may be relied on so far as it indicates whether or not that behaviour should be taken to amount to market abuse'.
2   The definition of market abuse is found at sections 118 and 118A.
3   See Freshfields Bruckhaus and Deringer, *Financial Services Investigations and Enforcement* p 622 (2005) (Tottel).

THE CODE SPECIFYING BEHAVIOUR

4.20   The Code may specify behaviour which, in the FSA's view, amounts to market abuse; or which, in its view, does not amount to market abuse. It may also specify factors which should be taken into account in determining whether, in the FSA's view, behaviour should amount to market abuse; and it may specify behaviour which is accepted market practice in relation to one or more specified markets, and that which is not accepted market practice.

BEHAVIOUR WHICH DOES NOT AMOUNT TO MARKET ABUSE

4.21   Section 118(1)(c) states that where behaviour does amount to market abuse, it will not give rise to a penalty or remedy if the person accused of market abuse believed on reasonable grounds that its behaviour did not amount to market abuse; or it took all reasonable precautions and exercised all due diligence to avoid committing market abuse. The FSA applied this reasonable person test in the *Harrison* case involving a portfolio manager who was given inside information about the refinancing plans of a company whose shares he later bought before the information became public.[1] The FSA acknowledged that Mr Harrison, a fund manager with Moore Credit Fund, did not realise that he was given inside information at the time, but that he should have realised it was inside information, and because he profited from it, he was required to provide restitution of £44,000 which included his employer's profits from the transaction, to cover the FSA's enforcement costs and he was suspended as a fund manager for one year. The case shows the importance of investors taking reasonable care to recognise inside information when they see it and not to misuse it. It was the first FSA market abuse case involving fund managers in the credit markets and is applicable to hedge fund managers who are often provided legitimately with inside information in the course of their business. The FSA expects fund managers in receipt of such information to observe high standards of conduct and not to profit from their privileged access to inside information.

1   *FSA Final Notice* (08 Sept 2008), FSA/PIN/101/2008.

4.22   The Code is intended to provide more clarity to the definition of market abuse and greater flexibility in applying that definition to changing market conditions and thus serves as a source of regulatory innovation. Nevertheless, under the FSMA, the Code has a limited role in determining whether market abuse has occurred. The only legal certainty it provides is its description of behaviour as *not amounting* to market abuse.[1] In contrast, the

Code only plays an evidentiary role in determining whether or not behaviour amounts to market abuse.[2] In both situations, the Code provides an important set of definitions and guidelines for behaviour that does not amount to market abuse, but its evidential factors that suggest that certain behaviour could constitute market abuse are subordinate to the statutory definition of market abuse.

1   FSMA 2000, s 122(1).
2   FSMA 2000, s 122(2).

SAFE HARBOURS

4.23   Section 122(1) provides that if a person behaves in a way that is determined by the Code not to be market abuse, then the person cannot be taken to have committed market abuse. This occurs, for example, if a person's behaviour has conformed to the safe harbour conditions described in the Code. The Market Abuse Directive enumerates an exhaustive list of safe harbours which a Member State must incorporate into its market abuse regime. The implementation of the Directive into UK law had the effect of reducing the number and scope of safe harbours which the FSA had originally incorporated into the Code of Market Conduct. The FSA had resisted eliminating the safe harbours that were not enumerated in the Directive on the grounds that they were merely descriptions of practices that did not constitute market abuse and therefore irrelevant to implementation of the amended regime under the Directive.[1] The Committee of European Securities Regulators (CESR), however, took a strict position prohibiting the FSA from adopting express 'safe harbours' in the Code that were not enumerated in the Directive or the Regulation.[2] Accordingly, the FSA amended the Code to include the following safe harbours that are required in the Directive.

1   HM Treasury and FSA, 'UK Implementation of the EU Market Abuse Directive' (Directive 2003/6/EC), *A Consultation Document*, June 2004, p 3 [HM Treasury].
2   This approach has been criticised on the grounds that the original safe harbours in the UK Code added clarity for practitioners and therefore by limiting those safe harbours under the Directive the Code's guidance may create further uncertainty, especially in view of the fact that the Directive has been often criticised for providing vague definitions of offences and the conditions for those offences. See CESR (December 2002) *Feedback statement for Level 2 Implementing Measures CESR/02–287b* (CESR, Paris)

Share buy-backs

4.24   This is the buying back of shares from a corporation to reduce the number of shares on the market. It is carried out in the interest of investors to improve shareholder dividends or strengthen the demand for an issuer's equity capital. By allowing corporate management to decide whether to buy-back shares while in possession of relevant information that has not been disclosed to the market, an important exception to the market abuse regime is created that is justified on the economic rationale that management should not have unnecessary regulatory restrictions on their efforts to maintain or enhance the value of shares held by investors. Share buy-back plans are nevertheless heavily regulated under EU company law directives to prevent issuers from using these programmes to engage in abuse through buying back shares before the relevant disclosure to the market is made with a potential impact on the price of the shares.[1]

The safe harbour is limited to share buy-back programmes and has restrictions upon the price and volume allowed. For instance, not more than ten per cent

(10%) of the subscribed share capital can be repurchased; a maximum of twenty five per cent (25%) of the average daily volume can be purchased, but it cannot be purchased at a price higher than the value for which it was bought.[2] Industry representatives have expressed the concern that the scope for permitted buy-backs in the safe harbour is too limited, particularly in relation to price and volume restrictions, and many believe the safe harbour should have been expanded to include debt repurchases and sales of own shares.[3]

1   Procedurally, share buy-back schemes must accord with the Second Company Law Directive 77/91/EEC and CESR (December 2002) *Advice on Level 2 Implementing Measures for the Market Abuse Directive* CESR/02–089d (CESR, Paris), p 34.
2   See CESR Advice (Dec 2002), p 36.
3   CESR's Feedback Statement (Dec 2002), p 30. CESR responded to these criticisms by saying that its discretion for expanding the scope of the safe harbour is limited due to the prescriptive requirements of the Directive.

Price stabilisation

4.25   This is an important economic mechanism to maintain the price of securities during an initial public offering. As in the UK Code, this is included in the Directive as a safe harbour, and is subject to strict rules rather than forming part of a blanket exemption. The rationale is that stabilisation measures taken over an extended period of time could be used as a form of market manipulation to increase or maintain share prices at an artificial level.[1] A stabilisation programme must meet a number of conditions before safe harbour status can be granted. Stabilisation may only occur during a certain period that has been disclosed to the market in advance. For example, during an IPO, the period will begin when the security is traded on a regulated market and end no later than thirty days after allotment, while the price may not exceed the offering price.[2] There must also be adequate levels of disclosure, including disclosure of possible risk factors.

1   See discussion in G A Ferraini (2004) 'The European Market Abuse Directive' 41 (3) *Common Market Law Review* 711–741, p 735.
2   CESR's Advice (Dec 2002), pp 39–40.

Accepted market practice

4.26   The final safe harbour involves an exemption if behaviour complies with accepted market practices, as established by the competent Member State regulatory authority.[1] This is defined as 'practices that are reasonably expected in one or more financial markets and are accepted by the competent authority'.[2] The FSA has not produced a definitive list, most probably because it wants to retain its discretion to approve a variety of covered practices. By not being too prescriptive with this requirement, the FSA leaves adequate room for market and regulatory innovation in how it addresses appropriate market practices. CESR has provided advice, however, but has avoided using prescriptive approaches that would inhibit market innovation in this area.[3] The discretion afforded Member State regulators to approve acceptable market practices, though necessary to respond quickly to changing practices in financial markets, compromises the aim of harmonisation of regulatory approaches across EU states, as different regulators will interpret it in their own way to reflect the needs of practitioners in their markets. This has led to a diversity of approaches amongst EU state regulators in determining what acceptable market practices should be for this safe harbour.

1   Although we focus primarily on acceptable practices in the UK financial markets, UK and non-UK issuers with securities trading on prescribed exchanges in other EU/EEA states should be cognisant of the different practices in those markets.

2   CESR (August 2003) 'Advice on the second set of Level 2 Implementing Measures for the Market Abuse Directive' CESR /03–212c, (CESR, Paris), p 6.

3   CESR (August 2003) 'Feedback Statement for Level 2 Implementing Measures' CESR/03–213b, (CESR, Paris), p 5.

Implications for practitioners

4.27   The Market Abuse Directive's amendments to the UK market abuse safe harbour rules have important consequences for practitioners. The cost and effort to revise risk management practices for firms has been significant. This is compounded by the fact that compliance practices were redesigned just after the first UK market abuse regime came into effect in 2001, which was a costly adjustment for many firms.[1] Most of these additional costs of complying with the Market Abuse Directive will be borne by the financial services and listed company sector which will have to pass the costs on to consumers and investors. The consolidation of the Code that has occurred because of the Directive's implementation has meant greater reliance on the Directive's prescriptive requirements and less discretion for the regulator to craft rules that are more sensitive to market practice. This has arguably limited FSA efforts to develop safe harbours that reflect appropriate market practices in the UK financial markets. Also, a stricter EU regime, due to the UK policy of super-equivalence and elimination of the regular user test, has meant that some EEA jurisdictions have only implemented the Directive's minimum standards, which may mean that the UK could become less competitive with other EEA jurisdictions because of the more stringent requirements of their super-equivalent provisions that are vestiges from the earlier regime. On the other hand, the UK should not lose its competitiveness if the super-equivalent requirements, not required in the Directive, have actually increased investor confidence by making it more difficult to engage in market misconduct without legitimate market efficiency justification. This is the tension confronting UK policymakers and regulators. Moreover, it has become more difficult for practitioners with large cross-border firms in Europe to settle upon acceptable practices that comply with the rules of those jurisdictions, while simultaneously complying with the super-equivalent requirements of the UK regime or similar super-equivalent practices in other EEA states.

1   See J Coffey *The Market Abuse Directive – the first use of the Lamfalussy Process.*

SANCTIONS

4.28   FSMA 2000[1] requires the FSA to issue a statement of its policy with respect to the imposition of penalties for market abuse and the amount of the penalty. The FSA's policy regarding sanctions is contained Chapter 6 of the Decision Procedures and Penalties (Manual).[2] In deciding whether to exercise its enforcement power under section 123 regarding any particular behaviour, the FSA must have regard to this statement. The FSA will also take into account any relevant provisions of its Enforcement manual as they are in force at any particular time.

The FSA can impose penalties, including fines and public censure, against a person who commits market abuse *or* against persons who require or encourage others to engage in behaviour which would have amounted to market abuse had it been engaged in by that first person.[3] The FSA can also petition a court of law for remedies against those engaged in market abuse or those who encourage or require behaviour that amounts to market abuse by seeking injunctions to freeze the assets of the abuser or other third parties or petition the court for restitution and/or compensation.

1 FSMA 2000, s 124(1).
2 See Chapter 10.
3 FSMA 2000, s 123.

REGULATORY POLICY AND THE MARKET ABUSE DIRECTIVE

4.29 The Market Abuse Directive's objectives are to consolidate and update previous legislation and expand the scope of conduct subject to liability to include both civil and criminal offences under the general offence of market manipulation. It also requires each Member State to establish a single regulatory authority with responsibility for both investigating and enforcing the requirements of the Directive. The creation of the single authority was intended to increase certainty, accountability and transparency regarding which agency has responsibility for investigating and enforcing the regulations and law. This means that under the UK market abuse regime the Financial Services Authority should have sole responsibility for investigating and enforcing the market abuse regime and the related criminal offences of misleading statements and misleading conduct under section 397.[1] Although this appears to be the policy of HM Treasury, several UK government agencies retain responsibility to investigate and enforce the criminal offences of insider dealing, misleading statements and market manipulation.

Implementation across EU Member States has been criticised as not being consistent or uniform due to differences in governmental institutions, legal traditions and business culture.[2] Generally, the Directive provides two broad descriptions of the market abuse offence: (1) the insider uses inside information that is not publicly available to his/her advantage, and (2) he/she prohibits market manipulation, and provides false or misleading impressions about certain financial instruments. This could potentially involve disturbances of the broader financial system without involving a breach of fiduciary duty to a shareholder or other company official.

1 See **5.3**.
2 Charlie Pretzlik (10/05/2004) 'UK warned not to obey EU's rules too strictly', *FT*, p 21.

UK IMPLEMENTATION

4.30 The FSA's and HM Treasury's consultation paper[1] discusses the FSA's approach to implementation, which aims to maintain its 'super-equivalence' in parts of the regime that exceeds the Directive's minimum requirements, while amending portions of the regime that do not meet the Directive's minimum standards.[2] The policy objective was to allow the provisions of the UK market abuse regime to remain unaltered where it met the Directive's minimum standards. This would cause less disruption to the UK regulatory regime and make it easier for compliance in the financial sector. Nevertheless, this has potentially created greater compliance costs because of the perceived complexity by business professionals who would be expected to have in depth knowledge of the previous regime as well as understanding how the Directive's amends and changes practice under the current regime. The FSA has reduced some of the complexity by amending the Code of Market Conduct and publishing guidance that assists firms in complying with the new requirements of the Directive.

Nevertheless, when adopting the 2005 Market Abuse implementation regulations, the Treasury decided to reduce what it had perceived to be the broad scope of the offence under the original section 118(2)(a)-(c), which had defined market abuse as misuse of information, creating false or misleading impressions and market distortion based on the application of a regular user test, in order to comply with the Directive's more precisely drafted classifications of market abuse. This complicated policy manoeuvre was described by the Treasury in an explanatory note as:

> '[The 2005 Market Abuse] Regulations amend sections 118 and 118A of the Financial Services and Markets Act 2000 (c.8) ("the 2000 Act") which were substituted, together with sections 118B and 118C, for the original section 118 by the Financial Services and Markets Act 2000 (Market Abuse) Regulations 2005, SI 2005/381 as from 1 July 2005. Such Regulations implemented, in part, Directive 2003/6/EC of the European Parliament and of the Council of 28 January 2003 on insider dealing and market manipulation ("the Market Abuse Directive").

> Subsections 118(4), 118(8), 118A(2) and 118A(3) of the 2000 Act retain the definitions of market abuse which are broader than those in Articles 1 to 5 of the Market Abuse Directive and were already in the original section 118. Section 118(9) provides that these provisions will cease to have effect on 30 June 2008; section 118A(6) does the same for the related provisions in section 118A.

> Regulations 3(2) and 3(3) amend sections 118(9) and 118A(6) of the 2000 Act to change the date on which the provisions affected by those sections will cease to have effect. The result of these amendments is that subsections (4) and (8) of section 118 of the 2000 Act and related ancillary provisions will remain in force until 31 December 2009.'[3]

One of the important effects of the Market Abuse directive, therefore, has been to define the market abuse offence in a more precise way, and to limit what the UK government had perceived to be its broad application through the three types of market abuse in section 118(2)(a)-(c) combined with the regular user test. Nevertheless, it is submitted that the overall effect of the Market Abuse Directive has been to make the UK market abuse regime stricter by providing more precision to the definitions of the relevant offences and removing many of the safe harbours under the previous regime with a view to enhancing investor confidence in the UK market and across European markets.

1   HM Treasury and FSA, 'UK Implementation of the EU Market Abuse Directive' (Directive 2003/6/EC), *A Consultation Document*, June 2004, p 3.
2   *Ibid*, p 15.
3   Financial Services and Markets Act 2000 (Market Abuse) Regulations 2008, SI 2008/1439.

Chapter 5

FSMA criminal offences of market manipulation

INTRODUCTION

5.1   An intrinsic characteristic of financial markets is that prices move in response to individual transactions and to supply and demand factors in the market. An efficient market for securities can often lead to volatile price movements that might reflect sharply changing investor preferences based on the dissemination of price sensitive information. Volatile movements in securities prices might also reflect significant adjustments in demand and supply of the relevant assets. Nevertheless, more sinister motivations of market participants can create distortions from the regular patterns of demand and supply which can undermine the efficiency and integrity of the market. Some commentators would agree that a price is likely to be distorted when price movements deviate from the norms expected by a regular user of the market. This could potentially lead to some forms of legitimate behaviour attracting civil liability for market abuse because of the sudden movement of asset prices that respond to different information in the market. Indeed, Keynes noted that changing investor sentiments regarding their perception of average investor opinion in the market could suddenly change based on rational and irrational factors which could result in a liquidity shock to financial markets.[1]

The FSA has recognised that distortion as a form of market abuse was very controversial. There was a concern that some types of legitimate behaviour would be restricted or prohibited by the market abuse regime. The civil and criminal law should acknowledge and make exception for market users who legitimately trade at times and in sizes most beneficial to them in maximising profit, but yet with a potentially volatile impact on the market. The criminal law of market distortion or manipulation accepts that where prices are trading outside of their normal range, this will not necessarily indicate that they are trading at a distorted or manipulated level. For the criminal law to impose liability, a person's 'purpose' or 'intent' is particularly relevant to whether they are engaged in distortion or manipulation of the market. This chapter addresses FSMA's criminal law of market manipulation and examines some of the challenges for the FSA in determining whether behaviour manipulates the market, given that market transactions inherently affect the price of the market.

1   JM Keynes *The General Theory of Employment, Interest, and Money* (1936), Chapter 12.

MANIPULATION

5.2 The term 'manipulation' in the context of financial markets has pervaded markets from the Dutch tulip bulb mania in the early seventeenth century to the collapse of the share prices of internet dotcom companies and Enron and WorldCom in the early 2000s. Some major jurisdictions, such as the United States, do not define 'manipulate' or 'manipulation'.[1] The US Securities and Exchange Commission has adopted rules, instead, that describe 'manipulation' by relating it to specific acts or activities that are then proscribed as 'manipulation' or 'manipulative'. The term 'manipulate' or 'manipulative' is often described as involving 'motive' or 'intent' to punish a result that is socially undesirable. A strict interpretation of the term would lead one to deduce that many types of acts could be characterised as manipulation, including activities regularly engaged in by securities professionals and others, but not necessarily in contexts predetermined to be undesirable. A less than rigid standard may be used to define 'manipulation' as it could cover many activities in the marketplace that are not viewed as harmful or socially undesirable. Indeed, the concept of manipulation is a constantly evolving one that takes on a less than objective standard that is similar to the 'he knows it when he sees it' definition used by US Supreme Court Judge Potter Stewart. For instance, the Seventh Circuit Court of Appeals adopted a definition of 'manipulation' as 'the creation of an artificial price by planned action'.[2] The Eighth Circuit utilises a definition that describes manipulation to occur when a price does not 'reflect basic forces of supply and demand',[3] yet no agreement exists regarding the types of behaviour that would qualify as market manipulation. Some agreement has coalesced around certain conduct that can be termed as artificial factors that result in manipulation in financial markets, such as 'corner', 'squeeze', 'domination and control', 'rumour manipulation', 'investor interest' manipulation and even 'price effect' manipulation, but these criteria appear to be hard to define in practice as the US courts have been contradictory in the application of these terms to conduct that is allegedly manipulative. In contrast, UK policymakers have since 1986 defined market manipulation, first under the Financial Services Act 1986, and later under the Financial Services and Markets Act 2000. This chapter examines the statutory provisions of FSMA that have defined the criminal offence of market manipulation.

1   The US Securities and Exchange Act 1934 does not define 'manipulative' or 'manipulation'.
2   *General Foods Corpn v Brannon* 170 F 2d 220, 234 (7th Cir, 1948).
3   *Cargill Inc v Hardin* 452 F 2d 1154 at 1163 (8th Cir, 1971).

UK CRIMINAL OFFENCES FOR MISLEADING STATEMENTS AND ACTS

5.3 FSMA subjects misleading statements and market manipulation to both a criminal regime and a civil penalties regime.[1] Section 397 of the FSMA establishes the criminal regime by creating two criminal offences.[2] First, it creates an offence of making misleading statements, whether dishonestly or recklessly, with a view to inducing a person to enter into an investment agreement.[3] Misleading statements can be made in one of three ways: (1) making a misleading statement whilst knowing that it is false, (2) concealing facts about such statements with dishonest intent, or (3) recklessly making (dishonestly or otherwise) a misleading statement.[4]

1   FSMA 2000, s 397(1)–(3) creates criminal offences for misleading statement and manipulative practices.

2   The statutory predecessor of the market manipulation provisions of section 397 is section 47 of the Financial Services Act 1986 (FSA 1986). Section 47(1) prohibited misleading statements, while section 47(2) prohibited misleading practices. Under the FSA 1986, the number of prosecutions for violations of section 47 was less than 10. The conviction rate was 50%. The FSA has had little more success with section 397, while bringing few prosecutions.

3   Section 397(1) states that it applies to a person 'who – (a) makes a statement, promise or forecast which he knows to be misleading, false or deceptive in a material particular; (b) dishonestly conceals any material facts whether in connection with a statement, promise or forecast made by him or otherwise; or (c) recklessly makes (dishonestly or otherwise) a statement, promise or forecast which is misleading, false or deceptive in a material particular.'

4   Section 397(1)(c).

5.4   An individual or firm can commit a criminal offence if it makes false statements in the manner described above with the intention of inducing or preventing another to enter into an agreement or exercising (or refraining from exercising) particular rights in relation to an agreement.[1] It must be proven that the person in question either acted dishonestly and was therefore fraudulent in making the particular statement or was reckless in doing so. In the case of recklessness, it must be shown that there was a high degree of negligence in the absence of fraud and dishonesty. Unlike previous criminal offences for insider dealing, the making of false and misleading statements may be committed either within or outside the market and applies to all natural persons including legal persons, such as companies, limited partnerships, limited liability partnerships (LLPs), limited liability companies (LLCs), or other business organisations. The aim of this particular offence is to prevent deliberate market manipulation by inducing investors to enter transactions based upon false statements.

1   Section 397(2). It states: '(2) A person to whom subsection (1) applies is guilty of an offence if he makes the statement, promise or forecast or conceals the facts for the purpose of inducing, or is reckless as to whether it may induce, another person (whether or not the person to whom the statement, promise or forecast is made) –

(a)   to enter or offer to enter into, or to refrain from entering or offering to enter into, a relevant agreement; or

(b)   to exercise, or refrain from exercising, any rights conferred by a relevant investment'.

5.5   The second criminal offence involves misleading conduct for the purpose of inducing another to acquire investments. It provides:

'(3)   Any person who does any act or engages in any course of conduct which creates a false or misleading impression as to the market in or the price or value of any relevant investments is guilty of an offence if he does so for the purpose of creating that impression and of thereby inducing another person to acquire, dispose of, subscribe for or underwrite those investments or to refrain from doing so or to exercise, or refrain from exercising, any rights conferred by those investments.'

In each of the above criminal offences, recklessness is sufficient *mens rea* – with the exception of section 397(1)(b) which requires the accused to have acted dishonestly in concealing material facts, involving recklessness as to whether it induced a person to enter into an investment agreement. Unlike the actual knowledge standard for the insider dealing offence under Part V of the Criminal Justice Act 1993, recklessness is an objective test. The objective test of recklessness involves the following question: did the accused make the statement while recklessly disregarding the known risks? Some practitioners have interpreted this to mean section 397 criminalises 'grossly negligent' statements and conduct.[1]

1   Charles Marquand *Comments on FSMA market abuse and market manipulation requirements* (2003) (London).

5.6   The making of reckless or grossly negligent statements which attract criminal liability under section 397 would also be a concern for a person engaging in financial promotions, whether as a authorised or unauthorised person. It may also be relevant to firms or individuals involved in making public statements during takeovers and in other circumstances governed by the FSMA regime.

DEFENCES

5.7   Section 397 contains several defences. Under both sections 397(2) and 397(3), the accused can assert that its conduct was in conformity with price stabilisation rules, or other acceptable market practices, such as control of information rules. These defences are similar to defences which may be asserted for committing the market abuse offence. Moreover, under section 397(3), the accused can assert the defence that it believed reasonably that its conduct would not create a false or misleading impression. This requires active conduct to corroborate its belief that its conduct did not create false or misleading impressions, not simply subjective perceptions.

Two particular types of market distortion identified by the Code of Market Conduct under the original market abuse regime were price positioning and abusive squeezes. These practices could also constitute market manipulation under section 397. Although the statutory conditions governing the market manipulation offences do not specifically refer to distortions of supply and demand in market, the FSA could potentially bring a criminal action against those engaging in such behaviour.

MARKET DISTORTION AND MARKET MANIPULATION

5.8   If the behaviour engaged in interferes with the proper operation of market forces with the purpose of positioning prices at a distorted level, then such behaviour could attract criminal liability for market manipulation. The necessary *mens rea* may be shown even if the defendant had other objectives for entering into the transaction so long as the manipulative practice was the actuating purpose of the transaction, and that there was a real and not fanciful likelihood that the behaviour in question will have such an effect, though the effect need not be more likely to occur than not. The 'behaviour' may, or may be likely to, give rise to more than one effect, including the manipulative behaviour in question.

5.9   A type of market distortion or manipulation can be caused by price positioning. For example, price positioning can occur if a person enters into a transaction or series of transactions with the purpose of positioning the price of a 'qualifying investment' or 'relevant product' at a distorted level. The positioning need not be the sole purpose for entering into the transaction or transactions, but must be an 'actuating purpose', defined as a purpose which motivates or incites a person to act.

5.10   In considering whether to bring a criminal action for market manipulation based on price positioning, the FSA will examine the legitimate commercial rationale and how the transaction could have been implemented in a proper way. Some of the factors that are taken into account in considering whether price positioning has taken place are much more detailed and can provide more certain guidance to market users, but there is a recognition that market practices evolve and the notion of what is acceptable market conduct can evolve to influence a determination by the regulatory authority of whether to bring an action.[1]

1 Specific examples of price positioning that could potentially be market distortion or market manipulation were listed in the Code at MAR 1.6.12.

ABUSIVE SQUEEZES

5.11   An abusive squeeze is behaviour which could amount to both market abuse and market manipulation. For instance, the Code of Market defined an abusive squeeze as occurring when (Code at MAR 1.6.13) a person had a significant influence over the supply of or demand for, or delivery mechanisms for, a 'qualifying investment' or 'relevant product'; and had a position (directly or indirectly) in an investment under which quantities of the 'qualifying investment' or 'relevant product' in question are deliverable. Abuse would occur if the person engaged in behaviour with the purpose of positioning at a distorted level the price at which others have to deliver, take delivery or defer delivery to satisfy their obligations (the purpose need not be the sole purpose for such conduct, but must be an actuating purpose).

5.12   Moreover, it should be emphasised that a significant influence over supply, for instance where there is market tightness, is not in itself abusive.[1] Regulators and enforcement authorities might rely on several factors that will be taken into account when considering whether a person has engaged in an abusive squeeze. These factors include: the extent to which a person is willing to relax his control or other influence in order to help maintain an orderly market and the price at which he is willing to do so; and the extent to which the person's activity causes or risks causing settlement default by other market users on a multilateral basis and not just a bilateral basis. The more widespread the risk of multilateral settlement default, the more likely that the market has been distorted.[2]

1 See discussion of factors as it relates to market distortion for the civil offence of market abuse in MAR 1.6.14.
2 The Code of Market Conduct gives a specific example of an abusive squeeze at MAR 1.6.18 to assist market users. It seems likely that the FSA will give specific examples of price positioning when giving guidance to market users.

FSA PROSECUTION

5.13   The FSA's authority to prosecute the criminal offences of insider dealing, misleading statements and market manipulation is provided in section 402. Civil and criminal sanctions can be imposed on those who violate section 397. The FSA may impose criminal sanctions for misleading statements or practices based on a conviction before jury trial that can result in custodial sentences of up to seven years and/or a fine. As discussed above, proving the requisite state of mind of the defendant will also be relevant in cases of market manipulation. For the offences of misleading statements in section 397(1)(a) and (c), the objective standard of 'recklessness' will be an adequate *mens rea*.

THE AIT CASE AND SECTION 397

5.14 The FSA enforced the market manipulation offence based on misleading statements in a criminal prosecution in 2005 against certain of the directors of the UK company AIT.[1] The facts of the case were as follows. On 2 May 2002, AIT directors Rigby & Bailey issued a statement via the Regulatory News Service that both turnover and profit were in line with expectations. The forecasted profit depended on revenue from three contracts worth £4.8 million. The announcement was rendered false because the contracts did not exist. Rigby and Bailey were found guilty by a jury in August 2005 of one count of recklessly making a statement, promise or forecast which was misleading, false or deceptive. Rigby was chairman & CEO of AIT and Bailey was AIT's finance director. Rigby served a custodial sentence of three and a half years, while Bailey served a custodial sentence of two years.

1   *R v Rigby, Bailey, and Rowley* (2005). Defendant Rigby was convicted of one count of recklessly making a statement to the market which was misleading, false or deceptive in a material particular; and Bailey was convicted of one count of recklessly making a statement, promise or forecast which was false, misleading or deceptive in a material particular, and Rowley was convicted on all counts. See FSA/PN/106/2005 (7 October 2005).

CIVIL SANCTIONS

5.15 Section 150 of the FSMA, however, confers a private action right for certain breaches of FSMA, such as the market abuse regime, but not for section 397. Under section 380 of the FSMA, the FSA can apply to court for an injunction to restrain a breach of the relevant requirement (or against a person 'knowingly concerned' in a violation). Section 382 authorises the FSA to apply to court for a restitution order against a person who has violated a 'relevant requirement' of FSMA. The FSA may also seek a court order to require a defendant to disgorge profits or pay compensation to any party suffering losses arising from a breach of (section 397 or all FSMA) FSMA, including for market abuse and market manipulation. Although a private right of action exists for those who suffered losses because of market abuse, no private right action exists for persons who have suffered losses as a result of market manipulation.

ANALYSIS AND CONCLUSION

5.16 Manipulation of the price of securities is a form of securities fraud that undermines the efficiency and integrity of financial markets. Today, market manipulation occurs across national borders through a variety of means, including the use of the internet to manipulate stock prices by, among other things, disseminating information that is false and negative about an issuer in an effort to drive down the price of its securities, or, alternatively, disseminating false information in order to drive a company's share price higher. UK authorities have brought few prosecutions of market manipulation as defined in section 397 or insider dealing as defined under Part V of the Criminal Justice Act 1993, as a number of obtsacles, including high evidentiary standards of proof and the complexity of bringing enforcement actions against white collar criminals, have made it difficult for UK authorities to show much success in this area. Indeed, the low number of prosecutions brought since FSMA became effective in 2001 can be explained in part by inefficient use of resources and poor training and skills of UK enforcement authorities. Moreover, inadequate pre-trial criminal procedures and the absence of effective negotiation mechanisms (eg plea bargaining) have also undermined the effectiveness of UK enforcement authorities.

5.17 FSMA supplements the market abuse regime by creating a broad market manipulation criminal offence of making misleading statements, both dishonestly or recklessly, with a view to inducing a person to enter into an investment agreement.[1] The market manipulation offence also includes engaging in misleading conduct for purpose of inducing another to acquire investments.[2] The FSA, however, has not undertaken many enforcement actions to impose criminal sanctions for the market manipulation offences. The poor record of the FSA and other UK enforcement authorities such as the Serious Fraud Office has led the FSA to bring many cases which could have been brought as criminal market manipulation cases instead as regulatory enforcement actions for market abuse, breach of the FSA's listing rules or general principles of business.[3] Even in civil enforcement actions, the FSA has had little success in reaching substantial settlements and admissions of wrongdoing by firms acting in concert with sophisticated trading strategies that resulted in arguably unlawful market distortions.[4] As discussed in chapters 10 and 11, the enforcement regime for civil and regulatory offences has been restructured to take into account the Tribunal's devastating criticisms of the FSA's procedural safeguards for investigations and enforcement in the *Legal and General* case. Other regulatory and enforcement complexities arise from the liberalisation and globalisation of financial markets and the associated cross-border dimension of market manipulation and the need to coordinate national investigations and enforcement actions with other national authorities, especially with EEA states whose prescribed exchanges and regulated markets attract the jurisdiction of the FSA and other EEA states. Finally, in light of the 2007–2008 credit crisis, it can also be argued that securities market regulators need to adopt a broader view of what market manipulation or market abuse is. Indeed, the credit crisis teaches us that effective cross-border regulation in Europe and at the global level should address not only traditional sources of market manipulation such as spreading false rumours and manipulative practices (eg abusive squeezes) in the market, but also follow a global approach to monitoring the level of leverage in the UK and European financial system which can be manipulated by firms to achieve unlawful market distortion.

1   FSMA 2000, s 397(1) and (2).
2   Section 397(3).
3   For example, a number of FSA regulatory enforcement actions for market abuse could have been brought as criminal enforcement actions for making material misstatements or engaging in manipulative conduct. The FSA's enforcement action against Royal Dutch/Shell Group for making knowingly false statements and other misrepresentations about its oil and gas reserves that had a significant impact on the group's share prices could also have been brought as a case of criminal misstatements to the market about Shell's future prospects. FSA, Final Notice, *the Shell Transport and Trading Company and the Royal Dutch Petroleum Company* NV (Oct 2005).
4   The FSA investigation into the activities of certain fund managers and brokers operating in the split capital investment trust sector led to settlement that was inadequate to compensate most of the claims of investors who had invested in zero-dividend preference shares and other unit trusts and financial products that invested in these risky instruments. See FSA Release (24 Dec 2004) 'FSA and firms announce details of Split Capital Investment Trust Settlement', FSA/PN/114/2004.

Chapter 6

Fraud and financial crime

INTRODUCTION

6.1   While it has long been recognised that one of the most important justifications for regulating conduct in the financial markets and financial services industry is the protection of investors, there has been surprisingly little discussion as to what this really means. For example, should all investors, no matter how professional or sophisticated they are, be given the same level of protection, and what type or quality of risk should this cover? In the context of our present discussion of insider dealing and market abuse, however, it is widely accepted that all investors should be protected from the risk of being defrauded. To the extent that we regard insider dealing and market abuse as a form of 'fraud', we can be reasonably confident that most would agree that it is reasonable for the law to intervene to protect investors. While some legal systems appear to be quite happy to regard those who abuse inside information as 'defrauding' at least the market, if not individual investors, in the United Kingdom, we have tended to adopt a rather different analysis. In English law, before we characterise something as 'fraudulent', we generally require some kind of knowing representation that is materially false with the intention that some identified person will rely upon to their harm. We would normally describe such conduct as 'dishonest'. While, as we have seen, in certain and generally exceptional circumstances, it is possible to regard an omission to disclose information as amounting to a form of representation, in the context of most instances of insider dealing, a failure to disclose the information in question will not be so regarded. When we consider the new offences of market abuse, in some respects we are closer to the normal conception of fraud, but in others even further away. When the market abuse involves the commission of an act intended to create a false or misleading impression or where a statement is actually made with the same intention, we are in the realm of fraud. Where, however, there is merely a taking advantage of privileged information, it is difficult to conceive this as fraud in any sense known under traditional English law.

6.2   It is obviously the case that investors' legitimate interests may be harmed by conduct which is not undertaken with the intention that it should cause harm or in circumstances where the person concerned appreciates that it could, but just does not care whether in fact it does or not. Indeed, it is probable that investors are more likely to be harmed by negligent rather than fraudulent conduct in most developed markets. While there are many laws and procedures designed to address this problem, this chapter focuses on what might be described as 'sharp practice' and not the competence of financial intermediaries. We are concerned here with what the Financial Services and Markets Act 2000 ('FSMA 2000') describes as 'financial crime'. There has been considerable concern, over many years, as to whether the law and the various agencies that are required or rather expected to enforce it, have or for that matter can, adequately police 'sharp practice' in the financial sector. Despite the early development of laws and even the recognition that specialised enforcement machinery might be necessary, the general view is that the traditional criminal justice system has not delivered. The Fraud Trial Committee, sitting under Roskill LJ, observed in 1986:

> 'the public no longer believes that the system ... is capable of bringing the perpetrators of serious fraud expeditiously and effectively to book. The overwhelming weight of evidence laid before us suggests that the public is right'.[1]

1   *Report of the Fraud Trial Committee* (1986, HMSO), para 1.

6.3   One of the driving forces behind the restructuring of the supervision of the financial sector and the FSMA 2000 was the concern to address financial crime and deal with it on a broader basis than the ordinary criminal justice system. Consequently, the FSMA 2000, s 2(2) provides that the reduction of financial crime is one of the four objectives that the Financial Services Authority should pursue to discharge its various statutory and regulatory functions. This objective is 'fleshed out' in the FSMA 2000, s 6, where it is made clear that the FSA is to be concerned with reducing the extent to which financial intermediaries are 'used for a purpose connected with financial crime'.[1] In particular, the FSA must have regard to ensuring that financial intermediaries are aware of the risks of being used in connection with financial crime and the importance of installing and adequately maintaining systems designed to prevent, detect and monitor the incidence of financial crime. The meaning of 'financial crime' is spelt out in section 6(3) as including any offence involving fraud or dishonesty, misconduct in, or misuse of information relating to, a financial market or the handling of the proceeds of crime. This is very broad and would cover most, if not all, of what we have previously labelled 'sharp practice'. It also includes 'handling the proceeds of crime', whatever that crime may be. The notion of handling is wide enough to include laundering the proceeds of crime and the FSA is given specific authority to promulgate rules on this by the FSMA 2000, s 146. It should also be noted that section 6(4) makes clear that an 'offence' includes an act or omission which would be an offence if it had taken place in the United Kingdom, even if it actually occurred overseas. It is, of course, important to appreciate that these provisions do not require the FSA to do anything other than in the exercise and discharge of its powers to pursue the reduction of crime as an objective. They do not mandate the FSA to pursue financial crime outside its limited statutory remit.

1   FSMA 2000, s 6(1).

6.4   On the other hand, it is clear that, in pursuing its objectives, the FSA is not only confined to utilising the weapons of the traditional criminal justice system. In addition to its various and many powers relating to prevention and compliance, it is now armed with significant investigative and civil enforcement powers which are discussed in Chapter 9. While there have been criticism of the resources that the FSA has deployed in pursuing its statutory mandate against financial crime, in recent years it has clearly taken its responsibilities more seriously. It must always be remembered, however, that the various provisions in FSMA aimed directly or indirectly at fraud and abuse represent only some of the weapons that can be used to promote and ensure integrity in the markets and wider financial services industry. In this chapter we will consider the general law as it applies to fraud and related abuses. While the FSA has attempted to co-operate much more closely with other authorities with wider responsibilities in the criminal justice system, the perception that the FSA operates a discreet system of enforcement which is not entirely in tune with, for example, the concerns of the police and agencies such as the Serious Organised Crime Agency, remains. On the otherhand, it must always be remembered that the FSA has rather wider concerns that the enforcement of the criminal and regulatory laws in its over arching responsibility to promote stability.

THE CREATION OF FALSE MARKETS

6.5   The early English law recognised that certain forms of conduct could undermine the efficient and fair operation of markets and there were common law offences, such as 'forestalling, regrating and cornering', as early as the eleventh century.[1] These were later superseded by statutory offences and today survive, to some degree, within the offence of conspiracy to defraud. While scandals were certainly not unknown in the financial markets, it was not until the early part of the last century that legislation was introduced specifically to outlaw certain frauds in the context of investments. The Prevention of Fraud (Investments) Act 1939, which was replaced and slightly amended by the Prevention of Fraud (Investments) Act 1958, made it a serious offence to induce an investment transaction by making a false statement, either dishonestly or recklessly, or by dishonestly concealing a material fact. This provision was more or less re-enacted in the Financial Services Act 1986, s 47(1) and with some useful redrafting as the FSMA 2000, s 397. While few prosecutions were successfully brought under these provisions, until the Financial Services Act 1986, there was no attempt to address, through legislation, attempts to manipulate the market, other than through making false statements. Before the Financial Services Act 1986, s 47(2), creating a false market by conduct was left to the general criminal law and various self-regulatory provisions. Consequently, the statutory control of manipulative practices, as opposed to the inducement of transactions by fraudulent misrepresentation, is relatively new in the United Kingdom. It follows that English law does not have the wealth of experience in addressing the many problems that arise from attempting to curb and control the creation of false markets that, for example, US law has.

1   See W S Holdsworth, *A History of English Law* (1922–1938, Little Brown) IV, p 375.

THE COMMON LAW

6.6   The most significant area of law in England with regard to manipulation was, prior to the enactment of the Financial Services Act 1986, s 47(2), the common law. The judiciary have rarely shown much sympathy for those involved in manipulating public markets. For example, in *Rubery v Grant*,[1] Sir Robert Malins VC considered that to allege that a person was a member of a share rigging syndicate amounted to an allegation that they were dishonest. He added:

'going into the market pretending to buy shares by a person whom you put forward to buy them, who is not really buying them, but only pretending to buy them, in order that they may be quoted in the public papers as bearing a premium, which premium is never paid, is one of the most dishonest practices to which men can possibly resort'.

The learned judge went on:

'there is a class of people who think it is a legitimate mode of making money, but if they would only examine it for a moment they would see that a more abominable fraud, and one more difficult of detection, cannot be found'.

1   (1871–1872) LR 13 Eq 443.

6.7   Perhaps the first English case to be decided by the English courts, or at least reported, is that of *R v De Berenger*.[1] This case involved one of the most audacious frauds ever perpetrated on a stock market. The United Kingdom had been at war with France for over two years and the price of British government stock was naturally depressed. The conspirators sought to raise the price of stock on the London Stock Exchange, enabling them to dump securities that they had already acquired, by spreading rumours that Napoleon had been killed and that peace was certain. The London Stock Exchange appointed a committee of inquiry which discovered the relevant facts. De Berenger and seven others were indicted of:

'unlawfully contriving by false reports, rumours, acts and contrivances, to induce the subjects of the King to believe that a peace would soon be made ... thereby to occasion without any just or true cause a great increase and rise of the public government funds and the government securities of the Kingdom ... with a wicked intention thereby to injure and aggrieve all the subjects of the King who should, on 21 February, purchase or buy any part or parts, share or shares of and in said public government funds and other government securities'.[2]

The defendants contended that seeking to raise the price of securities in the market was not of itself a crime and that there was no criminal conspiracy without some allegation that they had intended to cheat certain investors or cause harm to the government. Indeed, it was argued that it was in the government's interest that the price of its securities should be kept high.

1   (1814) 105 ER 536.
2   (1814) 105 ER 536.

6.8   The court, however, had little sympathy for such arguments and held that it was not necessary for the Crown to allege, let alone prove, that anyone had in fact been misled and injured. Both the means used, along with the object of the enterprise, were unlawful. The public had the right to expect that the market had not been interfered with by wrongful means. Lord Ellenborough stated:

'A public mischief is stated as the object of this conspiracy; the conspiracy is by false rumours to raise the price of the public funds and securities and the crime lies in the act of conspiracy and combination to effect that purpose and would have been complete although it had not been pursued to its consequences, or the parties had not been able to carry it into effect. The purpose itself is mischievous, it strikes at the price of a vendible commodity in the market and if it gives a fictitious price, by means of false rumours, it is a fraud levelled against all the public, for it is against all such as may possibly have anything to do with the funds on that particular day. The excuse is that it was impossible that they should have known, and if it were possible, the multitude would be an excuse in point of law. But the statement is wholly unnecessary, the conspiracy being complete independently of any persons being purchasers. I have no doubt it must be so considered in law according to the cases'.

The decision in *De Berenger* does not address directly, however, the issue as to whether it is an indictable conspiracy to interfere with the proper operation of the markets, not through the circulation of false rumours and information, but by a course of dealing. Under the ordinary law, it is possible to make a statement by word or by conduct, so, as a matter of principle, manipulative conduct could be regarded as constituting a false and misleading representation. Nonetheless, in *De Berenger*, one of the learned judges said:

> ' ... the raising or lowering the price of the public funds is not per se a crime. A man may have occasion to sell out a large sum, which may have the effect of depressing the price of stocks, or may buy in a large sum, and thereby raise the price on a particular day, and yet he will be guilty of no offence. But if a number of persons conspire by false rumours to raise the funds on a particular day, that is an offence and the offence is, not in raising the funds simply, but in conspiring by false rumours to raise them on that particular day'.

6.9 In a subsequent civil case involving an action for rescission against a stockbroker who had agreed to purchase shares on the Stock Exchange on behalf of the plaintiff for the sole purpose of creating trading on the market at a premium in order to create the impression that there was a thriving market and thereby induce other investors to purchase, in denying rescission, the court expressed the view that the relevant agreement amounted to a criminal conspiracy to defraud the public.[1] The view was expressed by Lopes LJ that there is 'no substantial distinction between false rumours and false and fictitious acts'.

1   *Scott v Brown, Doering, McNab & Co* [1892] 2 QB 724.

THE FAIR PRICE

6.10 On the other hand, it is also clear that not every concerted intervention into the market to hold a price will be considered manipulative. In *Sanderson and Levi v British Westralian Mine and Share Corpn*,[1] a contract was enforced pursuant to which a jobber on the Stock Exchange had made a market at a fair price, while the defendant distributed a substantial block of shares. In the rather less authoritative decision in *Landon v Beiorly*,[2] where a new trial was ordered,[3] the court also denied rescission of an allotment on the basis that the pegging of share prices during the launch of the company was to prevent 'undue depreciation below their actual worth'.

1   (1898) 43 Sol Jo 45.
2   (1849) 10 LTOS 505.
3   (1849) 13 LTOS 122.

6.11 Thus, it is clear on the English authorities that there is a distinction between manipulation and what we describe today as stabilisation. It is not without interest, however, that the courts of other jurisdictions have not always been prepared to accept such a distinction. For example, in *Harper v Crenshaw*,[1] the US Court of Appeals for the District of Columbia went further than the English Court of Appeal in *Scott v Brown*[2] and held that an agreement to stabilise the price of shares, while a large block of shares was brought onto the market, was illegal and unenforceable. There was no evidence that the agreement sought to create a fictitious price for the securities in question or to raise the price higher than the real value of the relevant securities. In *Bigelow v Oglesby*,[3] an Illinois appellate court declined to enforce a syndicate agreement among underwriters because it contained what was then a standard clause for stabilisation. The court distinguished the English case of *Sanderson & Levi* on the basis that in the present case the agreement was to stabilise the price of the relevant shares at a level which had not already been determined by the market itself.

1   82 F 2d 845 (DC Cir, 1936).
2   [1892] QB 724.
3   303 III App 27, 36, 23 NE 2d 382 (1939).

CONSPIRACY

6.12   It is important to remember when considering these authorities that the law might not necessarily be the same in the case of a criminal and a civil conspiracy and different considerations apply as to whether the persons concerned are being prosecuted for a criminal offence, are seeking to enforce an agreement inter-party or are being sued before the civil courts by an innocent third party. Unfortunately, the judges, in categorising certain conduct as illegal, do not always observe these distinctions. It would seem that a conspiracy to influence the price of shares or other securities on a market by making false statements or by engaging in purposeful conduct, such as a series of transactions with the intention of misleading the market, will be a conspiracy at criminal law. Conspiracy to create a public mischief no longer exists, but the facts in the relevant cases would fall within the scope of conspiracy to defraud today. Generally speaking, however, it would be appropriate for the prosecution to allege a statutory conspiracy to breach the FSMA 2000, s 397(1)(a), (b) or (c).[1]

1   See *R v Cooke* [1986] AC 909 modifying the strict rule in *R v Ayres* [1984] AC 447 to the effect that a conspiracy to defraud could not be charged where a substantive offence could be made out.

6.13   Considerable discussion has taken place over the years as to the proper scope of conspiracy in the criminal law. The Law Commission's working party published a consultation document in 1973[1] in which it concluded that the crime of conspiracy should be confined to an agreement to commit a specific offence. In other words, the mere agreement to engage in a course of conduct, no matter how malicious, should not of itself constitute a crime, unless the conduct in question was itself a specific offence. The Law Commission took the view, however, that there were situations covered by the crime of conspiracy to defraud which might not be susceptible to this approach.[2]

1   Working Paper 50, *Inchoate Offences*.
2   Working Paper 56, *Conspiracy to Defraud*.

6.14   The Criminal Law Act 1977, s 1 enacted a statutory offence of conspiracy to replace the common law offence of conspiracy. This reflected the Law Commission's view that the crime of conspiracy should be limited to circumstances where the object of the agreement is to commit an act which would itself be a substantive offence already known to the criminal law. However, the Criminal Law Act 1977, s 5(2) excepted the common law offence of conspiracy to defraud which remains outside s 1. Discussion has taken place as to whether conspiracy to defraud should remain an exception to the general rule. The Law Commission report Criminal Law: *Conspiracy to Defraud*[1] takes the view that it still has a role to play. This is illustrated in *Adams v R*.[2] The Privy

Council was of the opinion that an agreement to conceal transactions with regard to which there was a fiduciary duty of disclosure, so that those responsible might avoid being called to account for their unauthorised profits, amounted to an indictable conspiracy to defraud.

1   1994, HMSO.
2   [1995] 1 WLR 52.

ENFORCING THE BARGAIN

6.15   The agreement between the parties to the conspiracy would generally be unenforceable before the civil courts as being contrary to public policy. Indeed, Sir Frederick Pollack[1] referred to *Scott v Brown*[2] in which an attempt was made to enforce such an agreement, describing it as reminiscent of the 'well-known legal legend … of a highwayman coming into equity for an account against his partner'. Indeed, some US courts have taken this approach quite far and refused to enforce agreements involving the touting of shares, such as *Ridgely v Keene*.[3] In England, the courts have certainly declined to allow a wrongdoer to enforce such a transaction against the other party when that party is innocent and where both parties are involved in the wrongdoing. The general rule is that the courts should remain aloof. Losses and profits remain where they fall.

1   In an article published in the Law Quarterly Review in 1893 (9 LQR 105).
2   [1892] 2 QB 724.
3   134 AD 647, 119 NYS 451 (2nd dept, 1875).

6.16   In a case involving insider dealing, Knox J, despite a statutory provision to the effect that breach of the then insider dealing law did not make the relevant contract void or voidable, declined to lend the court's support to the enforcement of a partially completed transaction.[1] It has long been the English law that an innocent party can seek rescission or cancellation of a fraudulent transaction and the courts will not be keen to allow formalities or technical arguments to stand in the victim's path.[2] It is rather less likely that the courts would be prepared to see such an agreement enforced rather than rescinded by an innocent party. This is particularly so when the purpose of the agreement is to achieve something which is contrary to the public interest. In such circumstances, an innocent party would generally have other remedies than those based on the relevant agreement.

1   *Chase Manhattan Equities Ltd v Goodman* [1991] BCLC 897.
2   See *Gillett v Peppercorne* (1840) 3 Beav 78.

6.17   It is unclear to what extent a 'third party' such as an investor in the market, who claims to have been harmed by the manipulation, can pursue those responsible in the civil courts for deceit. In *Bedford v Bagshaw*, Pollock CB, stated:

> 'all persons buying shares upon the Stock Exchange must be considered as persons to whom it was contemplated the representations would be made …
> I am not prepared to lay down a general rule, that if a person makes a false representation, everyone to whom it is repeated and who acts upon it may sue him. But it is a different thing where a director of a company procures an artificial and false value to be given to shares which he professes to offer to the public'.[1]

1   (1859) 4 H & N 538.

6.18   The Chief Baron thought that where the person responsible contemplated that the plaintiff was 'one of the persons' to whom the representation could be made or 'ought to have been aware he was injuring or might injure', a cause of action might be found. Of course, in this case, the defendant had effectively procured a false value for stock by fraudulently securing a quotation and settling date. The plaintiff reasonably assumed that the sufficient shares had been taken up to justify the quotation. In *Barry v Croskey*,[1] while agreeing with Pollock CB's comments, Page Wood VC, referring to the contention that 'every person, who in consequence of (the defendant's) frauds on the Stock Exchange, was induced to purchase stock at an advanced price in reliance on the false rumour he had circulated, was entitled to maintain an action against (the defendant)' questioned whether 'such consequences' would not be too remote to form grounds for action. In *Peek v Gurney*,[2] Lord Chelmsford also thought it highly dubious that those who had made an assumption on the basis that, according to the rules and practices of the market, certain underlying facts must exist or have been represented to exist, had a viable complaint. In *Salaman v Warner*,[3] a remedy was denied to a jobber who had acted on his 'own judgment' as to a presumed state of affairs, rather than on a direct representation to himself. Of course, these cases are primarily concerned with false representations made to the market authorities, which result in securities being traded at an inflated price. Where there is a direct representation, such as the issue of a false statement directly to the market, then it is not unlikely, at least in the case of fraud, that all those who can establish direct loss will be able to sue for the full extent of that loss.

1   (1861) 2 John & H 1.
2   (1871) LR 13 Eq 79.
3   (1891) 7 TLR 484, CA.

6.19   The real problem in cases of manipulation, in particular by conduct, is whether it is possible to contend that the market price is itself a representation of, for example, compliance with all the rules and procedures which contribute to the availability of the market and, thus, price. Where a market has been manipulated and a 'false price' achieved, all those who come to the market or rely upon the market, at the relevant time, are harmed. In the leading US case of *US v Brown*,[1] Woolsey J, at first instance, referring to some of the English decisions, observed:

> 'when an outsider, a member of the public, reads the price quotations of a stock listed on an exchange, he is justified in supposing that the quoted price is an appraisal of the value of the stock due to a series of actual sales between various persons dealing at arm's length in a free and open market on the exchange'.

In other words, the investor is entitled to assume that the price is a true reflection of the proper interaction of supply and demand. While similar sentiments can be found in cases such as *Scott v Brown*,[2] it is questionable whether an English court would, on the basis of the common law, find liability to market participants for their loss. The twin hurdles of reliance and causation are likely to prove insurmountable.

1   5 F Supp 81 (SDNY, 1933).
2   [1892] 2 QB 724.

6.20   To what extent it may be possible to base an action for manipulation on some other cause of action than fraud is debatable. The courts have not been particularly sympathetic to arguments that seek to invoke allegations of conspiracy. At the end of the day, for a civil claim based on this particular tort, it is necessary to show that the plaintiff's legitimate interest has been harmed. In the context of our present discussion, this would be problematic to say the least. While it may well be appropriate to frame an action in the tort of negligence, the courts are notoriously reluctant to contemplate open-ended liability and in most cases that can reasonably be conceived of as manipulation, it is most unlikely the courts would find sufficient proximity between the wrongdoer and a person who simply comes into the market. The most likely civil claim for manipulative conduct that violates the FSA's rules and, in particular, the market abuse provisions, is under the FSMA 2000, s 150. This creates a right of action for 'private persons' who suffer loss as a result of such a contravention by an authorised person. A plaintiff may recover simply by showing a breach of the rules which has resulted in him suffering loss. Of course, as with the Financial Services Act 1986, ss 62 and 62A, it has to be shown that the loss in question occurred as a result of the violation. This was and remains a major stumbling block. It is, however, important to remember that the cause of action under s 150 is in addition to any rights that may exist at common law.

FRAUD (BY REPRESENTATION OR CONDUCT)

6.21   The early common law recognised the importance of punishing conduct that involved fraud and also providing those harmed by it, with recompense. However, in common with many other legal systems the law has had difficulty in determinining exactly what is fraud. In the context of the civil law one of the leading works on the subject (*Kerr on the Law of Fraud and Mistake*)[1] states 'It is not easy to give a definition of what constitutes fraud in the extensive signification in which the term is understood by the Civil Courts of Justice. The Courts have always avoided hampering themselves by defining or laying down as a general proposition what shall be held to constitute fraud. Fraud is infinite in variety. The fertility of man's invention in devising new schemes or fraud is so great, that the courts have always declined to define it ... reserving to themselves the liberty to deal with it under whatever form it may present itself. Fraud, in the contemplation of a Civil Court of Justice, may be said to include properly all acts, omissions, and concealments which involve a breach of legal or equitable duty, trust or confidence, justly reposed, and are injurious to another, or by which an undue or unconscientious advantage is taken of another. All surprise, trick, cunning, dissembling and other unfair way that is used to cheat any one is considered fraud. Fraud in all cases implies a wilful act on the part of anyone, whereby another is sought to be deprived, by illegal or inequitable means, of what he is entitled to.'

1   (7th Ed) by Denis Lane McDonnell and John George Monroe (1952), Sweet & Maxwell, page 1.

6.22   In the context of the criminal law there has been concern as to the fairness of such vagueness and in many countries attempts have been made to provide what passes for a definition. In reality most do little more than recite the ways in which the courts have identified something as fraudulent. Paradoxically, in Britain after much discussion and an extensive Fraud Review[1] ordered by the Attorney General in July 2006, a new law was enacted which in many respects broadens the crime of 'fraud'. Judge Alan Wilkie QC, then one of the Law Commissioners of England and Wales in referring to an earlier report by the English and Welsh Law Commission on Fraud, published in July 2002, stated that the objectives of a new law should be 'to make the law of fraud clearer and simpler ...(and) as a result all concerned whether jurors, police, victims, defendants or lawyers, will be better placed to understand who has committed a crime and who has not.'[2] In so far as the new Fraud Act 2006 bases liability on the concept of 'dishonesty' it remains to be seen whether there is any greater certainty.

1   Reference should be made generally to S Farrell, N Yeo and G Ladenburtg, *The Fraud Act 2006*, (2007) Oxford University Press and D Ormerod and D Williams, *Smith's law of Theft* (9th Ed) (2007), Oxford University Press.
2   See generally the *Fraud Report No 276*, Law Commission, http://www.lacom.gov.uk/docs/lc276.pdf; *Law Commission, Legislating the criminal Code: Fraud and Deception* (*Consultation paper No 155, 1999*).

6.23   In the United Kingdom there is only one offence of fraud in this new Act. It may be committed in three broad ways under section 1. Firstly, by a false representation.[1] Secondly, by failing to disclose information in regard to which there is a legal duty to disclose[2] and thirdly, by abuse of a position in which one is expected to safeguard, or not to act against, the financial interests of another person.[3] The offence is committed if what is done is done dishonestly with a fraudulent intention. Thus, it is the state of mind that is the determinant factor in liability.

1   Section 2.
2   Section 3.
3   Section 4.

REQUISITE STATE OF MIND – MENS REA

6.24   Dishonesty is a core and, indeed, protean concept, in fraud. Dishonesty is a question of fact, not law. Thus, the appropriate instruction, according to English law, to the jury is – where the prosecution has proved that what the defendant did, was dishonest by the ordinary standards of reasonable and honest people, must the defendant have realised that what he was doing would be regarded as dishonest by those standards?[1] It is important to note that it is for the jury to decide what the relevant standards of honest behaviour are. Furthermore, in considering whether the defendant actually appreciated that what he was doing violated these standards, the jury must consider the defendant's own state of mind at the relevant time.

1   See *R v Ghosh* (1982) 75 Cr App R 154.

6.25   The second element that must be established is that of fraudulent intent. In establishing that a fraud has been committed, it must be proved that in making the false representation, failing to disclose information, or abusing the position, the defendant intended to make a gain for himself, or for another, or to cause loss to another, or expose another to a risk of loss. It is important to note that the offence is complete if what is done is done with the requisite intention, the fact that a gain or loss occurred or did not, is irrelevant. It is the defendant's intention that is determinant. It is not without interest that the English Law Commission in its *Report on Fraud* (2002, para 7.53) stated that 'fraud is essentially an economic crime, and we do not think the new offence should extend to conduct which has no financial dimension'. Thus, gain or loss is stated in the Act only to apply to 'money or other property'. However, gain or loss does extend to a temporary gain or loss. There is no need for the defendant to intend to achieve a permanent gain or loss.

PROOF OF DISHONESTY AND FRAUDULENT INTENTION

6.26   Establishing dishonesty to the satisfaction of the court has been said to be one of the main stumbling blocks to securing more convictions. Juries have been criticised for not having the expertise and understanding to properly understand the facts that are placed before them and on occasion a similar complaint has been made about judges. The complexity of information and in particular documents placed before the court is often perceived to be a significant hurdle in achieving the level of appreciation upon which a sound determination of the facts can be made. On the other hand in common law jurisdictions it is often said that once the jury or judge 'sniffs' the stench of dishonesty, it is not difficult to find it. Given that the determination as to what amounts to dishonest conduct is in most cases a issue for the jury, proof of intention is probably more problematic. It is important to distinguish the question as to what the defendant's intention was, from what his motive may have been. Generally speaking, motive is an irrelevant issue in the determination of criminal liability. While it may be of significance, for other reasons such as classification, profiling and detection, motive is generally no concern of the court until sentencing. Intention is generally a straightforward issue, as a person intends something if he acts with the purpose of causing that result. Thus, juries will often be instructed to be sure that the defendant did the act he intended.

6.27   Intent may, however, not always be so simple. In many systems of law, the courts distinguish between direct and indirect or oblique intent. Direct intent is as we have set out, that is where the consequence is desired and the defendant seeks to bring it about, or, at least strives to. Indirect intent is where the defendant realises that the consequence is certain, or virtually certain, as a result of what he does or does not do, but he does not in any positive sense desire it, and yet proceeds. Oblique intention would normally be sufficient for a determination that the defendant has the required fraudulent intention. Thus, a result is intended when it is the defendant's purpose to cause it, or though it is not the defendant's purpose to cause it, the result is a virtually certain consequence of the act or omission, and he knows that it is a virtually certain consequence. It is necessary, however, to distinguish intention from recklessness. If the defendant foresees a consequence as likely or even possible as a result of his actions and yet proceeds, and in the result that consequence does in fact occur, the defendant can be said to have caused the result recklessly. It is important to note that even a very high degree of foresight as to a given consequence is not the same thing, in law, as an intention. Nevertheless, if the jury accept that the defendant was virtually certain that a specific result would occur and it did, it would not be unreasonable for the jury to conclude that the defendant did in fact intend it.

MISREPRESENTATION BY WORDS OR CONDUCT

6.28   The offence of fraud will be committed if the defendant, with the requisite *mens rea*, makes a false representation. The representation may be made by word or conduct, express or implied, in regard to any fact, including the state of mind of the person making the representation or another. It may also, unlike generally in the civil law, be a representation as to the law. It will be a false representation if it is untrue or misleading and the person responsible for the representation knows that it so. The Fraud Act also provides that a representation may be regarded as made if it, or anything implying it, is submitted in any form to any system or device designed to receive, convey or respond to communications, with or without human intervention. It should be noted that under the new English law the offence is based on the making of a misrepresentation by the defendant and not the deception of the victim. The focus for liability is the conduct of the defendant and not the effect of that on the mind of the victim.

6.29   This is important in the case of, for example, the unauthorised use of a payment card. It may well be that the merchant who takes the card, does not rely in any way on the implied representation of the person presenting the card for payment that he has authority to use it in that transaction, as the merchant will normally be reimbursed either way. Under the new provisions it is not necessary for the prosecution to allege, let alone prove, that the merchant was misled. It is enough that the defendant falsely represented that he had authority. By the same token, a merchant participating in a 'sting' operation, having been warned by the police, need not be deceived. It is enough that the defendant made the relevant false representation.

6.30   Returning to the issue of what is a representation, the English criminal law is based very much on the law of contract. A representation in the law of contract is a statement, by word or conduct, of material fact, made by one person to another during the negotiations leading up to contract, which was intended to be relied upon, and was in fact relied upon, but which was not intended to be a binding contractual term. Where that representation is false or misleading it is properly termed a misrepresentation. The state of a man's mind, is according to the law, as much a statement of fact as the state of a man's digestion.[1] It follows that a false statement as to one's current intention is a misrepresentation of fact. By the same token an assertion of belief in the existence of certain facts, even the likelihood of future events, may be a misrepresentation of the fact that the person making the statement actually had, at that time, such a belief.

1   *Edgington v Fitzmaurice* (1885) 29 Ch D 459 at 483 per Bowen LJ and *British Airways Board v Taylor* [1976] 1 All ER 65 at 68, per Lord Wilberforce.

SILENCE

6.31   Attributing responsibility for mere silence is always a problem in the law. Generally speaking there is no duty to disclose material facts and therefore mere silence cannot be considered to amount to a representation. There is no indication in the Fraud Act that the law has changed. Having said this, it has been argued that where an ordinary and honest person would consider it right to speak out, and such a person appreciating this, does not, then the very dishonesty of his conduct might justify liability. The problem with this argument is that there is still no representation as such. It is highly doubtful whether dishonesty can in itself create an obligation of disclosure. This issue has arisen in the context of whether a failure to disclose price sensitive information might amount to a dishonest concealment within the scope of section 397 of FSMA, which is discussed in more detail at **5.3**. In the context of the predessessor provision, section 13 of the Prevention of Fraud (Investments) Act 1958, prosecutions were considered but not initiated. In other jurisdictions, cases have ben brought under similar provisions. The argument in Britain against proceeding was that it cannot be dishonest not to disclose information which you may well be under a duty to treat with confidence. However, this is debateable, and is in any case a question of fact for the jury.

6.32   In the general law of contract, there are only three situations where silence may be regarded as being tantamount to a representation. Firstly, where there is a half-truth. If only half the truth is told, and the result is misleading, then the civil law normally imposes on the person responsible for the half-truth an obligation to correct the false impression. Thus, a statement by a lawyer that he was not aware of any adverse provisions in a draft contract was held a misrepresentation, because he omitted to say that he had not examined it. Secondly, a representation that is true when made, but is later falsified by events or in some cases a change of intention, would normally require correction. This reflects the notion that a representation continues to operate as an inducement to contract until the contract is entered into. Thirdly, there is a special category of contracts of utmost good faith – *uberrimae fide*. In these exceptional circumstances the law, by tradition, imposes an obligation to affirmatively disclose all material facts relating to the contract. Fiduciaries are under duty in dealing with their principals and beneficiaries to act in good faith and this, while not entirely accurate, may be considered to be to all intents and purposes within the scope of the duty of *uberrimae fide*. However, in the case of fraud by persons in a fiduciary position, it would probably be better to resort to the provisions in the new statute imposing liability for fraudulently taking advantage of one's special position. Indeed, it was partly because of the uncertainties as to the scope of the obligation to disclose in the course of fair dealing that justified the enactment of these specific provisions. Having said this, the dishonest failure to disclose information that should be disclosed, even on the basis of a fiduciary relationship, such as between a director and his company, may amount to a conspiracy to defraud.

6.33   For liability, the representation must be untrue or misleading. Under the English law it would seem that there might be liability in the criminal law for the making of an untrue statement, which the defendant does not know is untrue, but does appreciate might in the circumstances be misleading. Misleading means less than wholly true and capable of an interpretation to the detriment of the victim. In the case of the criminal law, where it is not necessary, at least in the United Kingdom, to consider whether it actually influenced the mind of the person to whom it was addressed, issues of reliance are irrelevant. Of course, where what is said is so ridiculous no reasonable person would rely upon it, the jury or court may find the defendant's conduct does not fail to meet the standards of ordinary and honest people. Of course, this is all rather subjective.

6.34   As we have pointed out, the reformed criminal law in the United Kingdom in regard to fraud has a different emphasis than in many other jurisdictions. One point that is worthy of note is that the United Kingdom law does not require proof of materiality. This is an important issue in many provisions relating to false statement in other countries. A good example in the US Federal law is section 1001 of Title 18 USC. This makes it a criminal offence to falsify, conceal or cover up by any trick, scheme or device a material fact, the making of any materially false, fictitious, or fraudulent statement or representation or making or using any false writing or document knowing that it contains any materially false, fictitious, or fraudulent statement or entry. In determining whether a false statement or concealment is material the US courts examine whether the statement has a natural tendency to influence, or be capable of influencing, the decision of the other party. It is not necessary to prove that the victim was actually influenced let alone that the victim relied on it. The Supreme Court considers that the issue of materiality involves questions of both fact and law and should therefore be submitted to the jury.

CONCEALMENT

6.35   We have already noted that section 3 of the Fraud Act in the United Kingdom provides that the offence of fraud may be established if a person dishonestly fails to disclose to another person information which he is under a legal duty to disclose, intending thereby to make a gain for himself or another, or to cause loss to another or to expose another to a risk of loss. We have already seen that generally the law does not place an obligation on a person, even during the negotiation of a contract, to disclose information that he appreciates would be material to the other party's decision. However, there are situations where by statute, contract, custom and fiduciary obligation a duty to disclose facts arises. We have also seen that in certain circumstances there may be a duty to correct the misleading impression resulting from a half-truth or the falsification of a continuing representation. Where the person failing to disclose is not under a specific legal duty to disclose the relevant information, then it may still be possible to find liability, but based on the notion of an implied representation. For example, in one case a defendant who asked a bureau de change to exchange obsolete foreign currency for sterling was convicted on the basis that he impliedly represented that the relevant currency was still in circulation. He was under no legal obligation to inform the cashier, but by tending the money he made a representation.[1]

1   *R v Williams (Jean Jacques)* [1980] Crim LR 589.

6.36   We have already raised the issue of whether a mere moral obligation to disclose information should be enough to provide a basis for liability. It is important to remember that legal rules do not operate in isolation of each other and there is an interaction between the civil and criminal law. Generally speaking the civil law does not obligate persons to disclose information simply because it would be the right thing to do. For example, the information might well have a proprietary value, which the owner would not wish to share. A duty to disclose information, simply because the other party is unaware of it or maybe could not have acquired it, would, for example, undermine the valuable role of research in the financial markets. Indeed, it was partly for this reason that the American courts somewhat pragmatically developed the so called 'abstein or disclose' rule in regard to price sensitive information in the USA. It is not without interest, however, that the English Law Commission[1] did recommend that the offence be wide enough to cover information of a kind that the defendant knows or is aware that the other party trusts him to disclose and that in the circumstances it would be reasonable for him to disclose it. The Government rejected this as it considered to impose liability where there is not a pre-existing duty under the civil law would have far reaching implications for the general approach of *caveat emptor*. On the other hand, for liability under the Fraud Act it is not necessary for the prosecution to establish, as the Law Commission also suggested, that the defendant is aware that he is under a legal duty to disclose the information in question. Of course, if he did not, it may well be that he is not dishonest.

1   The Fraud Report No 276, Law Commission, http://www.lacom.gov.uk/docs/lc276.pdf

CRIMINAL BREACH OF TRUST (CBT)

6.37   Before the enactment of the Fraud Act it has been claimed that English law did not recognise the offence of criminal breach of trust. Interestingly, this is an important offence in combating financial and other misconduct in many other Commonwealth jurisdictions. In the various Criminal Codes drafted and implemented during Imperial rule, it is not without interest that specific provisions were included in regard to dishonest breach of trust. Of course, it is true that most situations covered by such laws, would have been offences in Britain, but almost certainly not all. The Fraud Act 2006 now specifically addresses this in section 4. A person will be guilty of fraud if he occupies a position in which he is expected to protect or safeguard, or at least not act against, the financial interest of another person and he dishonestly abuses that position, intending thereby to make a gain for himself or another, or to cause loss to another, or to expose another to a risk of loss. It is expressly provided that a person may be regarded as having abused his position even though his conduct consists of an omission rather than an affirmative act.

6.38   The real issue revolves around who can properly be said to occupy a position where he is expected to safeguard, or not act against, the financial interests of another. It is clear that the formulation is wider than those in a conventional trust relationship, or for that matter fiduciary relationship. It is unclear whose expectation is relevant. Is it the expectation of the victim or a more objective determination? It is also unclear whether the expectation must be reasonable. It seems that it is the intention of the Government that this is a question of fact to be determined by the jury, in the same way as the issue of dishonesty. On the other hand there is a strong argument for contending that it is a question of mixed law and fact as it is in the USA. For example, should not the court rule as to whether in law the relationship is capable of giving rise to such expectations?

6.39   The concept of fiduciary obligation was authoritatively set out by Millet LJ in *Bristol and West Building Society v Mothew*.[1] The learned judge stated 'a fiduciary is someone who has undertaken to act for or on behalf of another in a particular matter in circumstances which give rise to a relationship of trust and confidence. The distinguishing obligation of a fiduciary is the obligation of loyalty. The principal is entitled to the single-minded loyalty of his fiduciary ...' Therefore company directors in their dealings with the company, partners in dealing with each other, an agent in dealing with his principal, a trustee in dealing with his beneficiary, a public official in regard to his office and a professional adviser in dealing with his client would all be included. It is also probable that an employee in his dealings with his employer would also be covered. While employees are not generally considered to be fiduciaries,[2] they are within a duty of fidelity which has much in common with the obligations cast upon a fiduciary. An employee is 'trusted' by his employer not to make use of the employer's property or premises for the employee's benefit. It is important to note, however, that unlike an ordinary fiduciary relationship, the obligations, albeit different, flow both ways. As we have seen directors of a company owe fiduciary duties, arising by virtue of their office, only to the company and not its shareholders.[3] Whether it could be argued that the shareholders have a reasonable expectation that directors will not act against their financial interests, such as by insider dealing, remains to be seen. It has been accepted that in the context of a takeover, directors are under a duty to shareholders to act honestly and shareholders therefore might well have a reasonable expectation that they, as directors, would not act contrary to the advice and information that they have given to the members.[4] It is also clear that there are family, domestic and other personal relationships, even within a business context[5] that might also give rise to such expectations and therefore be within the scope of the offence. It is probable that the criminal and civil law will not be entirely matched on such issues.

1   (1998) Ch 1 at 118.
2   Employees who in senior management positions act on behalf of a company, may well be considered to owe fiduciary obligations much the same as the company's directors, see *Canadian Aero Services Ltd v O'Malley* (1973) 40 DLR (3d) 771 and 381.
3   See **2.12** *et seq.*
4   See *Heron International Ltd v Lord Grade* [1983] BCLC 244. The expectations of other 'stakeholders' such as employees and creditors are rather more problematic in this regard, see generally *Winkworth v Edward Baron Development Co Ltd* [1986] 1 WLR 1512.
5   See *Peskin v Anderson* [2001] 1 BCLC 372, *Re Chez Nico (Restaurants) Ltd* [1992] BCLC 192 and *Platt v Platt* [1999] 2 BCLC 745 and in particular *Coleman v Myers* [1977] 2 NZLR 225. See **2.12** *et seq.*

6.40   In the past there have been problems with imposing criminal liability for diverting so called corporate opportunities and the taking of secret profits. As we have seen, corporate opportunity is a contract or other advantageous arrangement that should in fairness have gone to a particular company, but which has been diverted by insiders, typically the directors, for their own personal benefit. The approach of the courts differs and may have rather more to do with the perceived integrity of what has occurred rather than any underlying jurisprudence. There are decisions which treat the opportunity as some kind of expectant property which in good conscience belongs to the company. Therefore, when directors divert it they are in effect stealing or at least misappropriating an asset that belongs to the company. Other courts have been reluctant to treat this as property and have simply sought to impose personal obligations based on conflict of interest on the relevant insiders. There are very few cases where it has ever been thought appropriate to consider a charge theft. Such conduct does, however, in most instances amount to a breach of trust. Directors are under an obligation to safeguard the financial interest of the company and the dishonest diversion or such opportunities would be an offence under the Fraud Act.

6.41   We have also seen that those in a fiduciary position are forbidden from making a 'secret profit.' This is essentially a profit that arises in the course of the fiduciary obligation and which has not been specifically authorised or consented to by the person to whom the fiduciary obligation is owed. In most legal systems, the secret profit is owed much in the same way as a debt to the principal, but is not owned by him. In other words, the taking of a secret profit does not involve the misappropriation of another person's property. Provided the taking of a secret profit is now dishonest, it may well amount to a criminal breach of trust. This is important as the law relating to the taking of secret profits is potentially onerous. For example, in *Regal (Hastings) Ltd v Gulliver*,[1] Lord Russell of Killowen, stated 'the rule of equity which insists on those, who by the use of a fiduciary position make a profit, being liable to account for that profit, in no way depends on fraud, or absence of bona fides; or upon such questions or considerations as whether the profit would or should otherwise have gone to the plaintiff, or whether the profiteer was under a duty to obtain the source of the profit for the plaintiff, or whether he took a risk or acted as he did for the benefit of the plaintiff, or whether the plaintiff has in fact been damaged or benefited by his action. The liability arises from the mere fact of the profit having, in the stated circumstances, been made. The profiteer, however, honest and well intentioned, cannot escape the risk of being called to account'. Of course, it must be remembered in this case the issue was one of civil liability and not criminal liability. None the less, it does indicate how wide the 'duty' not to profit from one's position is.

1   [1942] 1 All ER 378.

MISAPPROPRIATION (INCLUDING THEFT)

The offence of theft

6.42   Theft in English law is rendered an offence under section 1 of the Theft Act 1968. This provides that a person is guilty of theft if he dishonestly appropriates property belonging to another with the intention of permanently depriving the other of it and it is immaterial whether the appropriation is made with a view to gain, or is made for the thief's own benefit. There are those who have argued that a charge for theft would have been rather more appropriate in a number of cases of misconduct in the City than the way in which the authorities in fact proceeded. This contention is based on the view, that has some justification, that traditionally those responsible for the integrity of the markets and financial services industry have been reluctant, for a variety of reasons, to treat those whose engage in misconduct as 'real criminals'.

6.43   There is a fundamental difference between the offences of theft and fraud, although in some situations there may be a potential overlap. In the case of fraud the victim is deceived into handing over property and therefore the notion of misappropriation is inappropriate. The victim thus, effectively 'consents' to the taking of the relevant opportunity or property. This 'consent' albeit based on a misapprehension will continue to operate in law until steps are taken to rescind the contract. However, there are cases which show that the effect of a fraud can be to induce a mistake which renders the contract void *ab initio*.[1] Consequently, in such circumstances the law of theft may well be relevant. Having said this, the Courts have become increasingly reluctant to accept that fraud operates other than within the law of misrepresentation.[2] Of course, fraud involves rather more than the dishonest appropriation of property. Issues have arisen not so much as to the nature of an appropriation, but in regard to what is capable of being appropriated. In the context of corporate law, for example, we have already mentioned the issue as to whether an opportunity that should in good conscience have been delivered up to a company, can be regarded as a form of expectant property capable of belonging to the company. There is also an issue in regard to bribes and secret profits. Do they belong to the person who can assert a right to their recovery? Until relatively recently it was thought that in such cases the law of theft was irrelevant. However, in the civil law, it has been held that as equity looks as done that which should be done, it will regard the bribe or secret profit as having been transferred, thereby justifying property based remedies. The issue as to whether confidential information can amount to property and therefore be capable of being misappropriated, is also a potentially important issues. In the USA the courts have attempted to develop the law penalising the abuse of inside information largely on the basis of misappropriation. Those who acquire price sensitive information in circumstances where they appreciate it 'belongs' to another are not allowed to misappropriate it for their own or another person's benefit.[3] The English Courts have held that confidential information is not property for the purposes of the law of theft,[4] although in the civil law, it can be protected almost as if it is a form of property. It has been said in Britain 'it is not too much to say that we live in a country where ... the theft of the boardroom table is punished far more severely than the theft of the boardroom secret'.[5] It is interesting that both the Law Commission and the Government decided not to include trade secrets and confidential information as a species of property in the Fraud Act 2006.

1   *Cundy v Lindsay* (1878) 3 App Cas 459.
2   *Phillips v Brooks Ltd* [1919] 2 KB 243 and *Lewis v Averay* [1972] 1QB 198.
3   See *US v O'Hagan* 117 S.Ct 2199(1997) and *Carpenter v US* 484 US 19 (1987) discussed at **3.66** *et seq.*
4   *Oxford v Moss* (1979) 68 Cr App R 183.
5   Sir Edward Boyle MP, Hansard HC 13 December 1968, vol 775, col 806.

Requisite state of mind – mens rea

6.44   Theft requires proof of two mental elements, dishonesty and an intention to permanently deprive the person of possession of the relevant property. We have already discussed what dishonesty means in this context. However, the relevant statutes have gone further, by setting out circumstances in which as a matter of law a person does not act dishonestly for the purposes of the law of theft. For example, section 2(1) of the Theft Act 1968 provides that a person is not dishonest if he believes he has in law the right to deprive the other person of the property; where he believes that the other person would have consented to the appropriation if he had known of the appropriation and the circumstances, and, except where he is a trustee or personal representative, he acts in the belief that the true owner cannot be found by taking reasonable steps. The section does, however, make it clear in subsection (2) that a person can be found to be dishonest notwithstanding his willingness to pay for the property in question. Thus, generally speaking a genuine belief of right or consent, will exonerate a person from allegations of dishonesty. It is important to appreciate that in English law the belief of the accused need not be reasonable. However, the more unreasonable it is, the more difficult it will be for him to convince the jury that he had a genuine belief and was not therefore subjectively dishonest. If a jury does consider that the accused did in fact have a genuine belief in his right or the consent of another, as a matter of law – in England, this is an end of the matter. He is entitled to an acquittal and the issue of dishonesty will not be put to the jury. This is not the case in regard to a prosecution for fraud under the Fraud Act 2006. In the case of fraud, the Act does not include similar provisions as in the Theft Act and therefore, even if the jury consider that the accused did in fact genuinely believe he had a right, the issue of dishonesty is not resolved. It is in law possible for the jury to still find that he was dishonest for the purposes of the fraud law. Of course, in practice it is difficult to conceive of a situation where it would be reasonable for a jury to find dishonesty in such a case.

6.45   In theft cases, as we have noted, it must also be shown that the accused has the intention to permanently deprive the owner of the property in question. Merely taking a briefcase and examining its contents to see if there is anything worth stealing is not in English law theft. Under section 6 of the Theft Act it is provided 'a person appropriating property belonging to another without meaning that other permanently to lose the thing itself is nevertheless to be regarded as having the intention of permanently depriving the other of it if his intention is to treat the thing as his own to dispose of regardless of the other's rights; and borrowing or lending of it may amount to so treating it if ... the borrowing or lending is for a period and in circumstances amounting to an outright taking or disposal'. It has long been held by the English courts that a person in possession or control of another person's property who, dishonestly and for his own purpose, deals with the property in such a manner that he knows he is risking its loss, may be guilty of theft.

What can and cannot be stolen

6.46 While there are differences in the law from one country to another, generally speaking the law of theft is quite comprehensive in what is considered to be property. Section 4 of the Theft Act provides that property, for the purposes of theft, may include real and personal property, money and intangible property, such as the credit in a bank account. Thus, in one case the accused, a builder, dishonestly over-billed for work which he had undertaken. The owner of the house gave the accused a cheque for this amount which was paid in to his account. In paying this cheque into his account the accused was held to have dishonestly appropriated part of the credit standing in his customer's bank account.

6.47 For a charge of theft the property must 'belong to another'. Section 5 of the Theft Act provides that property is regarded as belonging to anyone having possession or control of it or having a proprietary right or interest in it. Thus, merely an equitable right in property will be sufficient. It should also be noted that the owner of property can be guilty of stealing his own property from someone with a lesser interest, such as a lien for an unpaid bill. There may be circumstances where full legal ownership passes to the accused, but nonetheless, for the purposes of theft the law deems the original owner as still entitled. For example, section 5(3) of the Act provides that 'where a person receives property from or on account of another, and is under an obligation to that other to retain and deal with that property or its proceeds in a particular way, the property or proceeds shall be regarded, as against him, as belonging to the other'. This provision is, of course, particularly important when money is given to a person to pay certain expenses and is used for something else. Given the required state of mind, the crime of theft will have occurred. It is important, however, to note that the money or other property must be entrusted for a specific purpose.

6.48 As we have seen[1] in cases where a person receives property by virtue of another's mistake and is under an obligation in the civil law to make restoration in whole or in part, of the property or its proceeds, then to the extent of this obligation, the relevant property or proceeds will be regarded, in English law, as belonging to the person entitled to restoration.[2] Thus a person who receives property or payment by mistake, at the point when they form the necessary state of mind – which is to dishonestly and permanently deprive the owner of the relevant amount, they are guilty of theft. Of course, this means that they must actually be aware of the mistake and that they are under a legal obligation to make restoration. If they had a genuine belief in their right to retain it, as we have seen, they would not be dishonest, as a matter of law.

1   See **6.41** above.
2   Section 5(4) of the Theft Act 1968.

Unjust enrichment

6.49 The common law has not been eager to base liability on the unjust acquisition of wealth in circumstances where a specific wrong has not been committed. Indeed, there are cases in the English courts which affirm that characterising something as unfair or even unjust does not of itself establish a cause of action or enable the court to intervene. Of course, where there is an obligation such as in a fiduciary relationship to act fairly, the situation is different. The imposition of criminal liability for the acquisition of unexplained wealth, while controversial, is not as radical as some would suggest. Britain imposed in many of its territories and dominions[1] provisions relating to the acquisition of unexplained wealth, particularly in the case of public officials. These have been adopted in other jurisdictions and now the United Nations Convention against Corruption 2006 urges all countries to enact such laws. Article 20, provides:

> 'Subject to its constitution and the fundamental principles of its legal system, each State Party shall consider adopting such legislative and other measures as may be necessary to establish as a criminal offence, when committed intentionally, illicit enrichment, that is a significant increase in the assets of a public official that he or she cannot reasonably explain in relation to his or her lawful income.'

1 One of the best examples of the criminalisation of unexplained wealth is to be found in the Prevention of Bribery Ordinance (Cap 201) in Hong Kong. Section 10(a) provides that any person who is or has been a Crown Servant who maintains a standard of living above that which is commensurate with his present or past official emoluments or is in control of pecuniary resources or property disproportionate to his present or past official emoluments, shall be guilty of an offence, unless 'he gives a satisfactory explanation to the court as to how he was able to maintain such a standard of living or how such pecuniary resources or property came under his control'. Furthermore, under subsection 2 of this section, where a court is satisfied in proceedings for an offence under the first subsection, that 'having regard to the closeness of his relationship to the accused and to other circumstances, there is reason to believe that any person was holding pecuniary resources or property in trust for or otherwise on behalf of the accused or acquired such resources or property as a gift from the accused, such resources or property shall, in the absence of evidence to the contrary, be presumed to have been in the control of the accused'.

6.50   It is important to remember that many officials are in a position in which they are expected to safeguard or not to act against the financial interests of another person, including the public at large or the state. Consequently, many cases of abuse of office would be potentially an offence under the Fraud Act 2006. In cases where a public official, without reasonable excuse or justification, wilfully neglects to perform his public duty or wilfully misconducts himself, to the extent that he abuses the public's trust in the office, he is guilty of the common law offence of misfeasance in public office.[1] The collapse of the Bank of Credit and Commerce International (BCCI) led to allegations in Britain and elsewhere that the authorities and in particular the Bank of England had been 'willfully negligent' in their duty to protect depositors. Suits were brought alleging that the Bank of England and certain officers were guilty of the tort of misfeasance.[2] These actions failed in part because it could not be established that the Bank of England had acted with wilfulness in the breach of its duties. However, in the USA and certain other jurisdictions, this liability has become an important factor in the policing of misconduct, both in attributing responsibility and rathess less comendably in inhibiting the authorities.

1   *Attorney General's Reference* (No 93 of 2003) (2004) 2 Cr App R 23.
2   *Three Rivers District Council v Bank of England* (No 3) [2003] 2 AC 1.

FALSE STATEMENTS AND MANIPULATION

6.51   We have already discussed in Chapter 5 the offences in section 397 of FSMA relating to the inducement of investment transactions by false statements and the dishonest concealment of material facts. The law has long recognised that those responsible for promoting new issues of stock have a special responsibility to ensure that those who are likely to subscribe are given all the information that they need to make an informed decision. In addition to requiring full disclosure of material facts, there are statutory obligations on those responsible for promoting new issues and placing securities in the market to ensure that due care is exercised in complying with the relevant disclosure requirements. For example, under the FSMA 2000, s 90, persons responsible for a false or misleading statement or omission in listing particulars will be liable to compensate any person who has acquired the securities in question for any loss that they have suffered unless it can be proved by them that they had reasonable grounds for believing what was said was not false or misleading. Indeed, under the FSMA 2000, s 91, the FSA can impose financial penalties on the issuer or its directors if they were 'knowingly concerned' in the breach.

6.52   When discussing the common law's stand against the deliberate creation of false markets, mention was made of the fact that, apart from some very ancient statutes relating to the integrity of markets, it was not until the enactment of the Financial Services Act 1986, s 47(2) that there were UK statutory provisions specifically designed to outlaw the manipulation of markets other than by the making of false statements. It is possible, of course, to make a representation by conduct, but in the context of the financial markets, seeking to establish a charge or claim on such a basis would in practice be exceedingly difficult, albeit not impossible. Section 47(2) has been re-enacted as the FSMA 2000, s 397(3) and has been discussed in detail in Chapter 5.

HIGH PRESSURE SELLING

6.53   The high pressure selling of securities at a greater price than they are worth has long been identified as a major issue in investor protection. High pressure selling operations, some times referred to as 'boiler room' operations, are often associated with other fraudulent schemes and this form of crime has attracted organised criminals. As early as 1936, the government established a committee under Sir Archibald Bodkin 'to consider operations commonly known as share pushing and share hawking and similar activities'. The result of the committee's recommendations was the enactment of the Prevention of Fraud (Investments) Act 1939 which, in addition to addressing fraudulent statements, as we have seen, regulated the selling practices of share dealers and the dissemination of investment related information and, in particular, advertisements. The Financial Services Act 1986, s 56 went somewhat further than this and in effect made it a 'civil offence' to make unsolicited calls to procure an investment agreement, to or from the UK, unless such were made in conformity with rules drawn up by the Securities and Investments Board. In *Alpine Investments BV v Minister van Financien*,[1] the European Court accepted that while such rules curbing 'cold calling' were a restriction on a person's freedom to offer cross-border services, they could be justified on the basis that a member state had the right to ensure the protection of investors and the integrity of its markets.

1   Case C-384/93: [1995] All ER (EC) 543.

6.54   The Financial Services Act 1986, s 56 has been replaced by the FSMA 2000, s 30. At the cornerstone of the new regulatory regime is the FSMA 2000, s 21 which prohibits a person, in the course of business, communicating an invitation or inducement to engage in investment activity unless that person is an authorised person or the communication is approved by an authorised person. The rules promulgated by the FSA on financial promotion by authorised persons achieve more or less the same result as the earlier regime. If a person enters into 'controlled agreement' (that is one within the purview of s 21) as a result of an 'unlawful communication', then, subject to the discretion of the court, the customer is entitled to compensation for any loss or restitution of any moneys or property transferred and the agreement is unenforceable against him. Where the other party to the claimant is not the communicator, that person will be liable for any losses, subject to the discretion of the court. It must also be remembered that activity in breach of the prohibition in s 21, in addition to amounting to a criminal offence, will also bring into play the full enforcement powers of the FSA under the FSMA 2000, s 25.

FRAUDULENT TRADING AND INSOLVENCY RELATED OFFENCES

6.55   It is sadly too often the case that a fraud will only be discovered once an insolvency occurs. While to some the insolvency provisions may appear to be 'shutting the stable door after the horse has bolted', they have an important role in attributing responsibility, tracing misappropriated funds and facilitating compensation and restitution. The procedures provided for by these laws also assist in attempting to resolve the conflicts which inevitably arise between various parties when there is not enough money to meet every obligation. Perhaps the most important in the control of fraud and sharp practice are those provisions which address misconduct on the part of those who manage insolvent enterprises and which enable the authorities to intervene. For example, under the UK's Financial Services and Markets Act, section 367, the Financial Services Authority may petition the court for a winding up, not only of an authorised person, but also any unauthorised person who is engaged in activity in contravention of the general prohibition on conducting unauthorised investment business. Of course, these statutory provisions are in addition to those in the general law relating to companies and insolvency.

6.56   In most systems of law there will be a number of specific offences relating to malpractice and abuses before and during liquidation. Obviously it is not possible here to give more than a brief indication of their nature. Frauds against creditors may be divided into three broad categories. Firstly, there are cases where debts are incurred, albeit there is no intention of making payment. Long firm frauds are a good example. Here crooks will form a company or create some other form of trading vehicle, establish some degree of credibility and then place orders on credit for goods that they have no intention of paying for. These will then be sold, often at a discount, and the criminals will abscond with the proceeds leaving the creditors to pursue a mere shell. The second situation is the fraudulent evasion of debts and obligations that have already been incurred. Here assets may be transferred and siphoned off to prevent creditors getting their hands on them. The third situation, involves the concealment of the true state of affairs and perhaps the resurrection of the insolvent company's business in a 'phoenix company' to which the insolvent company's undertaking has been transferred at an undervaluation – thereby leaving the creditors with a shell. Of course, in all three categories it is probable that numerous non-insolvency specific offences may be committed.

6.57   The Fraud Act 2006 creates a new offence which is of particular relevance. It provides that 'a person is guilty of an offence if he is knowingly a party to the carrying on of a business' otherwise than as a company with intent to defraud creditors or for any other fraudulent purpose. Section 993 of the Companies Act 2006, provides that whether or not a company has been or is in the course of being wound up, if any business of the company is carried on with an intent to defraud creditors of that company or creditors of any other person, or for any fraudulent purpose, 'every person who is knowingly a party to the carrying on of the business in that manner commits an offence'. These two offences effectively catch all those who engage in fraudulent trading in the course of business. While fraudulent trading has a long history in the company laws of most countries, in Britain it became increasingly evident that there was widespread use of business forms other than companies engaging in bogus trading and long firm frauds. As we have seen, it is also not uncommon to discover that what appear to be companies are in fact phantoms – never having been properly incorporated. As the Law Commission observed (Law Commission No 277) 'it is anomalous and illogical that fraudulent trading should be an offence where it is done through the medium of a … company, but not where the individual who is trading fraudulently does not do so through the medium of such a body'.

6.58 For these offences a single fraudulent transaction is sufficient, provided 'it can properly be described as fraud on a creditor perpetrated in the course of carrying on business'.[1] The notion of being 'a party' to the fraudulent trading has caused some difficulty in the courts. Some judges have indicated that at least in the case of companies the person must have a relatively senior position in 'running the business' whereas other courts have held that the term 'must on its natural meaning indicate no more than 'participates in' 'takes part in' or 'concurs in' and involve some positive steps of some nature in the carrying on of the company's business in a fraudulent manner'.[2] Indeed, it has been held that the person who it is claimed is 'a party' to the fraud might even be an outsider. The breadth and scope of these provisions should not be under-estimated and in particular it should be noted that they are not, as are most of the provisions that we are about to discuss, relevant in or near an insolvency.

1   Templeman J in *Re Cooper Chemical Ltd* [1978] Ch 262.
2   Pennycuick VC, *In Re Maidstone Building Supplies* [1971] 1 WLR 1085.

6.59 A convenient starting point in our analysis of the insolvency law is section 89(1) of the Insolvency Act 1986. This provides that a majority of the directors of a company can make a statutory declaration, affirming that after their inquiries, they are satisfied that the company is solvent. The company can then, within a year, be subject to a members winding up as a solvent company. However, section 89(4) provides that if a director made such a declaration without having reasonable grounds for his opinion, he is guilty of an offence. It is important to note that it need not be proved that he knew the situation, his negligence is sufficient for criminal liability and if, indeed, within five weeks of the making of the declaration or such reasonable time as set out in the declaration, the company's debts are not discharged, it may be presumed that the directors did not have reasonable grounds for their opinion.

6.60 It is also provided in the Insolvency Act 1986, section 206 that a present or former officer of a company in liquidation who, within the previous year, conceals, fraudulently removes or pawns any of the company's property or conceals or falsifies any records relating to the company's property, will be deemed to have committed an offence. By the same token, an officer or former officer who is privy to any of these actions will also be deemed to have committed an offence. It should be noted that the term 'officer' includes shadow directors. Section 206 not only applies to things done prior to and in anticipation of a liquidation, but also to things done during a winding up. The defendant is entitled to a defence if he can establish that he had no intent to defraud, conceal information from the company or defeat the law. Section 207 provides when a company is being wound up, a person is deemed to have committed an offence if he, being at the time an officer of the company, has made or caused to be made any gift or transfer of, or charge on, or has caused or connived at the levying of any execution against, the company's property, unless the transaction in question took place more than five years before the commencement of winding up or if he proves that, at the time of the conduct constituting the offence, he had no intent to defraud the company's creditors. There has been debate as to whether the defendant has a legal burden of proof – that is to a balance of probabilities, or merely an evidential burden. In *Attorney-General's Reference (No 1 of 2004)*,[1] the House of Lords considered that 'it can be tempting to those involved in the management of a company or a bankrupt to conceal or dispose of ... assets to the disadvantage of creditors. Furthermore, such concealment or disposal may be done by a person alone and in private: a failure to record or disclose an asset, or a disposal of stock at an under value or the making of a disposal for nil consideration, may be known only to those involved in the transaction. There will be no independent witnesses to the act in question. Whether there has been fraud will often be known only to the individual, or individuals who are alleged to have committed the fraud'. Given the considerable benefits of incorporation and the operation of the personal bankruptcy laws to debtors, the House of Lords considered it was not unreasonable that the defendant has the full legal burden of proof – which is, of course, even in criminal matters, the civil burden.

1   [2004] 1 WLR 2111.

6.61   There are further offences that are worth considering. Section 211(1) provides that a past or present officer of a company that is being wound up, commits an offence if he makes any false representation or commits any other fraud for the purposes of obtaining the consent of the company's creditors to an agreement concerning the company's affairs. Furthermore, he is deemed to have committed such an offence, if prior to the winding up, he has made any false representation, or committed any other fraud, for this purpose. False representations require that the accused either knew the representation was false or that it might be. However, proof of dishonesty is not required. Under section 210(1) a past or present officer of a company that is being wound up, commits an offence if he makes a material omission in any statement relating to the company's affairs. He will also be deemed to have committed this offence, as in the case of section 211, if the company is ordered to be wound up by the court or passes a resolution for voluntary winding up, and he has previously made any material omission in any such statement. The scope of this offence is unclear. It has been argued that it cannot extend to all omissions that are or could become material. The better view, is that only omissions which render what has been said misleading are caught. It should be noted, however, there is no way to establish that the omission is fraudulent or even deliberate. However, if the defendant can show that he has no intent to defraud, he is entitled to an acquittal. Another potentially useful provision is found in section 208. This states that a person will be guilty of an offence if a company is being wound up and, being a present or past officer of the company, he 'does not to the best of his knowledge and belief fully and truly discover to the liquidator all the company's property' and how and to whom and for consideration and when the company disposed of any part of that property. Property that has been disposed of in the course of the company's ordinary business is excluded from this obligation. Such a person also commits an offence if he does not deliver up to the liquidator all the company's property and books and papers under his control. He is also obliged, 'knowing or believing that a false debt has been proved' by any person in the winding up to notify the liquidator. As in the case of the other offences, if the defendant proves that he had no intent to defraud he is not guilty. It is also an offence under section 208(2) if after the commencement of a winding up, any past or present officer 'attempts to account for any part of the company's property by fictitious losses or expense'. He is deemed to have committed this offence, if he is proved to have attempted to do this at any time within a year of the commencement of the winding up.

6.62 Perhaps one of the most important provisions is, however, the Insolvency Act 1986, s 213. This provides that if in the course of a winding up it appears that any business of the company has been carried on with the intent to defraud creditors of the company or creditors of any other person, or for any fraudulent purpose, the court on the application of the liquidator, may declare that any person who was knowingly party to the carrying on of the business in the manner mentioned, is liable to make such contributions to the company's assets as the court thinks proper. Given the requirement of intent to defraud, as in the case of a prosecution brought under the Insolvency Act 1986, s 206, and see *Re Patrick and Lyon Ltd*,[1] it is necessary to prove 'actual dishonesty, involving real moral blame'. Consequently, the provision is of limited use and proceedings for wrongful trading under the Insolvency Act 1986, s 214 are usually far more efficacious.

1   [1933] Ch 786.

6.63 This section empowers the court to declare that a person who is or has been a director, of the company in certain circumstances, must make a contribution to the assets of the company as the court considers proper. The circumstances in which an order can be made are, that that company is in insolvent liquidation, and at some time before the commencement of the winding up, the relevant person knew or ought to have concluded that there was no reasonable prospect that the company would avoid going into insolvent liquidation, and that at that point in time, he was a director of the company. However, the court should not make an order if its is satisfied, that after those circumstances occurring, the relevant person 'took every step with a view to minimising the potential loss to the company's creditors, assuming that he knew that there was no reasonable prospect that the company would avoid insolvent liquidation, which he ought to have taken. In section 214(4) it is provided that the facts which a director ought to know or ascertain, the conclusions which he ought to reach and the steps which he ought to take are those 'which would be known or ascertained, or reached or taken, by a reasonably diligent person having both: (a) the general knowledge, skill and experience that may reasonably be expected of a person carrying out the same functions as are carried out by that director in relation to the company, and (b) the general knowledge, skill and experience that that director has'. It should be noted section 214 applies with equal force to shadow directors.

6.64 In addition to these provisions, there are others facilitating investigation and recovery. For example, section 212 provides for summary proceedings in cases of misfeasance. Where, in a winding up, it appears that a person involved in the management or promotion of the company has misapplied or retained, or become accountable for, any money or other property of the company, or been guilty of any misfeasance or breach of any fiduciary or other duty in relation to the company, the court may, on the application of the liquidator or a creditor, examine the person concerned and make an order requiring restoration or contribution.

6.65 Our above discussion has focused on offences, primarily by those involved in the management, of a company that has become insolvent and is being wound up. Of course, it is important to remember that these offences operate in the context of the general criminal law and in particular the relevant corporate law. There may well be other proceedings. In our brief discussion of insolvency related financial crimes it is desirable to also refer to crimes involving the bankruptcy of an individual. Of course, in practice those involved in insolvency proceedings might also be involved in personal proceedings for their own bankruptcy.

6.66 Generally speaking, the relevant crimes apply to an individual who has been declared a bankrupt. Such a person will under section 352 of the insolvency Act 1986 be entitled to a defense if he can establish, in most cases to a balance of probabilities, that he at the material time had no intent to defraud or conceal the state of his affairs. However, where the offence is worded so widely as to catch conduct that would not normally be dishonest, the courts have taken the view that the burden imposed on the defendant is only evidential. Let us now look at two substantive offences which illustrate this. Section 357(1) renders it a crime if the bankrupt makes or causes to be made, or has in the five years ending with the commencement of his bankruptcy made or caused to be made any gift, or transfer of, or any charge on, his property. Under section 357(3) he is guilty of an offence if he conceals or removes, or has at any time before the commencement of the bankruptcy concealed or removed, any part of his property after, or within two months before, the date on which a judgment or order for payment has been made against him. Given the breadth of these offences, it is not unreasonable that the defendant has only to introduce evidence that he had no intention to defraud.[1] On the other hand, it is arguable that the defendant would have the full legal burden if he made the relevant dispositions after being declared a bankrupt and in regard to the offence under section 357(3) of concealing property after such a declaration. As in so many areas of the law, it is possible to find similar offences in other statutes. Section 13 of the Debtors Act 1869 makes it a criminal offence for any person with intent to defraud his creditors to make a gift or dispose or conceal his property. It should be noted that for this offence it is not necessary for the defendant to be bankrupt.

1   See *Attorney-General's Reference (No 1 of 2004)* [2004] 1 WLR 2111.

6.67 A declared bankrupt might also be charged with offences under section 354 if he conceals any debt that is due to or from him or any other property which he is required to deliver up to the receiver or trustee in bankruptcy. If he removes such property he also commits an offence. Furthermore, if he does any of these acts within a year before the petition for his bankruptcy, he commits an offence. Again he is entitled to a defense if he proves he had no intent to defraud. Under section 358 a bankrupt who leaves or attempts or makes preparations to leave the jurisdiction with any property that he is required to hand over, commits an offence. The same is true in regard to such conduct within six months before the petition, but as in regard to the other offences, he has the defense that he had no intent to defraud. The falsification, alteration and hiding of records is rendered a specific offence under section 355. Section 356 mirrors the provisions in the case of officers of insolvent companies in sections 210 and 211 discussed above. There is also a similar duty under section 353, to disclose property to the receiver or trustee.

6.68   In the case of insolvent companies the company will, at the end of the legal process, cease to exist. It may well be that proceedings will be initiated against the director of the company under the Company Directors Disqualification Act 1986 which has the effect of banning under criminal penalties former directors from being involved in the management of a company. Of course, there are many other grounds for such an order than being involved in the affairs of an insolvent company. Section 11 of this Act, however, renders it an offence, without the leave of the court, for an undischarged bankrupt to serve as a director or become directly or indirectly involved in the management of a company. Section 360 of the Insolvency Act renders it a crime for a declared bankrupt to engage in any business in a name other than that in which he has been adjudged bankrupt. Merely operating behind a sham company will not assist him. In *R v Doubleday*,[1] the Court of Appeal thought that the offence was committed where the prosecution established that the accused was 'in fact the proprietor of a business set up under another name'. The courts will, as we have seen in the misuse of companies, look at the reality of the situation. By section 360 an offence is also committed by a bankrupt if he obtains credit without disclosing his status. Finally, section 362(1) is of some interest in that it makes an offence for the bankrupt in the two years before the petition, to have 'materially contributed to, or increased the extent of, his insolvency by gambling or by rash and hazardous speculation …'. In determining whether any speculation was rash 'the financial position of the bankrupt at the time when he entered into' the relevant activity 'shall be taken into consideration.'

1   (1964) 49 Cr App R 62.

BLACKMAIL AND EXTORTION

6.69   The FSA and more recently the Serious Organised Crime Agency (SOCA) have emphasised the risks facing those engaged in the financial services industry as a result of the activities of organised crime and other professional criminals. We address the issues presented by the misuse of financial institutions and intermediaries for the laundering of the proceeds of crime in Chapter 7. However, in recent years evidence has come to light of criminals deliberately penetrating financial institutions not merely to facilitate the laundering of money, but to facilitate other crimes against the financial sector and others. Indeed, Sir Cullum McCarthy, the former Chairman of the FSA issued a warning to the financial services industry specifically about this threat in November 2005.[1] Consequently, in the context of our discussion of the offences relating to the financial sector, it is necessary to consider extortion and blackmail. While such crimes are often motivated by greed, they have another and more sinister aspect. It is the preying on persons, making unjustified threats to them or their loved ones, that gives these crimes a particularly unpleasant character. It is also the case that such crimes are often used by organised crime and in particular criminal groups who would not stop at extreme violence.

1   See 'warning over mafia gangs infiltrating British banks', *The Times*, 16 November 2005. This led to the European Commission initiating a five-country study of this problem with the assistance of the City of London Police under its AGIS Programme.

6.70   The crime of blackmail is set out in section 21 of the English Theft Act 1968. It provides that a person commits the crime 'if with a view to gain for himself or another or with intent to cause loss to another, he makes any unwarranted demand with menaces.' For the purposes of this offence 'a demand with menaces is unwarranted unless the person making it does so in the belief: (a) that he has reasonable grounds for making the demand; and (b) that the use of the menaces is a proper means of reinforcing the demand'. The concept of gain or loss in this context is confined to money or property. A demand is made for the purposes of the offence when it is spoken or mailed. The better view, on the authorities, is that it need not be heard, understood or even received.[1] The issue as to whether the demand is unwarranted or not is subjective, the accused does not have to be reasonable. On the other hand if the way in which an accused has acted is not proper, then even a reasonable belief in his right to, for example, pursue a debt, is criminal.

1 *Treacy v DPP* [1971] AC 537.

6.71 The term menaces is not defined in the Act, but one judge has said that it involves conduct or a threat of conduct 'of such a nature and extent that the mind of an ordinary person of normal stability and courage might be influenced or made apprehensive'.[1] It is to be noted that a threat to reveal another person's criminal activity, if made with a view to gain, can be sufficient for liability. The moral obligation to report crimes to the authorities should not be capable of being 'bought off' – indeed, in the United Kingdom, accepting payment, other than as compensation, for not reporting a crime is an offence under section 5 of the Criminal Law Act 1967. Thus, a threat to expose the crime or other wrongdoing of another unless payment is made, would be a crime. But so would a threat to attack a company in a newspaper article to depress price of its shares[2] or the threat to disclose sensitive commercial information[3] or probably the threat to initiate civil proceedings.

1 *R v Clear* [1968] 1 QB 670.
2 *R v Boyle and Merchant* [1914] 3 KB 339.
3 *R v Cox and Jenkins* (1979) 1 Cr App R(S) 190.

COMPUTER-RELATED CRIME

6.72 In the modern world it is difficult to imagine a situation where a sighificant financial crime can be perpetrated without the use or misuse of a computer. While the advent of technology has greatly facilitated the commission of many forms of fraud and abuse, the essential crimes remain much the same. Computers are used to assist in the execution of crime. Of course, it may be that threats are made against the security and integrity of computer systems, however, this is in essence no different than crimes involving criminal damage against any other form of property. It should also be noted that under section 13 of the Theft Act there is a specific offence of dishonestly abstracting or diverting electricty, which may well be technically relevant. Howver, the more significant law is found in the Computer Misuse Act 1990. This Act created three new and specific offences. Section 1 makes it an offence to access without authority computer material, that is a programme or data; section 2 renders it an offence to access without authority a computer system with intent to commit or facilitate the commission of a serious crime and section 3, provides that it is an offence to without authority modify computer material. While the computer and hardware might be adequately protected by the law relating to criminal damage, information is, as we have seen, not so easily protected. Section 3 seeks to address this, by providing that anyone who does any act which causes an unauthorised modification of the contents of a computer and has the requisite intention and knowledge, commits a crime. A modification is defined to include alteration or erasing any program or data on the computer. The requisite intention is an intention to impair the operation of any computer, to prevent or hinder access to any program or data, or impair the operation of any program or the reliability of any data. It is enough for the knowledge element that the accused knows that what he is doing is unauthorised. It is immaterial whether the alteration is merely temporary, the offence is still committed. The 1990 Act was amended in 2006 to make it clear that section 3 covers conduct designed to disrupt and deny computer related services. A new section 3A also, much in the same way as section 6 of the Fraud Act 2006, renders it a criminal offence to have or distribute 'tools' to be used for hacking computer networks.

6.73   Of course, one of the serious problems about addressing computer crime is the fact that it may often be perpetrated from overseas. As we have seen under section 2 of the Computer Misuse Act 1990 in the UK it is a crime to cause a computer to perform a function with intent to secure unauthorised access to programs or data with the intention of committing or facilitating the commission of some other offence. An offence under section 1 which simply renders it an offence to access without authorisation may be committed abroad provided that there is a 'significant link' with the UK. Thus, if the defendant does what he does to secure access from abroad, if the computer is physically in the UK there would be an offence. However, in the case of section 2, it is enough that the offence that it is intended to facilitate is within the jurisdiction of the UK. Thus, both the defendant and the computer could be outside the UK provided crime that he intends to facilitate is in the UK.

CORRUPTION

6.74   The law relating to corruption in the United Kingdom, albeit in the context of the ancient common law, has in recent years become controversial. Reform of the present law, which in certain respects fails to meet the various international obligations on the United Kingdom,[1] has been actively considered by the Law Commission and Home Office for a number of years.[2] There have also been recent institutional changes in the responsibility for the investigation of allegations of corruption which cast primary responsibility on the City of London Police. This area of law given the controversy that has been occasioned, particularly in regard to the investigation by the Serious Fraud Office into allegations relating to certain payments made by BAE Systems in the context of a major arms deal with Saudi Arabia,[3] is in a state of flux and it is probably that the recommendations of the Law Commission for radical reform will be implemented in the relatively near future.[4] We will, however, discuss the law as it is now.

In Britain there has traditionally been little dependence on specific provisions relating to corruption and much more use has been made of the general criminal law and in particular fraud. As in other countries, specific legislative concern has focused on those in public office. Section 1 of the Public Bodies Corrupt Practices Act 1889 provides that 'every person who shall by himself or by or in conjunction with any other person, corruptly solicit or receive, or agree to receive, for himself, or for any other person, any gift, loan, fee, reward or advantage whatever as an inducement to, or reward for, or otherwise on account of any member, officer, or servant of a public body … , doing or forbearing to do anything in respect of any matter or transaction whatsoever, actual or proposed, in which the said public body is concerned, shall be guilty of an offence'. It is further made an offence for any person 'by himself or by or in conjunction with any other person to corruptly give, promise, or offer any such benefit as an inducement or reward to such a person. Thus it is rendered a crime to take and to give an inducement, in such circumstances. It is only an offence if the bribe is given or offered to or solicited by a member, officer or servant of a 'public body'. While initially concerned with local government bodies, by the Prevention of Corruption Act 1916, it is extended to 'local and public authorities of all descriptions'. Thus, a body which has public or statutory duties to perform on behalf of the public will be a public body for the purposes of this offence. Having said this, there are areas of uncertainty. For example, while officials of a nationalised company would be caught, those of a company in partial public ownership would not. It is also questionable as to whether members of the House of Commons are included. Since 2002 bodies in other jurisdictions performing an equivalent function to a body that would be properly considered to be a public body in the United Kingdom are also covered.

1   See, for example, *United Kingdom: Phase 2bis: Report on the Application of the Convention on Combating Bribery of Foreign Public Officials in International Business Transactions and the 1997 Recommendation on Combating Bribery in International Business Transactions* (2008) OECD.
2   See *Legislating the Criminal Code: Corruption* (1998) Law Com No 248; Joint Committee on the Draft Corruption Bill, Session 2002–2003, HL Paper 157, HC 705 (2003); *The Government's Reply to the Report of the Joint Committee on the Draft Corruption Bill*, Session 2002–2003, HL Paper 157, HC 705 (2003) Cm 6086 and *Reforming Bribery: A Consultation Paper* (2007) Law Com Consultation Paper No 185.
3   See *R (on the application of Corner House Research) v Director of the Serious Fraud Office* (2008) 4 All ER 927.
4   See in particular *Reforming Bribery* (2008) The Law Commission Law Com No 313.

6.75   The scope of the offence in terms of benefit to be taken or given is extremely wide and includes 'any office, or dignity, and any forbearance to demand money or money's worth or valuable thing, and includes any aid, vote, consent, or influence, and also includes any promise or procurement of an agreement or endeavour to procure, or the holding out of any expectation of any gift, loan, fee, reward or advantage ...' The advantage must be give, solicited or offered, as an inducement to the members, officer or servant of a public body to do something or forbear from doing something in respect of a matter or transaction, actual or proposed, in which that public body is concerned, or as a reward for so doing, or otherwise on account of such. Thus a bribe may serve as a reward for past favours and an inducement to repeat them. However, a reward for past favours is sufficient for liability, even if there was no agreement in advance. The requirement that what is done must be proved to be done 'corruptly' has caused difficulty. It is not necessary to show dishonesty as such. Under section 2 of the Prevention of Corruption Act 1916 where in any proceedings it is proved that 'any money, gift, or other consideration has been paid or given to or received by a person in the employment of Her Majesty or any Government Department or a public body or from a person, or agent of a person, holding or seeking to obtain a contract from Her Majesty or (other public body)' the advantage 'shall be deemed to have been paid or given and received corruptly as such inducement or reward ... unless the contrary is proved'. In *R v Brathwaite*[1] it was explained that 'the burden of proof' in such circumstances 'descends on the shoulders of the defence. It then becomes necessary for the defendant to show, on a balance of probabilities, that what was going on was not 'corrupt'. It is not without interest that the reversal of the burden of proof has been criticised as unnecessary in Britain by the law

Commission (Law Commission No 248 (1998)) on the basis that under the Criminal Justice and Public Order Act 1994 (section 34) adverse inferences may be drawn from the failure of a defendant to explain certain circumstances in all cases.

1   [1983] 1 WLR 385.

6.76   The corruption of agents is addressed in section 1 of the Prevention of Corruption Act 1906. This provides 'if any agent corruptly accepts or obtains, or agrees to accept or attempts to obtain, from any person, for himself or for any other person, any gift or consideration as an inducement or reward for doing or forbearing to do ... any act in relation to his principal's affairs or business, or for showing or forbearing to show favour or favour to any person in relation to his principal's affairs or business ...' he commits a crime. The section also provides for mirror liability for anyone who corruptly seeks to induce an agent in this manner. Thus, as in the case of public officials, both the taker and giver of favours potentially commit a crime. Agents are defined to include 'any person employed by or acting for another; and the expression 'principal' includes an employer'. It is also made clear that a person serving under the Crown, any public body, or under any corporation, or local authority or board of guardians, is an agent. While in theory interesting legal issues could arise in regard to the scope of agency and whether if, for example, an employee acting outside his authority, is still an agent, in practice these have not arisen. The Anti-Terrorism, Crime and Security Act 2001 in section 1(4) provides that for the purpose of determining whether a person is within the scope of this offence it is immaterial if the principal's affairs or business have no connection with the UK and are conducted outside the UK and the agent's functions have no connection with the UK and are carried out in a foreign country. We have already noted that this Act also extended the definition of public body to overseas public bodies.

6.77   Bribery of a public officer is a common law offence and the receipt of a bribe, as we have seen, by an official may well be the crime (and tort) of misconduct in public office. It is probable that the notion of public officer, in regard to the common law offence in England, is wider that the statutory provisions. The 2001 Act also extended the scope of the common law offence making it clear that 'it is immaterial if the functions of the person who receives or is offered a reward have no connection with the UK and are carried out' outside the UK. The bribe must be proved to be intended to influence the officer's discharge of his public duties, by inducing him to act otherwise than what his duty would dictate.

6.78   The Anti-Terrorism, Crime and Security Act 2001 in section 109 provides that if a national of the UK or a body incorporated under the law of any part of the UK does anything in an country outside the UK and that act would, if done in the UK, constitute the crime of corruption, it will be so considered and proceedings may be taken in the UK. It is immaterial that what occurs is not a crime in the place it takes place. The crimes included within this 'long arm' provision include all that we have discussed above, including conspiracy, attempt or incitement to do so.

FALSE REPORTING

6.79   It is of fundamental importance to the proper operation of so many aspects of the legal and regulatory systems that information is properly and accurately recorded and reported. Indeed, in recent years, some of the most dramatic financial scandals have involved misconduct in this process. Under the English law, directors of a company must prepare accounts for each financial year and also a directors' report. The accounts must be audited and under section 499(1)(b) of the Companies Act 2006 an auditor can require various persons including the directors, officers and employees of the company to provide him with such information and explanations as he thinks necessary for the proper performance of his duties. Under section 501(1) of the Act a person who knowingly or recklessly makes an oral or written statement to an auditor that conveys or purports to convey information or explanations which the audit requires, or is entitled to require, and is misleading, false or deceptive in a material particular, commits an offence. It is also provided, much in line with the Sarbanes-Oxley provisions in the USA, that a director is required to state, in the directors' report, that so far as he is aware, there is no information needed by the auditor of which the auditor is unaware and that he has taken all the steps that he ought to have taken to make himself aware of any information needed by the auditor and to establish that the auditor is aware of it. It is sufficient for this purpose that he has made such enquiries of his fellow directors and of the auditors, and taken such other steps, as are required by his duty to exercise reasonable care, skill and diligence. If such a report is approved and the statement turns out to be false, the director commits a crime under section 418(5). Furthermore, the offence is committed by every director who knew that the statement was false or was recklessly indifferent as to whether it was true or false, and failed to take reasonable steps to prevent the report being approved. This places an affirmative obligation on directors to ensure that auditors are placed in a position to discharge their own duties in verifying the information that the company is required to disclose to the shareholders and other stakeholders. It is not now possible for directors to hide behind a veil of ignorance.

6.80   Every company, under section 386(2) of the 2006 Act, is required to keep and maintain proper accounting records. In particular, they must be sufficient to show and explain the company's transactions, be such as to disclose with reasonable accuracy, at any time, the company's financial position and be such as to enable the directors to ensure that the accounts comply with the statutory requirements. Furthermore, detailed information to be included in the records is set out in other provisions of the Act. If the company fails to discharge its obligations in this regard, every officer of the company who is in default commits an offence under section 387(1). It is a defence for a director to show that he acted honestly and in the circumstances in which the company's business was carried out his default was excusable. In like terms, there is a statutory obligation to ensure that such records are kept available in the UK for officers of the company to inspect by virtue of section 388(2).

6.81   These provisions do not stand alone. Section 17(1) of the Theft Act 1968 renders it an offence for any person, 'dishonestly, with a view to gain for himself or another or with intent to cause loss to another to (a) destroy, deface, conceal or falsify any account or any record or document made or required for any accounting purpose; or (b) in furnishing information for any purpose produces or makes use of any account, or any such record pr document as aforesaid, which to his knowledge is or may be misleading, false or deceptive in a material particular.' This offence covers documents 'if it is made for some purpose other than an accounting purpose, but is required for an accounting purpose as a subsidiary consideration …'.[1] If a document is required for an accounting purpose it matters not what it was created for. Furthermore, it should be noted that this is in no way confined to companies or established businesses, an individual may have accounting purposes. It is further provided in section 17(2) that for the purposes of the offence, 'a person who makes or concurs in making in an account or other document an entry which is or may be misleading, false or deceptive in a material particular, or who omits or concurs in omitting a material particular from an account or other document, is to be treated as falsifying the account or document'.

1   *Attorney-General's Reference (No 1 1980)* [1981] 1 WLR 34.

6.82   Section 18(1) of the 1968 Act provides that where an offence under section 17 is committed by a company and 'is proved to have been committed with the consent or connivance of any director, manager, secretary or other officer' of the company, or any person purporting so to be, that individual will also be guilty of the offence. It would seem from this, that once knowledge is established, then passive acquiescence would be enough for liability. By section 19 'an officer of a body corporate or unincorporated association, or person purporting to act as such, with intent to deceive members or creditors of the body corporate or association about its affairs, publishes or concurs in publishing a written statement or account which to his knowledge is or may be misleading, false or deceptive in a material particular..' commits an offence. This offence does not extend to oral statements. However, if, for example, a director orally made a false statement to the press which is then written up this would be sufficient. Section 1(1) of the Prevention of Corruption Act 1906 also includes a provision of interest. It provides that 'if any person knowingly gives to any agent, or if any agent knowingly uses with intent to deceive his principal, a receipt, account, or other document in respect of which the principal is interested, and which contains any statement which is false or erroneous or defective in any material particular, and which to his knowledge is intended to mislead the principal' is guilty of an offence.

6.83   Of course, there are many other provisions and procedures concerned with the integrity of disclosure and the reporting of information. In the case of companies that have their securities listed or registered for trading on an organised securities market, there will be many additional and specific reporting and disclosure obligations. We have already discussed the significance of these and in particular the obligation to make continuous and timely disclosure in the context of insider dealing. These obligations may give rise to liability at many levels within the legal system. The obligation to disclose will bring in fraud and possibly anti-manipulation laws. These may well result in criminal and civil liability. Those who are harmed by false and misleading information may also have a civil claim against those responsible, including the company. Those responsible for the false or misleading statements in the company may find that they are in breach of their duties to the company and be liable accordingly in the civil courts. In certain cases, in some jurisdictions, they might also be liable to anyone, including dealers in the market, who relied on this false information. The securities exchange upon which the relevant securities are listed or traded may also have grounds for complaint. In many countries the listing agreement is regarded as a contract and even where it is not, there are usually legal devices under which those responsible for the market can initiate injunctive and other actions against those responsible for each of the terms of listing and possibly misleading the market. It is also probable that the market regulator will also have powers to intervene and pursue those responsible. Finally in this regard, it is important to note that failure to disclose information as it should be, may well result in other problems for those in management. Insiders in such circumstances will generally not be able to deal.

FORGERY AND THE RELIABILITY OF DOCUMENTATION

6.84   The significance of documentation in the perpetration of so many financial crimes need not be laboured here, suffice it to say that in the commercial and financial sector documentation is vital and therefore a fraudster or money launderer will need to be able to manipulate and control the documents which establish his credibility and ability to operate. Section 1 of the Forgery and Counterfeiting Act 1981 provides 'a person is guilty of forgery if he makes a false instrument, with the intention that he or another shall use it to induce somebody to accept it as genuine, and by reason of so accepting it to do or not to do some act to his own or any other person's prejudice'. In the context of this offence 'instrument' includes any document whether formal or informal in character, stamps and any disc, tape, sound track or other device on or in which information is recorded or stored by mechanical, electronic or other means. In *Attorney-General of Hong Kong v Pat Chiuk-Wah*[1] the Privy Council stated that it includes 'any document intended to have some effect, as evidence of, or in connection with, a transaction which is capable, or giving rise to legal rights and obligations ...'. The notion behind forgery is that the instrument must not only tell a lie, but a lie about itself. The English Law Commission said, 'the primary reason ... for ...the law of forgery is to penalise the making of documents which, because of the spurious air of authenticity given to them, are likely to lead to their acceptance as true statements of the facts related in them.' (Law Commission No 55). Section 9(1) sets out what is meant by a false instrument. Basically an instrument will be false if it purports to be made in a form in which it was not in fact made, or in a form, or on terms that the person did not have authority to make, or has been altered, or made on a date or place or in other circumstances where it was not, or by a person who does not exist. Thus, the document may lie about itself in terms of the identity of the person making or authorising the statement, the circumstances of its making and the circumstances of any alteration.

1   [1971] AC 835.

6.85   It must be remembered that the wrongful conduct – the so called *actus reus* of forgery – is the making of a false instrument. This includes making an instrument which is false when it is made, altering a genuine instrument to render it false and altering an instrument which is already false by making it false in some additional way. The maker of this false instrument must intend that he or another shall use it to induce someone to accept it as a genuine instrument and that the person so accepting it by reason of so accepting it will do or not do some act and that act or omission shall be to his or another person's prejudice. It should be noted that the offence of forgery is complete on the making of a false instrument with the relevant intention. It matters not that no one was in fact prejudiced. It follows that an accused cannot escape liability '... merely because at the time when he is creating the document he has not made up his mind about the method of despatch ...'.[1] Section 10(3) provides that 'references to inducing someone to accept a false instrument as genuine ... include references to inducing a machine to respond to the instrument ...as if it was genuine'. Furthermore, section 10(4) adds that 'the act or omission intended to be induced by the machine responding to the instrument ... shall be treated as an act or omission to a person's prejudice.' The notion of prejudice is set out in section 10(1) where it is provided 'an act or omission intended to be induced is to a person's prejudice if, and only if,' it is one which, if it occurs will result in his temporary or permanent loss of property, or deprivation of an opportunity to earn remuneration or to gain a financial advantage, or will result in somebody being given an opportunity to earn remuneration or gain a financial advantage or will be the result of his having accepted a false instrument as genuine in connection with his performance of any duty.

1   *R v Ondhia* [1998] 2 Cr App R 150.

6.86   The offence of forgery is extended to the copying of a false instrument by section 2 of the 1981 Act. It is an offence 'for a person to make a copy of an instrument which is, and which he knows or believes to be, a false instrument, with the intention that he or another shall use it to induce somebody to accept it as a copy of a genuine instrument, and by reason of so accepting it to do or not to do some act to his own or any other person's prejudice'.

6.87   Section 3 of the Forgery and Counterfeiting Act 1981 provides that 'it is an offence for a person to use an instrument which is, and which he knows or believes to be, false, with the intention of inducing somebody to accept it as genuine, and by reason of so accepting it to do or not to do some act to his own or any other person's prejudice'. It should be noted that if the person uttering or using the false instrument knows or believes that the instrument is false and in fact it is false, it matters not that the person actually making the instrument has not been guilty of forgery. It is necessary, however, to establish some kind of nexus between the user and the instrument. It is not sufficient that someone acts in a manner where he knows someone else will supply a forged document, he must himself use it. Section 4 creates a similar offence in regard to use of a copy of a false instrument.

6.88   Given the ease with which forged documents can be transferred and hidden, it is under the English law an offence to merely be in possession of certain specified forged instruments. These include forged money and postal orders, postage stamps, share certificates, cheques and other bills of exchange, travellers' cheques, bankers' drafts, promissory notes, cheque, debit and credit cards and certificates relating to entries in official registers. It is an offence under section 5(1) of the Act 'for a person to have in his custody or under his control an instrument' to which this provision applies, 'which is, and which he knows or believes to be, false, with the intention that he or another shall use it to induce somebody to accept it as genuine and by reason of so accepting it to do or not to do some act to his own or any other person's prejudice'. It should be noted, however, that there is a lesser offence where the person will be guilty, if he has 'in his custody or under his control without lawful authority or excuse' a false instrument within the scope of this provision and 'which is and which he knows or believes to be false'. It is also an offence to have in possession 'a machine or implement, or paper or any other material' which to that person's 'knowledge is or has been specially designed or adapted for the making of an instrument' to which this provision applied with the intention that he or another will in fact make such an instrument and use it to another's prejudice (section 5(3)). The accused must actually know that the equipment has been so adapted or designed, but it is important to note that they need not have been adapted or designed to create a 'false' document. Section 5(4) creates an offence of merely being in possession of such equipment or materials without lawful excuse.

6.89   Suppression of documents in the commission of fraud is addressed in the English law under section 20 of the Theft Act 1968. This provides that 'a person who dishonestly, with a view to gain for himself or another or with intent to cause loss to another, destroys, defaces or conceals any valuable security, any will or other testamentary document or any original document of or belonging to, or filed or deposited in, any court of justice or any government department shall' be guilty of an offence. The notion of defacement is broad and might extend to altering a document and thus, this might be an alternative charge to one of forgery.

ACTS PREPARATORY TO FRAUD

6.90   Most frauds require the assistance of others and a considerable amount of preparation. However, generally speaking there is a reluctance in the law to punish mere acts of preparation other than in the context of terrorist related crime. While fraud is a crime of intent and the offence is complete whether or not the accused actually manages to dupe someone, there may be situations where all the requirements for a charge of fraud are not present and yet justice demands intervention.

6.91   Where a person agrees with another to carry out a course of conduct that would amount to the crime of fraud, he may in many jurisdictions be guilty of conspiracy to defraud. We have already referred on a number of occasions to the important crime of conspiracy and noted that it remains in England a common law conspiracy although it may also be charged as a conspiracy to commit the substantive crime of fraud as a statutory conspiracy. Section 1 of the Criminal Law Act 1977 renders it a statutory offence if a person agrees with any other person, including a company, that a course of conduct shall be undertaken, where if the agreement is carried out in accordance with their intentions it will amount to or involve the commission of a specific crime. Before a conviction can take place the jury must be satisfied that there was in fact an agreement between two or more persons to commit the crime in question; that the particular accused was a party to that agreement in the sense 'that he agreed with one or more of the other persons that the crime should be committed and at the time of agreeing to this, he intended that they (and he) should carry it out'.[1] It is not necessary that the agreement be to commit a specific offence under a statute. For example, an agreement to launder the proceeds of insider dealing or another crime, may be charged as a single conspiracy. The Criminal Law Act in section 1(2) provides that a person shall not be guilty of conspiracy under the Act unless he and at least one other party to the agreement intend or know that the facts necessary to the commission of the offence shall or will exist at the time of the conduct. This would seem to have the effect of blocking charges for conspiracy to commit crimes under, for example, the Fraud Act and the anti-money laundering provisions, where the accused might in the substantive offence be liable for reckless conduct or in the case of certain money laundering offences 'having reasonable grounds to suspect ...'.

1   Judiciary Studies Board, England and Wales, Specimen Direction 2005.

6.92   The common law conspiracy to defraud is preserved by the Act, as we have seen.[1] It was said by Buckley J in *London and Globe Finance Corporation*[2] that 'to defraud is to deprive by deceit; it is deceit to induce a man to act to his injury'. It would seem on the authorities that an agreement by two or more persons by dishonesty to deprive a person of something which he is or to which he is or would be or even might be entitled and an agreement by which two or more by dishonesty to injure some proprietary right of another is a conspiracy at common law. Furthermore an agreement to deceive a public official, as we have seen, into doing something, or not doing something, that he would not have done but for the deceit is also a conspiracy to defraud.[3] It is important to appreciate that it is the risk of prejudice not actual prejudice that is necessary for the offence. Thus, in *Attorney General of Hong Kong v Wai Yu-Tsang*,[4] the fact that the bank accountant covered up bad cheques passing through the bank to prevent a run on the bank still amounted to a conspiracy to defraud the bank. The Privy Council stated 'it is ...important to distinguish a conspirator's intention or immediate purpose ... from his motive (or underlying purpose.) The latter may be benign in that he does not wish the victim ... to suffer harm; but the mere fact that it is benign will not of itself prevent the agreement from constituting a conspiracy to defraud'. The scope and arguable vagueness as to the perimeters of this offence have resulted in criticism over many years. Where it is possible to charge a conspiracy to commit a specific statutory offence – such as fraud under section 1 of the Fraud Act 2006, then the common law should not be used. There are situations, however, where the crime of conspiracy to defraud is wider than the statutory law. For example, in the case of a statutory conspiracy to commit fraud, it would need to be shown that at least one of the parties to the agreement was intended to commit the fraud. In a situation where the agreement is to enable or facilitate someone else to commit the fraud, who is not a party to the agreement, the only charge would be conspiracy to defraud at common law. The creation of a general false impression over a period of time, such as in a long firm fraud along the lines we have already discussed, might be charged as a conspiracy to defraud.

1   See **6.14** *supra*.
2   [1903] 1 Ch 728.
3   See generally *Scott v Metropolitan Police Commissioner* [1975] AC 819 and *DPP v Welham* [1961] AC 103.
4   [1992] 1 AC 269.

6.93   If a person does an act which is more than merely preparatory to the commission of a crime then he or she may well be guilty of an attempt to commit that crime and generally punished in the same manner, under section 1 of the Criminal Attempts Act 1981. He or she must have moved beyond the stage of planning and preparation to that of starting to implement his or her intention. Merely putting oneself in a position to commit a crime is different from actually trying to commit it. In the case of fraud, given what has been said above, there is relatively little scope for the offence of 'attempt' to operate. It might be relevant where, for example, the accused makes a representation which he or she intends to be false, but which as a result of a mistake of fact, is true, or where he or she tries to communicate a false representation but this fails. However, in regard to other financial crimes there is rather more scope for charging attempt.

6.94   The law will in certain specific contexts punish the mere possession of certain substances, articles and equipment. In the context of burglary, for example, section 25 of the Theft Act 1968 renders it an offence for an accused to be found at a place 'other than his place of abode' with 'any article for use in committing a burglary or theft ...'. Furthermore, 'proof that he had with him an article made or adapted for us in committing a burglary or theft shall be evidence that he had it with him for such use'. In the case of fraud, under section 6 of the Fraud Act 2006 a person will be guilty of an offence if he has in his possession or under his control any article for use in the course of or in connection with any fraud. Under this offence the accused can be charged for possession of equipment, such as skimmers and letters used for 'flash' purposes, in his home. It should also be noted that section 8 makes it clear that 'article' includes 'any program or data held in electronic form'. It is only necessary for the prosecution to prove that the accused was in possession and intended the article to be used by himself or another, in the commission of a fraud or merely in connection with a fraud. It is interesting to compare the breadth of this provision with section 16 of the Terrorism Act 2000. This renders it a crime to possess money or other property but only if 'he intends that it should be used, or has reasonable cause to suspect that it may be used, for the purpose of terrorism'. This provision has been used effectively against those engaged in various frauds and other fund raising activities in support of terrorists. Finally, in this regard, section 7 of the Fraud Act 2006 makes it a crime for a person to make, adapt, supply or offer to supply any article 'knowing that it is designed or adapted for use in the course of or in connection with fraud, or intending it to be used to commit, or assist in the commission of a fraud'.

PERJURY AND FALSE DECLARATIONS

6.95 From our discussion above, it is clear that a number of abuses have occurred as a result of the 'crooks' misleading the market authorities and other regulators into permitting a state of affairs to come about or continue, which of itself creates an impression that certain underlying and justifying events have satisfactorily taken place. In *R v Aspinall*,[1] it was held that it is an indictable conspiracy at common law to obtain a listing of securities on the Stock Exchange by falsely representing that the required number of shares have been allotted and paid for. In this case, it was emphasised that it was enough for the prosecution to show that the defendants' purpose was to mislead the Stock Exchange's officials; it was not necessary to prove that the defendants intended to injure investors by securing a higher price for the shares they were floating than would otherwise have been obtainable. It might also amount to the crime of conspiracy to defraud, to agree with others to induce, by false statements, made by word or conduct, a public official to do, or not to do, an act in the course of his official duties. For example, it has been argued that furnishing the executive of the City Panel on Takeovers and Mergers with false information designed to mislead it in exercising its responsibilities under the Code might well fall within the scope of this offence. The FSMA 2000, s 398 makes it a criminal offence for a person knowingly or recklessly to give 'in purported compliance with any requirement imposed by or under this Act' false or misleading information to the Authority or, under the FSMA 2000, s 399, to the Director-General of Fair Trading. This provision is somewhat narrower than the offence which was created under the Financial Services Act 1986, s 200 and which was not confined to misleading officials of the Securities and Investments Board.

1   (1876) 1 QBD 730; affd (1876) 2 QBD 48, CA.

6.96 There are many situations where documents and statements are required to be made under oath or pursuant to some solemn legal undertaking to tell the truth. For example, section 5 of the Perjury Act 1911 renders it a crime to 'knowingly and wilfully make (otherwise than on oath) a statement false in a material particular' if the statement is made in a statutory declaration, 'in any abstract, account, balance sheet, book, certificate, declaration, entry, estimate, inventory, notice, report, return, or other document' which the person concerned is authorised, or required to make, attest, or verify by an 'public general Act of Parliament' and in any oral declaration or oral answer which he is required to make by, under, or in pursuance' of any such law. The statement must be intentionally false and under section 13 of the Act its falsity must be corroborated.

6.97   There are, however, many other statutory offences under various Acts imposing liability for false statements made in purported compliance with statutory obligations to tell the truth or affirm the veracity of certain facts or the genuineness of certain documents. For example, section 1112(1) of the Companies Act 2006 provides for an offence where a person for any purpose knowingly or recklessly delivers or causes to be delivered to the Registrar of Companies a document or makes to the Registrar a statement that is misleading, false or deceptive in a material particular.

CIVIL FRAUD

6.98   When examining the law relating to the manipulation of markets, reference was made to the possibility of suing in the civil courts for compensation. Mention has also been made of the statutory tort action that is expressly provided for under the FSMA 2000, s 150 in relation to violations of the various rules promulgated by the FSA. In the context of restitution and compensation, it is also important to remember the various powers that the FSA has to initiate civil actions. None of the statutory provisions, however, displaces the traditional common law remedies based on fraud. It is therefore worthwhile examining the civil law relating to fraudulent misrepresentation.

6.99   The dividing line between the criminal and civil law with regard to fraudulent conduct has never been entirely clear in English law. Indeed, one of the earliest causes of action, that of deceit, involved considerations of almost a penal nature. Given the harm that allegations of dishonesty can cause to individuals, particularly if they are in business, the courts have always been concerned by way of procedure and proof to ensure as far as is practical that such allegations are not made and pursued wantonly. Therefore, as a matter of pleading in the civil law, averments of fraud must be specially pleaded with all the relevant facts establishing the specific averment set out. While there is a difference between the standard of proof in an ordinary criminal trial and one for fraud in the civil law, judges have often emphasised that as the seriousness of the allegation increases in criminal proceedings, the standard of proof that is required to be met will be more exacting. Therefore, in practice, there may not be a great deal of difference between the standards of proof required to establish fraud in the civil and criminal law, particularly when it is remembered that in most cases considerable reliance will need to be placed on documentary evidence. Where allegations of fraud or deliberate misconduct involving moral turpitude are made and persisted with in circumstances which the court considers unjustified, there will be serious cost implications for the plaintiff and on occasion judges have expressed their disapproval of counsel.

6.100   The issue of fraud may arise in the civil law in a number of ways. However, since *Paisley v Freeman*,[1] it has been the rule that if a person knowingly or recklessly, ie not caring whether it is true or false, makes a statement to another with the intention that it shall be relied upon by that person, who in fact does rely on it and as a consequence suffers harm, then an action in deceit will be available. It is the need for the plaintiff to establish that the defendant acted with actual knowledge or could not care less whether what he said was true or not, which distinguishes liability in fraud from, for example, liability in the tort of negligence.[2] In the case of negligent misstatement, the defendant will be liable if an ordinary reasonable person would have known that what was said was untrue, ie the standard is objective. Where a person has been induced to enter into a contract as a result of a fraudulent misrepresentation, the law provides remedies or rescission and damages. While rescission may be a more attractive remedy in the case of investment transactions, it will not always be available. There is a strict rule which requires full restoration of property transferred under the relevant contract, ie the parties must be restored to their original position. It follows that if the victim of the fraud, rather than run the risk of a further, perhaps unrelated, diminution in the value of his securities, disposes of them, he will have lost his right to rescind. In *Smith New Court v Scrimgeour Vickers*,[3] Nourse LJ observed that, in the case of a fungible asset like quoted shares, the rule which requires restitution *in specie* is a hard one and in cases of fraud it was clear that the court had little sympathy with it, although in the circumstances it was not appropriate to depart from it. The rule works harshly, particularly in the case of an omission to disclose information which does not give rise to an independent cause of action for damages.[4]

1   (1789) 3 TR 51.
2   See *Derry v Peek* (1889) 14 App Cas 337.
3   [1994] 4 All ER 225.
4   See *Banque Keysey Ullman v Skandia* [1989] 2 All ER 952.

6.101   In an action for damages, the courts have been concerned to ensure that a fraudster takes no benefit from his fraud or the false circumstances that he has created. In *Clark v Urquhart, Stracey v Urquhart*,[1] Lord Aitkin emphasised that the measure of damages is the 'actual damage directly flowing from the fraudulent inducement' and this includes consequential loss.[2] On the other hand, deprecations of the value of shares by market forces operating after the date of acquisition do not flow directly from the fraudulent inducement, but from the purchaser's decision to retain the shares and accept the hazards of the market rather than sell at once.[3] The measure of damages will therefore be the difference between the price that the plaintiff paid and the 'true value' of the securities at the time he was fraudulently induced to acquire them. Valuation is always a difficult task and determination of the price depends upon a number of assumptions, one of the most important being what assumption should be made about the information which was available to the market.[4] In *Smith New Court v Scrimgeour Vickers*,[5] the Court of Appeal considered that there were only two plausible possibilities in determining what assumption should be made as to information in the case of fraud. First, to assume that the market knew everything it actually did know, but was not influenced by the misrepresentation itself or, secondly, to assume that the market was omniscient. The Court of Appeal thought that the first approach was rational, but the second arbitrary and therefore disagreed with Chadwick J who at first instance appeared to have assumed that the market was omniscient. In the result, the Court of Appeal held that the correct measure of damages in a case where a person is induced to acquire shares by deceit is the difference between the price that was actually paid and the price which, in the absence of the misrepresentation, the parcel of shares would have fetched on the open market at that time.

1   [1930] AC 28 at 68.
2   See *Doyle v Olby (Ironmongers) Ltd* [1969] 2 All ER 119.
3   See *Waddell v Blockley* (1879) 4 QBD 678.
4   See *Lynall v IRC* [1971] 3 All ER 914 and with regard to insider trading.
5   [1994] 4 All ER 225.

6.102   The relationship between actions for deceit and in the tort of negligence have already been alluded to. As it is not necessary for a plaintiff in an action for damages to specify the particular tort which he is seeking to rely on for a remedy, provided he asserts and establishes the facts required for liability under at least one accepted cause of action, there may in practice be little lost in not alleging to being able to prove dishonesty, given the court's attitude to allegations of fraud. Apart from the desire to brand a person as a fraudster, it remains possible to obtain exemplary damages in cases of proven fraud and the statue of limitation may be more favourable,[1] but in the majority of cases plaintiffs are well advised to refrain from specific averments of fraud. In the case of misrepresentation inducing a contract between the parties, the statutory remedies for negligent statements provided by the Misrepresentation Act 1967, s 2(1) are, in practical terms, superior to an action in tort. Under section 2(1), the person responsible for the misrepresentation has the burden of establishing that he had reasonable grounds for believing and did in fact believe what he said to be true.

1   Limitation Act 1980, s 32.

6.103   As we have seen, the issues of fraud may also be relevant in other actions such as conspiracy and under specific statutory provisions giving rise to a civil remedy. Equity follows the law and will not enforce a bargain that has been procured by fraud. Furthermore, the courts have developed a form of restitutionary liability for those who receive property transferred in breach of trust or who facilitate the laundering of such property with the requisite degree of dishonesty.[1] It must also be remembered that whilst there have been significant developments in the criminal law facilitating the taking and receipt of evidence from overseas, the civil law provides far greater weapons in obtaining evidence and discovery, in freezing funds and in enforcing orders of the court. Whilst the criminal courts possess statutory power, in certain circumstances, to order restoration and even compensation, as we have seen in the context of insider dealing, such orders are rarely appropriate in the case of securities related fraud.

1   See *Agip (Africa) Ltd v Jackson* [1992] 4 All ER 385 at 451; *El Ajou v Dollar Land Holdings plc* [1993] 3 All ER 717 and *Royal Brunei Airlines Sdn Bhd v Tan* [1995] 2 AC 378.

DISCLOSURE ORDERS AND FREEZING ORDERS

6.104   The range of orders that the court can make in theory may be limited only by the judge's imagination, but in practice orders tend to follow precedents and in most countries the law has been settled into recognised procedures and orders. Perhaps the most significant from our perspective are orders for the freezing of monies in bank accounts or the immobilisation of wealth. Section 37 of the Supreme Court Act 1981 enables the High Court to grant injunctions 'in all cases in which it appears to the court to be just and convenient to do so' and within this wide power the courts are prepared to issue a freezing injunction to restrain a party from removing from the jurisdiction assets located there or dealing with any assets whether located in the jurisdiction or not. Freezing orders were previously referred to as Mareva injunctions. In *Mareva Compania Naviera SA v International Bulkcarriers SA*,[1] the court issued an injunction restraining the defendant from improperly disposing of his assets or concealing or moving them overseas and thereby making himself 'judgement proof'. A freezing order may be obtained in the English Court and most other common law jurisdictions whenever there is a real risk of dissipation of assets. Such orders play a most significant role in fighting financial crime and render the courts of common law jurisdictions attractive to those who wish to pursue the assets of fraudsters and their confederates. While many non-common law jurisdictions may order the interdiction of property, few have procedures as effective and as wide reaching in terms of their personal jurisdiction. It is important to remember that in so far as the order enjoins individuals to whom it is addressed or who have proper notice of it, it is in no way confined, unless it so provides, to territorial jurisdiction. The order may have world-wide application. A considerable amount of law has been developed as to the availability, reach and terms of such orders given the devastating impact that they can have on a person's business and life.

1 [1975] 2 Lloyd's Rep 509.

6.105 Application is usually made without notice possibly before the action has even commenced. There will be three primary issues for the High Court judge hearing the *ex parte* application. Firstly, whether there is a good arguable case; secondly, whether the claimant can adduce sufficient evidence as to the existence and location of assets which the injunction, if made, would affect; and whether there is a real risk that the defendant may deal with those assets so as to render nugatory any judgment which the claimant may obtain. The application must identify as precisely as possible the bank accounts or other assets that the injunction is to be aimed at. Generally speaking if there is sufficient wealth within the jurisdiction to satisfy a likely judgment, the order will be confined to the jurisdiction. It might apply to bank accounts and other wealth in the name of other people if there is evidence that in fact it belongs to the defendant.[1] If the defendant is the majority shareholder in a company than an order can be made against the assets of that company and the company will become a co-defendant in the cause.[2] The risk of dissipation will be decided on the facts of each case. However, dishonesty or any proof of lack of integrity on the part of the defendant will be relevant, as will the use of offshore banking facilities in suspect jurisdictions.

1 *SCF Finance Co v Masri* [1985] 1 WLR 876.
2 *TSB Private Bank International SA v Chabra* [1992] 1 WLR 231.

6.106 Section 25 of the UK Civil Jurisdiction and Judgments Act 1982 empowers the court to grant all forms of interim relief in aid of foreign courts unless 'in the opinion of the court, the fact that the court has no jurisdiction apart from this section in relation to the subject matter of the proceedings in question makes it inexpedient for the court to grant it'. Thus an application can be made to an English High Court judge to freeze assets relevant to a proceeding in any foreign court. The Court have been careful to in effect issue a world-wide freezing order when the foreign proceedings have nothing to do with the UK and the parties are not resident here. However, in *Motorola Credit Corporation v Uzan (No 2)*[1] the court was prepared to uphold on appeal certain orders in regard to various defendants based in Turkey, who were accused of participating in an international fraud and who were subject to local freezing orders in New York. While the court accepted that the requirements for an order on behalf of a foreign applicant in foreign proceedings were much the same as those for an application in regard to proceedings in the English courts, it recognised the need for caution. For example, in the present case the New York court did not have the 'unusually wide powers against a foreign defendant' that the English courts had, Furthermore, there was sensitivity in Turkey and an order had been obtained in the Turkish Courts attempting to restrain the claimants from resorting to the New York and UK courts.

1 [2004] 1 WLR 113.

6.107 It is important to realise that the making of an order gives the claimant no property rights in the relevant monies and he does not become a secured or preferential creditor. He will also have to give undertakings in damages, as in the case of any interim injunction. The applicant will have to undertake to indemnify any person upon whom notice of the order is served in respect of expenses and liabilities they may incur in seeking to comply with the order. This is in addition to the claimant's cross undertaking to compensate the defendant if the case is not substantiated. Of course, these undertakings present a serious hurdle to the claimant. However, in *RBG Resources PLC v Rastogi*,[1] Laddie J accepted a limited cross undertaking where there was strong evidence of the defendant's wrongdoing and the claimant was financially weak.

1   (2002) LTL May 31 2002.

6.108   A curious feature of freezing orders is that although it is made against the defendant it may be effective only if notice of it is given to the relevant bank or person in possession of the assets. It would seem on the authorities that a claimant cannot sue a bank or other person for failing to preserve the relevant assets, even after proper notice has been served, as they do not owe him a duty of care.[1] Nonetheless, it may be that such a person would be subject to a tracing claim or liable to pay compensation if they dishonestly assisted the defendant to transfer assets. Their primary liability is, however, to the contempt jurisdiction of the court. If they knowingly ignore an order of the court they will stand in contempt. However, to be guilty of contempt it must be shown that the bank or other person had notice of the probability that the monies would be disposed of in breach of the terms of the injunction.[2] It should be noted that the courts in such cases have the power to order the person in contempt to pay compensation. Of course, if the parties are outside the jurisdiction and the order has been made without notice, then it is unlikely foreign courts would give effect to an order of the English Courts, as in like circumstances in all probability an English court would not. The issue of enforceability is a real one, as the courts will not act in vain and if there is no real prospect of an order being obeyed or enforced out of jurisdiction the courts will be reluctant to issue one.

1   *Commissioners of Customs and Excise v Barclays Bank PLC* (2006) 3 WML 1.
2   *Bank Mellat v Kazmi* [1989] QB 541.

6.109   Once an order has been made, the claimant is under an obligation to forge ahead with his claim. He is also under a continuing duty of disclosure to the defendant in regard of any matter which may render his cross undertaking unreliable. Of course, it is always open to the defendant to seek discharge or variation of the order. While the courts will generally allow release of monies for living expenses, outstanding debts and legal fees, the courts will be alert to any attempt to use up the monies within jurisdiction. They will be prepared to inquire into the financial resources of the defendant on a world-wide basis. Of course, it is also open to third parties to intervene in regard to relevant assets and obligations.

6.110   Perhaps as important as freezing orders in dealing with financial misconduct are civil search orders. This is in addition to the various system that operate in different legal systems to require parties in civil litigation to make proper disclosure and respond to interrogatories. It may well be that one party will suspect that the other is about to destroy or conceal information. Consequently in some countries the civil courts have authority to authorise essentially a civil search. It is important to appreciate that this is not the same as a search warrant as it gives no authority to force entry on to private property. The sanction for non-compliance is the court's contempt power. A search order compels the defendant to permit the claimant's agents, usually his solicitor, to enter the defendant's property to search for and in most cases seize certain documents or property. In England this is a special form of mandatory injunction the object of which is to preserve evidence. While some commonwealth jurisdictions have similar procedures most civilian countries do not, nor do the US courts. These injunctions used to be referred to as Anton Piller orders after the case *Anton Piller KG v Manufacturing Processes Ltd.*[1] The order must be made by a High Court judge and the applicant must make a cross undertaking in damages as in the case of a freezing order. In the nature of the case, the application will normally be made without notice and the applicant must show that there is a strong case that serious harm or injustice will occur.

1   [1976] Ch 55.

6.111   Of course, the court may order the defendant in proceedings, even interim proceedings, to disclose information. In the case of an application for a freezing order the defendant can be required to disclose immediately and then subsequently in affidavit, for example, the whereabouts of his assets. An issue that has arisen in this context is whether the defendant is bound to disclose information that might incriminate him in future criminal proceedings.[1] If the defendant does assert the privilege against self-incrimination and the court considers it is not made out, then he will be in contempt. Furthermore, there is no privilege against exposure to criminal proceedings in other jurisdictions. The Courts have also held that even threats of violence overseas do not justify refusal to disclose information that has been ordered to be revealed. Courts in the UK and USA have also held that where a question is properly put to a defendant it is still contempt if he refuses to answer on the ground that to do so would constitute a criminal offence under the secrecy or blocking laws of another state. In cases where information can only be disclosed under the relevant laws of another state with the consent of the person to whom the information 'belongs', certain US courts have been prepared in both civil and criminal cases to order the defendant or another within their jurisdiction to furnish this authorisation for disclosure to the appropriate person. Failure to do so is treated as contempt. Of course, it goes without saying that furnishing false or misleading information to the court is contempt and it may constitute a specific offence, as we have seen. It might also result in the court deciding a matter against the interests of that party. In *Canada Trust Co v Stolzenberg*,[2] Neuberger J held that where a foreign defendant, with no assets in the UK, failed to comply with an order for disclosure and there was a strong case against him, it may be appropriate to debar him from defending the case, if he persisted in his failure to comply with the terms of the injunction. His contention that compliance with the order would involve a breach of the laws of another jurisdiction was, while a factor to be taken into account, not determinant.

1   See *Coca-Cola Company v Gilbey* [1995] 4 All ER 711.
2   *The Times*, November 10 1997.

6.112   There will always be a temptation for those under investigation to flee the jurisdiction. While there have been significant developments facilitating co-operation and mutual assuistance, particularly within the European Union, it is always more problematic to ensure justice is served once a suspect or material witnesses leaves the jurisdiction. In criminal cases arrest will effectively prevent this, at least, in regard to those suspected of a criminal offence. In civil cases the position is more difficult. The courts are not, however, without power. In *Bayer AG v Winter*[1] an injunction was issued against the defendant ordering him to deliver up his passport and restraining him from leaving the jurisdiction of the English courts. The courts have, as we have seen, significant powers over property and can make a wide range of orders including the appointment of receivers to get in property and monies. In *International Credit and*

Investment Co (Overseas) Ltd v Adham (Appointment of Receiver)[2] the court held that it could pierce the veil of incorporation of a company and appoint a receiver over property in a case where a world-wide freezing order had been granted over property and where there was a real risk that the order would be breached.

1   [1986] 1 WLR 497.
2   [1998] BCC 134.

DISQUALIFICATION PROCEDURES

6.113   While fraud does not always involve the use of a company, it often does. Consequently, it is sensible to deprive those who have committed fraud and other misconduct, of the opportunity to misuse the privilege of using a company as a vehicle for their dishonesty. This is one of the justifications for disqualifying certain persons from being involved in the management of companies. Disqualification proceedings under the Company Directors Disqualification Act 1986 play an important role in preventing further abuses and constitute an additional sanction with regard to conduct that has already taken place.

6.114   It should be noted that in certain circumstances an order may be made with regard to a foreign citizen in relation to conduct taking place outside the United Kingdom. In construing the Company Directors Disqualification Act 1986, s 6, Arden J decided that the fact that modern communications enabled companies to be controlled across frontiers, given Parliament's intention to create an effective and integrated response to misconduct, justified an interpretation of the provisions which could extend to foreigners and conduct out of the jurisdiction.[1] An order made under the Act against a director or, in many cases, a shadow director makes it unlawful for him to be a director, liquidator, administrator or receiver of a company or be in any way, either directly or indirectly, concerned with the promotion, incorporation or management of a company in the United Kingdom during the currency of the order.

1   See *Re Seagull Manufacturing Co Ltd (No 2)* [1994] 1 BCLC 273.

6.115   There are a number of statutory grounds upon which an application can be made by the Secretary of State, or in some instances the liquidator or even a creditor, to the court under the Company Directors Disqualification Act 1986. Conviction for an indictable offence in connection with the promotion, formation, management or liquidation of a company is a ground under the Company Directors Disqualification Act 1986, s 2. It has been held that a conviction for insider dealing, when the conduct in question clearly had a relevant factual connection with the management of the company, was sufficient to justify a disqualification order.[1] Under the Company Directors Disqualification Act 1986, s 3, a court may make a disqualification order where there has been persistent default in making returns or delivering accounts and other documents required under the Companies Act 1985. The Company Directors Disqualification Act 1986, s 5 empowers the court to make an order on summary conviction for failing to comply with the statutory provisions relating to the filing of returns where there has been three such convictions within a period of five years.

1   See *R v Goodman* [1994] 1 BCLC 349.

6.116 The Company Directors Disqualification Act 1986, s 4 empowers the courts to make an order where it appears to the court in the course of insolvency proceedings, which need not necessarily end in a determination of insolvency, that there has been fraudulent trading or a breach of duty to the company. It should be noted that a conviction is not a prerequisite to the court exercising its powers under this section. The Company Directors Disqualification Act 1986, s 5 gives the court power to disqualify a person.

6.117 The Company Directors Disqualification Act 1986, s 6 relates to the disqualification of a director who has been associated with an insolvent company and is found to be unfit to be a director. It has been accepted by the courts that deliberately concealing transactions from the company and its shareholders is sufficient for the court to determine that a person is unfit to be a director.[1]

1   See *Re Godwin Warren Control Systems plc* [1993] BCLC 80.

6.118 By the Company Directors Disqualification Act 1986, s 8, the Secretary of State is empowered to seek an order for disqualification when he has received a report from inspectors appointed under the Companies Act 1985 or the Financial Services Act 1986, or information pursuant to his own powers of investigation, indicating that it is in the public interest that an individual should be so disqualified. Before the court can make an order, it must be satisfied that the conduct in relation to the company makes the person concerned unfit to be involved in corporate management under the Company Directors Disqualification Act 1986, s 9. In determining the issue of unfitness, it is further provided that the court has regard to the matters set out in the Company Directors Disqualification Act 1986, Sch 1, Pt 1 which relates to the question of unfitness in cases brought under the Company Directors Disqualification Act 1986, s 6. Thus, a director who abuses his power in circumstances indicating a lack of commercial probity was held to be unfit.[1] The House of Common's Select Committee on Trade and Industry severely criticised the refusal of the Secretary of State to initiate such proceedings against the Fayed brothers following a recommendation by inspectors appointed to inquire into the House of Fraser affair. Although there was evidence that the Fayeds and their advisers had misled the City Panel on Takeovers and Mergers, the Department of Trade and Industry took the view that their conduct was not related to the management of a company, albeit that it is arguable that their misconduct facilitated the acquisition of the House of Fraser.[2]

1   See *Re Looe Fish Ltd* [1993] BCLC 1160.
2   See *Company Investigation*, Third Report of the Trade and Industry Committee (1990, HMSO).

6.119 Finally, with regard to the grounds for disqualification, the Company Directors Disqualification Act 1986, s 10 permits a court to disqualify a person against whom it decides to make an order under either the Insolvency Act 1986, s 213 for fraudulent trading or the Insolvency Act 1986, s 214 for wrongful trading.

6.120 Breach of a disqualification order constitutes a criminal offence under the Company Directors Disqualification Act 1986, s 13, as well as contempt of court. Under the Company Directors Disqualification Act 1986, s 15, a person who is involved in the management of a company in violation of an order made under the Act, or a person who acts or is willing to act as a 'frontman' for a person whom he knows to be subject to disqualification, will be personally liable for all debts of the company. It should be noted that the same rules apply with regard to undischarged bankrupts.[1]

1   See the Company Directors Disqualification Act 1986, ss 11 and 15.

6.121   Under the FSMA 2000, s 56, the FSA is empowered to issue 'a prohibition order' prohibiting an individual from performing a specified function or any function falling within a specified description if it appears to the Authority that the individual 'is not a fit and proper person to perform' the relevant functions in relation to regulated activity carried on by an authorised person. Before the Authority makes such an order, it is necessary for the individual concerned to be given a warning notice and he may request that the decision is referred to the Financial Services Tribunal. While the notion of 'fit and proper' is open textured, it is clear that fraud and many of the other forms of misconduct described in this chapter would justify the Authority in concluding that the person responsible is not a fit and proper person to be involved in investment business. The same may well also apply to those responsible for supervising that person's activities. It is a criminal offence under section 56(4) to perform or agree to perform a function in breach of a prohibition order, although it is a defence to show that the person concerned took all reasonable precautions and exercised all due diligence to avoid committing the offence. Furthermore, under section 56(6), an authorised person must take reasonable care to ensure that no function of his, in relation to the carrying on of a regulated activity, is performed by a person who is prohibited from performing that function pursuant to a prohibition order. If an authorised person violates this, any private person who suffers loss as a result has a right of action against him under the FSMA 2000, s 71.

6.122   In this context, it is also important to note the provisions in the FSMA 2000, Pt XII relating to control over authorised persons. Obviously, the safeguards that have been put in place to ensure that only fit and proper persons become authorised, or employ persons that are fit and proper, would count for very little if authorised persons could come under the control of unscrupulous individuals. The obligations to give notice and comply with orders by the FSA are reinforced by the criminal law under the FSMA 2000, s 191.

OFFENCES BY BODIES CORPORATE

6.123   Mention has already been made of the use that fraudsters make of companies as a vehicle for fraud. While the common law is well able to cut through corporate personality and fix liability directly on the individuals responsible when the corporate form is a sham or has been employed merely as an engine of fraud, the position is more difficult when a 'real' company that is not purely a device for the fraudster is involved. The law is able to attribute knowledge and even a guilty intent to a company, provided that knowledge or intent reposes in an individual who is sufficiently senior to be regarded as the company's mind or at least determinant over the function in question.[1] Indeed, in some cases, the courts have gone even further and held that the acts of an individual may be attributed to the company, even if that person is acting outside the duties of his employment and in breach of his employer's instructions, if acts are carried out in the course of his employment. In such cases, the attempts that the employer has gone to in ensuring compliance with the law are merely an issue for mitigation.

1   See generally Cheong-Ann Png, *Corporate Liability* (2001, Kluwer).

6.124 The FSMA 2000, s 400 addresses the reverse problem when it is appropriate to hold individuals responsible for offences committed by a company. Of course, it is necessary that the company be guilty and thus has the requisite state of knowledge before this issue arises. The section states that if an offence under the Act committed by a company is shown to have been committed with the consent or connivance of an officer or to be attributable to any neglect on his part, that officer, as well as the company, will be guilty of the offence in question. The concept of 'officer' is defined to include all those who have managerial responsibility, including directors and 'an individual who is a controller' of the company. Similar rules are applicable to partnerships. The exact implications of this provision are difficult to state. Provided a company could be given the requisite degree of culpability to justify a charge under the FSMA 2000, s 397(2) or (3), it is possible that charges could be brought against an 'officer' who was only guilty of 'neglect'.

CONCLUSION

6.125 Given the emphasis that has been placed on the protection of investors, the need to maintain confidence in the integrity of the markets and the desirability of reducing financial crime, the policing of fraud and other abuses will inevitably attract a great deal of attention. The FSA cannot complain that it has not been given the weapons to police at least those offences within its statutory purview. The civil enforcement powers that have been entrusted to it are considerable and there has been a significant 'tidying up' of the relevant legislation which will no doubt render enforcement less hazardous. On the other hand, experience has shown in the UK and elsewhere that the problems in dealing effectively with serious fraud are far ranging and intractable. Obviously, much will depend upon the level of co-operation and collaboration that the FSA is able to achieve, not only with other authorities in the UK, but also with its counterparts overseas. A great deal will also depend upon how much it can rely upon those in the industry and in particular those working in compliance to get their own houses in order and work effectively with the authorities. While civil enforcement by or through the FSA is destined to become a more significant feature of policing the markets, it remains very doubtful whether private litigants will become the champions of integrity to the extent that some think they are in the United States.

Chapter 7

Anti-money laundering

THE CORPORATE AND FINANCIAL DIMENSION

7.1   Evidence was presented in 1995 to the Home Affairs Select Committee during its investigation into the threat of organised crime in the United Kingdom as to the misuse of the privilege of incorporation to assist in the perpetration of fraud and other financial crimes. National risk assessments by the Serious Organised Crime Agency have confirmed that this remains a matter of concern. There can be little doubt that criminals have found the organisational advantages of the corporate form beneficial in their illicit enterprises. More importantly the ability to hide behind corporate nominees and obscure the ownership and control of business, whether legal or illegal, has proved invaluable. While the Courts have long been prepared to look at the real purpose for which a company has been incorporated[1] and will not allow criminals and fraudsters to hide behind the legal fiction of incorporation, to distort responsibility and avoid accountability,[2] it is in the context of the relatively recent significance that has been attached to pursuing the proceeds of crime, that concern about the misuse of incorporation has become most pressing. The facility that easily incorporated business forms offer those engaged in hiding the proceeds of crime, or at least seeking to sever the nexus between the predicate crime that produces the illicit sum its present location, has been recognised throughout the world. While there has always been a variety of reasons why those in possession of wealth, whatever its source, may wish to hide it,[3] the development of laws that allow the proceeds of crime, actual or even presumptive, to be seized by the authorities, has given a real incentive to those capable of laundering wealth. In this process the company plays a vital role. Consequently, there are a number of legal issues thrown up directly by these new laws and perhaps more importantly, in terms of risk, indirectly, by virtue of the shift of responsibility to fight serious crime, on to those who in the ordinary course of their commercial and financial business mind other peoples' wealth. Indeed, such is the concern, that as we have seen in Chapter 6, one of the four statutory objectives set for the Financial Services Authority in section 2(2) of the Financial Services and Markets Act 2000 is the reduction of financial crime and this is defined to include 'handling the proceeds of crime'. The impact of anti-money laundering laws on the way in which financial and wealth business is conducted, in many respects has probably been greater than any other substantive body of law. In assisting in the interdiction of the proceeds of serious crime and the flow of funds to terrorist organisations, company law clearly has a role to play.

1   See *Bowman v Secular Society Ltd* [1917] AC 406. Normally incorporation should be denied, *R.v Registrar of Joint Stock Companies* [1931] 2 KB 197. Once incorporated, it should be wound up, rather than struck down – *Princess of Reuss v Bos* (1871) LR 5 HL 176, Lord Hatherley LC at 193.

2   *Smith v Hancock* [1894] 2 Ch 377; *Gilford Motor Co Ltd v Horne* (1933) Ch 935 and *Jones v Lipman* [1962] 1 WLR 832 and (refer to relevant GB section).

3   See generally B Rider, *Memorandum 15, Organised Crime, Minutes of Evidence and Memoranda, Home Affairs Committee SI Session* 1994–95, HMSO and B Rider and M Ashe (eds), *Money Laundering Control* (1996), Sweet & Maxwell, Ch 1.

7.2   Having regard to the risks both legal and otherwise, that can arise for those involved, innocently or not, in the laundering of the proceeds of crime or the transfer of terrorist funds, ensuring proper and effective compliance with the statutory and other obligations is an important task of management. Oversight in terms of the establishment and support of such systems is an important issue in governance. In certain situations the failure of management and those responsible for governance might well result in legal and regulatory liability. It is also important to note the complex web of law and regulation thrown up by anti-money laundering laws often has the effect imposing obligations with the risk of legal consequences, internationally. For example, generally speaking under most laws, the offences relating to money laundering apply to conduct within jurisdiction, even if the criminal activity generating the property in question took place entirely out of jurisdiction. It is also the case that some provisions operate on wider notions of jurisdiction than would traditionally be encountered in most criminal justice systems. The significance that governments and, in particular inter-governmental organisations, now attach to combating serious crime, corruption and the funding of terror, through inhibiting the transfer and concealment of funds associated or representing such activity, means that regulators and indeed, even the courts, have been robust in the administration and application of relevant laws and procedures. A powerful illustration of the importance now attached to depriving criminals of their illicit wealth is provided in the new United Nations Convention Against Corruption.[1] Article 51 states that pursing the proceeds of corruption is a fundamental principle of the Convention. It should be noted that many of the Conventions provisions might well have impact on the business world.[2] Furthermore, it must also be borne in mind that as it has proved in practice difficult to interdict property associated with crime and terror, law enforcement and regulatory authorities have adopted strategies designed rather more to disrupt criminal and subversive enterprises than interdict specific property. The Serious Organised Crime and Police Act 2005 places considerable emphasis on this. Indeed, the winding up of the Asset Recovery Agency and the transfer of its powers to the Serious Organised Crime Agency, is thought by many to give emphasis to the role of disruption, rather than depriving criminals, through lengthy and often expensive, legal procedures of their ill-gotten gains. The problem with this approach is that the perimeters of what is acceptable, let alone lawful, disruptive conduct are not clear. It is also the case that often those being used knowingly or otherwise in the processes of disruption will be individuals and companies engaged in business or the financial sector. The legal risks in placing such persons in the 'front line' have not been sufficiently determined, or for that matter considered.

1   See generally B Rider, 'Recovering the Proceeds of Corruption', 10 *Journal of Money Laundering Control* (2007) 5.

2   See, for example, article 12 in regard to anti-corruption initiatives in the private sector; article 20 on unjust enrichment and articles 21 and 22 in regard to bribery and embezzlement in the private sector.

7.3   Few laws can or do operate in a legal vacuum and the inter-relationship of rules is not always predictable or doesn't always produce desirable results. A serious problem, in many jurisdictions, is that those laws relating to the imposition of criminal and increasingly, what might be described as administrative, penalties for misconduct, impact on the way business is conducted. The laws facilitating and controlling business and in particular financial business may not adequately or comfortably interface with these essentially criminal laws. A good example is the obligation not to reveal, to anyone other than the appropriate public authority, one's suspicion of money laundering. In the United Kingdom the unauthorised disclosure of this information may well amount to the serious crime of 'tipping off'. While this offence is intended to facilitate effective law enforcement by allowing the secret monitoring of transactions by the authorities, the relationship of this crime with the obligations occasionally imposed under the civil law were not sufficiently recognised. For example, there are situations where a person, in a fiduciary relationship or in a position which may result in the imposition of fiduciary obligations, is under a duty, in the proper discharge of those fiduciary responsibilities, to search out and inform those who may, in line with the suspicions that he has properly formed, have a claim against the property in question.[1] There are other situations, in which, there would be a duty in the civil law, to take steps on protect the relevant property, which might have the effect of 'tipping off' those under suspicion.[2] The Courts have been required to consider such situations, but have not always found it possible to provide a degree of guidance, let alone protection, that would meet the expectations of those engaged in legitimate business.[3] Again, while it is clear, under the relevant statutory provisions, that liability for breach of contract or disclosure of confidential information, when reporting a bona fide suspicion to the proper authorities, is unlikely, although in certain cases not entirely unthinkable, there are real and unresolved issues in the law of defamation. Therefore, in seeking to comply and ensure proper compliance, with these laws and the various rules they have spawned, care needs to be taken in regard to the general law as well. It is often the case that compliance systems and advice focus almost exclusively on the criminal and administrative laws and ignore the legal environment within which the relevant transactions or conduct occur. This is particularly important in the context of corporate life given the many relationships that, for example, a director will find himself in, both to his company and others. This is not a simple or straightforward area of law.

1   See for example, *Finers v Miro* [1991] 1 WLR 35. See generally, *Banking on Corruption, The Legal Responsibilities of those who Handle the Proceeds of Corruption* (Sir Richard Scott and Lord Steel of Aikwood, 2000), Society of Advanced Legal Studies.
2   See for example *Bank of Scotland v A Ltd* [2001] EWCA Civ 52.
3   See *C v S* [1999] 2 All ER 343, *Amalgamated Metal Trading Ltd v City of London Police Financial Investigation Unit* [2003] EWHC 703 Com and *Hosni Tayeb v HSBC and Al Farsan International* [2004] EWHC 1529 Comm.

MONEY LAUNDERING IN CONTEXT

7.4   Given the significance, for various reasons, that has been attached to attacking the proceeds of crime and now the wider concept of 'criminal property' as a means of disrupting criminal enterprises, all legal systems have complex laws facilitating the identification, pursuit, seizure and then either confiscature or forfeiture[1] of the property in question. This is not the place to enter into a discussion of these provisions. Suffice it to say, that in the vast majority of cases, by the time that these statutory powers are properly invoked by the appropriate authorities, the situation in terms of the probable legality of the relevant transactions or conduct, will be sufficiently obvious. A director or officer acting in good faith in the proper performance of his duties would not normally be at risk. Having said this, the expansion of these powers, which are often very far reaching, to cases where no crime has actually been proven and their re-casting into the civil law,[2] has increased the potential for uncertainty. The relevant provisions whether in the criminal or the civil law do not, however, present a major problem for those who act and continue to act within the scope of, for example, the traditional duties of directors. Of rather greater impact, in practice, is the use of the civil law in essentially a restitutory role.[3] The perimeters of liability for receipt of property that is subject to a fiduciary obligation, and providing assistance in the handling and concealment of such property, are far more uncertain and potentially dangerous.[4] This important and dynamic area of the law, has in recent years had a significant impact on the law relating to directors duties and in particular the recovery of the proceeds of fraud and breaches of fiduciary duties.[5] It is not without interest that the United Nations' Convention Against Corruption places significant emphasis on the ability of litigants, public and private, to pursue the proceeds of corruption and fraud and impose liability to make restoration on those who facilitate, with the requisite degree of culpability, the laundering of such property. It is this area of the law that has created issues for banks and other financial institutions in attempting to comply with the criminal law and in particular the offence of 'tipping off'.[6] It must also be born in mind that invariably cases that do arise, involve a number of different jurisdictions with differing legal standards. The vitality of civil law in ensuring integrity on the part of those who are stewards of other peoples' wealth is increasingly being recognised around the world and private actions in pursuit of fraudsters and in particular corrupt officials and those complicit in such crimes are likely to increase significantly.

1   See generally T Millington and M Sutherland Williams, *The Proceeds of Crime, Law and Practice of restraint, Confiscation, Condemnation and Forfeiture* (2nd Ed 2007), Oxford.
2   See generally the Proceeds of Crime Act 2002 and in particular Parts 1 and 5. Note in particular the ability to recover unlawful property, by civil process, irrespective of criminal guilt.
3   See for example *Attorney General of Hong Kong v Reid* (1994) 1 AC 324.
4   Reference should be made to, for example, G Virgo, *The Principles of the Law of Restitution* (2nd Ed. 2006), Oxford, at Ch 20.
5   Refer to relevant GB section.
6   See below at **7.19**.

7.5   Before we examine the specific offences relating to the laundering of criminal wealth, it is also important to flag the importance of other areas of the criminal law. It has been held that conspiring to evade a civil duty of disclosure, such as might arise under statute or, for example, the fiduciary obligations of director to his company, can amount to a conspiracy to defraud in the criminal law.[1] Indeed, dishonesty may well be established, simply by the desire of those involved to act in secret.[2] After all, secrecy is the badge of fraud! Charges for handling stolen property may also be appropriate.[3] It is important to remember that this offence is not confined merely to the property that is stolen in the narrow legal sense. Money or other property that results from fraud or even blackmail may well be handled in the criminal sense. Many money laundering operations will involve fraudulent conduct. Indeed, in some cases those involved in laundering might well be susceptible to a substantive change of theft. There is also the prospect of offences under the insolvency law, in appropriate cases, and invariably implications under the relevant tax laws. Indeed, the significance of the role of Her Majesty's Revenue and Customs (HMRC)[4] in pursuing the proceeds of crime and in particular the disruption of criminal enterprises has been clear in a number of major cases. The extension of the Revenue's powers in this regard to other agencies, attests to their potential success in combating serious crime.[5] Finally in this context, the level of international co-operation,[6] at all levels, in this area is second to none. The law enforcement authorities, regulators and courts have been zealous in providing assistance to the authorities of other jurisdictions in the tracking of funds and their interdiction.

1   See for example *R v Adams* (1995) 1 WLR 52.
2   *Norris v Government of the United States* [2007] EWHC 71 (Admin), 25 January 2007, QBD.
3   See section 22 of the Theft Act 1968.
4   It is important to remember that HMRC, under a number of statutory provisions, have considerable powers to identify, interdict and charge funds and property that is or may be subject to taxation in one form or another. The proceeds of crime are, of course, taxable income in the hands of the criminal or anyone in control thereof.
5   See for example, the powers of the Director of the Asset Recovery Agency, under Part 6 of the Proceeds of Crime Act 2002, which will be transferred to the Director General of the Serious Organised Crime Agency in due course.
6   See generally T Millington and M Sutherland Williams, *supra* at n 9, Ch 25.

7.6   The law relating to money laundering suffers from having been developed on an ad hoc basis without a great deal of regard to the different characteristics of the laundering process in relation to the nature of the underlying criminal or subversive activity. The process of laundering will be rather different in the case of a continuing criminal enterprise, than in, for example, an isolated case of fraud, insider dealing or corruption. The law relating to money laundering has also been adopted and applied, more or less without modification, to those who provide financial support for terrorist activity. The processes involved in channelling such funds to terrorist organisations are different in character from most cases involving profitable crime. While there is disappointment in most jurisdictions that the amounts of money and other property seized, let alone actually confiscated or forfeited, are relatively small compared with the guesstimates as to the amount of wealth that could be subject to such procedures,[1] the offences relating to money laundering have proved rather useful. The regime of reporting, recording and monitoring suspicious funds, has generated useful intelligence and has served to place a hurdle in front of those who seek to conceal their ill gotten gains.[2] It has created additional risk and cost for criminals, particularly organised crime. It has also fostered a greater degree of awareness of the dangers of serious crime, and co-operation among those who, in the ordinary and legitimate course of their business or profession mind or assist in the minding of other peoples' wealth. To some extent it has placed such persons in the forefront of the 'financial war' against organised crime and even terrorism. Whether the use to which intelligence has been deployed justifies the considerable costs and risks, legal and otherwise, to those in the financial community, remains to be seen. The effect of the law and the various systems of compliance that have been developed, is to facilitate the reconstruction of financial transactions by providing a 'paper trail' and assist in the financial profiling of suspects. Of course, the laws also have the effect of essentially criminalising those who facilitate profitable and enterprise crime, thereby placing yet another risk and financial hurdle in the path of organised crime. Prosecutions simply for breach of the substantive offences of money laundering are not common. In most jurisdictions a charge of money laundering is added to other substantive charges. However, it is noticeable that in the USA prosecutors appear to prefer charges for money laundering than basing prosecutions on the so called predicate offence in many cases of securities and corporate related fraud and abuse. Having said this, however, it is important to recognise that in the USA laws relating to integrity, whether in the corporate or market context, tend to be enforced through civil enforcement proceedings rather than the traditional criminal law. As has already been emphasised, in this area of law, the environment and in particular the institutional aspects of law enforcement, in particular jurisdictions, play a very significant role in the way matters are brought before the courts and are disposed of.

1   See for example, *Recovering the Proceeds of Crime*, (2000), Cabinet Office; *Asset Recover Action Plan, A Consultation Document*, (2007), Home Office; and *The Financial Challenge to Crime and Terrorism* (2007), Treasury, Home Office, Serious Organised Crime Agency and Foreign and Commonwealth Office.
2   *Review of the Suspicious Activity Reports Regime*, S Lander (2006), Serious Organised Crime Agency.

PROCEEDS OF CRIME

7.7   The law in the United Kingdom relating to money laundering developed after the creation of statutory powers to seize the proceeds of particularly profitable crimes. Indeed, there is a view that the failure to criminalise the laundering of the proceeds of crime at the time such statutory powers were given to the courts, may have constituted another incentive for criminals to develop money laundering in Britain. In common with most legal systems, the early law focused exclusively on the proceeds of illicit drug related crime. The difficulty in law and practice of establishing that particular property was related to specific drug offences rendered these provisions of relatively little value. Consequently, the offences were extended to the proceeds of all serious crime and even such crimes committed overseas.[1] There are a number of international instruments relating to the criminalisation and control of money laundering, including no less than three EU Directives specifically on the subject.[2] Generally speaking, the English law has run ahead of the various international obligations and therefore, in this brief discussion we will not refer to the various and many international documents.[3] The importance of the international community in developing this area of the law, should not, however, be underestimated. For example, almost a third of the provisions in the new United Nations Convention Against Corruption relate directly or indirectly to the identification, interdiction, recovery and laundering of wealth related to corruption. It is also important to appreciate the strength of the political imperative, largely set by the US Government, but taken up by many others, to foster 'stability' through integrity of the financial system. Of course, cynics may argue that all this has rather more to do with fostering and strengthening western banking and facilitating the recovery of tax, than promoting integrity and frustrating organised crime.

1   See generally on the development of the law, T Graham, E Bell and N Elliott, *Money Laundering* (2003), Butterworths; K Hinterseer, *Criminal Finance*, (2002), Kluwer; S Savla, *Money Laundering and Financial Intermediaries* (2001), Kluwer; P Alldridge, *Money Laundering Law* (2003), Hart and S Bazley and C Foster, *Money Laundering – Business Compliance* (2004) LexisNexis.
2   See generally R Alexander, *Insider Dealing and Money Laundering in the EU: Law and Regulation*, (2007) Ashgate; G Stessens, *Money Laundering – A New International Law Enforcement Model*, (2000), Cambridge University Press; V Mitsilegas, *Money Laundering Counter-Measures in the European Union*, (2003) Kluwer and in particular to *Implementing the Third Money Laundering Directive: Draft Money Laundering Regulations 2007*, (2007) Treasury.
3   P Schott, *Reference Guide to Anti-Money Laundering and Combating the Financing of Terrorism* (2003), World Bank/IMF. Reference should also be made to the relevant websites of the Financial Action Task Force, United Nations, European Union, World Bank and International Monetary Fund.

7.8   The principal legislation relating to money laundering is now the Proceeds of Crime Act 2002. However, there are also important provisions, the Terrorism Act 2000, the Anti-Terrorism, Crime and Security Act 2001 and the Terrorism (United Nations) Order 2001. The Proceeds of Crime Act 2002 has also been amended on several occasions and not least by the Serious Organised Crime and Police Act 2005. As the relevant statutory provisions have been brought into effect in stages, by Order, care needs to be taken in ascertaining, at any point in time, exactly what provisions are pertinent. The new Money Laundering Regulations 2006[1] are of particular significance, although the Money Laundering Regulations 2003[2] still play a very important role in determining the administration of the law, particularly in terms of the subsidiary obligations. Our analysis and discussion here, must needs be general and cannot descend to the considerable detail that is required for proper compliance with the many and varied obligations. Of course, given the significance of authoritative guidance from such bodies as the Financial Services Authority, British Bankers Association and Law Society, which impact on the determination of liability, businesses engaged, in particular, in regulated activities and especially in the financial sector, will need to have specific regard to industry standards and advice. Having said this, here we will focus rather more on the substantive law.

1   SI 2006/308.
2   SI 2003/3075, but note Draft Regulations 2007 referred to *supra* n 24. See also *The Regulation of Money Service Business: A Consultation*, (2006), Treasury.

7.9   Part 7 of the Proceeds of Crime Act establishes three basic crimes. Section 327 makes it a criminal offence to conceal, disguise, convert or transfer criminal property, or remove it from the jurisdiction. Section 327, renders it criminal to make an arrangement to facilitate the acquisition, retention, use or control of criminal property, by, or on behalf of, another person. Section 329 makes it an offence to acquire, use or have possession of criminal property. Under section 338, in regard to all three basic offences, a person does not commit a crime if an authorised disclosure is made to the relevant authority and when appropriate, the necessary consent to continue the relevant transaction is given. By the same token, there is no offence if the person concerned intended to make such a disclosure, but had a reasonable excuse for not doing so. In regard to all the substantive offences it is also a defence, to establish that what has been done is in fact merely carrying out a function that the accused has in relation to enforcing any provision in the Act or other statute relating to the benefits of criminal activity. Given the panoply of provisions allowing the interdiction of property that is suspected or proven to be the proceeds of criminal conduct, the burden placed on officials and others charged with preserving and managing it, before final determination by the courts, is considerable and would present certain risks of prosecution under the anti-money laundering laws, but for such a defence. By section 329, in the case of the offence under section 329, namely acquisition or use of property, no offence will be committed if this has been done for 'adequate consideration'. The substantive offences are supported by a number of provisions which oblige certain persons to ensure that they know for whom they act and the character of their business and transactions. As we have already seen, other provisions require disclosure of suspicions to the authorities and outlaw 'tipping off'.

7.10   While we are concerned essentially with the proceeds of crime, the legislation is concerned to impose criminal responsibility on any person who benefits from property derived from criminal conduct or uses or comes into possession of such. It is important to note that this responsibility applies whenever or wherever the crime 'creating' the property is committed and it is irrelevant whether the 'launderer' is aware of who was involved in that original criminal activity. The Act defines property extremely widely as it does the concepts of obtaining, possession and use. Any involvement in the use, possession or realisation of the property or any interest in such will be caught. The provisions bite, however, on 'criminal property' and this is defined to include any property that represents a benefit from criminal conduct, whether directly or indirectly, in whole or in part. Provided the person charged, knows or suspects that the property is so derived he is potentially liable. It is important to note, as has already been pointed out, it is irrelevant when this criminal conduct giving rise to the relevant property occurred or that the person accused of laundering is ignorant of the identity of those involved. What is in issue is his knowledge or suspicion as to the legitimacy of the property in issue, not those creating it. Of course, knowledge that those individuals are engaged in crime would be sufficient, but such is not necessary. The law focuses on the status in law of the property and rights in it. The concept of criminal conduct is set out in section 340(2) of the Act. It is broad in every respect. It includes offences in the United Kingdom, or conduct overseas, whether criminal there or not, which had it occurred in the United Kingdom would constitute such an offence.

7.11 The substantive offence of concealment is contained in section 327 of the Act, as we have seen. This section sets out five types of concealment which are potentially criminal; namely concealment, conversion, transfer, removal and disguising the property in question. Concealing and disguising the property's nature, source, location, disposition, movement, ownership or any right in regard to it, are potentially an offence. For liability all that need be proved is that such took place in regard to criminal property and the person concerned knew or suspected that it constituted the benefit of criminal conduct. Of course, it should be noted that this offence will invariably be committed by the perpetrator of the crime that gives rise to the criminal benefit. Consequently the practice has developed of adding to the substantive offences of fraud and theft, a charge under this section.

7.12 Under section 327(2C), which was introduced by the Serious Organised Crime and Police Act 2005, a deposit taking body that converts or transfers criminal property will not commit an offence, provided it does the act, in the context of operating an account that it maintains, and the value of the criminal property does not exceed the relevant threshold amount. At present this threshold, set by the Treasury, is only £250.

7.13 Section 328 is concerned with assisting another to retain the benefit of his or another person's criminal conduct. An offence will be committed under this provision where a person has entered into, or become concerned in an arrangement, under which another person is assisted in laundering property that, is known or suspected by the first person, to represent criminal property derived from the criminal conduct of another person, and he fails to make a proper disclosure to the appropriate authorities. It is this offence that is most likely to be of concern to those involved in business and advising those in business. Thus, a bank employee or professional adviser who suspects that the property in question has resulted from criminal activity would be at risk. Of course, as we have already seen, such a person would also, in many instances, be under certain duties in the civil law. The assistance that is provided, whether for reward or not, must be known or suspected to facilitate the retention or control of the criminal property by or on behalf of the other person, or to enable him to have access to his property, or facilitate its use for investment for his benefit. As has already been emphasised, this crime is committed, whether the benefiting from the criminal property is by the person who committed the original criminal activity, or others. For a conviction under this provision, the prosecution must establish that the accused knew or suspected that the arrangement related to the proceeds of criminal conduct, whether on the part of the person with whom he is dealing or another, and that he knew or suspected that by the arrangement he was facilitating retention or control or access to the funds by that person. No offence is committed if the accused makes an authorised disclosure of his knowledge or belief to the authorities and receives permission to proceed, or where he does not disclose before acting and has a reasonable excuse for not having done so. An authorised disclosure is defined in section 338 as disclosure to a constable, a customs officer or nominated officer on the individual's own initiative as soon as it is reasonable for him to do so. The term constable is defined in section 340(13), as amended, to include any person authorised by the Director General of the Serious Organised Crime Agency. In the case of a person who is employed, and this includes persons whether remunerated or not, then disclosure to a person nominated by his employer, according to certain procedures within the organisation of company, will amount to disclosure to a constable. Of course, that person must then pass the information on. Under section 309 of the Act the then National Criminal Intelligence Service, whose functions under the Act have now been transferred to SOCA, is authorised to prescribe the form of disclosure and effectively the scope of disclosure. It should be noted that if, after proper disclosure, consent is not given within seven working days, no offence would be committed under section 328 in continuing the transaction. Of course, this would not absolve the person concerned and in appropriate circumstances his employer and organisation from civil liability. Indeed, in the civil law his head is already on the block, as he has documented the fact that he suspects that the relevant property may well be subject to legal claims by third parties. To proceed, without regard to the obligations that the civil law may on the facts impose, would be rash.

7.14   As has already been pointed out, the transmission of 'suspicion based' reports to the Financial Intelligence Unit of SOCA is at the very heart of the Government's initiative to disrupt organised crime and discourage career criminals.[1] Unlike the obligation to report all transactions above a certain amount in value, as exists in most jurisdictions, reports based on a reasonable suspicion, particularly those that have already gone through a process evaluation within a financial institution, by experts, are of particular value to the police. They often provide real and valuable intelligence. Of course suspicions, no matter how reasonable and well founded, are not evidence. Action based on such may need to be justified in the end before a court, and it is the ability to convert information into intelligence and then into evidence which presents the biggest challenge to law enforcement, and for that matter regulatory agencies. The emphasis that is now being placed on intervention and disruption of criminal activity may be, in practice, justified by intelligence, but those who are exposed to legal risk and possible claims will need the reassurance of evidence behind their actions. It is also important, in the context of disclosure of suspicious activity, to consider the impact of the general law relating to 'whistle blowing' and, of course, data protection.

1   See *Proceeds of Crime: Consultation on Draft Legislation*, (2001), Home Office, Cm 5966 and in particular *One Step Ahead, A 21st Century Strategy to Defeat Organised Crime*, (2004), Home Office and *supra* at n 22. Reference should also be made to FIU's *In Action*, (2001), Egmont Group.

7.15   The third substantive money laundering offence is provided for in section 329 of the Act. This renders the acquisition, use and possession of the proceeds of criminal activity a specific crime. However, section 329(2) states that the offence is not committed if the person concerned makes an authorised disclosure as in the case of section 328, or has acquired or used or had possession of the property, albeit criminal property, for adequate consideration. The notion of adequate consideration is explained in section 329(3). A person acquires property for inadequate consideration if the value of the consideration is significantly less than the value of the property; or in the case of use or possession, the value is significantly less than the consideration. It is also provided that the provision by a person of goods or services which he knows or suspects may help another to carry out criminal conduct is not consideration. Indeed, in the case of the civil law it is probable that such would not be considered good consideration. It is, of course, necessary for the prosecution to establish that the accused knew or suspected that the property in question is criminal property. In practise, the manifest inadequacy of the consideration required, might itself indicate this. However, with all three substantive offences, it must be remembered that the knowledge or suspicion of the accused is subjective. It must be proved beyond a reasonable doubt that the accused did in fact have knowledge of the status of property in question or at least a suspicion.

7.16   The three substantive offences apply to everyone. There are, however, offences which apply only to those in what is termed the regulated sector set out in Schedule 9, as amended, of the Act. The scope of this sector is ever expanding, but the notion justifying the imposition of a greater responsibility on such persons, is that they engage usually for remuneration in a specific activity which gives rise to a reasonable expectation of professionalism. Consequently, it is reasonable to hold such persons to a standard of greater diligence in the provision of their essentially facilitative services and impose an objective standard of culpability upon them. Thus, in regard to certain offences, it will not be necessary for the prosecution to establish that the accused did actually have knowledge or was suspicious, it will be enough for criminal liability that an ordinary and reasonable person in their line of work would have known or, more likely, have been at least suspicious. Of course, it is rare in crimes based on a state of mind, that objective knowledge or belief is sufficient for the imposition of criminal liability. The scope of these provisions is those engaged in 'relevant financial business' as set out in Schedule 9 of the Act.

7.17   Section 330 imposes an obligation on those in the regulated sector to report to the authorities their suspicions of laundering activity. Where a person fails to make the required disclosure as soon as is practicable, when he knows or suspects, or has reason for knowing or suspecting, another person is engaging in money laundering, and this information came to him in the course of his trade, profession, business or employment within the regulated sector, he commits a crime. Thus, a suspicion that property represents the benefit of criminal conduct committed overseas, including from inchoate offences such as conspiracy, would be caught under this provision. There is some protection, although not much, in that a person who does not in fact know or suspect that laundering is taking place, and has not had the benefit of the training that is required to be given the Regulations, will not be guilty of an offence. There are other limited defences. Where there is a reasonable excuse for non-disclosure then no offence is committed. Furthermore, a professional legal adviser will not be guilty for failing to disclose information that comes to him in privileged circumstances, provided such information is not in furtherance of criminal activity. Of course, under the general law, privilege is restricted in that it cannot serve to hide and facilitate crime. However, in this context it should also be noted in *Bowman v Fels*,[1] the Court of Appeal confirmed that the obligation to report, in that case as a defence under section 328, did not override the common law legal professional privilege.

1 [2005] EWC Civ 226. See also section 106 of the Serious Organised Crime and Police Act 2005.

7.18 Section 331 of the Act imposes responsibility on nominated officers commonly referred to as Money Laundering Reporting Officers (MLROs) to pass on information that they receive. They are under an obligation to forward this information, in the prescribed manner, to the authorities as soon as practicable. However, in considering whether an offence has been committed, courts are required to consider whether the officer in question followed guidance issued, with the approval of the Treasury, by appropriate designated bodies under Schedule 9 of the Act. Thus, compliance with, for example, the Guidance Notes of the Joint Money Laundering Steering Group of the British Bankers Association, the Law Society or the Financial Services Authority would be relevant in the determination of guilt. In the case of the non-regulated sector, section 332 imposes similar obligations on nominated officers to report, as soon as practicable, knowledge or suspicion based on information that they have received. However, as we have seen here the test for liability is subjective rather than objective. Furthermore, they are not guilty if they have a reasonable excuse for non-compliance.

7.19 Reference has already been made to the offence of 'Tipping off' contained in section 333 of the Act. This crime involves making a disclosure that is likely to prejudice a money laundering investigation. If a person knows or suspects that a protected or authorised disclosure has been made to the authorities or an employer and he makes a disclosure which is likely to prejudice any investigation that may be undertaken as a result of the protected or authorised disclosure, he commits an offence. This provision applies to everyone, including professional advisers. However, in the case of a professional legal adviser no offence will be committed in regard to the disclosure of information to a client or the client's representative, in regard to the provision of legal advice, or to any person in contemplation of, or in connection with, legal proceedings for the purpose of those proceedings, unless, of course, the disclosure was made with a view to furthering a criminal purpose. If the accused did not know or suspect that the disclosure was likely to prejudice an investigation, no offence is committed. Furthermore, as in the case of all the offences, there is no crime if what is done is pursuant to statutory authority or in the enforcement of the law.

7.20 Under section 342 of the Act any person who, knowing or suspecting that someone is acting or proposing to act in connection with a confiscation or money laundering investigation makes a disclosure that is likely to prejudice the investigation or interferes with evidence, is guilty of an offence. There are defences rather similar to those relating to an offence under section 333. Of course, where there is a deliberate interference with the administration of justice or destruction, concealment or falsification of evidence, then there would be the prospect of prosecution for offences under the general criminal law.

7.21 Mention has been made of the possibility of liability resulting from the disclosure of information, pursuant to the statutory obligations in the Act, under the general law. In the case of disclosure by persons within the regulated sector, section 337 provides that they are protected from any legal or other obligation that might otherwise prevent them from revealing confidential information, provided the information upon which they acted came to them in the course of their trade, profession, business or profession. Such disclosures are referred to as 'protected disclosures'. Section 338(4) extends a similar protection to all authorised disclosures made under the provisions of the Act, whether by persons in the regulated sector or not. It is important to note that these provisions protect against liability, based on a breach of any restriction on the disclosure of information, however, imposed. Thus, there would be no liability for breach of confidentiality arising, for example, by contract or a fiduciary relationship. However, this protection does not extend to, for instance, liability in the law of defamation. While it would be possible in most cases to assert a defence of qualified privilege, the threat of suit is a significant inhibition. Furthermore, it must not be forgotten that these statutory defences under the Act can only apply to proceedings within jurisdiction.

7.22   As far as penalties are concerned, section 334 provides that, anyone convicted on indictment of an offence under sections 327 to 329, is liable to a prison term of up to fourteen years and an unlimited fine. In the case of sections 330 to 333, on conviction on indictment, the maximum penalty is five years imprisonment and an unlimited fine. Of course, in the case of summary convictions the maximum term of imprisonment is six months. Offences under these provisions might well be suitable for triggering proceedings for confiscature or asset recovery.

TERRORIST FINANCE

7.23   It has long been recognised, particularly in the context of terrorist activity in Northern Ireland, that there is value in attempting to disrupt the flow of funds to terrorist organisations. There is also value in being able to subject such organisations to financial investigation and profiling. There is, however, an important difference between attempting to interdict the funds of terrorist organisations and those of organised crime. Generally speaking a significant proportion of the funding for criminal and other activity by organised crime will be derived from criminal activity. In other words, it will be the proceeds of crime. However, while terrorists may be indistinguishable from organised crime in what they do, some organisations derive their financial support from legitimate sources. To take action against such funds, it is necessary to 'taint' them by virtue of the purpose for which they are given. Thus, it is the intention or at least, knowledge of the donor that renders the property 'criminal property'. This is an important difference and one that is rarely encountered in the general law.

7.24   The principle offences in regard to terrorist funds are found in the Terrorism Act 2000, as amended.[1] Section 14 defines terrorist property as money or other property which is likely to be used for the purposes of terrorism and this includes the resources of a proscribed organisation. Section 14(2)(b) further provides that any money or other property which is applied or made available or is to be applied or made available for use by such an organisation is also included. It is also made clear that the proceeds of the commission of acts of terrorism as well as the proceeds of acts carried out for the purposes of terrorism will be considered to be terrorist property. In this context, the proceeds of such crimes have a similarly wide meaning to that of 'criminal property' in the general anti-money laundering law. Raising funds and providing property for terrorism is outlawed in section 15 of the Act. Under section 15(1) a person commits an offence if he invites another to provide money or other property and intends that it should be used, or has reasonable cause to suspect that it may be used for the purposes of terrorism. Section 15(2) renders it a crime to receive money or other property with the intention that it will be used for the purposes of terrorism. It is also an offence to receive funds or property where there is reasonable cause to suspect that will be so used. Section 15(3) renders the financing of terror a crime, in that a person commits a crime if he provides money or other property and knows or has reasonable cause to suspect that it will or may be used for the purposes of terrorism. It is made clear that a reference to the provision of funds or other property includes it being lent or otherwise made available, whether or not for consideration. The objective aspect to this crime should be noted.

1   SI 2001/3365. See also *Review of Safeguards to Protect the Charitable Sector from Terrorist Abuse; A Consultation Document*, (2007), Home Office. There are provisions in the anti-terrorist law that may be relevant in the context preparatory activity and investigation, see generally C Walker, *The Anti-Terrorism Legislation* (2002), Oxford and A Jones, R Bowers and H Lodge, *The Terrorism Act 2006* (2006), Oxford. See also *The Funding of Terror, The Legal implications of the Financial War on Terror* (R Cranston, 2002), Society of Advanced Legal Studies.

7.25   The use and possession of money and property for the purposes of terrorism is rendered an offence under section 16. It is a crime to possess money or property with the intention that it should be used for the purposes of terrorism, or where there is reasonable cause to suspect that it may be. Section 17 renders it a criminal offence to enter into or become concerned in an arrangement as a result of which money or other property is made available or is to be made available for a terrorist purpose, provided that he knows or has reasonable cause to suspect that this is the case. Section 18 provides that it is a crime to become concerned in an arrangement which facilitates the retention or control of terrorist property by or on behalf of another whether this is done by concealment, removal from the jurisdiction, transfer to nominees, or in any other manner. However, an accused is entitled to a defence if he can prove that he did not know and had no reasonable cause to suspect that the arrangement related to terrorist property. It should be noted that it is not enough for the defence to raise this issue it must actually be proved, albeit to the civil standard of proof.

7.26   Section 19 imposes a duty on those who acquire information, as a result of it coming to their attention in the course of a trade, business, profession or employment. Where such a person believes or suspects that another person has committed an offence under sections 15 to 18 of the Act, he commits an offence if he does not report his belief or suspicion and the information upon which it is based, as soon as is reasonably practicable, to the police. It is a defence for an accused to prove that he had a reasonable excuse for not making a report or that he did in fact report his suspicions to his employer in accordance with an established compliance procedure. The obligation to disclose does not extend to professional legal advisers, in regard to information obtained in privileged circumstances, or a belief or suspicion based upon such. Of course, information relevant to furtherance of criminal activity would not be privileged, as we have seen in regard to the general law on anti-money laundering. The scope of section 19 is significantly extended by virtue of section 19(7). It is there provided that for the purposes of determining whether a person has committed a crime activating the obligation to report, if that person has taken an action or been in possession of a thing, and he would have committed an offence under sections 15 to 18 if that had taken place in the United Kingdom, he will for the purpose of section 19 be considered to have committed the relevant crime. There is protection from any liability arising from the restriction on the disclosure of information, for disclosures to the authorities, or in accord with compliance procedures, both generally and in regard to section 19. Of course, as we have seen, this would only provide legal protection within jurisdiction and not from actions based on, for example, the law of defamation or malicious prosecution. Section 21 provides that no offence is committed under any of these substantive provisions if disclosure is made before he becomes involved and the authorities consent, or afterwards, on his own initiative as soon as is reasonably practicable, along the same lines as in the general anti-money laundering law. There are also similar penalties for breach of these provisions as discussed above under section 334 of the Proceeds of Crime Act 2002.

MONEY LAUNDERING LIABILITY IN THE CIVIL LAW

7.27   We have already referred to liability in equity for breach of trust and other fiduciary obligations.[1] While every breach of trust will amount to a breach of fiduciary duty, not every breach of a fiduciary relationship will amount to a breach of trust. Trusts, even remedial constructive trusts, involve property and rights in property. The relationship between the trust and the trustee is a proprietary relationship. It is upon this basis that trustees are under a strict obligation that does not depend upon culpability or a state of mind, to replace property that has been improperly removed or diverted from the trust.[2] Trustees are also held to the general and strict fiduciary obligations to avoid all conflicts of interest, to act in good faith in the best interests of their beneficiaries and to act with prudence and diligence. They have an overall obligation of loyalty and fair dealing. While the obligations of a trustee are expressed in proprietary terms, many of the obligations are also personal, and the remedies that are applied may well be compensatory. One area which has caused difficulty is the situation where a person receiving property, including rights in or to property, appreciates that it is being transferred to him in breach of trust. Generally speaking in terms of priorities a *bona fide* purchaser of such property, without actual knowledge, will be able to take the property unencumbered. The original owner's rights in the property, which are equitable, will be defeated by the stronger right of the so called 'equity's darling'. The position may be different if the 'original' owner has been able to re-establish his legal ownership in the property. For example, in cases of theft, or fraud where there has been an effective rescission of the contract, the legal ownership remains in or reverts in full to the owner and even 'equity's darling' will, save in exceptional circumstances, in most common law as opposed to most civilian jurisdictions, have no right to the property against the owner. Of course, in such cases as where the original owner's equitable interest is defeated, the remedy will be in damages against the fraudster – who sadly is likely to have disappeared. Where a third party takes property with knowledge of a breach of trust, then in many legal systems he will become a constructive trustee and hold the property on much the same terms as the trustee in breach. There are cases which indicate that in such circumstances, actual knowledge of the breach does not need to be established. Knowledge of facts that would put a reasonable man on inquiry would be sufficient to create the obligation of trustee. Reckless indifference to the rights of another would be enough, but whether negligence is an appropriate standard has been questioned. Deliberately refusing to make inquiries in circumstances where you are suspicious is generally considered to place on you the risk of what you might have found had you made proper and reasonable inquiry. Of course, if the person who takes the transfer is a volunteer, that is, does not provide consideration, then he will not be considered a *bona fide* purchaser and the issue of knowledge is irrelevant. He will not be able to resist a claim by the beneficial owner and may well be considered to possess the property as a constructive trustee. While the courts as a matter of contract law generally do not consider the adequacy of consideration, in cases such as we are discussing a wholly inadequate consideration might not be considered as dealing in good faith.

1   See **2.7**.
2   See *Clough v Bond* (1838) 3 My & C 490, *Target Holdings v Redferns* [1996] 1 AC 421 and *Attorney General for Hong Kong v Reid* (1994) 1 AC 324.

7.28   The circumstances where a fiduciary obligation is imposed are not fixed. The courts may be prepared to find that in the circumstances of a case, a person has stepped into a fiduciary relationship and is thus subject to fiduciary obligations. There are many factors influencing the courts in this regard, but issues such as a reposing confidence in another and reasonably expecting fairness and good faith play a role.[1] As do deliberate taking advantage of an imbalance of opportunity in unfair circumstances. Having said this, given the onerous obligations attaching to fiduciary status, the courts do not find such a relationship easily. Where a person is a fiduciary, however, then the obligations are strict and remedies generally do not depend upon the state of mind of the fiduciary in breach. If a fiduciary enters into a conflict of interest or takes a secret profit he will be liable irrespective of whether he was dishonest or not. His breach of stewardship is sufficient harm and justification for a remedy.[2] The state of mind of the fiduciary may, however, have an impact on the way in which the court deals with him and in regard to such issues as ratification and indemnity. The more dishonest a person is the less easy will it be for him to persuade a court that there has been agreement, express or implied, to his conduct.

1   See **8.9** *et seq.*
2   See **6.41**.

7.29   Mention has been made of the liability that equity has developed for those who assist others in the breach of their fiduciary obligations. Where the trust property is actually transferred to the third party, then it is often appropriate to talk in terms of liability based on a constructive or resulting trust, as we have just seen. There is a proprietary relationship. Of course, there are issues as to what can be considered trust property for the purposes of imposing or rather finding a trust relationship. In equity it seems that confidential information and opportunities to profit, such as by virtue of an embryo contract, may be considered, unlike in the criminal law, to be a form of property.[1] We have already seen that in certain circumstances secret profits and bribes may be considered to amount to trust property on the basis that equity looks as done that which should be done and will look to the stage after the fiduciary has been ordered to account for the illicit benefit.[2] However, what is the position of a third person who does not actually receive into their control or possession, property that can be the basis of a tracing claim, but nonetheless assists the fiduciary to breach his duties or launder the proceeds of such? It is misleading to describe such a person as coming into a constructive trust relationship with the ultimate beneficiary as there is no proprietary nexus – there is no property upon which equity can focus. Of course, imaginative lawyers and occasionally sympathetic judges – who do not like to see fraudsters retaining their ill-gotten gains, invent arguments by which rights to call to account or even sue, are transmuted into something resembling a right in property. However, this is not really good law and creates uncertainty and potential unfairness, particularly for relatively innocent third parties.

1   See *Boardman v Phipps* [1967] 2 AC 46 and *Cook v Deeks* [1916] 1 AC 554.
2   *Attorney General for Hong Kong v Reid* (1994) 1 AC 324.

7.30   Rather than bend property law, in many common law jurisdictions the courts have found liability for culpable third parties on the basis of their dishonest assistance in the breach of another. This form of accessory liability is based purely on their dishonesty and not upon notions of property or for that matter the viability of a tracing claim. In a number of cases the courts in many Commonwealth and even some non-common law jurisdictions, have imposed personal liability on those who dishonestly assist others to breach their fiduciary duties, including the laundering of the proceeds of such. In providing assistance it is not necessary that the accessory has at any time control over or possession of the illicit wealth. On the other hand, the assistance must be material. There has been debate as to the state of knowledge that the accessory must be proved to have to justify his personal liability. Actual knowledge of the facts relating to the breach of duty by the fiduciary is obviously sufficient. It has also been held that the reckless disregard of the rights of another might well be sufficient.[1] It is on this level of knowledge that dishonesty can be found. Of course, unlike in the criminal law, the test is in civil cases objective.[2] Thus, the defendant will be taken to know or appreciate what a person in his position, with his knowledge and skill, would appreciate. It has, for example, been held that an accountant who refrains from asking why his client wants companies registered in England with bank accounts, might well be taken to know the facts that would have come out if he had received answers.[3] By not asking, he deliberately put himself in a position of ignorance. He had what has been termed 'Nelsonian' knowledge. When Admiral Nelson was asked if he saw his commander's flag signals requiring that he withdraw from a navel engagement he held his spyglass to his blind eye and asserted he saw nothing!

1   *Royal Brunei Airlines v Tan* [1995] 1 AC 378 and *Selangor v Cradock (No 3)* [1968] 1 WLR 1555.
2   But it has been held that the defendant must realise that his actions would be considered dishonest by ordinary reasonable people, see *Twinsectra Ltd v Yardley* [2002] 2 All ER 377.
3   *Agip (Africa) v Jackson* [1991] Ch 547.

NAUGHTY KNOWLEDGE AND MENS REA

7.31   It is useful here to briefly consider in the context of the criminal law what the prosecution needs to prove, beyond a reasonable doubt, in the case of a prosecution under the relevant statutory provisions. It will be noted that most of the substantive offences require either knowledge or suspicion. As we have seen in the case of certain of the offences relating to terrorist finance, it will suffice to prove that the accused has reasonable cause to suspect. In other words an ordinary reasonable man, in the position of the accused, would have formed a suspicion. Of course, it has to be proved even under this objective standard, that the accused knew such facts as would have properly grounded such a suspicion. In the case of handling charges, under section 22 of the Theft Act 1968, it is necessary to prove that the accused knew or believed that the relevant goods were stolen or were the proceeds of fraud. Some of the commentaries on the anti-money laundering provisions refer to belief as suspicion. This is certainly wrong in the criminal law and probably misleading in the civil law. Knowledge in the criminal law is certain knowledge of the relevant facts. Belief is something less than certain knowledge. Belief is, for example, when a person might say to himself: 'I cannot say I know for certain that those goods are stolen, but there can be no other reasonable conclusion in the light of all the circumstances, in the light of all that I have heard and seen.'[1] A suspicion would not be sufficient. However, it has been accepted that wilful blindness, that is deliberately not acquiring knowledge, is sufficient to establish a belief.[2] Suspicion is defined in the Oxford Dictionary to include: an impression of the existence or presence of; belief tentatively without clear grounds; being inclined to think; being inclined to mentally accuse or doubt innocence and to doubt the genuineness or truth of a suspected person. In *R v Da Silva*, the Court of Appeal, in regard to an earlier provision, thought that the accused must be shown to think that there is a 'possibility, which is more than fanciful, that the relevant facts exist' and that the resulting suspicion should be of a 'settled nature'.[3] However, in *Squirrell Ltd v National Westminster Bank plc*[4] Laddie J rather unhelpfully noted that there was no direct authority on what 'suspect' means under the anti-money laundering provisions. He did recognise that there is no need for the suspicion to be reasonable.[5] In practice, it may well be possible to establish the requisite state of mind from circumstantial evidence, although this is problematic. The conduct of the accused may well indicate, beyond a reasonable doubt, that he or she was in fact suspicious. It is clear that negligence is not sufficient. While culpable and gross negligence are terms that rather distort the criminal law, it may well be that self-interested negligence[6] may be a sufficient basis. Wilfully shutting one's eyes to what would have been obvious,[7] would be sufficient in most cases. An accused who deliberately prevented himself acquiring certain knowledge, would, in the vast majority of situations, be doing so because he suspected the truth. Having said all this, the notion of suspicion is a difficult one, especially for the criminal law.[8]

1   *R v Hall* (1985) 81 Cr App Rep 260.
2   *R v Moys* (1984) 79 Cr App Rep 72 and see also in regard to a 'great suspicion' and a refusal to believe, *R v Forsyth* [1997] 2 Cr App Rep 299.
3   [2006] EWCA Crim 1654.
4   [2005] EWHC 664 and also *K Ltd v National Westminster Bank* [2006] EWCA Civ 1039. In *Hussein v Chong Fook Kam* [1970] AC 942, Lord Devlin, observed 'suspicion in its ordinary meaning is a state of conjecture or sumise where proof is lacking.' He also added that suspicion did not require admissible evidence or, for that matter, evidence.
5   Note the contrast between the subjective standards in the substantive offences in sections 327 to 329 as compared with the objective standard in the reporting obligations imposed under sections 330 and 331 of the Proceeds of Crime Act 2002.
6   See for example, albeit in a rather different context, *Daniels v Daniels* [1978] 2 WLR 73 discussed in B Rider 'Amiable Lunatics and the Rule in Foss v Harbottle' (1978) CLJ 270.
7   See for example Millett J's comments in *AGIP v Jackson* (1990) Ch 265, affirmed (1991) Ch 547, see *supra* at **7.30**.
8   While Courts generally take the view that it is wrong to try and define concepts such as knowledge and belief for juries (see *R v Harris* (1986) 84 Cr App Rep 75 and in particular *R v Smith* (1976) 64 Cr App Rep 217), 'where much reference is made to suspicion, it will be prudent to give (a direction)' to the jury, R Toor (1986) 85 Cr App Rep 116.

COMPLIANCE

7.32   Mention has been made of the importance of secondary legislation in this area of the law, particularly in regard to what might be described as compliance issues. The legislation requires those within the regulated sector and in many respects those outside, to establish procedures for identifying and knowing clients (Know Your Client – KYC) and others with whom one deals, the recording or relevant information, training of staff and the development and implementation of procedures for monitoring, reporting and handling suspicions.[1] As has already been pointed out, the actual requirements differ, at least in emphasis, from one business or profession to another. It is also the case that the requirements, in law and good practice, differ in regard to whether one is considering, for example, serious crime, market abuse,[2] corruption, tax fraud or terrorist related activity. Added to this is the need to incorporate into such systems and procedures provisions to address other areas of legal and other risk, such as that presented by restitutory actions or proceedings for the interdiction of property.[3] There has been concern that the burdens placed on particularly financial institutions are not cost effective and produce little of real value in discouraging crime or in assisting law enforcement. This has been a concern that has been taken up by the Financial Services Authority.[4] The FSA has abandoned its detailed and prescriptive rules relating to money laundering in favour of a risk based approach, which places the burden on particular businesses to identify and address the peculiar risks facing them. Consequently, while the FSA is concerned to take action, including enforcement action,[5] where records are not adequately maintained, or there is a failure of KYC, in practice it is concerned with failure to establish and adequately operate and supervise systems.

1   See Chapter 12 and S Bazley and A Haynes, *Financial Services Authority Regulation and Risk-based Compliance*, (2nd Ed, 2007), Tottel, and *Money Laundering and Terrorist Financing, Reporting Officer's Reference Guide 2007*, British Bankers Association, in particular the Joint Money Laundering Steering Group Guidelines, www.jmlsg.org.uk, and the website of the International Compliance Association www.int-comp.com.

2   In particular note the Financial Services and Markets Act 2000, s 131A in regard to protected disclosures.

3   See generally *Laundering and Tracing* (P Birks ed) (1995), Oxford and J Ulph, *Commercial Fraud* (2006), Oxford, Part B.

4   See for example, *The Fight Against Money Laundering; Promoting Effectiveness* P Robinson, 22 June 2005. Reference should be made to the FSA website www.fsa.ov.uk . See also *Anti-money Laundering current customer review cost benefit analysis: Report prepared by Pricewaterhouse Coopers for the FSA* (2003), *FSA and Anti-Money Laundering Requirements; Costs, Benefits and Perceptions* (X/Yen, 2005), Corporation of the City of London.

5   See for an early example, *Final Notice: The Governor and Company of the Bank of Ireland*, 31 August 2004, FSA.

Chapter 8

Conflicts of interest

A FUNDAMENTAL RULE

8.1 The significance of the law relating to conflicts of interest in the control of abuse and in particular insider dealing has already been emphasised on several occasions in this work.[1] We have seen that much of the traditional fiduciary law is based on the fundamental obligation to avoid conflicts of interest and account for any benefit that results from an actual conflict of interest.[2] In this regard it is probably worth quoting Lord Herscell LC in *Bray v Ford*[3] that 'it is an inflexible rule of a Court of Equity that a person in a fiduciary position ... is not, unless otherwise expressly provided, entitled to make a profit; he is not allowed to put himself in apposition where his interest and duty conflict.' And Lord Russell of Killowen in *Regal (Hastings) Ltd v Gulliver*:[4] 'The rule of equity which insists on those, who by the use of a fiduciary position make a profit, being liable to account for that profit, in no way depends on fraud, or absence of bona fides; or upon such questions or considerations as whether the profit would or should otherwise have gone to the plaintiff, or whether the profiteer was under a duty to obtain the source of the profit for the plaintiff, or whether he took a risk or acted as he did for the benefit of the plaintiff, or whether the plaintiff has in fact been damaged or benefited by his action. The liability arises from the mere fact of the profit having, in the stated circumstances, been made. The profiteer, however, honest and well intentioned, cannot escape the risk of being called to account'. We have already seen in our discussion of the liability of those who abuse unpublished price sensitive information in the civil law[5] the 'codification' of these principles, in so far as they relate to company directors, in the Companies Act 2006.

1 See **2.2** *et seq* and generally C Nakajima and E Sheffield, *Conflicts of Interest and Chinese Walls*, (2002), Butterworths.
2 See **2.7** *et seq*.
3 [1896] AC 44.
4 [1967] AC 152 and see **2.7** and **7.27** *et seq*.

DIRECTORS AND THEIR DUTY OF LOYALTY

8.2 Section 175(1) of the Companies Act 2006 provides that 'a director of a company must avoid a situation in which he has, or can have, a direct or indirect interest that conflicts, or possibly may conflict, with the interests of the company'. It is made clear in section 175(7) that the 'no conflict rule' applies also to conflicts of duties.[1] It has been argued that all the relevant fiduciary obligations are based on this fundamental principle. Consequently, the obligation to account for secret profits is but a manifestation of this strict obligation of loyalty. This is, however, an over simplification.[2] Indeed, it is clear even in the context of directors' duties that there are at least three relatively distinct, albeit often related, situations. This is underlined by the fact that section 175(3) states that the duty set out in section 175(1) 'does not apply to a conflict of interest arising in relation to a transaction or arrangement with the company'. Self-dealing in such transactions, on the part of a director, is governed by a specific set of rules relating to disclosure, control and approval.

1   See also section 176(5) in regard to benefits from third parties.
2   See for example, *Bhullar v Bhullar* [2003] 3 BCLC 241 and *Plus Group Ltd v Pyke* (2002) 2 BCLC 201.

8.3   The common law imposed a very strict obligation on directors. Lord Cranworth LC in *Aberdeen Railway v Blaikie*[1] stated 'it is a rule of universal application that no one' having duties of a fiduciary nature 'shall be allowed to enter into engagements in which he has, or can have, a personal interest conflicting, or which possibly may conflict with the interests of those whom he is bound to protect' and 'so strictly is this principle adhered to that no question is allowed to be raised as to the fairness or unfairness of a contract so entered into …'. To hold directors to the duties of a trustee was not practical, or perhaps in many cases in the commercial interests of the company. Consequently, despite the strict law, the courts permitted directors to deal with their own companies provided the shareholders, after full disclosure, ratified what had occurred. Indeed, in the case of prior authorisation by the shareholders, it is arguable that the potential conflict is avoided. The exigencies of business led to the Courts going somewhat further and accepted that provided adequate disclosure was made to an appropriate body, determined by the company's constitutional documents, which may be merely the board of directors, the so called 'universal' rule of Lord Cranworth was effectively avoided. Commercial practice went perhaps too far and since the Companies Act 1929 there has been a statutory obligation of disclosure to the board which cannot be excluded or modified by the articles of association.[2] Section 177(1) of the Companies Act 2006 places a statutory obligation on a director who is 'in any way, directly or indirectly' interested in a proposed transaction or arrangement with his company to declare to the other directors the 'nature and extent' of the interest before the relevant arrangement is entered into. It is important to note that this obligation goes beyond contract and includes non-contractual arrangements. The purpose of this provision is to alert the board to the existence of a conflict and therefore obligate it to address it in the interests of the company. It follows that changes in the nature and extent of the relevant interest must also be disclosed and recorded. While the scope of this obligation is wide in so far as it includes 'indirect' interests such as a shareholding in another company with which a transaction is proposed, section 177(6)(a) provides that a director need not declare an interest 'if it cannot reasonably be regarded as likely to give rise to a conflict of interest'. Furthermore, he need not disclose any interest that his fellow directors are already aware of and 'the other directors are treated as aware of anything of which they ought reasonably to be aware' under section 177(6)(b). A similar obligation to disclose interests is imposed on directors and shadow directors by section 182 in regard to existing transactions or arrangements. It should be noted that failure to disclose existing interests, usually upon appointment, is made a specific criminal offence under section 183.

1   (1854) 2 Eq Rep 1281.

2   See generally *Gower and Davies, Principles of Modern Company Law* (8th Ed, Sweet and Maxwell 2008), Ch 16.

8.4   Section 180 of the Companies Act 2006 provides that compliance with the disclosure obligation means that the director will not be in breach of his duty to the company if the relevant transaction is then entered into. Compliance will also ensure that 'the transaction or arrangement is not liable to be set aside by virtue of any common law rule or equitable principle requiring the consent or approval of the members of the company'.[1] While section 178(1) of the Companies Act 2006 provides the consequences of breach of section 177 are to be the same as under the corresponding common law or equitable rules,[2] it should be noted that the imposition of a statutory obligation to disclose may well render the law of fraud relevant.[3] A dishonest failure to disclose might well constitute the offence of fraud, and connivance on the part of others might well amount to a conspiracy to defraud.[4]

1   Section 180(1). Note, however, 'this is without prejudice to any enactment, or provision of the company's constitution, requiring such consent or approval'.
2   Section 178(2) provides 'the duties …are, accordingly, enforceable in the same way as any other fiduciary duty owed to a company by its directors'.
3   See **6.21** *et seq.*
4   See **6.14**.

8.5   The Companies Act 2006 as the previous legislation, recognises that there are certain situations where the temptation and consequent risks of self-dealing are of such significance that mere disclosure to the board is not enough. Consequently in regard to substantial property transactions[1] and loans to directors[2] and those connected with them,[3] and certain aspects of their service contracts,[4] there must be full disclosure to the shareholders and a vote in general meeting. While of importance in promoting and ensuring the integrity of directors and in certain respects other insiders, we need not address these provisions here in detail. The Act provides specific civil remedies, which while resembling the general law, are specifically honed to deal with the involvement of persons connected with the director.[5]

1   See sections 190 to 196. Note in particular section 194, which excludes transactions on a recognised investment exchange through an independent broker.
2   See sections 197 *et seq.*
3   See sections 252, 253 and 254.
4   See sections 188 and 189 and generally Part 10, Chapter 5.
5   See section 195 and also section 213.

8.6   The other two areas of liability that arguably flow from the general rule against conflict of interest, in the context of corporate law, relate to the misuse of corporate property, information and opportunities and the making of secret profits. In our discussion of civil liability we have already noted that section 175(2) specifically refers to the misuse of information.[1] It also refers to the exploitation of property and so called corporate opportunities.[2] We have examined the liability that can arise where a person in a fiduciary relationship, without proper consent or approval, derives profit from the exploitation of information or property, including expectant property[3] or receives a benefit from a third party. It has been argued that the strict obligations of stewardship should render any risk of a conflict of interest or duty unacceptable. However, in the case of directors who are in the commercial world, the law is less exacting. Section 175(4) in regard to the avoidance of conflicts of interest, in the context of exploiting information, property and opportunity, states 'the duty is not infringed if the situation cannot reasonably be regarded as likely to give rise to a conflict of interest.' By the same token section 176(4) in the context of outlawing benefits from third parties, provides 'this duty is not infringed if the acceptance of the benefit cannot reasonably be regarded as likely to give rise to a conflict of interest'. Consequently, theoretical and unrealistic conflicts actual as well as potential should not expose a director to the prospect of liability.[4]

1 See **2.7**.
2 See **2.9**.
3 See **2.23** *et seq.*
4 See generally *Island Export Finance Ltd v Umunna* [1986] BCLC 460; *Framlington Group Plc v Anderson* [1995] 1 BCLC 475 and *Ultraframe (UK) Ltd v Fielding* [2005] EWHC 1638.

MULTIPLE APPOINTMENTS

8.7   An issue that has caused controversy is the position of directors who hold multiple directorships. We have seen that the courts have tended to treat directors less strictly than other fiduciaries, recognising the commercial environment within which they are required to operate. Indeed, there is authority, albeit not particularly strong, that a director cannot be restrained from serving as a director of another company actually competing in the same line of business.[1] Without informed consent this would not be permissible in the case of an ordinary fiduciary. The situation is complicated where the director is also an employee. While the duty of fidelity owed by an employee to his employee is less demanding than the ordinary fiduciary obligations, it has been held that an employee cannot work for a competitor even in his spare time.[2] Of course, if the director makes adequate disclosure and secures permission under section 175, which provides that the 'no conflict rule' will not be breached if the matter has been authorised by the board – presumably in such a case of both companies, he should not be at risk. However, any material change in the nature of the conflict will need to be disclosed for this to provide protection. Of course, it goes without saying that if a director does exploit information, property or opportunity belonging to another company personally or for the benefit of another, then he will be liable, as may well the company or person for whose benefit that property or information is used.[3]

1 *London & Mashonaland Exploration Co v New Mashonaland Exploration Co* [1891] WN 165 approved by Lord Blanesburgh in *Bell v Lever Bros* [1932] AC 161 at 195, but see *In Plus Group Ltd v Pyke* [2002] 2 BCLC 201 where doubts were expressed as to whether today this is appropriate. Of course, a director should not subordinate the interests of one company to another, even within the context of a group, see *Scottish Co-op Wholesale Society Ltd v Meyer* [1959] AC 324 at 366.
2 See *Hivac Ltd v Park Royal Scientific Instruments Ltd* [1946] Ch 169. See also *Industrial Development Consultants v Cooley* [1972] 1 WLR 433.
3 See **2.23**.

MODIFICATION OF DUTIES

8.8   We have seen that in regard to the various obligations associated with the 'no conflict rule', directors are able to secure authorisation or obtain ratification of their conduct from the shareholders and in some cases simply the board. We have also referred to the practice of attempting to redefine fiduciary obligations in the company's constitutional documents and in particular articles of association. Successive legislation has intervened to curb this. Section 232(1) provides that any provision that purports to exempt a director or shadow director from any liability that would otherwise attach to him in connection with any negligence, default, breach of duty or trust in relation to the company is void. On the other hand section 232(4) states that 'nothing in this section prevents a company's articles from making such provision as has previously been lawful for dealing with conflicts of interest'.[1] The problem is that the law before the enactment of these provisions was not entirely clear. In *Movitex Ltd v Bulfield*[2] Vinelott J distinguished between the fundamental principle that directors would be accountable for any benefit resulting from a conflict of interest regardless of whether it was fair or not, and the obligation of directors to always pursue the best interests of the company. This second obligation could not be varied or excused. In the case of the obligation to yield up benefits, the articles or shareholders could essentially redefine what might be considered to be a conflict of interest. If what might otherwise have been considered to be a conflict is rendered no longer a conflict then there is nothing for the fundamental rule to bite upon and therefore there is no breach to be excused. Thus, would it be acceptable to provide that directors could exploit information that came to them in their capacity as directors? Of course, it may be difficult in practice to distinguish information from property or opportunity. We have seen that the courts, at least in the civil law, are willing, in certain circumstances, to regard information as resembling property and to protect it accordingly.[3] There is also an informational element in every case of so called 'corporate opportunity. Indeed, some cases that have been regarded as illustrating the taking of an opportunity might equally be considered examples of insider trading on the basis of price sensitive information.[4] It would seem that where the company has itself an interest in exploiting the information or opportunity, then a misappropriation or diversion by the directors would be contrary to their obligation to place the interests of the company first. In such a case a purported modification of their duty would be void. However, if the relevant organ of the company has made a *bona fide* decision not to use the information or pursue the opportunity then there may be no objection, as there is no actual conflict. Of course, this in the context of insider dealing may not be as simplistic. As we have seen it would not generally be in the interests of a company for its directors to be seen to be utilising unpublished price sensitive information improperly.[5]

1 See also section 180(4)(b) in the same vein.
2 [1988] BCLC 104.
3 See **2.7**.
4 See *Boardman v Phipps* (1967) AC 46 and see in this context B Rider 'The Fiduciary and the Frying Pan' (1978) *Conveyancer* 114.
5 See **2.10** and *Diamond v Oreamuno* (1969) 24 NY ed 494.

8.9   The cases indicate that in regard to most, but not all, fiduciary obligations, the person to whom they are owed may after full disclosure decide to waive their performance or excuse their nonperformance. However, in the case of companies there is a problem. We have seen that directors owe their fiduciary duties to the company. While there are situations where the board of directors is the proper organ of the company to decide on performance, there are situations where the decision falls to the shareholders in general meeting. In such cases what is the position of a director who wishes to see his duties modified or excused, if he is also a shareholder. May he vote his own shares to change or excuse performance of his duties as a director to the company? Traditionally the law has taken the view that as shares are proprietary rights and shareholders are not in a fiduciary relationship with the company, there is no inhibition on director shareholders exercising their votes in general meeting as they choose. Having said this there are cases which indicate a willingness of the courts to have regard to the actions of directors in such circumstances as an indication of their good faith.[1] If a director who is in breach of his duties is prepared to have the matter resolved by an independent majority of the shareholders, after full disclosure, this surely indicates integrity. Furthermore, an independent resolution better reflects what is in fact considered to be in the best interests of the company. Section 239(4) in regard to the *ex post facto* ratification of directors' breaches of duty and trust provides that the ordinary resolution is to be considered passed 'only if the necessary voting majority is obtained disregarding the votes in favour of the resolution by the director ... and any member connected with him'. In some respects this section is narrower than the common law, which is not necessarily pre-empted. The recent approach of some judges when considering the effect of a resolution on the ability of minority shareholders to raise a challenge on behalf of the company is rather wider and more searching. The section only 'disqualifies' the votes of the specific director and those connected with him as defined in the provisions relating to substantial property transactions.[2] Thus, cronies and others who may be very interested in the wrongdoing, but who are not connected in a formal sense, will be able to vote as they choose.

1   See *Smith v Croft (No 2)* [1988] Ch 114. Vinelott J's more extreme view expressed in *Prudential Assurance Co Ltd v Newman Industries Ltd (No 2)* (1981) Ch 257 is probably not good law. But see also *Daniels v Daniels* [1978] Ch 406.
2   See sections 252 to 254 of the Companies Act 2006.

8.10   We have noted that it is the better view that there are certain duties which cannot be excused even after full disclosure and purported ratification. It has been argued that it would be against public policy to allow ratification of fraudulent conduct or other misconduct that amounts to a serious crime, such as, presumably, money laundering or for that matter insider dealing. The perimeters of what might be considered excusable as a matter of public policy, albeit from merely the perspective of the civil law, are unclear. We have seen that courts have taken differing views on insider dealing.[1] Perhaps assistance can be obtained from the law of insurance? Directors and Officers indemnity cover does not extend to allegations of fraud or deliberate wrongdoing. However, there has been uncertainly in regard to regulatory misconduct and civil enforcement. It is argued that a breach of duty involving the misappropriation of property belonging to the company cannot be excused. For example, in *Cook v Deeks*[2] directors who misappropriated a corporate opportunity which 'belonged' to their company were not allowed to exercise their votes, which constituted a majority, to 'make a present to themselves'.[3] Whether the position would have been different had the vote been by a disinterested majority is open to question. It is important in this regard to remember that section 239 only applies to breaches of duty and trust that the law has considered capable of ratification. The traditional interpretation of *Cook v Deeks* is that as a misappropriation of corporate property was in issue, ratification was not possible. On the other hand there are cases involving forms of self-dealing where the courts have allowed or contemplated allowing ratification. It is argued that in these cases company's claim was simply for an account of unauthorised profits and did not involve a misappropriation of corporate property.[4] This analysis has always been open to question given the different ways in which courts have regarded the misuse of information. In some, the courts have regarded it as giving rise to a personal claim for the benefit that the fiduciary has received and in others to a proprietary claim based on the misuse of information as a species of corporate property.[5] Of course, the explanation may be rather more to do with whether the benefit remains in the hands of a fiduciary and can therefore be subjected to a personal claim. After the approach of the Privy Council in *Attorney General of Hong Kong v Reid*[6] it is doubtful whether a sensible distinction can be made between these cases on the traditional distinction between a personal and proprietary claim. Perhaps a better approach is to return to the issue of honesty and fair dealing.[7]

1   See **2.47**.
2   [1916] 1 AC 554.
3   [1916] 1 AC 554 at 564 and see Templeman J in *Daniels v Daniels* [1978] Ch 406 discussed on this point in B Rider 'Amiable Lunatics and the Rule in *Foss v Harbottle*' (1978) *Cambridge Law Journal* 270.
4   *North West Transportation Co v Beatty* (1887) LR 12 App Cas 589 and *Regal (Hastings) v Gulliver* [1967] AC 152.
5   For example *Phipps v Boardman* [1967] AC 46; *Attorney General of Hong Kong v Reid* (1994) 1 AC 324 and *Daraydan Holdings Ltd v Solland International Ltd* [2005] Ch 119.
6   *Supra* at 5.
7   See B Rider *supra* at 3. Of course, where actual dishonesty is alleged then the allegations of fraud have allowed judges to cut through procedural and other barriers, see *Atwood v Merryweather* [1867] LT 5 Eq 464. Having noted this, however, the courts do not like allegations that are justified purely as procedural devices.

8.11   Our discussion has focused on the ratification of conduct which, without such informed approval, would have amounted to a breach of fiduciary duty. The effect of the ratification is to render the conduct no longer objectionable. Of course, it may well be that a particular transaction that could be avoided for breach of duty might be affirmed by the board or the shareholders, albeit the liability of those responsible for the wrong not excused. There is also the issue which we have touched upon of prior authorisation. We have noted the attempts, primarily through the articles of association, to authorise actions which would otherwise constitute a breach of fiduciary duty. The Companies Act 2006 does not as in the case of *ex post facto* ratification address the issue whether the directors as shareholders might use their votes in this context. It is probably the case that, save in exceptional circumstances, there is no objection to those who might well be interested in some other capacity – even as a potential wrongdoer, utilising their own votes to amend the articles to include a relevant provision. Of course, we have seen that there are limitations on what can be excluded or modified in terms of duty to the company.[1] Finally in this context, it is important to remember that directors who have acted honestly and reasonably and who in fairness ought to be excused from all or part of liability for a breach of duty can apply to the court under section 1157 for the judge to exercise his discretion.

1   See **8.8**.

8.12   Section 232 of the Companies Act 2006 prohibits any provision by which the company provides directly or indirectly an indemnity to a director or a director of an associated company.[1] However, under section 233, companies are permitted to purchase insurance cover for their directors even in regard to liability arising for breach of their duties to the company. It is most unlikely that this cover would extend to deliberate misconduct and in particular fraud, as we have seen. By the same token it is questionable whether such cover is available for secret profits as opposed to losses actually occasioned to the company. The company may also provide indemnity, directly or indirectly, in regard to liability to third parties. However, under section 234, this may not extend to fines imposed as a result of criminal proceedings, costs incurred in unsuccessfully defending a prosecution, a penalty imposed by a regulatory authority[1] and the costs of defending civil proceedings brought by the company or an associated company in which judgment is given against the director.[2] It should be noted that under this section there is no objection to a company indemnifying a director against the costs of unsuccessfully defending an action brought by a regulator, such as the FSA, although this would not extend to the penalty.

1   However, see sections 205 and 206 in regard to loans for defending civil actions and regulatory procedures.
2   Of course the company cannot, by any provision, cover a director in regard to liability for any breach of duty to the company. Therefore, this provision is directed at actions where it is not the director's own breach of duty to the company that is in issue.

OTHER FIDUCIARIES

8.13   Our discussion has so far focused on the directors of companies and in particular the issue of conflict of interest. Of course, in the context of financial service industry the range of fiduciary relationships is somewhat wider. There will be many individuals and companies that find themselves owing fiduciary obligations who are not in the position of directors.[1] The regulatory system has, as we shall see, imposed obligations relating to the control and management of conflicts of interest and duty on persons who would not, in law be considered fiduciaries.[2] It is also the case that the regulatory system and its rules have not always been in compliance with fiduciary law[3] and certainly the reliance that some have placed on following industry practice and even regulatory guidance may as a matter of law be misplaced.[4] There are numerous conceivable situations where conflicts of interest and duty may arise in the conduct of financial business. This is not the place to try and identify these let alone address them. It is also the case that the intervention of law on a much broader basis has made a considerable difference in resolving certain conflicts. For example, today it could not be sensibly argued that a stockbroker who learnt unpublished price sensitive information is under a duty to use it for the benefit of his client.[5] The same would also be true of a trustee in the prudent management of the trust funds.[6] However, potential conflict issues arise that have perhaps not been considered with as much thought in the past. For example, the position of members of a shari'ah council advising financial institutions on issues of shari'ah compliance in regard to different products and funds may raise issues of conflict and handling of price sensitive information.[7] It will not always be clear, where fiduciaries operate in multiple functions or for different clients, who is entitled to primacy and on what basis. The traditional rules of equity that give primacy in the discharge of a duty to those who are first in time – subject to issues of notice – is not in the context of the realities of financial life, practicable.[8] Attempts to expand and apply rules based on simple conflicts between two principals, in the context of simple commercial transactions or agency agreements, have also proved inadequate for the task.[9] Referring to the strict rules of confidentiality and no conflict developed, for example, in the practice of law, tends to neglect the public policy issues that dictate exacting standards as a matter of justice, which are arguably inappropriate in the world of business. Reliance on so called 'Chinese walls' and other methods of segregating information, focus on liability attaching to the flow of information and knowledge rather than the issue of conflict of duty.[10] While as we shall see the regulators and professions have attempted to deal with some of these issues, given the complexity of the issues and vested interests, successive governments have been reluctant to resort to legislation and the matter has somewhat pragmatically been left largely in the hands of the courts.[11]

1   See generally C Nakajima and E Sheffield, *Conflicts of Interest and Chinese Walls* (2002 Butterworths); B Rider and TM Ashe (eds), *The Fiduciary, the Insider and the Conflict* (Sweet and Maxwell 1995) and C Hollander and S Salzedo, *Conflicts of Interest* (3rd Ed Sweet and Maxwell 2008).
2   See **8.21** *et seq.*

3   See generally *Law Commission, Fiduciary Duties and regulatory Rules, A Consultation Paper (LC No 124) (1992) HMSO; Law Commission, Fiduciary Duties amd Regulatory Rules, Report (LC No 236) (1995) HMSO* and B Rider (Ed), *The Regulation of the British Securities Industry* (Oyez 1979) Ch 5.

4   See B Rider and T M Ashe *supra* n 1 above.

5   See G Cooper and R Cridlan, *The Law and Procedure of the Stock Exchange* (Butterworths 1971) at page 104 and also see the allegations in *Briggs v Gunner*, Chancery Division 16 January 1979 discussed in B Rider, *supra* at 3.

6   But see *Phipps v Boardman* [1967] 2 AC 46 also discussed in B Rider *supra* at n 3 and B Rider 'The Fiduciary and the Frying Pan' (1978) *Conveyancer* 114.

7   See B Rider and C Nakajima, Chapter 18 in S Archer and R Karim, *Islamic Finance, the Regulatory Challenge*, Wiley, 2007.

8   See generally C Nakajima and E Sheffield *supra* n 1 above.

9   See for example *Anglo-African Merchants Ltd v Bayley* [1969] 1 All ER 421 and *North and South Trust Company v Berkeley* (1971) 1 All ER 980.

10 See for example *Financial Services in the UK, A new framework for investor protection*, DTI (1985) Cmnd 9432 HMSO para 7.4 'the Government is not convinced that total reliance can be placed on Chinese Walls because they restrict flows of information and not the conflicts of interest themselves'. See also *Dunford & Elliott Ltd v Johson & Firth Brown Ltd* [1977] 1 Lloyds Rep 505 at Roskill LJ at 515.

8.14   At the heart of the modern law is the colourful case of *Prince Jefri Bolkiah v KPMG*.[1] Essentially this involved the issue of whether KPMG, by constructing various informational barriers, could act for the government of Brunei in investigating the dispersal of certain funds to companies possibly associated with Prince Jefri, when KPMG has undertaken work relating to these issues on instruction from Prince Jerfri. At first instance Pumfrey J granted an injunction on the basis that KPMG had not convinced the court that its arrangements would satisfactorily protect Prince Jefri's confidential information.[2] The court considered that KPMG in providing forensic services were in much the same position as a solicitor and accordingly a very high burden was upon them. Lightman J had adopted a similar stance in *Re Solicitors (A Firm)*.[3] The Court of Appeal disagreed with Pumfrey J and thought on the facts that there was no real danger of information leaking across the Chinese Wall and the matter was one for the court to take a balanced view on.[4] The House of Lords agreed with the court at first instance. It is interesting to note that the House of Lords emphasised that KPMG were under no fiduciary obligations to Prince Jefri as he had been a former client. The matter was therefore to be resolved purely on the issue of protection of confidential information. Prince Jefri's right to protection was unqualified. It was not an issue of balance and unless KPMG could persuade the court that there was no risk other than a fanciful one of disclosure, he was entitled to an injunction.[5] Lord Millett who delivered the leading speech attempted to set out principles of wider application than to the facts before the court. It is worth considering these here.

1   [1999] 2 AC 222.
2   (1999) BCLC 1.
3   [1997] Ch 1 and see also *Re Solicitors (A Firm)* [1992] QB 959.
4   (1999) BCLC 1.
5   (1999) 2 AC 222.

8.15   In circumstances where a person is in a fiduciary relationship with two clients at the same time he cannot discharge his duties of loyalty to both and he will be in a conflict of interest.[1] In such circumstances the issue is wider than that of the protection of confidential information. Where there is such a conflict the fiduciary must obtain the informed consent of both parties. However, Lord Millett considered that there are circumstances where the conflict is such that even written consent after full disclosure may not resolve the problem. Of course, if one of the fiduciary relationships ceases then the only issue will be protection of confidential information obtained during the currency of that relationship.[2] As we have seen, the duty of loyalty exists only during the currency of a fiduciary relationship except possibly where an opportunity to exploit it continues. This is similar to the situation of a director whose office ends. As there was in the *Jefri* case and also in other cases relating to solicitors, if there is confidential information the person seeking to enter into another relevant relationship must be able to show that there is no risk of this information being misused. While the courts in practice, if not in law, probably do adopt a higher standard in cases involving privileged information in the hands of lawyers,[3] the burden of showing that there is no real risk of leakage or misuse is a very exacting one. Of course, where it is possible to show that the information has been effectively isolated within a firm or company, the problem is not necessarily resolved. In many cases the business or professional adviser will have duties of care involving obligations to search out relevant information and use it for the benefit of other clients. While it has been accepted that in the discharge of such duties a fiduciary is under no obligation to acquire inside information,[4] it is not clear that it would have a defence to an action based on negligence.[5] Would it be acceptable to argue that the firm was not negligent because in its own commercial interests it had disabled those responsible for advising the relevant client from access to certain material information in its possession? Of course, this is not likely to be an appealing argument for most firms. It must be remembered that in many cases the action will be brought against the firm and not necessarily against individuals. Where the quality of advice is tested solely at the level it was in fact given, then it may be arguable that the individual professional could not reasonably be expected to have access to information that in any case had been acquired by the firm in confidential circumstances. The issue would be whether in the discharge of his duties the relevant professional adviser or manager should have acquired this or similar knowledge from another unobjectionable source? However, the courts have shown themselves to be relatively unsympathetic to banks and other financial institutions who for purely their own commercial reasons find themselves in a conflict of duties in money laundering cases.

1   *Bristol & West Building Society v Mothew* [1998] 1 Ch 1 and *Clark Boyce v Mouat* [1994] 1 AC 428.
2   Albeit a different issue, the court have held that an impression of impropriety will be enough to involve the 'no conflict rule,' see *Supasave Retail v Coward Chance (a firm) see Lee (David) & Co (Lincoln) Ltd v Coward Chance (a firm)* [1991] Ch 259, [1990] 3 WLR 1278, [1991] 1 All ER 668at 674, per Brown-Wilkinson VC.
3   Of course, information should be used only for the purposes for which it was given, *Barclays Bank Ltd v Quistclose Investments Ltd* [1970] AC 567. Furthermore, in certain cases it may not be appropriate to terminate the relationship, see *Young v Robinson Rhodes* [1999] 3 All ER 524.
4   See *Briggs v Gunner* (Unreported) Ch D 16 January 1979 discussed in B Rider *Insider Trading* (1983) Jordans, at 224.
5   See generally B Rider and TM Ashe *supra* at **8.13** n 1. See also *Jones v Canavan* [1972] 2 NSWLR 236 and *Daly v The Sydney Stock Exchange Ltd* (1986) 160 CLR 371.

CONTRACTING OUT

8.16   We have already raised the issue in the case of directors of companies seeking to redefine or exclude their fiduciary and other duties by contractual provisions.[1] Of course, in most situations involving activity in the financial services industry, there will be a contractual as well as fiduciary relationship. The terms of the relevant contract may well be pertinent in regard to many of the issues discussed in this book. We have already seen that contractual terms may well determine the scope of disclosure obligations there by having relevance in both the civil and the criminal law.[2] The parties may agree by contract to vary and inhibit the enforcement of other legal obligations including those arising by virtue of a fiduciary relationship. While responsibility for fraud and certain other criminal acts cannot be excluded by contractual terms, we have seen that the law is by no means certain. Much will depend upon a construction of the contractual terms. Obviously, the courts will be unsympathetic to those who seek to abuse their position or act unfairly. We have already seen that judges have indicated in certain cases a dislike for directors who seek to manipulate circumstances in furtherance of dishonest designs.[3] However, the courts must give effect to the clear and unambiguous intentions of the parties, determined objectively, unless such is contrary to statute or public policy. In *Clark Boyce v Mouat*[4] the Privy Council accepted that a solicitor could act for two parties with conflicting interests provided he had the informed consent of both. It is important to note, however, that the Board of the Privy Council were most concerned to determine exactly what the scope of the solicitor's duties were on the facts of the case. Lord Jauncey stated that 'when a client in full command of his faculties and apparently aware of what he is doing seeks the assistance of a solicitor in the carrying out of a particular transaction, that solicitor is under no duty whether before or after accepting those instructions to go beyond those instructions by proffering unsought advice on the wisdom of the transaction'. This is important in the context of fiduciaries operating in the financial sector. For example, absent a contractual provision it has been held that a stockbroker in the ordinary course of his business when instructed to execute a particular transaction is under no obligation to provide advice.[5] The express obligations imposed by a contract may not, however, be determinative. For example, additional contractual obligations may arise by implication or by virtue of a collateral contract. It is also the case that reasonable expectations may arise as a result of a course of dealing or the circumstances of the case. The obligations in the law of negligence[6] and equity are by no means confined within the precise terms of contract.

1   See **8.8**. Consideration also needs to be given to the general issues that arise when attempts are made to exclude or modify legal obligations by contract. In particular, section 3 of the Misrepresentation Act 1967 and the Unfair Terms in Consumer Contracts Regulations 1999 noting the Unfair Contract Terms Act 1977 excludes contracts relating to securities, may well be relevant and there are developed rules of construction which operate against the party seeking the benefit of the exclusion or limitation of liability. See *Cheshire, Fifoot and Furmston's Law of Contract* (Oxford 2007) at 202 *et seq*. It may also be relevant to consider pre-contractual negotiations in the context of the law of misrepresentation and as to whether other contractual obligations of a collateral nature have been entered into.

2   See **6.31** *et seq*.

3   See **8.9**.

4   [1994] 1 AC 428.

5   *Scheder & Co v Walton and Hemingway* (1910) 27 TLR 89. However, note in this case the client's instructions were unequivocal and irrespective of whether there is an obligation to proffer advice, if it is given it must be honest, see Allun KC at 89, accepted by Ridley J at 90. Furthermore, considerable caution needs to be exercised on the impact of obligations imposed by the FSA in regard to the conduct of business, particularly in regard to vulnerable investors.

6   In the law of negligence it is rarely true that the claimant will have contracted to have received the relevant advice. There may also be concurrent and overlapping duties in contract and tort, see *Pirelli General Cable Works Ltd v Oscar Faber & Partners* [1983] 2 AC 1, and for that matter in equity. It should be noted, however, the courts are reluctant to find duties to disclose information which would not otherwise require disclosure, see *Banque Financiere de la Cite SA v Westgate Insurance Co* (1991) 2 AC 249.

INFORMED CONSENT

8.17   There has been much discussion as to the adequacy of informed consent. In *Clarke Boyce* the Privy Council appear to accept that 'consent given in the knowledge that there is a conflict between the parties and that as a result the solicitor may be disabled from disclosing to each party the full knowledge which he possesses as to the transaction or may be disabled from giving advice to one party which conflicts with the interests of the other' is sufficient'.[1] The cases do indicate that where the fiduciary's conflict is as a result of a conflict with his own self-interest, the obligations to ensure proper understanding on the part of the client are somewhat more onerous.[2] Indeed, they are of the utmost good faith.[3] Disclosure must be full and complete as to the material facts and not serve merely as a warning to the client. Where the conflict arises between two or more clients, the law is not entirely certain as to exactly what needs to be disclosed. The better view is that it must be enough to allow those concerned to fully appreciate the risks. Of course, much will depend upon the circumstances and the status of the parties. Given that we are in the realm of fiduciary obligations, it is clear that the test will be subjective and take account of the circumstances and knowledge of the relevant parties. Thus, disclosure must be in a legal sense suitable to the parties. On the other hand, full disclosure might itself conflict with a specific obligation to one or more of the parties. For example, too much detail might involve a breach of confidence and even the disclosure as to the existence of a specific conflict or other party might prejudice a legitimate interest. In such cases, perhaps the fiduciary must just take the consequences of liability. As Donaldson J observed in *North and South Trust Company v Berkeley*, '... he cannot say to his principal "I have not discharged my duty to you because I owe a duty to another" '.[4] As Donaldson J emphasised, in such a case the fiduciary has to accept the 'consequences flowing from the unlawful nature' of the position in which he has deliberately got himself into, in most cases for financial reward! Of course, such strict principles do not sit well with the way in which business has traditionally been done in the City of London where the wearing of many hats has long been fashionable. The self-regulatory authorities and even the Securities and Investment Board took the view that these rules could be varied by practice and their own rules. The Financial Services Authority has been rather more circumspect, accepting that the law may only be changed by legislation specifically addressing the relevant issues.[5] Mere compliance with best City practice[6] or even non-statutory principles and rules will not protect a fiduciary who has breached his fundamental duty. As Donaldson J. pointed out, 'how do you train anyone to act properly in such a situation? What course of action can possibly be adopted which does not involve some breach of duty to one principal or the other? ... Neither skill nor honesty can reconcile the irreconcilable.'[7]

1   (1993) 4 All ER 268 Lord Jauncey at 273. Note that the FSA has expressed the view that reliance by a fiduciary on informed consent should be the last defence! See **8.21** *et seq.*
2   *New Zealand Society 'Oranje' v Kuys* [1973] 1 WLR 1126 and *Phipps v Boardman* [1967] 2 AC 46.
3   See **6.32**.
4   [1971] 1 All ER 980.
5   See *supra* **8.13** n 3.
6   See **8.19** below.
7   (1971) 1 All ER 980 at 991.

8.18   It has been argued that there are situations where it is reasonable to find that the parties, because of the circumstances or the nature of the business, can be taken to have given their consent to the conflict. In *Kelly v Cooper*[1] the

Privy Council accepted that an estate agent could act for a number of vendors and 'ring fence' the confidential information he received from each *vis a vis* other parties with admittedly competing interests. The Board considered that this was justified by the implication of a term in the relevant contracts and this determined the scope of the fiduciary obligations. The basis upon which the Privy Council found this implied term is not clear from their decision. In the *Jefri* case Lord Millett took the view that the Privy Council in Kelly based their opinion not so much on an implied term, but the deemed consent to a state of affairs on the part of the competing principals. Referring to firms of accountants engaged in audits for clients with possibly competing interests, Lord Millett stated 'their clients are taken to consent to their auditors acting for competing clients though they must of course keep confidential the information obtained from their respective clients'.[2] It would seem, however, that the courts require evidence that the relevant parties were aware of the conflicts and that such are common in the particular business or activity. While not entirely satisfactory, such a pragmatic approach has much to commend it.[3] Indeed, in Kelly their Lordships emphasised the advantage of such an approach, as a matter of expedience, in regard to stockbrokers with competing clients, who could not reasonably be expected to share inside information obtained in other capacities.[4]

1 [1993] AC 205.
2 [1999] 2 AC 222 at 235.
3 See B Rider 'The Fiduciary and the Frying Pan' (1978) *Conveyancer* 114 at 119.
4 [1993] AC 205 at 214.

8.19   The situation would therefore appear to be that provided the fiduciary can show that he has the informed consent of his clients, he will be at risk. The Courts will, however, be prepared to examine the scope of his contractual obligations and the terms, express or implied, might well fashion the extent of other obligations including those arising in equity. The basis upon which an implied term may be found, is not free from controversy and although there is no authority particularly in point, it has been argued that this may be as a result of an established trade practice.[1] Nonetheless, this would have to be something rather more than mere common practice.[2] The extent to which it is reasonable to infer a contractual agreement to reduce the expectations of a client on the basis of his knowledge of what takes place in a particular trade or business remains unclear. It is therefore perhaps better to take the approach that where certain practices, such as the acting for multiple clients, are well established and the client appreciates this, then consent may be inferred or deemed. On the basis of the knowledge that the client has of what goes on it is reasonable to assume he will not object! Indeed, to allow him so to do would be unconscionable. As Donaldson J stated in the *Berkeley* case, 'if X, a third party, knowing that A is the agent of P, the principal enters into an agreement with A involving duties which are inconsistent with those owed to P then in the absence of the fully informed consent of P, X acts at his peril'.[3] While this observation is in a somewhat different and perhaps easier context,[4] it does show that the courts have no sympathy with those who come into relationships in the knowledge that there are pre-existing obligations. Of course, much depends upon the degree of knowledge that the client has and the burden is on the fiduciary to ensure, in his own interests, that each client is aware of the circumstances.

1 See generally *Hutton v Warren* (1836) 1 M & W 466 and in particular Baron Parke at 475 and
   Cunliffe-Owen v Teather and Greenwood [1967] 3 All ER 561 (1967).
2 See **8.17** *supra* Lord Langdale MR in *Gillett v Peppercorne* (1840) 3 Beav 81 expressed the
   view that the fact that something might be 'every day practice in the City' did not necessarily
   mean it was not a fraud.

3   [1971] 1 All ER 993.
4   Of course, this approach as we have seen does not adequately address the situations where there
     are many potential principles with various expectations, perhaps changing over time. See in
     particular C Nakajima and E Sheffield at **8.13 n** 1.

A REAL CASE!

8.20   Having regard to the practical significance of many of the issues that
we have raised and the implications that such have for proper legal and
regulatory risk management, it is perhaps surprising that there is such a dearth
of directly relevant authority pertaining to the financial services sector. A recent
case[1] before the Federal Court of Australia has addressed many of the questions
that we have raised in this chapter. The case was brought by the Australian
Securities and Investments Commission against Citigroup Global Markets
Australia Ltd on the basis that Citigroup as an adviser to another company in the
context of a takeover – Toll Holdings Ltd, was in a fiduciary relationship and
was therefore obliged not to violate its duty of loyalty by virtue of undertaking
any activity which could amount to a conflict of interest. While Citigroup had
constructed a Chinese Wall, its own proprietary trading was characterised as
insider dealing. ASIC contended that to avoid allegations of breach of duty and
deception it was necessary for the bank to obtain the informed consent of Toll to
its own trading. The Commission maintained that the fiduciary relationship
arose from the contractual arrangement between the bank and Toll despite the
fact that Citigroup had inserted a term in the contract making it clear that the
bank was acting 'as an independent contractor and not in any other capacity
including as a fiduciary'. Jacobson J following other Australian cases took the
view that where a contractual and fiduciary relationship co-exist, the fiduciary
relationship must conform to the contractual terms.[2] He distinguished between
a pre-existing fiduciary relationship and one that comes about as a result of a
particular agreement of occurrence. In the later case the relevant contract or
agreement defines and determines to the scope of the fiduciary duties that arise.
With the exception of fraud and deliberate dereliction of duty, the court took the
view that all such duties were capable of being varied or excluded by the terms
of the contract.[3] As there was no pre-existing fiduciary relationship between the
parties, as there had been in for example some of the cases involving agents and
solicitors, the court doubted whether it was even necessary for the bank to
obtain the informed consent of Toll for its own share dealings. Jacobson J also
considered that given Toll's knowledge of the banks structure and operations
and its own sophistication, it had sufficient knowledge of the real possibility of
proprietary trading by Citigroup to amount to an informed consent. ASIC also
failed in its assertion that certain transactions amounted to inside information.
While the court considered that an un-communicated supposition could
constitute inside information within the relevant provision[4] it would not on the
facts have had the required material effect.[5] Furthermore, Jacobson J held that
the arrangements that the bank had put in place to reinforce its 'Chinese Wall'
were adequate within the statutory test.[6] He noted, however, that such
arrangements would not necessarily have addressed the conflict of interest had
one actually arisen. He referred to Lord Millett in the *Jefri* case where it was
emphasised that the efficacy of a Chinese Wall would depend upon the facts and
it being 'an established part of the organisational structure' and not created on
ad hoc basis.[7]

1   *Australian Securities and Investments Commission v Citigroup Global Markets Australia
     Pty Ltd* [2007] FCA 963.

2   *Hospital Products Ltd v US Surgical Corporation* (1984) 156 CLR 41 and *Breen v Williams* (1996) 186 CLR 71. See also *Chan v Zacharia* (1984) 154 CLR 178.
3   The Law Commission, see **8.13** n 3, has also adopted this view and was cited with approval by Jacobson J. However, on the older authorities the position is perhaps not as clear as it seems, see for example in regard to gross negligence *Ferguson v Paterson* [1900] AC 271 at 281 and *Re Poche* (1984) 6 DLR 40 at 55. We have already seen that the courts have been reluctant to allow directors to excuse themselves for self-dealing, see **8.9** at n 1.
4   See section 1043A of the Australian Corporations Act.
5   See section 1042D.
6   See sections 912A and 1043F.
7   (1999) 2 AC 222 at 239. Jacobson J also referred to Bryson J in *D & J Constructions Pty Ltd v Head & v Ors Trading as Clayton Utz* (1987) 9 NSWLR 118 at 123 where the practical efficacy of Chinese Walls was doubted. As we have seen the English courts have in practice been reluctant to accept that Chinese Walls actually do secure confidential information.

CONFLICTS, COMPLIANCE AND THE REGULATORY ENVIRONMENT

8.21

'In recent times it has become clear to us and other regulators around the world that the marketing of research to clients as being objective did not match reality. In particular, senior managers of firms did not, as they should have done, ensure that analysts producing this research were free from the influence of conflicting business interests in the production of research.'[1]

1   FSA Policy Statement 04/06, *Conflicts of Interest in Investment Research.*

8.22   The trading on price sensitive information relies on the exploitation of a conflict of interest. Furthermore, individuals and firms can use their position of conflict in a financial market to manipulate market trading. Section 147 of the Financial Services and Markets Act 2000 provides for the Financial Services Authority to make rules about the disclosure and use of information held by an authorised person.

8.23   In the early part of this decade, concern emerged in the US markets about the extent to which large regulated firms conducting and publishing research into securities might be able to exploit the impact that such research had in the market place for the benefit of their commercial relationship with the company. Although the US market conducted its own investigation into such activities, similar concerns about banking research activities extended to the UK markets and in 2004 the Financial Services Authority published its concerns in the form of a letter to all investment banking Chief Executives:[1]

'I am writing to remind you of your responsibility to implement appropriate processes and procedures for the effective risk management of conflicts of interest and risks arising from financing transactions. Where your business profile gives rise to these risks, you should expect to receive increasing scrutiny and challenge about current and developing practices from our supervisors in the coming months ...'

1   FSA 'Dear CEO letter 17 September 2004'. From Hector Sants, the then FSA Managing Director, Wholesale division. Many of the initiatives promoted by the FSA following this letter have since been modified by the provisions relating to conflicts management in the Markets in Financial Instruments Directive.

8.24   The FSA's 'Dear CEO letter' set out not only the basis for the FSA's regulatory concerns but also the conflict management controls that it expected banking organisations to have in place to deal with conflicts arising from research activities. In the letter the FSA addresses the point that in its view, the culture of an organisation is a key mitigating tool for the proper management of conflicts of interest and as is now so often the case, organisational culture is an essential element of compliance within an emerging Principles based system of regulation. The letter did, moreover, address specific issues expected of a firm's systems of conflicts management, providing in particular that investment banks' senior management should be fully engaged in conflict identification and management at their firms, take a holistic view of conflicts risk and conflict mitigation within the full range of business activities for which they are responsible, have some means of achieving a consistent treatment of conflicts of interest throughout their organisation, set out the type of mitigation they require for the different types of conflicts they have agreed to manage, and be getting management information on the extent and mitigation of conflicts of interest in their business in order to control their business effectively.

The FSA letter further announced that in future there would be increased regulatory activity resulting in the FSA reviewing the conflict management arrangements that firms had in place, in particular that senior management were taking full responsibility for transactions within the businesses for which they are responsible; the mechanisms designed to draw out information and analysis to permit decision-makers to reach appropriate decisions on risks; the need for a clear audit trail relating to the business intent of the transactions; the need for adequate disclosure and documentation; and the need for risk disclosures to recognise the possibility of the product being sold on to retail customers.

8.25   As can be seen from the FSA's work in investment research and conflicts management, it considers that the effective management of conflicts is a central regulatory control within the UK system of regulation, with regulatory standards being imposed through a combination of high level principles and detailed rules-based requirements.

8.26   Although the FSA has had in place since 2001 regulatory requirements imposing conflict management requirements on authorised firms, its regulation is now supported by conflict management obligations imposed on EU Member States competent authorities by the Markets In Financial Instruments Directive, (MiFID), which requires firms to identify and manage material conflicts of interest. We will consider further below the regulatory definition of material conflicts. While the conflict regulations within MiFID relate to an investment firm's general business operations, they do have a significant impact on how firms manage the conflicts present in the handling of price-sensitive information. It is important to remember that the current regulatory regime is concerned with the arrangements that firms have in place to manage conflicts of interest rather than seeking to prevent all conflicts from manifesting.

The FSA's rules on organisational systems and controls

8.27   UK regulation of conflicts management is established through a framework of rules specifically address at conflict situations and others addressing management systems and controls. The FSA places considerable importance on the need for authorised firms to have in place appropriate system and controls allowing the effective management of conflicts of interest. This can be illustrated by the obligations in the FSA high level principles for business, where Principle for Business 8 requires 'A firm must manage conflicts of interest fairly, both between itself and its customers and between a customer and another client.' Whereas High Level Principle 8 deals specifically with an obligation to manage conflicts of interest, other high level principles address conflicts management through obligations supporting the need to operate appropriate organisational systems and controls. For example High Level Principle 1 requires that 'A firm must conduct its business with integrity,' and High Level Principle 3 requires that, 'A firm must take reasonable care to organise and control its affairs responsibly and effectively, with adequate risk management systems.'

8.28   The FSA specific rules dealing with conflicts management are located in rules specifically addressed at firms' systems and controls obligations which are contained within the FSA sourcebook 'Senior Management Systems and Controls', (SYSC) and those rules governing the conduct of a firm's business set out within the FSA's 'Conduct of Business Sourcebook' (COBS). Moreover, the systems and controls rules are broken down between rules relating to all regulated firms that are targeted generally at fundamental systems of control and those applying only to firms to which MiFID relates and which set standards specifically for the management of conflicts of interest. A significant element of the FSA's rules in SYSC have been influenced by the Market in Financial Instruments Directive. MiFID Article 13 (3) provides an investment firm shall[1] maintain and operate effective organisational and administrative arrangements with a view to taking all reasonable steps designed to prevent conflicts of interest as defined in Article 18 from adversely affecting the interest of clients.[2]

1   In this context an Investment Firm is one that conducts business subject to the markets in the Financial Instruments Directive.
2   The definition of conflicts under MiFID is provided at **8.34** below.

8.29   The FSA rule at SYSC 3.1.1 R has general application and is used by the FSA to require systems of control that are appropriate to the individual business model and risks present within a firm's business model. While not directed specifically at conflicts management its coverage is broad enough to apply to standards of conflicts management. It provides: 'A firm must take reasonable care to establish and maintain such systems and controls as are appropriate to its business.' Guidance provided at SYSC 3.1.2 G[1] makes clear that the nature and extent of the systems and controls which a firm will need to maintain under SYSC 3.1.1 R will depend upon a variety of factors including:

(a)   the nature and scale and complexity of its business;
(b)   the diversity of its operations, including geographical diversity;
(c)   the volume and size of its transactions; and
(d)   the degree of risk associated with each area of its operation.

1   The FSA guidance at SYSC 3.2.3 G acknowledges the need for a firm's governing body to delegate its functions but that: 'When functions or tasks are delegated, ... appropriate safeguards should be put in place and that there should be arrangements to supervise delegation, and to monitor the discharge of delegates functions or tasks.'

8.30   The FSA rules on systems and controls also make specific general provision for compliance arrangements,[1] for MiFID firms that requirement is set out at SYSC 6.1.1R which requires that firms 'must establish, implement and maintain adequate policies and procedures sufficient to ensure compliance of the firm including its managers, employees and appointed representatives ... with its obligations under the regulatory system and for countering the risk that the firm might be used to further financial crime.' Undoubtedly there is overlap between the generic provisions with SYSC 3.1.1 and the special compliance arrangements within SYSC 6.1.1R. A more detailed analysis of the theory and regulation of compliance arrangements is provided at Chapter 12. However, in the context of conflicts of interest, we should in this Chapter, recognise firms' reliance on information barriers, commonly referred to as 'Chinese Walls', as a major control mechanism for the management of conflicts including the passage of price-sensitive information. In this context the effective control of price-sensitive information by way of a Chinese Wall preventing the flow of information from one part of a firm to another can act as a defence to criminal proceedings for misleading statements and practices under section 397(2) and (3) of the Act and Market Abuse under section 118. SYSC 10.2.2R is a control of information rule made under section 147 of the Act and recognises the role of the Chinese Wall. Before considering in more detail the provisions within SYSC 10.2.2R, it is useful to reflect on what the law says about the merits of Chinese Walls as an effective information barrier. The Law Commission's Consultation Paper on Fiduciary Duties and Regulatory Rules[2] (1992), considered the inherent features of a so called Chinese Wall and highlighted that to be considered effective it would normally involve some combination of the following organisational arrangements:

(a)   the physical separation of the various departments in order to insulate them from each other ...;

(b)   an educational programme ... to emphasis the importance of not improperly or inadvertently divulging confidential information;

(c)   strict and carefully defined procedures for dealing with a situation where it is felt that the wall should be crossed and the maintaining of proper records where this occurs;

(d)   monitoring by compliance officers of the effectiveness of the wall;

(e)   disciplinary sanctions where there has been a breach of the wall.

1   The general compliance obligation applying to Non-MiFID firms is set out at SYSC 3.2.6 R and provides 'A firm must take reasonable care to establish and maintain effective systems and controls for compliance with applicable requirements and standards under the regulatory system and for countering the risk that the firm might be used to further financial crime ...'

2   Consultation Paper on Fiduciary Duties and Regulatory Rules (1992) (Law Com No 124)

8.31   The role of the information barrier as a method for conflict management for a financial institution was also recognised in *Prince Jefri Bolkiah v KPMG*,[1] however while acknowledging the common usage of Chinese Walls, Lord Millett only considered such an arrangement as effective where it is an established part of a firms structure: '... Chinese Walls are widely used by financial institutions in the City of London and elsewhere. They are the favoured technique for managing the conflicts of interest which arise when financial business is carried on by a conglomerate ... In my opinion an effective Chinese Wall needs to be an established part of the organisational structure of the firm, not created ad hoc and dependent on the acceptance of evidence sworn for the purpose by members of staff engaged on the relevant work ...'

1   *Prince Jefri Bolkiah v KPMG* [1999] 1 All ER 517. See also **8.18** *supra*.

8.32   Moving forward to contemporary regulation, the FSA defines a Chinese Wall as 'an arrangement that requires information held by a person in the course of carrying on one part of its business to be withheld from, or not to be used for, persons with or for whom it acts in the course of carrying on another part of its business.' This definition is important for the purpose of SYSC 10.2.2R which recognises the role of a Chinese Wall both in terms of it forming part of an effective compliance arrangement, including that required in SYSC 10.1.7R, but also as an information barrier that will not give rise to attributions of knowledge by one side of a firm denied to them as a result of the barrier itself.[1] This later point is important in terms of demonstrating compliance with certain provisions of the rule book that apply to firms that 'act with knowledge' as without such recognition, one side of a firm denied information by its internal information barrier would nonetheless be treated for the purpose of regulatory compliance as if it had acted with knowledge of such information.

SYSC 10.2.2R provides that firm establishing and maintaining a Chinese Wall may:

(a)   withhold or not use the information held; and

(b)   for that purpose, permit persons employed in the first part of its business to withhold the information held from those employed in that other part of the business.

1   See SYSC 10.2.4R and guidance at SYSC 10.2.5G.

8.33   The provisions at SYSC 10 set out obligations addressing how firms are required to identify and manage conflicts of interest where a service is provided to clients in the course of carrying on regulated activities[1] or ancillary services.[2] MiFID Article 18(1), applied by FSA rules at SYSC 10.1.3R provides that investment firms must take all reasonable steps to identify conflicts of interest between themselves, including their managers, employees and tied agents, or any person directly or indirectly linked to them by control and their clients or between one client and another that arise in the course of providing any investments and ancillary services, or combinations thereof. SYSC 10.1.3, sets out the basic conflicts provision, providing that a common platform firm must take all reasonable steps to identify conflicts of interest between:

(1)   the firm including its managers, employees and appointed representatives, (or where applicable, tied agents) or any person directly or indirectly linked to them by control, and a client of the firm, or

(2)   one client of the firm and another client

that can arise or may arise in the course of the firm providing any service referred to in SYSC 10.1.1R.[3]

1   Those activities specified in Part II of the Regulated Activities Order (Specified Activities). This includes activities such as dealing in investments as principal or agent and arranging deals in investments.
2   Those services listed in Section B of Annex I to MiFID.
3   SYSC 10.1.1R provides that the rule in 10.1 apply to a common platform firm which provides services to its clients in the course of carrying on regulated activities or ancillary activities or providing ancillary services (but only where the ancillary services constitute MiFID business).

8.34   In the context of SYSC 10, the obligation to identify conflicts only arises, however, in relation to those conflicts that may give rise to a material risk of damage to the interests of either a client or the firm itself and provides that in identifying such conflicts, firms must take into account as a minimum the following matters, where the firm: (1) is likely to make a financial gain or avoid a financial loss at the expense of the client: (2) has an interest in the outcome of the service provided to the client or of a transaction carried out on behalf of the client, which is distinct from the client's interest in that outcome, (3) has a financial or other incentive to favour the interest of another client or group of clients over the interests of the client, (4) carries on the same business as the client, or (5) receives or will receive from a person other than the client, an inducement in relation to a service provided to the client, in the form of monies, goods or services, other than the standard commission or fee for that service. Recital 24 of the MiFID implementing directive makes clear that in those circumstances that give rise to a conflict of interest, it is not enough that the firm may gain a benefit if there is not also a possible disadvantage to a client, or that one client to whom the firm owes a duty may make a gain or avoid a loss without there being a possible accompanying loss to another such client. SYSC 10.1.6R requires that firms keep and regularly update a record of the kinds of service or activity carried out with or on behalf of the firm in which a conflict of interest gives rise entailing a material risk of disadvantage or damage to the interests of one or more clients which have arisen or may arise in the case of ongoing service activity.

Managing conflicts

8.35 SYSC 10.1.7R (applying MiFID Article 13(3) requires that a firm must maintain and operate effective organisational and administrative arrangements with a view to taking all reasonable steps to prevent conflicts of interest (as defined in SYSC 10.1.3 R, see **8.33** and **8.34** above) from constituting or giving rise to a material risk of damage to the interests of its clients. We have considered above the role of the Chinese Wall in a firm's compliance arrangements. Whilst much of the threat to possible insider trading and market abuse is manifested through misuse of confidential information, much of conflicts management is about ensuring that conflicts are effectively understood by the firm and the threats presented are appropriately controlled. As we have seen in the context of FSA rules at SYSC 3.1.1R the controls that might be relevant for one firm's business are not necessarily appropriate for another and it is for a firm to determine conflicts management arrangements that are appropriate for its business and the conflicts that might occur. SYSC 10.1.11 R, although in relation to conflicts policies, gives an indication of those matters that might be included within a firm's conflicts management arrangements. First, and consistent with the recognition of a firm's size and activities as in SYSC 3.1.1, it provides that the procedures should be designed to ensure that those engaged in different business activities involving a conflict of interest carry on those activities at a level of independence appropriate to the size and activities of the firm and of the group to which it belongs, and to the materiality of the risk of damage to the interests of clients. It further gives examples of the types of arrangements that might need to be present. In the context of Market Abuse it addresses information barriers, supervision and individuals' dual activities. With regard to information barriers[1] it provides that management procedures should include effective procedures to prevent or control the exchange of information between those engaged in activities involving a risk of a conflict of interest where the exchange of that information may harm the interests of one or more clients. Stressing the importance of supervision,[2] it requires the separate supervision of persons whose principal functions involve carrying out activities on behalf of, or providing services to, clients whose interests may conflict, or who otherwise represent different interests that may conflict, including those of the firm. In addressing the risk present when persons are able to exercise substantial control over a process, it requires measures to prevent or control the simultaneous or sequential involvement of a person in separate services or activities where such involvement may impair the proper management of conflicts of interest.[3]

---

1 SYSC 10.1.11 (2) (b) i.
2 SYSC 10.1.11 (2) (b) ii.
3 SYSC 10.1.11 (2) (b) v.

8.36 Where a firm is able to identify key and regular conflict situations from its business model, it would seem logical for it to have in place routine conflicts management arrangements to prevent damage to client interests. Firms, however, should not assume that freshly identified conflicts can always be appropriately managed by standardised arrangements and must be prepared to keep their conflicts management arrangements under regular review. It would be wrong, therefore to assume that conflicts management can be satisfied merely by information barriers. MiFID continues to promote regulation to deal with the inherent conflicts presented by firms' preparation if investment research and the FSA require at COBS 12.2.3 R that a firm ensure all of the measures for managing conflicts of interest in SYSC 10.1.11R are implemented in relation to the financial analysts involved in the production of investment research. Furthermore, the conflicts management arrangements in relation to investment research also seek to address many of the threats arising from the misuse of research material prior to its publication. In particular COBS 12.2.5 (1) limits pre-publication trading by providing that 'if a financial analyst or other relevant person has knowledge of the likely timing or content of investment research which is not publicly available or available to clients and cannot readily be inferred from information that is so available, that financial analyst or other relevant person must not undertake personal transactions or trade on behalf of any other person, including the firm ...',[1] and furthermore at 12.2.5 (2) personal trading must not take place contrary to the current research recommendations. Other restrictions on conflicts in investment research are designed to guard against manipulative behaviour that can arise from favourable treatment to issuers or inducements.

1 Trading as market maker in good faith and in the normal course of market making activity is permitted under SYSC 1.2.5 (1).

Disclosure of conflicts

8.37   Article 18 (2) and SYSC 10.1.8R make provision for disclosure of conflicts, providing that where organisational or administrative arrangements made by the investment firm in accordance with Article 13(3) to manage conflicts of interest are not sufficient to ensure, with reasonable confidence, that risks of damage to client interests will be prevented, the investment firm shall clearly disclose the general nature and/or sources of conflicts of interest to the client before undertaking business on its behalf. Where a disclosure is required it must be made in a durable medium; and include sufficient detail, taking into account the nature of the client, to enable that client to take an informed decision with respect to the service in the context of which the conflict of interest arises.[1] Guidance at SYSC 10.1.9 G makes clear that disclosure of conflicts cannot be used as a substitute for appropriate conflicts management and firms should aim to identify and manage the conflicts of interest arising in their various business under a comprehensive conflicts of interest policy. Indeed the FSA stresses at SYSC 10.1.9 G that an over-reliance on disclosure without adequate consideration as to how conflicts might be appropriately managed is not permitted.

1 See SYSC 10.1.8R (2) and Article 22(4) MiFID implementing Council Directive 2006/73/EC OJL241/26, implementing Directive 2004/39/EC as regards organisational requirements and operating conditions for investment firms and defined terms for the purpose of that Directive.

Maintaining and publishing a conflicts policy

8.38   Article 22(1) of MiFID's implementing Directive and SYSC 10.1.10R requires firms to establish, implement and maintain and set out in writing an effective conflicts of interest policy which is appropriate to the size and organisation of the firm and the nature, scale and complexity of its business. Furthermore the provision requires that where the firm is a member of a group, the policy must also take into account any circumstances, of which the firm is or should be aware, which may give rise to a conflict of interest arising as a result of the structure and business activities of other members of the group.

8.39   SYSC 10.1.11R (1), which adopts Article 22(2) and (3), sets out detailed provision for the content of firms' conflict policies, including provision that the policy must identify by reference to the specific services and activities carried out by or on behalf of the firm the circumstances which constitute or may give rise to a conflict of interest entailing a material risk of damage to the interests of its clients. It must also specify procedures to be followed and measures to be adopted in order to manage such conflicts. SYSC 10.1.11 R (2) adds further detail regarding the procedures and measures, including that the procedures must be designed to ensure that those engaged in different business activities involving a conflict of interest of the kind specified carry on those activities at a level of independence appropriate to the size and activities of the firm and to the materiality of the risk of damage to the interests of clients. A MiFID firm's[1] conflicts policy must be disclosed to retail clients[2] in good time before supplying services.[3] Although the policy only need be provided in summary form, where a client request it a firm is required to provide the client with further details regarding its conflicts policy.[4]

1   A non MiFID firm is required by COBS 6.1.4 R (8) b to disclose to its retail clients how and
    when a material interest or conflict of interest may or does arise and the manner in which the
    firm will ensure fair treatment of the client.
2   COBS 6.1.4R (8) and (9).
3   COBS 6.1.11R
4   COBS 6.1.4 R (9)

Chapter 9

FSA investigations

INTRODUCTION

9.1   In practice, the letter of the law alone is unlikely to influence behaviour or maintain consumer confidence. Consequently, the Financial Services and Markets Act 2000 ('FSMA 2000') underpins the substantive law of market misconduct with a wide range of investigation and enforcement powers.

9.2   Ms Melanie Johnson, the Economic Secretary to the Treasury, said of the powers of investigation:

> 'we make no apologies for wanting to be sure that investigations can take place as and when the circumstances suggest that they are needed. Nothing is gained by having a regulator that cannot respond quickly. Nothing is gained by encouraging wrongdoers to seek to prevent the launch of inquiries through procedural challenges in the courts'.[1]

Extensive powers of investigation were introduced in respect of all types of market misconduct (i.e. market abuse and the criminal offences of market manipulation and insider dealing). These powers of investigation are reinforced by a number of sanctions for failure to co-operate and comply (considered below). Furthermore, as explored in both this and the next chapters, the FSA is developing its use of its general investigation and enforcement powers to deal with market misconduct cases involving authorised persons. In such cases, the FSA is increasingly relying upon breaches of its High Level Principles instead of misconduct by reference to breaches of specific rules or statutory provisions.

1   Standing Committee A, 23 November 1999, column 887.

9.3   The FSA also has at its disposal a number of enforcement powers. The range of sanctions available in combating market abuse was one of the most fundamental innovations of the FSMA 2000, when introduced. The FSA may impose financial penalties and restitution orders administratively in all cases. Further, as regards authorised persons it may exercise its disciplinary powers. Those upon whom the FSA has imposed sanctions may then refer the matter to the Financial Services and Markets Tribunal ('FSMT'), run under the auspices of the Tribunal Service. The FSMT is central to preserving the right to a fair trial and correspondingly to the regime as a whole. The FSMT has to date been much more popular than the Financial Services Tribunal, which had only one referral since 1998.[1] The FSA also has power to apply to the civil courts for injunctions and restitution orders and request the court to impose a financial penalty.

Finally, the FSA has power to prosecute criminal offences of market misconduct. All these enforcement powers run in tandem with other regulatory provisions such as the City Code.

1   See the government's consultation paper 'Review of Tribunals'.

9.4   An effective and proportionate use of enforcement powers impacts considerably upon the FSA's ability to meets its Statutory Objectives.[1] There is a strong interconnection between the FSA's investigation and enforcement powers and effective prosecutions and regulatory proceedings. As a risk based regulator with limited resources, the FSA prioritises its resources towards the areas which pose the biggest threat to its Statutory Objectives and thus not every instance of potential market abuse or regulatory breach will result in an investigation or enforcement outcome. Such an approach very much supports the FSA's desire to achieve a balance between regulatory intervention and a regime that allows some risk to materialise. This approach is illustrated by the following comments by Kari Hale, the FSA's former Director of Finance, Strategy and Risk in a speech entitled 'Risk-based compliance for financial services' in which he stated,

> 'After all, most markets have some element of market failure. Often those who favour intervention argue that any market failure justifies intervention. But, the real test goes beyond that: there must be both market failure and the prospect that intervention will provide a net benefit. This involves recognising that regulatory intervention has a cost; and that regulatory intervention, like reliance on market operations, has a non-zero probability of failure …'[2]

1   Section 2(1) of the FSMA 2000 requires that the Financial Services Authority, in meeting its general regulatory function and in so far as is reasonably possible, meets the four Statutory Objectives of market confidence, public awareness, the protection of consumers and the reduction of financial crime. Indeed two of these Objectives affect specifically the Authority's work in both the Market Abuse regime and in addressing Insider Trading: the market confidence and reduction of financial crime objectives. The Market Confidence Objective is defined by section 3(1)–(2) of the FSMA as 'maintaining confidence in the financial system,' where 'financial system' is defined as including 'a) financial markets and exchanges; b) regulated activities; and c) other activities connected with financial markets and exchanges'. The reduction of financial crime objective is defined by section 6(1) of the FSMA as: 'reducing the extent to which it is possible for a business carried on by a regulated person, or in contravention of the general prohibition to be used for a purpose connected with a financial crime', where 'financial crime' is defined by section 6(3) of the FSMA as any offence involving 'fraud or dishonesty; misconduct in, or misuse of information relating to, a financial market; or handling the proceeds of crime.'

2   25 November 2004.

9.5   The FSA is also concerned to ensure that it conducts its investigations in accordance with principles of fairness, efficiency and transparency; in part its investigation procedures and policies are designed to meet such standards. The obligation to operate such standards in its investigations can be derived from a number of sources. Certainly the need to operate efficient investigation processes is an inherent part of the FSA's risk based approach to regulation, being in part derived from the its obligation under section 2(3) of the FSMA, that in performing its general functions[1] it must have regard to the need to use its resources in the most efficient and economic way. Furthermore, the close linkage between the FSA's investigation and enforcement processes can leave the standard of the FSA's investigation procedure open to close scrutiny during any reference of its decision making to the Financial Services and Markets Tribunal.[2] This in turn leads the FSA to have in place standards of fairness and transparency to ensure accuracy and consistency in its decision making.

Standards of fairness also arise from the obligation imposed on the FSA to separate its investigatory and enforcement decision making functions; this also limits the extent to which the FSA might otherwise act as legislator, investigator and enforcer of its own rules. In this regard, section 395 of the FSMA requires that the FSA procedures in relation to supervisory, warning and decision notices must be designed to secure that the decision which gives rise to the obligation to give any such notice is taken by a person not directly involved in establishing the evidence on which that decision is based.

1   The FSA's general functions are defined by section 2(4) of the FSMA as: (a) its function of making rules under this Act (considered as a whole); (b) its function of preparing and issuing codes under this Act (considered as a whole); (c) its functions in relation to the giving of general guidance (considered as a whole); and (d) its function of determining the general policy and principles by reference to which it performs particular functions.

2   See for example *Paul Davidson and Ashley Tatham v FSA* cost decision. Financial Services and Markets Tribunal, case number 40. Reported 11 October 2006. In which the the FSA's investigation report together with its decision making in the matter was considered by the Tribunal for the purpose of assessing whether the FSA had acted reasonably. It should be noted that the FSA's enforcement and decison making process applied during the Davidson and Tatham matter had been altered by the FSA as a result of its enforcement review published in July 2005.

9.6   To support the fairness and transparency of the FSA's investigations powers, the FSA publishes an enforcement guide (which we refer to throughout this chapter as 'EG'), which is available to the general public. In particular, the guide describes the FSA's approach to its information gathering powers and how it conducts investigations.[1] The EG is revised by the FSA from time to time and recourse should be made to the text of the guide itself at the relevant time.

1   The current Enforcement Guide took effect on 28 August 2007 and can be found on the FSA's website in the regulatory guide section of its handbook.

9.7   The FSA's enforcement guide expressly recognises the need for standards of fairness. While addressed at the FSA's wider enforcement process (integral parts of which are its powers of investigation) paragraph 2.2 of its enforcement guide recognises a number of principles underlying its approach to enforcement by making reference to the need to ensure fair treatment when exercising its enforcement powers as well as matters such as transparency and proportionality. A considerable element of fairness in any enforcement process is achieved through the consistency in which the process is applied, as without such standard the regime's application becomes considered as arbitrary by those caught up in the enforcement process. The need for consistency is also referred to by the FSA in paragraph 2.2 of the Enforcement Guide and, it is submitted, is central to the role played by the FSA's investigation process in meeting its Statutory Objectives.

INVESTIGATIONS AND INFORMATION GATHERING

The appointment of investigators

9.8   The Financial Services and Markets Act 2000 provides the FSA with a variety of formal powers of investigation enabling both the FSA and the Secretary of State to appoint persons to conduct an investigation where there are concerns regarding potential market abuse. The FSA has both 'general' powers of investigation under section 167 of the FSMA as well as the 'special' powers under section 168. The latter can be exercised in relation to specific concerns about insider trading and market abuse. In part, sections 167 and 168 draw a distinction between investigations into the conduct of authorised persons (section 167), and investigations relating to the conduct of unregulated persons (section 168 is unlimited as to the type of person in respect of whom such powers may be exercised). Further, section 168 allows the FSA to appoint an investigator where the FSA has identified a general concern that misconduct in the market may have occurred but where at the time of the appointment of investigators it has not identified specific persons to investigate. The FSA's enforcement guide at paragraphs 3.8 and 3.9 recognises that in cases where there is both a specific concern about potential market abuse and general concerns, then it may appoint investigators under both sections 167 and 168. Indeed, where an investigator appointed in relation to general matters under section 167 has identified specific concerns such as market abuse, the investigation may be extended to cover matters within section 168.

9.9   The FSA has indicated that it will normally use the power pursuant to section 168 where there are 'circumstances suggesting that contraventions or offences' set out in that section may have occurred [EG 3.8]. The power to appoint an investigator under section 167 is stated by the FSA to be more likely to be used where while although the circumstances 'do not suggest any specific breach or contravention covered by section 168', the FSA still has concerns relevant to the power under section 168 [EG 3.8]. Further, investigators may be appointed under both provisions [EG 3.9].

General power of appointment of investigator

9.10   Section 167 of the FSMA provides both the FSA and the Secretary of State with the power to appoint one or more competent persons to conduct an investigation on its behalf into the nature, conduct or state of the business of a recognised investment exchange or an authorised person or an appointed representative or any particular aspect of that business; or in relation to the ownership or control of a recognised investment exchange or an authorised person.[1] In general, the FSA's power under section 167 will be deployed in relation to concerns regarding allegations of breaches by authorised persons of the FSA's rules or principles. Further, given that the FSA will consider the extent of an authorised person's compliance with the FSA's rules on senior management systems and controls in the context of market abuse, the power of appointment under section 167 might be an appropriate response to such concerns.

1   An appointment under section 167 may also be exercised in relation to a former authorised person (or appointed representative) but only in relation to: business carried on at any time when he was an authorised person (or appointed representative); or the ownership or control of a former authorised person at any time when he was an authorised person (see section 167(4)).

9.11   While the main thrust of an investigation under section 167 is towards authorised persons, (as well as any of its appointed representatives or the authorised person's controllers) the appointed investigator may, if it is considered necessary for the purposes of his investigation, also investigate the business of a person who is or has at any relevant time been a member of the group of which the person under investigation is part or a partnership of which the person under investigation is a member (see section 167(2)). Section 167(5) defines 'business' in such a way as to allow the appointed person to conduct an investigation into any part of the business of the person under investigation, whether such business is regulated or not.

9.12   In order to make such an appointment, section 167(1) requires that there must be 'good reason for doing so'. It is submitted that such a threshold is easily achieved on the basis that the FSA is concerned that any breach of its rules or Principles that threatens its Statutory Objectives[1] requires only that the FSA is concerned to identify that there has been a breach of its rules or high level principles. Further, the FSA enforcement guide provides little assistance in determining how the FSA satisfies that it meets the threshold. Paragraph 2.10 of the guide merely states that before the FSA proceeds with an investigation it will satisfy itself there are grounds to investigate under the statutory provisions that give the FSA powers to appoint investigators. To assist its consideration of cases, the FSA utilises assessment criteria.[2] In framing the criteria, the FSA state[3] that they take into account the Statutory Objectives, its business priorities and other issues such as the response of the firm or individual to the issues being considered for referral.

1   See fn 1 in **9.4** above.
2   The criteria is currently published on the FSA's website under: Doing business with the FSA/being regulated/enforcing the law/enforcement referal criteria. The FSA apply additional criteria in cases of suspected market misconduct; these are set out in the FSA's Enforcement Manual Decision Procedure and Penalties manual and are referred to below at **9.60**.
3   See fn 2 and the FSA's introduction to the enforcement referral criteria.

9.13   The criteria include matters relevant to market abuse such as:

(a)   Has there been actual or potential consumer loss/detriment?
(b)   Is there evidence of financial crime or risk of financial crime?
(c)   Are there actions or potential breaches that could undermine public confidence in the orderliness of financial markets?
(d)   Is the issue to be referred relevant to an FSA strategic priority?
(e)   If the issue does not fall within an FSA strategic priority, does the conduct in question make the conduct particularly egregious and presenting a serious risk to one of the FSA's Objectives?

9.14   The powers of such an investigator are provided by section 171 of the FSMA 2000, save in the case of investigations into recognised investment exchanges which are expressly extended to include sections 172 and 173 (FSMA 2000, s 171(3A)).

Special powers to appoint investigators

9.15   The FSA and the Secretary of State both have power to appoint one or more investigators for particular cases 'if it appears that there are circumstances suggesting' that the criminal offences of market manipulation or insider dealing have been committed or where market abuse may have taken place.[1] These specific powers apply to all persons, irrespective of whether they are authorised. The powers of investigators appointed in these circumstances include those contained in sections 173 and 175 of the FSMA 2000. These powers are extensive and are easily triggered. Where an investigator considers that any person 'is or may be able to give information which is or may be relevant to the investigation' he may require such a person to attend before the investigator at a specified time and place and answer questions or otherwise to provide such information as the investigator may require for the purposes of the investigation.[2] Such power is extended, as considered at **9.36** *et seq*. In addition, the investigator may require such a person to produce at a specified time and place any specified documents or documents of a specified description 'which appear to the investigator to relate to any matter relevant to the investigation'.[3]

1   FSMA 2000, s 168.
2   FSMA 2000, s 173(2).
3   FSMA 2000, s 173(3).

9.16   Finally, the investigator may also require such a person to give the investigator all assistance in connection with the investigation 'which he is reasonably able to give'.[1] It is worth emphasising that the scope of those who may be subject to such powers is not expressly limited to the subject of the investigation.

1   FSMA 2000, s 173(4).

9.17   Considerable debate surrounded the low threshold for the appointment of an investigator under the power in section 168. Members of Standing Committee A argued that this drafting was an attempt by the government to immunise itself from judicial review.[1] The earlier text of the Financial Services and Markets Bill required 'reasonable grounds for suspecting that' certain circumstances existed before the power to appoint an investigator arose. The Economic Secretary said that this was 'an unnecessarily high test for launching an investigation' and justified the recast text on the basis of investigation powers contained in the Financial Services Act 1986, s 177 and the Companies Act 1985, s 432.[2]

1   Standing Committee A, 23 November 1999, column 879.
2   Standing Committee A, 23 November 1999, column 886.

9.18   It was noted in the course of debate regarding the investigation powers that the Secretary of State for Trade and Industry had retained the power to appoint an investigator for a number of reasons. First, such a body's expertise in company law investigations, secondly, the potential for a company investigation to move into one concerned with financial services issues and, finally, a fallback in the event of a conflict of interest with the FSA.[1]

1   Standing Committee A, 23 November 1999, column 862.

Other powers of investigation and information gathering

9.19   In addition to the powers of appointment noted above, there are wide powers to appoint investigators and gather information from both authorised persons and, in certain circumstances, non-regulated persons such as where there are suggestions that market abuse may have occurred (FSMA 2000, ss165–168 and 284).[1] These powers may be used alone or in combination depending upon the particular circumstances of the case, as confirmed in guidance given by the FSA [EG 3.1]. From a practical standpoint, the FSA's decision on which of its formal information gathering or investigation powers it might exercise will be determined by a number of factors including the extent to which it has available to it internal resource with the requisite skills, the extent to which it expects to receive co-operation from the person with whom it is making enquiries and whether or not such a person is or is not a regulated person. The FSA does, however, state in its enforcement guidance[2] that for reasons of fairness, transparency and efficiency, it will as a matter of standard practice generally use statutory powers to require the production of documents, the provision of information or the answering of questions in interview.

1   The FSA as the UK listing authority may also appoint investigators under section 97 of the FSMA 2000 where there are circumstances suggesting certain breaches of the listing rules.
2   FSA ENF Guide 2008, Chapter 4 Paragraph 4.8.

Information requests

9.20   The FSA will often find that as part of its routine supervisory work or as part of its enforcement activity that it is desirable to acquire information or documents from firms. There may be circumstances where the FSA considers it appropriate to obtain such material informally. Where information or documents are required as a precursor to a formal investigation, it is more common for the FSA to formalise information requests pursuant to powers under section 165 of the Act. Section 165 provides the FSA with power by notice in writing to require an authorised person[1] to provide specified information or documents, information or documents of a specified description (section 165(1)). Such information or documents must be provided by the end of such reasonable period as may be specified in the notice (section 165(2)). As an alternative to making a request for the delivery of information or documents under section 165(1), the FSA may under section 165(3) authorise one of its officers to require an authorised person without delay to provide to the officer in question specified information or documents or information or documents of a specified description. Although the terms of section 165 are widely drawn, allowing the FSA to seek disclosure of both specific and classes of information or documents, section 165 limits the FSA's powers by allowing it only to require production of such material when it is 'reasonably required in connection with the exercise by the FSA of functions conferred on it by the FSMA 2000'.

1   Section 165 powers may also be exercised against a person connected with an authorised person such as a member of the same group of companies as the authorised person, a controller of the authorised person, any other member of a partnership of which A is a member, or in relation to A, a person mentioned in Part I of Schedule 15. It may also be exercised against any person who was at any time an authorised person but who has ceased to be an authorised person (section 165(8)).

Reports from firms or skilled persons: introduction

9.21   Where the FSA identifies that a firm may have issues requiring more detailed assessment, it has to consider the availability of its own resources to undertake the necessary review. Where its concerns relate to matters where it has required or could require the provision of documents or information under section 165 to the Act, it can require a report from a skilled person to address the concerns it has relating to the firm.[1] In practice and in line with the FSA's policy on the use of skilled persons, skilled person reports are used in a variety of situations ranging from diagnostic purposes, enabling the FSA to identify, assess and measure risks; for monitoring purposes, enabling the tracking of how risk develops; as a preventative action to stop identified risks from crystallising or increasing; through to use as a remedial tool and responding to risks which have already been identified following an enforcement action.[2]

1   Section 166(1) of the FSMA.
2   See the FSA's policy on the use of Skilled Persons contained within the FSA's Handbook at SUP 5.31.

FSA policy on using skilled person reports

9.22   When making the decision to require a report by a skilled person, the FSA will have regard to all relevant factors at the firm and determines each case on its own merits and in reaching its decision will consider the objective of its enquiry and any legal and procedural issues surrounding the issues at the firm. It will have to consider the cost of using its own resource, against the cost to the firm flowing from the FSA requesting a skilled person report, which can (depending on the skilled person used) be considerable.[1] The FSA may conclude that the individual circumstances of the case may be better served by using alternative tools, including other statutory powers. The FSA's rules and guidance supporting the appointment of Skilled Persons is contained in its Supervision sourcebook, referred to as 'SUP'.

1   SUP 5.3.3G *et seq.*

9.23   One of the key drivers to the FSA decisions as to the use of a skilled person will be circumstances relating to the firm.[1] In particular, SUP 5.3.4G reveals that the FSA will be swayed by the attitude of the firm and its senior management to resolving and managing the identified risk or issues. If the firm and its senior management are cooperative, and the FSA has confidence about the firm's ability and willingness to provide the required information or an objective report, it is more likely to leave the firm to respond to the concerns itself. Where, however, the FSA is concerned that the subject matter of the enquiries or the report involves actual or potential misconduct, the issues might give rise to conflicts of interest, the firm lacks knowledge or expertise, or where there has been a history of similar issues within the firm which have not been dealt with in a timely fashion it is likely to conclude that it is inappropriate to rely on the firm's own enquiries into the matter and its objectives are better served through the involvement of a third party skilled person.

1   SUP 5.3.4G.

Appointment process

9.24   The skilled person appointment process is set out in section 166 to the Act and supported by provisions in the FSA handbook at SUP 5. The FSA is required to provide notice to the firm, which may be one of the following who is or was at the relevant time carrying on a business:[1]

(a)   an authorised person;
(b)   any other member of the authorised person's group;
(c)   a partnership of which the authorised person is a member;
(d)   a person who has at any relevant time been a person in a, b or c.

1   Section 166(2) of the FSMA.

9.25   In practice, the notice will set out the purpose of the report, its scope, the matters which the report is required to address, any other relevant matters and the timetable for its completion. The notice will also set out requirements as to the report's format. Section 166(3) permits the FSA to require the report to be in such form as the FSA may specify. It is usual for the FSA, prior to formally giving the written notice, to meet the firm to discuss its decision to require a report by a skilled person, the scope of the report, who should be appointed as the skilled person and the likely cost. This sometimes can present both the firm in question and the FSA with an opportunity to discuss whether there might be a more appropriate means of obtaining the information the FSA requires.

9.26   Section 166(4) of the Act requires that the skilled person is nominated or approved by the FSA and must have the necessary skills to report on the matter concerned. The skilled person appointment is the responsibility of the firm and it will be the firm that contracts with the skilled person for the commission of the report as well as the payment of their professional fees. The FSA will, however, need to be satisfied that the skilled person possesses the necessary skills to undertake the work required. The FSA state[1] that most likely a skilled person will be an accountant, lawyer, actuary or other person with relevant business, technical or technological skills. When the FSA determines whether to nominate or approve the skilled person's appointment it will consider:[2]

(1)   the skills necessary to make a report on the matter concerned;

(2)   the ability to complete the report within the time expected;

(3)   any relevant specialised knowledge, for instance of the firm in question, the type of business carried on by the firm, or the matter to be reported on;

(4)   any professional difficulty or potential conflict of interest in reviewing the matters to be reported on, for instance because the matters to be reported on may involve questions reflecting on the quality or reliability of work previously carried out by the proposed skilled person; and

(5)   whether the skilled person has enough detachment, bearing in mind the closeness of an existing professional or commercial relationship, to give an objective opinion on matters.

1   SUP 5.4.7G.
2   SUP 5.4.8G.

9.27   The firm's contract with the skilled person is governed by SUP 5.5.1R. The FSA require that the contract contain key provisions relating to the role of the skilled person as well as the firm. The contract must be governed by the laws of a part of the United Kingdom and overall must operate to give effect to the reporting requirements set out in the section 166(1) notice.

9.28   In respect of the skilled person SUP 5.5.1R specifies that the contract must:

(1)   require and permit the skilled person during and after the course of his/her appointment:

    (a) to cooperate with the FSA in the discharge of its functions; and

    (b) to communicate to the FSA information on, or his/her opinion on, matters of which he/she has, or had, become aware in his/her capacity as skilled person reporting on the firm in the following circumstances:

        (i)   where he/she reasonably believes that, as regards the firm concerned; there is or has been, or may be or may have been, a contravention of any relevant requirement that applies to the firm concerned; and that the contravention may be of material significance to the FSA in determining whether to exercise, in relation to the firm concerned, any functions conferred on the FSA by or under any provision of the Act other than Part VI. (Official Listing); or

        (ii) that he/she reasonably believes that the information on, or his/her opinion on, those matters may be of material significance to the FSA in determining whether the firm concerned satisfies and will continue to satisfy the threshold conditions; or

        (iii) he/she reasonably believes that the firm is not, may not be or may cease to be a going concern;

(2)   require the preparation of a report, as notified to the firm by the FSA, within the time specified by the FSA; and

(3)   waive any duty of confidentiality owed by the skilled person to the firm which might limit the provision of information or opinion by that skilled person to the FSA in accordance with (1) or (2).

9.29   In respect of the firm and the contract generally the contract must expressly provide:[1]

(1)   that the FSA has a right to enforce the provisions included in the contract relating to the role of the skilled person in SUP 5.5.1R and other general contractual requirements in SUP 5.5.5R (2);

(2)   that, in proceedings brought by the FSA for such enforcement, the skilled person is not to have available by way of defence, set-off or counterclaim any matter that is not relevant to those provisions;

(3)   (if the contract includes an arbitration agreement) that the FSA is not, in exercising the right in (a), to be treated as a party to, or bound by, the arbitration agreement; and

(4)   that the SUP provisions included in the contract are irrevocable and may not be varied or rescinded without the FSA's consent.

SUP 5.5.5R also requires that the skilled person contract cannot be varied or rescinded in such a way as to extinguish or alter the provisions referred to in SUP.

1   SUP 5.5.5R.

Preparation and delivery of the report

9.30   The FSA's section 166(1) notice will normally specify a time limit within which the skilled person is to deliver the report and the skilled person should take reasonable steps to achieve delivery by that time. Situations may arise of course that frustrate and delay the preparation or delivery of the report. The FSA will expect the skilled person to raise these and discuss them as they arise.[1] During the preparation of the report, particularly where difficulties might arise because of matters such as: complexity; the timescale for the report is lengthy or where serious issues have arisen, the FSA will expect there to be discussion with the skilled person and the authorised firm in question about the report progress and matters relevant to it. Once the report is finalised the FSA will usually wish to meet with the skilled person to discuss the report's findings. In most cases this meeting will involve senior management from the firm in question, although the FSA may decide to exclude the firm.

1   See SUP 5.4.12G.

Consequences for firms of skilled person report

9.31   The costs incurred by firms having to instruct skilled persons is often far in excess of the cost of deploying their own staff to undertake the same review. Firms subject to skilled persons' work often experience a major disruption to the operation of their business as the skilled person's review work progresses. Senior management often find they are required to manage and direct the skilled person's staff as well as attend for interview and respond to enquiries relating to the matter under review. SUP 5.5.9R requires that the firm must provide all reasonable cooperation to the skilled person. Ultimately the skilled person's report is to be submitted to the FSA and although most skilled persons will provide the firm and its management with an opportunity to comment on the report, the extent to which the firm is able to influence the report content is limited as the fundamental views and findings expressed in the report are to be those of the skilled person and not the firm.[1] Inevitably, any part of a firm's business operation that is subjected to scrutiny will display weaknesses. Indeed, where the FSA has identified issues or risk within a firm, the scrutiny of the skilled person is more likely to confirm the FSA's concerns.

1   See for example SUP 5.5.1R.

Voluntary production and the obligation to be open and honest with the FSA

9.32   The FSA high level Principle 11 (and Principle 4 of the Approved Persons Code for Approved Persons) reflects the importance placed on openness and cooperation between the regulated community and the FSA. The relationship between the FSA and the firms it regulates is intended to be an open and cooperative one. The regulatory system demands that firms take responsibility for their own standards of compliance with FSA rules extending to cooperating with the FSA during its supervisory activities as well as proactively drawing to the FSA's attention material failures within their business. Principle 11 is drafted generally and talks in terms of disclosures of anything of which the FSA would reasonably expect notice, providing that 'A firm must deal with its regulators in an open and cooperative way, and must disclose to the FSA appropriately anything relating to the firm of which the FSA would reasonably expect notice.' Principle 11 is widely drawn, and provides the FSA with sufficient scope to undertake enquiries into the conduct of the firm, expecting the firm's full co-operation. Indeed compliance with Principle 11 will require firms to proactively disclose information, including that which might be prejudicial to the firm's regulatory status, in advance of any formal investigation by the FSA and where such disclosure might be the first occasion that the FSA becomes aware of any regulatory breach. Although Principle 11 imposes upon authorised firms and approved persons a positive obligation to be open and co-operative, there may be occasion when the FSA will, during an investigation, rely on the duty imposed by the high level principle in an attempt to secure disclosure of information or documents without making a formal request under the FSMA. At paragraph 4.9 of its Enforcement Guide, the FSA states that in such circumstances it will make it clear to the person concerned whether it requires them to produce information or answer questions under the FSMA or whether the person is being asked to provide information on a voluntary basis.

9.33   Furthermore, there are occasions when the FSA will rely on the voluntary disclosure of information by non-regulated persons, such as those that might hold information relevant to a market abuse enquiry. At paragraph 4.8 of its enforcement guide, the FSA anticipates seeking information on a voluntary basis in the case of victims of an alleged fraud or misconduct, but also indicates that it might be appropriate to seek voluntary disclosure from suspects in criminal or market abuse investigations, albeit that the interview might be undertaken under caution.

Scoping discussions

9.34   Close to the start of the investigation, the FSA will generally attempt to provide the firm or individuals concerned in the investigation with an indication of the nature of and reasons for its concerns and the scope of the investigation. Such a scoping discussion will generally take place in a meeting between the FSA investigator, its supervisor, and representatives of the firm as well as any individuals that might be under investigation. Thereafter it is usually unlikely that an authorised firm's FSA supervisor will continue to have involvement in any investigation ensuring a clear distinction between the FSA's investigation and supervision activity. The FSA does nonetheless recognise the benefit in the investigation team having access to supervisory knowledge about the firm or any individuals that has been developed by the supervisor and at EG 4.14 the FSA sets out a policy on the provision of such supervisory expertise during an investigation. The FSA will in particular use the scoping discussion to provide an indication of the documents and individuals it will need access to and how the investigation is likely to proceed. The FSA provides some guidance to the role of scoping meetings within EG 4.12–4.13, but does make it clear that there is, however, a limit as to how specific the FSA can be about the nature of its concerns in the early stages of an investigation.

Time frame for responding to information and document requirements

9.35 The FSA expects responses to information and document requests to be made in a timely manner and that any appropriate deadlines are met. A failure to meet any such deadlines can expose those concerned to investigation or regulatory sanctions (these are discussed in further detail below). Investigations into complex matters, can however, give rise to practical concerns affecting the identification and delivery of information and documents and it is not unusual, providing that there is sufficient time within the FSA's investigation timetable, for the FSA to issue a draft information or document request allowing for comment on the practicalities of meeting the request, by the proposed deadline. Once the FSA has considered such comments it will duly confirm or amend the request and thereafter, save where there are compelling reasons the FSA will not usually agree to an extension of time for complying with the request.

Extended production powers, lawyers and bankers

9.36 The power to require the production of documents is extended by section 175 of the FSMA 2000 to include documents from a third person with possession of the same. The person to whom the document is produced may take copies or extracts from the document or require the person producing the document or any 'relevant person' to provide an explanation of it. The FSMA 2000, s 175(3) provides that if a person who is required to produce a document fails to do so, the FSA or an investigator may require him to state, to the best of his knowledge and belief, where the document is, no doubt with a view to an application for a search order pursuant to the FSMA 2000, s 176. The apparent scope of such power is tempered by the following specific limitations.

9.37 A lawyer may be required by an investigator to furnish the name and address of his client and to this extent the law goes beyond the Financial Services Act 1986, s 177.[1] However, legal professional privilege is preserved, as it was under the FSA 1986, s 177(7). The FSMA 2000, s 413(1) provides that a person may not be required under the FSMA 2000 to produce, disclose or permit the inspection of 'protected items'.[2] 'Protected items' are defined by section 413(3) and include a variety of communications between a professional legal advisor and his client. However, an item may not attract such protection if it is held with the intention of furthering a criminal purpose.[3] It should also be noted that where a person voluntarily discloses documents that benefit from legal professional privilege, such privilege may be waived unless the person making disclosure makes clear that it is waived for limited purposes.[4]

1 FSMA 2000, s 175(4).
2 FSMA 2000, s 413(1).
3 FSMA 2000, s 413(4).
4 As recognised by Standing Committee A, 7 December 1999.

9.38 While the obligation of confidence of those carrying on the business of banking is recognised at first, further consideration reveals that the powers of the investigators as regards bankers are extensive and go beyond the FSA 1986, s 177. Disclosure is not limited to circumstances in which the person owed the obligation of confidence consents. Pursuant to the FSMA 2000, s 175(5), disclosure may also be required where the person to whom the obligation of confidence is owed is the person under investigation or a member of that person's group or the banker himself or a member of that person's group is under investigation. The former appears to render the notion of banker's confidence virtually redundant in this context. However, given that the key evidence of market misconduct may lie in a person's bank account, such step is clearly significant to making powers of investigation effective.

Interviews

9.39 As noted above, the investigator has power to compel an interview whether appointed under sections 167 or 168. The FSA has indicated that it will not always use its statutory powers to require individuals to be interviewed and where appropriate will seek an interview on a voluntary basis.[1]

1 EG 4.8.

Use of statements obtained in investigations

Compulsory interviews

9.40 The general principle is that statements made to investigators pursuant to any of the requirements of sections 171, 172, 173 or 175 are admissible in evidence in 'any' proceedings, subject to principles of admissibility (see section 174(1) of the FSMA 2000). However and importantly, in most criminal proceedings and in 'proceedings in relation to action to be taken' against that person to impose penalties in cases of market abuse (pursuant to section 123 of the FSMA 2000), there is very little scope to introduce such statements. In particular, no evidence relating to that statement may be adduced and no question relating to it may be asked by the prosecution or (as appropriate) the FSA, unless evidence relating to it is adduced, or a question relating to it is asked, in the proceedings by or on behalf of that person (section 174(2) of the FSMA 2000).

9.41 This may be contrasted with the FSA 1986, s 177(6) which specifically provided that statements made to investigators could be used in evidence against such person. This change of approach probably derives from the criticism that without such provision the legislation was contrary to art 6 of the European Convention on Human Rights.[1]

1 See the joint opinion of Lord Lester of Herne Hill QC and Javan Herberg at Annex C of the Joint Committee on Financial Services and Markets First Report.

Voluntary interviews

9.42 However, different principles are likely to apply where a statement is made voluntarily. Such statements would not attract the protection from admissibility afforded by the FSMA 2000, s 174(2) as the decision of the European Court of Human Rights ('ECHR') in *Staines v United Kingdom*[1] illustrates. The applicant (who was tried in connection with insider dealing) had first given voluntary statements and then attended a formal interview where she gave evidence under oath. The prosecution later made use of the statements that she had given under compulsion. She objected on the basis that her right to a fair trial had been breached. The ECHR distinguished the renowned case of *Saunders v United Kingdom*[2] on the facts in part because the statement in the voluntary interview did not depart from the compulsory.

1　(16 May 2000, unreported).
2　(1997) 23 EHRR 313.

9.43 This distinction may account for the FSA's stated policy to prefer to question on a voluntary basis, possibly under caution, for suspects or possible suspects in criminal or market abuse investigations (EG 4.8). The FSA's guidance notes that in these circumstances 'the interviewee does not have to answer, but if they do those answers may be used in subsequent proceedings, including market abuse proceedings' (EG 4.8). However, the FSA also warns that 'an adverse inference may be drawn from the failure to attend a voluntary interview, or a refusal to answer any question at such an interview' [EG 4.19]. Irrespective of whether the interview is voluntary or under compulsion, those attending are entitled to be accompanied by a legal advisor if they wish (EG 4.20).

NOTIFICATION OF THE INVESTIGATION

9.44 There is no statutory obligation to give a person under investigation for market abuse or certain other misconduct outlined in section 168(2) written notice of such investigation.[1] This may be justified on the basis that many of the enforcement powers such as applications to freeze assets where there is a risk of dissipation of assets would be undermined by early notification of investigation. Indeed, at the time of an appointment of an investigator under section 168 for the purpose of investigating allegations of market abuse, the FSA may not be aware of any specific target of its investigation, thus making notification impossible. Nonetheless, in such circumstances, the FSA may consider it appropriate to publicise that an investigation has been commenced. For example during the difficult market conditions in 2008, the FSA announced publicly on 19 March 2008 that it had begun an investigation into potential market abuse following short selling of shares in HBOS.[2]

1　FSMA 2000, s 170(2) and (3).
2　See FSA press release 026/2008 19 March 2008.

9.45 The FSA has, however, indicated that it will notify those under investigation once it proceeds to exercise its statutory powers to require information from them, unless this would prejudice the FSA's ability to conduct the investigation effectively.[1] Similarly, the FSA will provide an indication of the nature and subject matter of the FSA's investigations to those who are required to provide information to assist with the investigation where the identity of the perpetrator may not be known or where the investigator is looking at market circumstances rather than a particular person.[2] In response to concerns raised following CP 65, the FSA gave guidance as to the circumstances in which it would give notice of the termination of an investigation. The current stated guidance is that where the FSA has given a person written notice that it has appointed an investigator and later decides to discontinue the investigation without present intention to take further action, it will confirm such decision where it considers it appropriate to do so bearing in mind the circumstances of the case [EG 4.6].

1   EG 4.3.
2   EG 4.4.

9.46   By contrast, where an investigator is appointed pursuant to the more general powers in section 167, considered above, the FSA must give written notice of the appointment of an investigator to the person who is subject to the investigation (section 170(2) of the FSMA). In such a case, if the scope or conduct of an investigation changes and in the opinion of the FSA the person subject to investigation is likely to be significantly prejudiced by not being made aware of it, the FSA must give that person written notice of the change.[1]

1   FSMA 2000, s 170(9).

9.47   Notwithstanding that notice has not formally been given, a person may know or suspect that an investigation is being or is likely to be conducted by the FSA. If such a person falsifies, conceals, destroys or otherwise disposes of a document which he/she knows or suspects is, or would be, relevant to the investigation or causes or permits the falsification, concealment, destruction or disposal of such a document, he/she is guilty of an offence unless he/she shows that he/she had no intention of concealing facts disclosed by the documents from the investigator.[1] Further sanctions underpinning the effectiveness of investigations are considered at **9.54** *et seq* below.

1   FSMA 2000, s 177(3).

SPECIAL CASES OF INVESTIGATION

Investigations into collective investment schemes

9.48   Part XVII of the Act makes special provision for the authorisation, regulation and control of Collective Investment Schemes. Section 284 specifically provides for the appointment of investigators and conduct of investigations into the affairs of: (i) an authorised unit trust scheme or its manager or trustee, (ii) a recognised scheme or (iii) certain other collective investment schemes or operators, trustees or depositories, if it appears to the FSA that it is in the interest of the participants or potential participants of the schemes to do so or that the matter is of public concern. Once appointed, the investigator under section 284 may, where it is considered necessary for the purpose of the investigation, extend the investigation to cover other persons as well as other collective investment schemes for which the manager, trustee, operator or depository also acts in that capacity. Section 284(3) provides the appointed investigator with power to gather information and documents relevant to the investigation from any person who is or may be able to give information which is relevant to the investigation and imposes on that person a duty to comply with such a request. Where the collective investment scheme manager, trustee, operator or depository is also an authorised person, then from a practical point of view there seems little distinction between the powers of investigation contained within section 284 and those within sections 165 and

167. Nonetheless the main purpose of the powers within section 284 would seem to be those that can be targeted towards the affairs of the collective investment scheme itself, which is not an authorised person and would thus not be directly subject to the information gathering and powers of investigation within sections 165 and 167.

Investigations to assist overseas authorities

9.49 Globalisation in the financial services industry has led to a proliferation of firms conducting investment business in countries beyond that in which their main or head office is based. This is particularly evident in the United Kingdom where overseas investment businesses have established business operations to facilitate international trading activities as well as to take advantage of the UK domestic market. Although some of these businesses might have obtained authorisation from the FSA to conduct their UK investment business, that business might be so closely aligned to its international parent that it is used to process transactions impacting upon another jurisdiction's regulatory regimes or in the case of the European Union is permitted to conduct its business in another European Member State. Such business structures can impose challenges for international regulatory investigations although section 169 of FSMA allows in certain circumstances for the FSA to support an investigation of an overseas regulator, by either exercising its information gathering powers under section 165 or appointing a competent person to carry out an investigation. Indeed section 169(7) goes as far as allowing the FSA to direct that the investigator permit a representative of the overseas regulator to attend and take part in any interview, which is being conducted as part of the investigation. Section 169 does not however impose upon the FSA a strict obligation of support, but rather allows the FSA to determine, based on a number of issues, whether or not to exercise its investigative powers. However, it need not consider such matters where it considers it necessary to exercise its investigation powers in order to comply with a European Community obligation. The provision within section 169 also needs to be considered in the context of the FSA duty of co-operation under section 354 which extends to overseas persons exercising functions similar to the FSA or in relation to the prevention and detection of financial crime. The FSA makes clear at paragraph 1.2 of its enforcement guide that it views co-operation with its overseas counterparts as an essential part of its regulatory functions, even to the extent that it has published at Chapter 7 of its Decision Procedures and Policy manual a policy statement dealing with interviews that may be attended by representatives of overseas regulators.

Interaction with other investigatory authorities

9.50 In matters involving serious allegations of financial crime or misconduct it is not uncommon for the matters under investigation to fall within the jurisdiction of a number of other UK authorities. In particular, allegations of market abuse might also fall within the jurisdiction of the enforcement division of the investment exchange on which the trading activity took place. In such circumstances the FSA might consider it appropriate to refer some of the issues to that exchange for consideration, refer the matter when it appears that the exchange is better placed to take action or investigate and perhaps ultimately take action in parallel with the exchange. In taking such a decision the FSA practice, confirmed at EG 2.15, is to consider the extent to which the relevant exchange has adequate and appropriate powers to investigate and deal with a matter itself.

9.51   The FSA has established guidelines set out in its enforcement guide as well as at DEPP 6.2.19 G to DEPP 6.2.28 G. These set out a framework for the liaison and co-operation between it and certain other UK authorities where each have an interest in investigating or prosecuting any aspect of a matter or where a rule breach might also result in action by other domestic or overseas regulatory authorities or enforcement agencies. That guidance at EG annex 2 provides in particular some broad principles on matters such as how they can determine which agency should investigate a particular case; co-operation where more than one agency is investigating a matter; preventing undue duplication of effort, and preventing unfair treatment of investigation subjects because of the unwarranted involvement of more than one agency.

CONFIDENTIALITY

9.52   In general, the FSA must not disclose 'confidential information', which includes information received by the FSA or Secretary of State during an investigation, unless the source of the information and, if different, the person to whom it relates, consents.[1] Disclosure of such information is a criminal offence (FSMA 2000, s 352). One of the characteristics of 'confidential information' for these purposes is information relating to the 'business or other affairs of any person' (FSMA 2000, s 348(2)). It should also be noted that a person obtaining 'confidential information' directly or indirectly from the FSA is also subject to these restrictions (s 348(1)).

1   FSMA 2000, s 348.

9.53   There are, however, a wide number of exceptions to this starting point. In particular, there are a range of circumstances involving 'the carrying out of a public function', both in this jurisdiction and overseas in which such information may be disclosed (FSMA 2000, s 349). Significant detail is given in the now much amended Financial Services and Markets Act 2000 (Disclosure of Confidential Information) Regulations 2001 [SI 2001/2188].

1   FSMA 2000, s 349.

ENFORCEMENT OF INVESTIGATIONS

Enforcement of investigations (including the responsibility of senior management)

9.54   In practice, senior management of authorised firms under investigation will usually be those given responsibility for ensuring that the firm meets the obligations imposed by the relevant information gathering or investigation notice. A failure to meet the specified obligations might result in the FSA seeking to enforce the requirements in the statutory notice through the investigatory enforcement powers within the FSMA 2000. Furthermore, a failure to comply with an information gathering or investigation notice can also expose the firm or its senior management to further disciplinary action including criminal prosecution (some of the offences are considered further below). It is essential that senior management ensure that they analyse and understand the precise terms of any statutory notice both in terms of any timescales stipulated for responding as well as its scope such as information or document requested or the areas that will be investigated. Where the terms of the notice are unclear, senior management should ensure that they promptly seek clarification from the FSA.

9.55 The FSMA 2000, s 177 creates a number of sanctions that reinforce the powers of the investigators. Each of these can be applied to both the person under investigation as well as any person that becomes in anyway involved in the course of the investigation. These include:

(a) being dealt with by the High Court (or the Court of Session in Scotland) as if in contempt of court, if the court is satisfied that such a person failed without reasonable excuse to comply with a requirement imposed upon him/her by the FSMA 2000, Pt XI;

(b) the criminal offence relating to falsification, concealment or destruction of documents which he/she knows or suspects are or would be relevant to such an investigation; and

(c) criminal offences in respect of the provision or reckless provision of false or misleading information.

9.56 Further, the FSA, the Secretary of State or the investigator may apply to a justice of the peace for a warrant, authorising a police constable amongst other things to enter and search premises specified in the warrant and to take possession of documents or information appearing to be documents or information of a kind in respect of which the warrant was issued (FSMA 2000, s 176). The FSA or Secretary of State or investigator must give or arrange on their behalf for information to be given to the magistrate on oath in order to satisfy the magistrate that the prescribed conditions for a search and seizure order are satisfied.[1] The conditions to be satisfied are wide ranging and relate not only to information concerning documents that have been withheld, but also, in the case of an authorised person, to documents or information which could be the subject of an 'information requirement' (defined by FSMA 2000, s 176(10)) in circumstances where such a requirement would not be complied with or the documents or information would be removed, tampered with or destroyed.[2]

1   FSMA 2000, s 176(1).
2   FSMA 2000, s 176(2), (3) and (4).
3   FSMA 2000, s 177(6).

Non-statutory routes to enforcement

9.57 We have discussed previously circumstances where the FSA might expect voluntary disclosure of information and considered the obligations to be open and co-operative with the FSA that are imposed upon authorised firms under High Level Principle 11 and Approved Persons under Principle 4 of the Approved Persons Code. Such an obligation might be relied upon by the FSA in an attempt to secure the disclosure of information without the need for it to rely on the information gathering powers in the Act. The obligations within those principles might also be used by the FSA as a method of enforcing its investigatory powers against authorised or approved persons as an alternative to the sanctions contained within section 177. The FSA indicates at EG 4.11 that a failure to comply with the exercise of the FSA's statutory investigation powers can be viewed as a serious form of non co-operation resulting in it bringing regulatory proceedings for breach of Principle 11 or Statement of Principle 4. It has to be questioned, however, whether an authorised or approved person's mere refusal to co-operate with a request for a voluntary interview or information request might expose that person to proceedings for breach of Principle 11 or Statement of Principle 4. From a strict regulatory point of view, a refusal to cooperate with the FSA is a breach of the obligation to be open and co-operative, and therefore authorised and approved persons need to weigh up carefully their motivation for not answering questions against their regulatory responsibilities. The FSA states at EG 4.10 that it will not bring disciplinary proceedings against a person under the principles simply because they choose not to attend or answer questions at a purely voluntary interview. The FSA goes on in EG 4.10 to make clear, however, that there may be circumstances in which an adverse inference may be drawn from the reluctance to participate in a voluntary interview.

PRELIMINARY FINDINGS LETTER

9.58   Following the outcome of its investigation, the usual practice of the FSA is to send a preliminary findings letter, annexing a preliminary investigation report, to the subject of the investigation before submitting a report to the Regulatory Decisions Committee (EG 4.30). The recipient then has an opportunity to respond and is usually allowed 28 days for this purpose (EG 4.32). However, there is no statutory requirement that the FSA send a preliminary findings letter. The FSA has indicated that it may decide not to send such a letter, for instance where action is urgently required to restore market confidence or no useful purpose would be achieved by sending such a letter (EG 4.31).

DISCIPLINARY POWERS, CRITERIA FOR DISCIPLINARY ACTION

9.59   Having concluded an investigation and assuming that regulatory breaches have been identified, the FSA in dealing with those breaches has a number of regulatory tools at its disposal. It is not always the case that the FSA will determine to impose a disciplinary sanction even though it does view its enforcement process as a necessary element of it providing a credible deterrent. The FSA places significance on the importance of maintaining a co-operative and open relationship with firms and thus considers in appropriate circumstances that in some cases, even though a contravention has taken place, formal disciplinary action may not be taken where it can expect the firm to act promptly in taking the necessary remedial action agreed with its supervisors. Nonetheless where a firm does not do this, the FSA makes clear at EG 2.4 that it may take disciplinary or other enforcement action in respect of the original contravention.

CASE SELECTION BY THE FSA

9.60   The FSA's selection method for cases involving authorised and approved persons and in market abuse is determined by both its strategic planning such as priority and thematic work and its decision-making on individual cases. The FSA will not, however, only take action in priority cases and underlying its case selection method is a determination, expressed in EG 2.8, to deal with particularly serious cases where enforcement action is necessary, such as those that have a particular significance in a market or involve financial crime. In respect of individual case assessment the FSA considers that the nature of its overall relationship with a firm has a bearing on whether or not the use of its enforcement powers will support its overall regulatory objectives. Confirming this point EG 2.33 provides that:

'... using enforcement tools will be less likely if a firm has built up over time a strong track record of taking its senior management responsibilities seriously and been open and communicative with the FSA ...'

9.61 One factor that can have a material impact on whether the FSA will determine not to seek a disciplinary sanction is whether the authorised person has self-reported, helped the FSA establish the facts and taken adequate remedial action. Any such response is likely to be an indicator to the FSA that a firm is sufficiently responsible to manage its own regulatory failings in an appropriate and responsible manner. Firms, cannot, however, assume that a strong regulatory relationship will keep them immune from disciplinary proceedings and the FSA will consider each case on its own merits as well as its overall regulatory priorities. We consider in more detail in Chapter 10 on Enforcement, the criteria the FSA uses to determine when it will take enforcement action in individual cases.

Chapter 10

Enforcement issues

INTRODUCTION

10.1

'... we intend to be bolder and more resolute about proceeding with market abuse and insider dealing cases so that we can actually bring about a change in the culture in the City. We've got to get all the market players to take this subject seriously ...'. [1]

In this chapter we will consider the statutory provisions and policy aspects of the FSA's enforcement powers under the Market Abuse regime, as well as provide an examination of the powers given to the FSA to make applications to the Courts to secure and recover assets in market abuse cases. Much of the FSA's focus on Market Abuse enforcement is centred on its civil powers under the Market Abuse regime in section 123 of the FSMA, as well as the enforcement powers it has against authorised firms and approved persons. The FSA, is however, increasingly using its powers of prosecution to deal with abuse in the financial markets. Indeed the profile of the criminal prosecution as an effective deterrent in market abuse cases has gradually gathered support and it is now viewed by the FSA as an essential tool in its enforcement armoury. In November 2008 the FSA's Head of Wholesale enforcement, Jamie Symington, commented on the merits that the FSA can gain from using its powers of prosecution, '... So the objective is to up the stakes for people who might risk committing market abuse so that they are deterred by the fact that they face a real prospect of a spell in prison and the publicity and stigma of a criminal conviction ...'.2 This Chapter will therefore conclude by considering in overview the FSA's powers of prosecution as well as its interaction with other law enforcement agencies. Although the Market Abuse regime extends to all users of the market, much of the FSA's work in this area involves the conduct of regulated firms. It is thus essential when considering Market Abuse enforcement to take into account the extent to which the FSA considers whether abuse in the market impacts on a regulated firm's authorisation to conduct regulated business and how it uses its Principles for Business and its general rules when dealing with misconduct. The term 'enforcement' is used generally, applying to both the powers available to discipline persons involved in market misconduct as well as to those powers available to the FSA to secure or confiscate assets.

---

1   From 'How Enforcement makes a difference', a speech by Margaret Cole, FSA Director of Enforcement. FSA Enforcement Law Conference, 18 June 2008.

2 From a speech entitled 'The FSA and enforcing the market abuse regime', by Jamie Symington, Head of Wholesale Department, FSA, City and Financial Market Abuse Conference, 6 November 2008.

SANCTIONS FOR MARKET ABUSE

10.2 The FSA's administrative powers for dealing with market abuse when introduced by the FSMA 2000, were entirely new and required their own set of procedures. The FSA's dual responsibility of maintaining confidence in the financial markets and reducing the extent to which it is possible for a business to be used in connection with financial crime lead the FSA to be concerned to ensure that its enforcement process appropriately contributes to its drive to improve cleanliness in the United Kingdom's financial markets. The FSA stresses that it will take enforcement action where it needs to publicise a specific or general deterrent. Margaret Cole, FSA Director of Enforcement stated in a speech on 29 June 2007, 'Enforcement outcomes contribute towards both the prevention and cure elements of our market abuse strategy. Published Final Notices are a useful tool for industry to understand better the types of behaviour we consider unacceptable. Last year supervisors observed that the publication of an enforcement action often led firms to consider whether the enforcement action had implications for their business, systems and controls.'[1]

1 Speech by Margaret Cole, FSA Director of Enforcement, at Securities House Discussion Group, 'The FSA's Market Abuse Strategy, Prevention and Cure', 29 June 2007.

10.3 The FSA's approach to its enforcement of the Market Abuse regime has not been without challenge. Evidential evaluation differences[1] between the FSA's Regulatory Decisions Committee and the Financial Services and Markets Tribunal[2] in the matters of Paul Davidson and Ashley Tatham and Timothy Baldwin and WRT Investments[3] have overshadowed the successes FSA has experienced in other market abuse cases such as in the matter of Philip Jabre and GLG Partners.[4] Notwithstanding the difficulties of evidential setbacks, the FSA remains committed to using the market abuse regime and to improve the cleanliness of the UK markets and has increased its resolve, in appropriate cases, to use criminal prosecution. However, it remains realistic about what it can achieve, acknowledging that in order to operate an effective regime and deterrent, some cases will be lost. Margaret Cole, FSA Director of Enforcement, has said[5] '... we face many challenges and we expect to lose some cases and to have setbacks. This won't dent our commitment and determination to stick to our objective ...'.

1 Financial Times 'City regulator's crackdown undermined by market abuse case defeat', 18 May 2006.
2 See further Bazley and Haynes, Chapter 13, *Financial Services Authority Regulation and Risk Based* Compliance, 2nd edition, Tottel Publishing, 2007.
3 *Paul Davidson v Financial Services Authority* (2006) Case Number 2003/016 and 2003.021; and *Baldwin and WRT Investments v Financial Services Authority* (2006) Case Number 2005/011.
4 Financial Services and Markets Tribunal reference *Philip Jabre v Financial Services Authority* (2006). Case 36 fin 06/2006 on a preliminary issue concerning the scope of the Market Abuse regime and FSA Final Notice to Phil Jabre and GLG Partners 1 August 2006
5 Margaret Cole, FSA Director of Enforcement, from a speech at the Cambridge Symposium on economic crime, 1 September 2008.

PRINCIPLES BASED ENFORCEMENT

10.4 Market abuse is an unusual aspect of FSA regulation as it applies to all persons, whether or not authorised. However, at the outset of this chapter, it should be noted that market abuse by authorised persons is often addressed by the FSA reference to a firm's failure to establish and operate appropriate systems and controls. Many of the FSA's rules on system and controls take the form of general principles of conduct rather than detailed or prescriptive rules. Indeed significant elements of the FSA's Code of Market Conduct are 'principles based' such that the FSA and authorised persons may focus more on the outcomes gained by compliance with principles rather than how to comply with prescriptive rules. To put it another way, it encourages compliance with the spirit of regulation as opposed to the letter. The FSA believes an approach focused more on outcomes will allow it to achieve its regulatory objectives in a more efficient and effective way and will lead to an increased focus on principles-based enforcement action.[1]

1 See FSA's Enforcement Guide, paragraphs 2.18–2.19.

10.5   Recent enforcement cases such as Roberto Chiarion Casoni[1] and Deutsche Bank AG[2] show that the FSA, when dealing with authorised and approved persons, will consider enforcement by reference to breaches of high level Principles for Business and failures in systems and controls obligations rather than by reference to allegations of specific breaches of the Market Abuse regime.[3] As part of its work in developing principles-based regulation, the FSA has identified positive outcomes for a move towards principles-based regulation. It has expressed the view that a large volume of detailed, prescriptive and highly complex rules can divert attention towards adhering to the letter rather than the purpose of regulatory standards,[4] Dan Watters FSA Director of retail policy stated:

'Why then is the FSA committing itself to a more principles-based regime? The short answer is that we believe it will enable us better to discharge our statutory duties.'

1 FSA Final Notice, Roberto Chiarion Casoni, 20 March 2007. The FSA imposed a financial penalty on Mr Casoni for breaching Principle 3 of the Statement of Principles for Approved Persons. Principle 3 provides: 'An approved person must observe proper standards of market conduct in carrying out his controlled function.'
2 FSA Final Notice Deutsche Bank AG 10 April 2006. The FSA imposed a financial penalty on Deutsche Bank AG for breaching Principles 2 and 5 of the Principles for Business. Principle 2 provides: 'A firm must conduct its business with due skill, care and diligence'; and Principle 5 provides: 'A firm must observe proper standards of market conduct.'
3 For further detail on principles-based enforcement see Freshfields Bruckhaus Deringer, Chapter 1, *Financial Services: Investigations and Enforcement*, 2nd edition, Tottel Publishing 2005.
4 Dan Watters, FSA director of retail policy, speech on the future of UK regulation. Securities and Investment Institute annual conference 23 May 2007.

10.6   In its enforcement case against Citigroup Global Markets Limited (CGML)[1] the FSA focused on breaches of High Level Principle 2 of due skill, care and diligence; and Principle 3 of organisation and control, highlighting how its high level principles can be used to good effect to deal with market conduct cases. In the Final Notice for the action it was reported that four traders on CGML's European Government bond desk had developed a trading strategy on European government bond markets involving the building up and rapid sale of long positions in government bonds resulting in a temporary disruption to the volumes of bonds quoted and traded, as well as a drop in bond prices and a temporary withdrawal by some participants from quoting on a certain trading platform. It was reported that although the traders that had developed the strategy had discussed their proposal with their head of desk, who in turn sought and gained approval of the strategy from CGML's head of interest rate trading, there was no common or clear understanding between them as to the size of the proposed trade and thus no effective communication of the arrangements CGML was to establish. FSA's Hector Sants when commenting on the case stated, '… the lack of adequate systems and controls meant that the strategy was never fully considered, as would be expected, at an appropriate senior level within CGML …'.

1   Citigroup Global Markets Limited. FSA Final Notice, 28 June 2005.

10.7   However, the regulatory flexibility offered by principles-based regulation does present issues relating to compliance certainty for firms, such as determining whether their adopted approach to compliance will meet FSA expectations and not expose the firm to a threat of enforcement. This point is not lost on the FSA, which recognises the importance of a regulatory environment in which authorised persons understand what is expected of them and that the principles-based regime encourages an exercising of judgement about how to comply in terms of how they conduct their business.[1] In addition it has promoted the importance of firms being able to predict reasonably, at the time of the action concerned, whether the conduct would breach the principles. However, rather than establishing a true legal test of reasonable predictability, the FSA indicates that it will not take enforcement action unless it was possible to determine at the time of an alleged breach that the conduct fell short of FSA standards.[2]

1   See Enforcement Guide, para 2.20.
2   See Enforcement Guide, para 2.20.

10.8   Therefore, the ability for authorised persons to identify the standards that are required is vital. In response to this need, the FSA points to the roles played by its guidance as well as any formally recognised industry guidance.[1] The clear distinction between industry guidance and industry practice is worthy of note as it is possible that business practice within a particular sector, even though widespread, can fall below the standards expected by the FSA and result in enforcement action for individual industry participants. Guidance is not, however, binding on authorised persons and the advantages of a principles-based regime allows authorised persons to develop approaches to regulatory compliance that are appropriate for their business in the context of its size, type and complexity provided of course that the underlying regulatory requirements are met. Analysis of guidance can however provide firms with a degree of predictability and the extent to which guidance is followed will be used by the FSA in its enforcement work. Indeed the FSA states in its Decisions Procedure and Penalties Manual (DEPP) at 6.2.1 (4) that it will not take action for behaviour that it considers is in line with guidance; other materials published by the FSA in support of its rules or FSA confirmed Industry Guidance, which was current at the time of the behaviour in question. The reference in DEPP 6.2.1(4) to 'other materials' raises the profile of the extent to which authorised firms should or can take into account so called 'soft' guidance published by the FSA, in documents such as FSA speeches, discussion and consultation documents and even correspondence from FSA supervision teams. The specific reference to 'other materials' in DEPP and reference to 'supporting materials' in the FSA's enforcements guide,[2] suggests that such other material can provide useful material, provided that authorised firms recognise that it can only be used to supplement the FSA formal guidance and the firm's own assessment of how it should meet its regulatory obligations.

1   The FSA has established a mechanism for the recognition of Industry Guidance. See FSA Policy Statement 07/16 which describes the FSA approach to the use of Industry Guidance and

the process that is to be followed to obtain recognition for Industry Guidance. For an example of industry guidance, see MiFID Connect at www.mifidconnect.com

2   Enforcement Guide, para 2.25

10.9   Of importance is the sense that compliance with principles-based regulation can give rise to so called 'regulatory creep' resulting in the expectations of compliance standards increasing over time. In essence, what might have been historically acceptable behaviour becomes unacceptable even though the strict wording of a principle does not change. Of concern to authorised firms is being confident that their historical behaviour will not, as a matter of course, be judged by the standards of today. This point was recognised by the Financial Services and Markets Tribunal in the matter of *Legal General Assurance Society Ltd v Financial Services Authority*.[1] Although the case does not relate to market abuse, it does provide useful information regarding the standards necessary to comply with principles. The Tribunal had to determine standards of behaviour derived from broad requirements of 'best endeavours', 'due skill care and diligence' and the obligation to establish procedures directed at all the 'Rules and Principles'. The Tribunal was concerned with the situation where standards changed over the course of the relevant period and ensured that the standards it applied were those considered acceptable at the time, appropriate to the facts of the case. It concluded that there was not a problem when a firm is being judged against an objectively measured standard or where there is explicit guidance indicating in reasonable detail what should or should not be done. The Tribunal made clear in its written decision that judging a past problem with today's standards was not appropriate. It stated,

'… it is common ground that L&G have to be judged against the compliance standards as they applied in the Relevant Period. The fact that procedures are changed and improved as they were in the latter part of 1999 does not mean that prior conduct was necessarily inappropriate or in breach of the rules …'

1   See *Legal and General Assurance Society v FSA*. Financial Services and Markets Tribunal case number 11. Published 18 January 2005.

10.10   Firms can take comfort from FSA's statement at paragraph 2.21 of its Enforcement Guide that it will not apply later, higher standards to behaviour when deciding whether to take enforcement action for a breach of the Principles.

THE FSA'S ENFORCEMENT OF DECISION MAKING

10.11   One of the major concerns voiced during the passage of the Financial Services and Markets Bill was the need to ensure proper separation between the exercise of the FSA's powers of investigation and enforcement. One member of Standing Committee A expressed the point as follows: 'various legal experts who made submissions on the matter referred frequently to Chinese Walls and I remain unclear as to how thick and sturdy the walls of the FSA's structure will be'.[1]

1   Per Mr Tim Loughton, Standing Committee A, 4 November 1999, column 717.

10.12   The FSMA 2000, s 395 obliges the FSA to maintain its own 'Chinese Wall'. Section 395(2) provides that the decision to initiate action against an alleged offender through supervisory notices, warning notices and decision notices (which are each referred to as 'Statutory Notices') must not be taken by a person directly involved in establishing the evidence on which that decision is based. The FSA has created the Regulatory Decisions Committee in order to comply with the obligation under section 395 (the structure of the regulatory decisions Committee and its role as an FSA decision maker in enforcement cases is considered further below). Further, the FSA has now isolated its enforcement decision-making procedure in a decision-making manual and penalties manual commonly referred to as 'DEPP'.

10.13   The FSA process supporting whether it will take the decision to issue Statutory Notices is centred on an FSA 'decision maker'. The selection of the most appropriate decision maker will be based in part on the nature of the decision to be taken but will also take into account the complexity of the matter, its urgency and importance.[1] Furthermore, in each case the decision maker will exercise their decision-making responsibilities by applying the relevant statutory tests and having regard to the facts of the case, the law relating to the matter in question and the FSA's priorities and policies.[2] The choice of decision maker will vary depending on the circumstances of individual cases as well as the stage that the case is at within the FSA process, but will be selected from either:

(a)   the Regulatory Decisions Committee;

(b)   an FSA staff member under its executive procedures, this includes individual members of staff or a senior staff committee;[3]

(c)   FSA staff under its settlement decisions procedure.[4]

1   DEPP 1.2.5.
2   DEPP 1.2.7.
3   The FSA senior staff committee consists of staff members appointed by FSA's senior executive.
4   DEPP 1.2.5. See further **10.62** *et seq* below concerning the FSA's settlement decisions process.

10.14   Since the FSA review of its enforcement process in 2005,[1] considerable adjustment has been made to its enforcement process and the FSA now operates a multi layered decision-making process allowing for simple and less contentious cases to be handled and concluded by its senior executive team, thus reserving for its Regulatory Decisions Committee more complex and contentious cases. Through the life of an enforcement case it is possible that the decision leading to the relevant FSA Statutory Notices (such as warning notices and decision notices) will be taken by different decision makers. For example, the FSA process, where the person against whom enforcement action is taken disputes the matter, will result in a warning notice decision being taken by FSA staff under executive procedures and the decision notice decision be taken by the RDC.[2]

1   See FSA Enforcement Process Review: report and recommendations, July 2005.
2   DEPP 2.5.2. Annex 1 to DEPP 2.5 sets out the decision makers in respect of each type of Statutory Notice under the Financial Services and Markets Act 2000 and other relevant statutory provisions.

REGULATORY DECISIONS COMMITTEE

10.15   The Regulatory Decisions Committee ('RDC') is a committee of the FSA board exercising certain regulatory powers on behalf of the FSA.[1] The chairman of the RDC is the only member who is an employee of the FSA.[2] The RDC has its own legal advisers and support staff all of which are separate from the FSA staff involved in conducting investigations and making recommendations to the RDC. The RDC is, however, fully accountable to the FSA for the decisions it takes.[3]

1   DEPP 3.1.1.

2 DEPP 3.1.2.
3 DEPP 3.1.1.

WARNING NOTICE AND REPRESENTATIONS

10.16 Following investigation, if the FSA staff consider that action is appropriate, they will recommend to the relevant decision maker that a warning notice be given.[1] Following such recommendation, it is possible that the decision maker may decide not to take further action and in such an event if the FSA had previously informed the person concerned that it intended to recommend action, it must communicate the decision not to take further action promptly to such a person.[2] However, if instead the FSA decides to take action, it is obliged by the FSMA 2000, s 126(1) to give a warning notice to a person against whom it proposes to impose a penalty for market abuse under the FSMA 2000, s 123. Such notice must state the amount of the proposed penalty. Further, a warning notice about a proposal to publish a statement must set out the terms of the proposed statement.[3] A similar procedure applies where the FSA proposes to require a person to pay restitution pursuant to its administrative powers.[4]

1 DEPP 2.2.1.
2 DEPP 2.2.4.
3 FSMA 2000, s 126(3).
4 FSMA 2000, s 385.

10.17 The mandatory contents of the warning notice are set out in the FSMA 2000, s 387. The warning notice must: (a) state the action which the FSA proposes to take, (b) be in writing, (c) give reasons for the proposed action, (d) state whether access to certain FSA material applies pursuant to the FSMA 2000, s 394, and (e) if that section applies, describe its effect and state whether any secondary material exists to which the person concerned must be allowed access under it. The warning notice must also specify a reasonable period (which may not be less than 28 days) within which the person to whom it is given may make representations to the FSA, which period the FSA may extend.[1] The period of time allowed for making representations is set by the FSA decision maker[2] and will usually be not less than 28 days although a subject may seek an extension of time to make any representations. A person dissatisfied with the time allowed for representations may request more time from the FSA decision maker in writing within 14 days of receiving the warning notice.[3] However, if a request for an extension of time will be considered by the decision maker, he will notify the recipient of the notice of the outcome of his request.[4] The FSA has also indicated that, where appropriate, it will include a statement that the mediation scheme is available.[5] Notwithstanding the requirements relating to a warning notice, should the FSA issue a decision notice that was preceded by a warning notice, the action to which the decision notice relates need only be under the same part of the FSMA 2000 as the action proposed in the warning notice according to the FSMA 2000, s 388(2).

1 FSMA 2000, s 387(2) and (3).
2 DEPP 1.2.6.
3 DEPP 3.2.16 where the RDC is the decision maker and as adopted by DEPP 4.1.13 for executive committee decision making.
4 DEPP 3.2.16 (3) where the RDC is the decision maker and as adopted by DEPP 4.1.13 for executive committee decision making.
5 See **10.62** *et seq* below concerning the FSA's settlement and mediation scheme.

10.18 Following receipt of a warning notice, the person concerned may make representations to the FSA in accordance with DEPP 3.2.7.[1] Making any representations following the warning notice and ensuring that these are made within the relevant time limits is critical. In particular, the FSMA 2000, s 123(2) provides that the FSA may not impose a penalty on a person if it is satisfied on reasonable grounds following representations by the person concerned in response to a warning notice that the person either believed on reasonable grounds that his behaviour did amount to market abuse (within section 123(1)) or took all reasonable precautions and exercised all due diligence to avoid behaving in a way which fell within section 123(1).

1   The process for representations at DEPP 3.2.7 applies directly to where the RDC is the decision maker, but a similar process is followed for executive decision making by virtue of DEPP 4.1.13.

10.19   Section 123(2) is significant for a compliance officer, as the defence to the matter will often rest on the compliance procedures in place within a firm. The following points at Chapter 6.3.2 of DEPP (at the time of writing) are important:

(1)   whether, and if so to what extent, the behaviour in question was or was not analogous to behaviour described in the Code of Market Conduct (see MAR 1) as amounting or not amounting to market abuse or requiring or encouraging;

(2)   whether the FSA has published any guidance or other materials on the behaviour in question and if so, the extent to which the person sought to follow that guidance or take account of those materials (see the Reader's Guide to the Handbook regarding the status of guidance.) The FSA will consider the nature and accessibility of any guidance or other published materials when deciding whether it is relevant in this context and, if so, what weight it should be given;

(3)   whether, and if so to what extent, the behaviour complied with the rules of any relevant prescribed market or any other relevant market or other regulatory requirements (including the Takeover Code) or any relevant codes of conduct or best practice;

(4)   the level of knowledge, skill and experience to be expected of the person concerned;

(5)   whether, and if so to what extent, the person can demonstrate that the behaviour was engaged in for a legitimate purpose and in a proper way;

(6)   whether, and if so to what extent, the person followed internal consultation and escalation procedures in relation to the behaviour (for example, did the person discuss the behaviour with internal line management and/or internal legal or compliance departments);

(7)   whether, and if so the extent to which, the person sought any appropriate expert legal or other expert professional advice and followed that advice; and

(8)   whether, and if so to what extent, the person sought advice from the market authorities of any relevant prescribed market or, where relevant, consulted the Takeover Panel, and followed the advice received.

ACCESS TO FSA MATERIAL

10.20   The FSMA 2000, s 394 confers a right of access to key documentation in the possession of the FSA on a person who has been given a warning or decision notice. In particular, access must be allowed to: (a) the material on which the FSA relied in taking the decision that gave rise to the obligation to give such notice, and (b) any secondary material that, in the opinion of the FSA, might undermine that decision. The FSA may refuse access to material in circumstances set out in the remainder of section 394, although such refusal must be given by written notice, together with reasons. The circumstances in which access may be refused include where material has been obtained under warrant, documents are subject to legal professional privilege and where disclosure would not be in the public interest or would harm the commercial interests of another party.

DECISION NOTICE AND NOTICE OF DISCONTINUANCE

10.21 After considering the representations made to it following a warning notice, the RDC or FSA executive committee will state its decision in a decision notice or, where appropriate, a notice of discontinuance. The FSMA 2000, s 388 imposes similar requirements to warning notices in relation to giving decision notices. In the case of a penalty, the amount of such a penalty must be stated in the decision notice[1] and similar provisions apply to restitution orders and publishing a statement.

1   FSMA 2000, s 127(2).

10.22 The decision notice is different from the warning notice in that any right to refer the matter to the Financial Services and Markets Tribunal ('FSMT') and the procedure for making such referral must be indicated at this stage. There is a rather curious provision allowing the FSA to give a further decision notice which relates to different action in respect of the same matter provided a person consents, which is expanded upon at DEPP 2.3.5 and 2.3.6.[1]

1   FSMA 2000, s 388(3)–(6).

10.23 The FSA may not take action specified in a decision notice during the period within which the matter to which the decision notice relates may be referred to the FSMT and if the matter is so referred, until the reference and any appeal against the FSMT's decision have been finally disposed of.[1]

1   FSMA 2000, s 133(10).

10.24 The FSA is obliged to give a notice of discontinuance to a person to whom it has given a warning or decision notice if it decides not to take the action proposed in the warning notice or the action to which a decision notice relates.[1] The FSA has also indicated that it will send such notice to a third party served with a warning or decision notice.[2]

1   FSMA 2000, s 389
2   DEPP 3.2.5.

THIRD PARTY RIGHTS

10.25 Where a warning notice is, in the opinion of the FSA, prejudicial to a third party and such a party is identified in a warning notice to which the FSMA 2000, s 393 applies, the FSA must give a copy of the notice to that third party.[1] This section does not apply if the FSA has given him a separate warning notice in relation to the same matter or gives him such notice at the same time as it gives the warning notice which identifies him.[2] Such notice must specify a reasonable period (not less than 28 days) within which such a third party may make representations to the FSA.[3] However, this right to be informed is qualified. The FSA is not obliged to give a copy to such a third party if the FSA considers it impracticable to do so.[4] The FSMA 2000, s 394 relating to access to material, considered above, applies equally to a third party served with a warning notice.[5] The FSMA 2000, s 393 makes similar provision for decision notices.

1   FSMA 2000, s 393(1).
2   FSMA 2000, s 393(2).
3   FSMA 2000, s 393(2).
4   FSMA 2000, s 393(7).
5   FSMA 2000, s 393(12).

10.26   The rights set out in section 393 ensure that third parties should not be identified and adversely criticised in a warning notice issued by the FSA without having had an opportunity to make representations in response and if they are identified and criticised in a decision notice, they should have the right to challenge such criticisms in the Tribunal.[1]

1   Section 392(1) of the Act deals with third parties that are identified in FSA warning notices, it provides:

'If any of the reasons contained in a warning notice to which this section applies relates to a matter which-

(a)   identifies a person ("the third party") other than the person to whom the notice is given, and
(b)   in the opinion of the Authority, is prejudicial to the third party

a copy of the notice must be given to the third party.'
Section 393(3) of the Act provides the right for a third party that has received copy of a warning notice to make representations to the FSA within 28 days of the warning notice.
Section 393(4) of the Act deals with third parties that are identified in FSA Decision notices it provides:

'If any of the reasons contained in a decision notice to which this section applies relates to a matter which

(a)   identifies a person ("the third party") other than the person to whom the decision notice is given, and
(b)   in the opinion of the Authority, is prejudicial to the third party,

a copy of the notice must be given to the third party.'

10.27   The purpose of section 393 was described by Lord Bach (the Minister who introduced the amendments the Financial Services and Markets Bill which became section 393) during the passage of the legislation through Parliament[1] as follows:

'The new clause on third party rights … rationalises the existing provisions dealing with the rights of third parties identified in warning or decision notices in a way that is prejudicial to them. These provisions were designed to deal with cases where there is some wrong-doing alleged on the part of a third party who is not himself the subject of action by the FSA. For instance, in disciplinary cases under Part XIV, it was felt that action might be taken against a firm for reasons which implied that there has been some failing by one of its directors or employees; or in market abuse cases, where other parties might well be involved in the transactions giving rise to the allegation that market abuse has been engaged in. The provisions give third parties, who are identified in prejudicial terms in the reasons for a warning or decision notice, the right to receive a copy of the notice, and to make representations or refer the matter to the tribunal in the same way as the person who is the subject of the FSA's proposed action. We took the view that although these rights create an administrative burden for the FSA, they are necessary to give the third party the right to defend himself against any implied blame arising from the reasons given for the action.'

1   Hansard HL col 1026, March 30, 2000.

10.28   In respect of the right to make a reference to the Financial Services and Markets Tribunal, section 393(9) makes provision for references in respect of both the FSA decision and any opinion expressed by the FSA in relation to the third party. There may be occasions where the FSA considers that it has no obligation to provide a person with a copy of a relevant notice, but the third party disagrees. In such circumstances the third party may make a reference to the Tribunal under section 393(11) which provides that:

'A person who alleges that a copy of the notice should have been given to him, but was not, may refer to the Tribunal the alleged failure and:

(a)   the decision in question, so far as it is based on a reason of the kind mentioned in subsection (4); or

(b)   any opinion expressed by the Authority in relation to him.'

1   Section 393(9) provides a person to whom a copy of the notice is given under this section may refer to the Tribunal:
> (a)   the decision in question, so far as it is based on a reason of the kind mentioned in subsection (4); or
> (b)   any opinion expressed by the Authority in relation to him.

10.29   In the reference of *Sir Philip Watts v Financial Services Authority Ltd 2005*, the Tribunal was required to consider the meaning of identification under section 393 in a preliminary hearing. The application turned on the meaning in section 393(4) and in essence, whether Sir Philip was identified in the Notice by virtue of the external publicity about him following the events that led to the FSA's enforcement activities against Royal Dutch Shell Corporation. Sir Philip Watts had been the Chairman of Royal and Dutch Shell. On 9 January 2004, Shell announced a re-categorisation representing 3.9 billion 'barrels of oil equivalent' of its proved hydrocarbon reserves. This was 20% of its proved reserves at that date. Following the announcement, Shell's share price fell 7.5%. In mid-April, after further adjustments, Shell announced that the total re-categorisation was about 4.3 billion 'barrels of oil equivalent'.

10.30   Shell's stock was traded in New York as well as London and the calculation of its reserves resulted in regulatory action in the UK and USA. On 29 July 2004, Shell announced that it had reached agreement in principle with the regulators, without admitting or denying their findings or conclusions. Shell agreed to the FSA issuing findings that Shell had breached the market abuse provisions of FSMA, as well as the Listing Rules. It agreed to pay a penalty of £17 million. Similar findings were made by the SEC and in the US Shell agreed to pay a $120 million civil penalty, and an additional $5 million to developing a comprehensive internal compliance program.[1]

1   See FSA Final Notice. Royal Dutch Shell Corporation. 2 August 2004.

10.31   The FSA's Final Notice to Shell was issued on 24 August 2004. Because of the agreed settlement, Shell did not contest these notices. The Applicant was given written notice of the FSA's investigation on 27 May 2004 as an additional subject of the investigation for the purposes of section 170(2) of the FSMA.

10.32   The applicant had been subject to extensive adverse comment in the media and was concerned to protect his reputation against what he considered to be unjust criticism. In the Tribunal reference the applicant asserted his rights as a third party under section 393 of the FSMA, claiming that even if he was not explicitly identified in the relevant notice, he was entitled to the statutory rights of a third party if he was identifiable by reference to publicly available sources as the individual responsible for the matters complained of.

10.33   The Tribunal concluded that the proper construction of section 393(4) affords third party rights to a person who is identified in the decision notice itself, and not as the Applicant had argued, to a person identified in the 'matter' as ascertained by looking at external sources. In reaching this conclusion the Tribunal determined that the term 'matter' as used in section 393 relates to the decision taken by the FSA as defined in the relevant notice and not to a wider context in which the individual may by identified or criticised. The Tribunal considered that this construction is consistent with other instances where the term 'matter' is used in FSMA. It provided a series of examples to illustrate this point, in particular section 127(4) which states 'if the Authority decides to take action against a person [for market abuse], that person may refer the matter to the Tribunal.' It considered, therefore, that there was no reason to give the term 'matter' a wider meaning in section 393(3). In the context of section 393(4), The Tribunal considered that the use of the term 'matter' serves to make it clear that identification can be found from the entire notice, and not from the reasons alone, or one of them.

10.34   In its decision in the Philip Watts case, the Tribunal stated,

'We have to say that we regard the contrary interpretation as a very artificial one. A company is (as the Applicant reminds us) an abstraction, but it is one which is basic to the law. There is no reason in our view why a market abuse allegation directed at a company must necessarily be taken to impute criticism to particular individuals. We doubt whether undertaking the threefold steps which are said to be required, and looking at "publicly available sources" to see whether any and if so which individuals were identified, would be a workable process.'

REFERRAL TO THE FINANCIAL SERVICES AND MARKETS TRIBUNAL

10.35   The independent check and balance on the powers of the FSA is the Financial Services and Markets Tribunal ('FSMT'), which is administered by the Tribunals Service, an executive agency of the Ministry of Justice. The FSMT has jurisdiction throughout the United Kingdom. Shortly before it became operational, the government described the FSMT as 'a single, fully independent tribunal which will safeguard the rights of individuals and firms.'[1] The FSMT has been widely recognised as the notional guarantor of the right to a fair trial.[2]

1   Miss Melanie Johnson, Standing Committee A, 4 November 1999, column 710.
2   See, eg, the joint opinion of Lord Lester of Herne Hill QC and Javan Herberg at Annex C to the First Report of the Joint Committee on Financial Services and Markets, para 2(d)(i).

10.36   By virtue of FSMA 2000, s 127(4) the right to make a reference to the FSMT arises where the FSA decides to take action against 'a person' by imposing a penalty for, or publishing a statement that a person has engaged in, market abuse. Similarly, where the FSA has imposed a restitution order administratively, a person may refer the matter to the FSMT.[1] Any such reference must be made within 28 days of the date on which the decision notice or supervisory notice is given.[2] However, the FSMT may allow a reference to be made after the end of such a period.[3] Further, the FSMT is given specific power pursuant to the Rules (defined below) to extend any time limit for making a reference under the Act or the Rules (Rule 10(1)(d)). An example of a case in which the Tribunal did extend the time limit is *Sonaike v the Financial Services Authority* (13 July 2005) in which a notice was filed one day out of time in circumstances where the applicant had acted promptly once he became aware of the relevant supervisory notice. The FSA is prohibited from taking the action specified in a decision notice both during the 28 day time limit until the reference to the FSMT and any subsequent appeal against the Tribunal's determination has been concluded (see FSMA, s 133(9)). Additionally, there is scope for a third person, being a person who, while not the person to whom a warning or decision notice is given but who is identified in the reasons given in such notice and which in the opinion of the FSA is prejudicial to such a third party, has rights to refer to the FSMT (FSMA 2000, s 393).

1   FSMA 2000, s 386(3).
2   FSMA 2000, s 133(1).
3   FSMA 2000, s 133(2).

10.37   In common with the practice of other Tribunals, the Tribunal comprises a legally qualified chairman who sits with lay persons with relevant experience (see generally FSMA 2000, Schedule 13). Both chairman and members are selected from panels constituted pursuant to FSMA, Schedule 13. Further, in cases involving a question of fact of special difficulty, the FSMT may appoint one or more experts to provide assistance (see paragraph 7(4) of Schedule 13). In matters apart from the determination of a reference or the setting aside of a decision, on a reference anything required or authorised by the Rules (defined below) to be done by the FSMT may be done by the Chairman (see Rule 29).

10.38   The FSMT is created by statute such that its powers are specified in or derived from rules made pursuant to the FSMA. A referral to the FSMT is not a true appeal, limited to a review of the FSA but a re-hearing; in accordance with its independent function, the FSMT reaches its own determination (FSMA, s 133(4)). The FSMT is not constrained by the consideration of evidence before the FSA and may consider any evidence whether or not it was before the FSA (FSMA, s 133(3) and Rule 19(3)). The FSMT is required to determine: (a) what (if any) is the appropriate action for the FSA to take in relation to the matter referred to it, and further (b) whether to remit the matter to the Authority with such directions (if any) as the Tribunal considers appropriate for giving effect to its determination (see FSMA, s 133(4) and (5)). Moreover, the FSMT has power on determining a reference to make recommendations as to the FSA's regulating provisions or its procedures (see FSMA, s 133(8)). However, in common with the FSA, the FSMT is constrained by FSMA, s 388(2), which prevents the taking of action following a decision notice preceded by a warning notice under a different Part of FSMA from that proposed in a warning notice (see FSMA, s 388(2)).

10.39   A legal assistance scheme has been set up pursuant to FSMA, ss 134–136. The availability of legal assistance is restricted by statute to individuals referring a matter to the Tribunal pursuant to section 127(4) of the FSMA (referral to the FSMT following a decision to impose penalties in cases of market abuse). The mechanics of the scheme are contained in two statutory instruments created pursuant to the powers contained in these sections, namely the Financial Services and Markets Tribunal (Legal Assistance)

Regulations 2001 (see SI 2001/3632) and the Financial Services and Markets Tribunal (Legal Assistance Scheme – Costs) Regulations 2001 (see 2001/3633). The first instrument contains the mechanics of applying for legal assistance, the criteria for the award of such assistance or any contribution thereto and indeed the withdrawal of assistance and duty to report abuse of the scheme. Any application for assistance must be made to the FSMT (see paragraph 4 of SI 2001/3632). The second instrument referred to addresses how and at what level work by legal representatives may be remunerated.

10.40 Some parts of the FSMT's procedure are prescribed by FSMA 2000, Schedule 13. However, in common with other tribunals, the primary procedural rules are contained in statutory instrument, namely the Financial Services and Markets Tribunal Rules 2001, SI 2001/2476 ('the Rules') made pursuant to the FSMA 2000, s 132. The following does not purport to be an exhaustive account of the rules and is intended simply to highlight certain aspects of procedure. The reference is initiated by a reference notice (see Rule 4) in response to which the FSA submits a statement of case accompanied by a list of those documents upon which the FSA relies in support of the referred action and further material which in the opinion of the FSA might undermine the decision to take that action (Rule 5). The applicant then replies to the statement of case, providing a list of all the documents on which the applicant relies in support of his/her case. There is a tight time limit of 28 days in respect of each event (see Rules 4, 5 and 6). The FSMT nevertheless retains power to vary any time limit pursuant to Rule 10(1)(d).

10.41 A further important requirement upon the FSA, assuring in principle an 'equality of arms' for the applicant, is secondary disclosure in respect of 'any further material which might be reasonably expected to assist the applicant's case as disclosed by the applicant's reply', any such list to be filed no later than 14 days after the day on which the FSA received the applicant's reply (Rule 7). However, there are specific exceptions to the disclosure required, listed in Rule 8. Amongst such exceptions is a document in respect of which an 'application has been or is being made under paragraph (4)'. Such sub-paragraph enables a party to apply without notice to the other party for a direction to exclude a document from its list 'on the ground that disclosure of the document: (a) would not be in the public interest; or (b) would not be fair, having regard to: (i) the likely significance of the document to the applicant in relation to the matter referred to the Tribunal; and (ii) the potential prejudice to the commercial interests of a person other than the applicant which would be caused by disclosure of the document.' The FSMT has power upon such an application to require both that the document be produced to it together with a statement of reasons in support of the ground(s) relied upon and invite the other party to make representations (Rule 8(5)).

10.42 Moreover, by virtue of Rule 8(8) 'protected items' (see FSMA, s 413) are an exception to those documents within a party's list which may be inspected or copied. A general indicator of a document that will be regarded as 'protected' is one that would be subject to legal professional privilege at common law. The definition is detailed and specific regard to section 413 will clearly be important in practice. It should be noted that protection ceases if 'a communication or item is ... held with the intention of furthering a criminal purpose' (FSMA, s 413(4)). It will be recalled that such items are exempt from production, disclosure or inspection 'under' FSMA by virtue of FSMA, s 413(1).

10.43 The FSMT also has power to require any person to attend at such time and place to give evidence or to produce any document in his/her custody or under his/her control which the Tribunal considers it necessary to examine by summons. A person who fails or refuses without reasonable excuse to attend following the issue of a summons by the Tribunal, to give evidence or to alter, suppress, conceal or destroy or refuse to produce a document which he/she may be required to produce for the purposes of proceedings before the Tribunal is guilty of an offence (see FSMA, paragraph 11 of Schedule 13). Further detail as regards such powers is set out in Rule 12, which provides for example that a person shall not be required to travel more than 16 kilometres from his/her place of residence unless the necessary expenses of his/her attendance are paid or tendered to him/her in advance (see Rule 12(5)). The exceptions to disclosure specified by Rule 8 and as regards 'protected items' are extended to these powers to order a person to file documents by Rule 12(2).

10.44 The procedure at hearings is flexible, the same being conducted under the Rules 'in such manner as [the Tribunal] considers most suitable to the clarification of the issues before it and generally to the just, expeditious and economical determination of the proceedings' (Rule 19(1)). Notwithstanding such apparent flexibility, procedure common to most forms of judicial process is maintained, the parties being entitled '(a) to give evidence (and, with the consent of the Tribunal, to bring expert evidence); (b) to call witnesses; (c) to question any witnesses; and (d) to address the Tribunal on the evidence, and generally on the subject matter of the reference.' (see Rule 19(2)).

10.45 Further, the general rule is that all hearings are in public (see Rule 17(2)). However, 'the Tribunal may direct that all or part of a hearing shall be in private: (a) upon the application of all the parties; or (b) upon the application of any party, if the Tribunal is satisfied that a hearing in private is necessary, having regard to: (i) the interests of morals, public order, national security or the protection of the private lives of the parties; or (ii) any unfairness to the applicant or prejudice to the interests of consumers that might result from a hearing in public, if, in either case, the Tribunal is satisfied that a hearing in private would not prejudice the interests of justice' (*see* Rule 17(3)). Moreover, the FSMT is obliged by Rule 17(5) to consider whether only part of a hearing should be heard in private. Finally, irrespective of whether the hearing is in private, the FSMT has power to 'direct that information about the whole or part of the proceedings before the Tribunal (including information that might help to identify any person) shall not be made public, and such a direction may provide for the information (if any) that is to be entered in the register or removed from it.' (see Rule 17(11)).

10.46 One aspect of hearings that provoked debate prior to the introduction of the regime was the applicable burden of proof in referrals to the FSMT. Tension arose in light of the argument that market abuse provisions are criminal in nature and therefore the burden of proof should be nearer the criminal standard of beyond reasonable doubt than the civil standard of balance of probabilities. It was suggested that the then recent decisions of SRO tribunals demonstrated an ability on the part of such tribunals to apply a fair sliding civil standard, ie requiring exacting evidence before imposing fines (see Joint opinion of Lord Lester/Javan Herberg at para 58).

10.47 The FSMT, while determining that the burden of proof on the FSA is the civil one, has recognised that the 'concept requires some refinement in its application' (*Parker v FSA* 2006 FSMT Case 037 at paragraph [21] of the decision). The FSMT there relied at [21] on Lord Nicholls judgment in *Re H* [1996] 1 All ER 1 at pp 16–17 where he said 'When assessing the probabilities the court will have in mind as a factor, to whatever extent is appropriate in the particular case, that the more serious the allegation, the less likely it is that the event occurred and, hence, the stronger should be the evidence before the court concludes that the allegation is established on the balance of probability'. The FSMT in *Parker* regarded the imposition of a penalty of £300 000 as a 'very grave charge' (see [23]) and that 'in a practical sense, even if not semantically, it is difficult to draw a meaningful distinction between the standard we must apply and the criminal standard' (see [23]).

10.48   The FSMT's powers in respect of the costs are different from those of the courts in mainstream commercial litigation in England and Wales. The power to award a party to pay the costs or expenses of another party incurred by the other party in connection with the proceedings arises in very limited circumstances. The Tribunal must consider that a party to any proceedings on a reference has acted vexatiously, frivolously or unreasonably. In such circumstances, it may order that party to pay to another party to the proceedings the whole or part of the costs or expenses (see FSMA paragraph 13(1), Schedule 13). Such a provision strikes a balance between ensuring that potential appellants are not inhibited by undue concern as to the threat of costs, and discouraging behaviour that wastes the Tribunal's time. There is further and specific power to order the FSA to pay to another party to the proceedings the whole or part of the costs or expenses incurred by the other party in connection with the proceedings where it considers that the relevant decision of the FSA was unreasonable (see FSMA paragraph 13(2), Schedule 13). A particularly interesting case by virtue of its analysis of the relevant statutory provisions is *Baldwin & ors v Financial Services Authority* FIN/2005/0011. The applicant had been accused of market abuse. The Tribunal concluded that he was not guilty of market abuse and no penalty should be imposed. The applicant sought his costs and failed in his application. As regards the power under paragraph 13(2), the Tribunal considered that the right approach was to ask themselves 'whether [they] consider that the Authority's decision was unreasonable, given the facts and circumstances which were known or ought to have been known to the FSA at the time when the decision was made' (see paragraph [15] of the decision). The Tribunal noted in particular that the process leading to the FSA's decision was 'not a full judicial hearing of the kind conducted by the Tribunal' [15]. Having considered possible rival constructions of paragraph 13(1), the Tribunal concluded that 'if there had been an intention to limit the conduct referred to (in that paragraph) to conduct in the course of the proceedings, the statutory wording would have said so expressly' [23]. However, for conduct before the proceedings to be relevant 'it must have some bearing on the proceedings' [26]. Further, the Tribunal distinguished 'wrong' and 'unreasonable' [17] and [27] as regards both paragraphs.

10.49   The costs provisions are amplified by Rule 21 of the Rules. The FSMT is required to give the paying party an opportunity to make representations against the making of the order. The FSMT may either fix the costs or expenses itself or refer the costs and taxes to be assessed on such basis as it shall specify by the appropriate body. Further, the FSMT has a power to order costs where a party without reasonable excuse fails to comply with either a direction made pursuant to or a provision of the Rules (see Rule 27(1)(i)).

10.50   Once the FSMT delivers its decision, a dissatisfied party may appeal on point of law (in contradistinction from any factual issues) only to the Court of Appeal or the Court of Session (in Scotland) (see FSMA, s 137). In common with many other appeals in mainstream litigation, an appeal may only be brought with permission either of the FSMT or the relevant appellate authority (see FSMA, s 137(2)). The appellate court has power on any such appeal either to remit the matter to the FSMT for rehearing and determination or to itself make a determination if it considers the FSMT was wrong in law (see FSMA, s 137(3)). In the event that the appeal is remitted, the Rules apply to the rehearing (see Rule 25). In common with mainstream cases, there is a final right of appeal to the Court of Appeal or Court of Session to the House of Lords. Permission must once again be sought either from the Court of Appeal, Court of Session (in Scotland) or the House of Lords (see FSMA, s 137(5)).

10.51 Apart from the appeal provisions, the Tribunal itself has power to 'review' and set aside its own decision (Rule 22). Such a review may be initiated either by a party or by the Tribunal. The power only arises where either: (a) its decision determining a reference was wrongly made as a result of an error on the part of the Tribunal staff, or (b) new evidence has become available since the conclusion of the hearing to which that decision relates, the existence of which could not have been reasonably known of or foreseen. In common with the provisions relating to referral, there are strict time limits in respect of such reviews (see Rule 22(2) and (3)).

10.52 In the event that no appeal is made, the FSA must act in accordance with the determination of and any direction given by the Tribunal (see FSMA, s 133(10)). Any order of the FSMT may be enforced as if it were an order of a County Court or as if it were an order of the Court of Session (in Scotland) (see FSMA, s 133(11)).

FINAL NOTICE

10.53 If the matter is not referred to the FSMT, the FSA must give final notice to the person concerned pursuant to the FSMA 2000, s 390. Similarly, if the FSMT or a court on an appeal on a point of law (pursuant to the FSMA 2000, s 137) gives the FSA directions to take certain action, the FSA must give the person to whom the decision notice was given a final notice pursuant to section 390(2). Section 390 sets out mandatory requirements that must be included within such a notice.

10.54 A penalty becomes a debt at the end of the period given for its payment in the final notice, which must be not less than 14 days beginning with the date the final notice is given.[1] Similar provisions apply to a restitution order, which may be enforceable by the FSA making application for an injunction.[2]

1   FSMA 2000, s 390(8). See further **10.56** *et seq* regarding FSA penalties.
2   FSMA 2000, s 390(10).

PUBLICATION

10.55 The FSA is required to publish such information about the matter to which a final notice relates as it considers appropriate and in such manner as it thinks fit, unless publication would, in the opinion of the FSA, be unfair to the person with respect to whom the action was taken or prejudicial to the interest of consumers.[1] Neither the FSA nor a person to whom a warning notice or decision notice has been given or copied may publish the details concerning it.[2] However, the FSA may publish such information as it thinks appropriate in relation to a matter in which a notice of discontinuance has been served provided that the person concerned consents.[3]

1   FSMA 2000, s 391(4), (6) and (7).
2   FSMA 2000, s 391(1)
3   FSMA 2000, s 391(2) and (3).

PENALTIES AND STATEMENTS

10.56   Chapter 6 of the Decision Procedure and Penalties Manual contains the FSA's current statement of policy as required by section 124 of the FSMA and regarding the imposition of penalties for Market Abuse under section 123. A similar policy is also required by section 66 in relation to regulatory penalties against approved persons and section 210 in relation to authorised persons.

10.57   The FSA has indicated that it will not institute enforcement action in all cases of market abuse.[1] The factors that the FSA has stated it will take into account form part of its enforcement guide and Decision Procedure and Penalties Manual. At the heart of any decision to take proceedings for market abuse is a consideration of a number of principles[2] including its desire to change the behaviour of the person who is the subject of its action, to deter future non-compliance by others, to eliminate any financial gain or benefit from non-compliance, and where appropriate, to remedy the harm caused by the non-compliance. In addition the FSA takes Market Abuse enforcement in the context of it meeting its statutory objectives, namely the maintenance of market confidence and protecting the interests of consumers.[3] The imposition of a penalty does not make the transaction in question void or unenforceable.[4]

1   DEPP 6.3.1.
2   Enforcement Guide 2.2.
3   See, eg, Enforcement Guide 2.1 and the FSMA 2000, ss 3–6.
4   FSMA 2000, s 131.

10.58   In relation to any enforcement proceedings, the FSA take into account a number of factors, some of these have particular relevance for market abuse cases. These factors are set out in the FSA's Decision Procedure and Penalties manual, which makes clear that the factors are not a substitute for an analysis of the full circumstances of each individual case and nor do they provide an exhaustive list of criteria. It is therefore possible that the unique features of an individual case may give rise to issues that warrant an enforcement outcome in order for the FSA to meet its Statutory Objectives[1] despite not obviously being identified by any of the FSA enforcement criteria.

1   Section 2(1) of the Financial Services and Markets Act 2000 requires that the Financial Services Authority, in meeting its general regulatory function and in so far as is reasonably possible, meets the four Statutory Objectives of market confidence; public awareness; the protection of consumers; and the reduction of financial crime. Indeed two of these Objectives affect specifically the Authority's work in the Market Abuse regime and with Insider Trading. The Market Confidence Objective is defined by section 3(1)–(2) of the FSMA as 'the maintaining confidence in the financial system,' where 'financial system' is defined as including: (a) financial markets and exchanges; (b) regulated activities; and (c) other activities connected with financial markets and exchanges and the reduction of financial crime objective is defined by section 6(1) FSMA as: 'reducing the extent to which it is possible for a business carried on by a regulated person, or in contravention of the general prohibition to be used for a purpose connected with a financial crime' and 'Financial Crime being defined by section 6(3) FSMA' as involving; fraud or dishonesty; misconduct in, or misuse of information relating to, a financial market; or handling the proceeds of crime.

10.59   The criteria set out in DEPP 6.2.1 include the following:

(a)   the likelihood that the same type of behaviour (whether on the part of the person concerned or others) will recur if no action is taken;

(b)   whether the breach was deliberate or reckless;

(c)   the amount of any benefit gained or loss avoided as a result of the breach;

(d)   the impact or potential impact of the breach on the orderliness of markets including whether confidence in those markets has been damaged or put at risk;

(e)   the degree of co-operation the person showed during the investigation of the breach;

(f)   whether the person concerned has complied with any requirements or rulings of another regulatory authority relating to his behaviour (for example the Takeover Panel or a Recognised Investment Exchange; and

(g)   the previous disciplinary record and compliance history of the person.[1]

1   DEPP 6.2.1.

10.60   It will be recalled that section 123 of the FSMA 2000 limits the circumstances in which the FSA may impose a financial penalty. The factors that determine whether the FSA may impose a financial penalty for market abuse are set out at DEPP 6.3 and are similar to those considered in the context of section 123 in the passage entitled 'warning notices' above.

FINANCIAL PENALTY OR STATEMENT OF MISCONDUCT

10.61   The FSA has power under the FSMA 2000, s 123(3) to publish a statement that a person has engaged in market abuse rather than impose a penalty. The FSA clearly regards the imposition of a penalty as more appropriate for serious cases. The publication of a statement as another sanction affords the FSA the flexibility to adapt to different situations. For instance, where a person has taken steps to ensure that those who have suffered loss due to the behaviour are fully compensated, it may be more appropriate to issue a public statement rather than impose a financial penalty.[1] Conversely the FSA will consider it more appropriate to impose a financial penalty on the basis that a person should not be entitled to benefit from their misconduct, if the person has made a profit or avoided a loss as a result of the breach.[2]

1   DEPP 6.4.2.
2   DEPP 6.4.2.

SETTLEMENT AND MEDIATION

10.62   Although the FSA is given statutory powers to impose enforcement sanctions for market abuse, many of the administrative cases brought by the FSA are concluded following an early managed settlement. Indeed the FSA has reported[1] that between 1 April 2007 and 31 March 2008 approximately three-quarters of all cases with a disciplinary outcome settled before reaching the FSA's Regulatory Decision Committee. The benefits offered by early settlement apply to both the FSA and those against whom the action is brought both in financial terms (by reducing cost and a recognised discount on any financial penalty) and by affording the opportunity to acknowledge any regulatory failing at an early stage, permitting rectification of any such failing. Indeed the FSA's settlement process is supported by a mediation facility to assist the parties to negotiate an agreed settlement.

1   Financial Services Authority Enforcement Annual Performance Account 2007/2008. Paragraph 30.

10.63   The FSA is clearly keen to encourage negotiations, informal settlement and mediation in appropriate cases.[1] Mediation has become increasingly popular as a method to assist in the settlement of enforcement cases and involves a neutral mediator helping the FSA and persons concerned to negotiate an agreed settlement. Mediation is available in enforcement cases involving market abuse, although the FSA does not consider it appropriate to deal with cases by this route where there are allegations of criminal conduct.[2]

1   FSA website www.FSA.gov.uk/enforcing the law/Enforcement in focus/Mediation and the FSA.
2   See FSA website pages on its Mediation scheme.

10.64   The FSA has introduced increased transparency supporting a formal settlement process which is set out at Chapter 5 of DEPP. That process allows for the subject of enforcement to enter into settlement discussions with the FSA at any stage of the enforcement process as well as for two FSA decision makers to agree to settle an enforcement case. In addition to setting out a formalised settlement process, Chapter 6.7 of DEPP also sets out a clear discount scheme for financial penalties that is applied to the stage at which during the FSA enforcement process settlement might be achieved. In essence the following discounts are applied.[1]

1   See DEPP 6.7.3.

10.65   Stage 1 being the period from the commencement of an investigation up to the time when FSA has communicated its assessment of the breach and allowed the person concerned a reasonable opportunity to reach agreement as to the amount of the penalty: A 30% discount.

Stage 2 being the period from the end of stage 1 until the end of the period for making written representations or the date on which the written representations is sent if sooner: A discount of 20%.

Stage 3 being the period from the end of stage 2 until the FSA gives a decision notice: A discount of 10%.

Stage 4 being the period after the end of stage 3: No discount.

DETERMINING THE LEVEL OF FINANCIAL PENALTY

10.66   The FSA does not apply a tariff of penalties, believing that the use of a tariff would not be of practical use given the wide range of different breaches in respect of which its enforcement activity can operate.[1] Consistent with the obligation imposed by the FSMA 2000, s 124(2), the FSA's policy in determining the amount of a penalty has regard to a considerable number of matters including: (a) whether the behaviour in respect of which the penalty is to be imposed had an adverse effect on the market in question and, if it did, how serious that effect was, (b) the extent to which that behaviour was deliberate or reckless, and (c) whether the person on whom the penalty is to be imposed is an individual.[2] The additional factors that the FSA has indicated that it will take into account in determining the level of financial penalty that it may impose are similar to those it takes into account in determining whether or not to take action. For instance, the FSA will consider conduct following the contravention and the previous disciplinary record and general compliance history of the person.[3]

1   DEPP 6.5.1.
2   DEPP 6.5.2.
3   DEPP 6.5.2(9).

REMOVAL OR VARIATION OF BUSINESS PERMISSIONS

10.67   In market misconduct cases against authorised persons or approved persons, the FSA may determine that the facts of the misconduct are so serious that it has to take action to withdraw or vary a firm's business permissions or prohibit an Approved Person. Part IV of the FSMA contains powers granted to the FSA to cancel or vary a firm's business permissions[1] and section 63 of the FSMA grants power to withdraw approved person status. The severity of the situation might reveal that the firm ceases to satisfy the threshold conditions[2] for authorisation or that the interests of consumers are at risk to such an extent that the FSA considers it desirable to impose limitations or restrictions on the firm's regulated activities. Indeed the FSA might have concerns that the facts of the matter show that an approved person ceases to be a fit and proper person.[3] If as a result of a withdrawal of a firm's business permission there remains no regulatory activity for which the firm has permission, then the FSA may under section 33 withdraw the firm's authorisation. The FSA's Enforcement Guide contains information at Chapter 8 on how it will use its powers in relation to business permissions and at Chapter 9 in relation to approved persons. At Chapter 8 a distinction is drawn between the grounds that might justify a variation to permissions including circumstances that warrant urgent action and grounds that justify cancellation. Clearly any steps taken to restrict or cancel an authorised firm's activities will have a profound impact on its commercial viability and thus it can be assumed that such action will only be taken where it is necessary for the FSA to meet its Statutory Objectives,[4] such as that to protect consumers.[5] In general terms the FSA states at 8.2 of its Enforcement Guide that formal action affecting the conduct of a firm's commercial business is taken only if that business is being or has been conducted in such a way that the FSA judges it necessary to act in order to secure compliance or address the consequences of non-compliance. Although business permission cancellation might be viewed as an extreme outcome necessary in the most serious of cases, the FSA also has power to vary or restrict business permissions. For example Enforcement Guide 8.11 and 8.12 states that limitations might be imposed on the number, or category, of customers that a firm can deal with or the activities of the firm so that they fall within specific regulatory regimes. As an alternative to a limitation the FSA may impose a requirement in a firm's business permission such as one not to trade in certain categories of specified investments.

1   Section 45 of the FSMA sets out the FSA's powers in relation to cancellation or variation of business permissions. The process the FSA must follow when cancelling or varying a permission is set out at sections 53 and 54.
2   Section 41(2) of the FSMA requires that the FSA must, when giving or varying permission for a person to carry on one or more regulated activities, ensure that that the person concerned must satisfy and continue to satisfy the threshold conditions in relation to all of the regulated activities for which he has or will have permission. The threshold conditions are the conditions set out in Schedule 6 to the FSMA and cover the following matters; legal status; location of offices; appointment of claims representatives (for certain types of insurance business only); close links; adequate resources and suitability.
3   Section 59 of the FSMA sets out the requirement for approved persons in relation to 'Controlled Functions'. Section 61(1) provides that when determining an application for an approved person the FSA must be satisfied that the applicant is a fit and proper person to perform the function to which the application relates and section 63(1) provides that the FSA

may withdraw an approval if it considers that the person in respect of whom it was given is not a fit and proper person to perform the functions to which the approval relates.

4 See **10.58** fn 1.
5 See section 5 which sets out the objective to protect the consumer.

APPLICATIONS TO THE COURT

10.68 The FSA has powers to apply directly to the High Court (or in Scotland the Court of Session) for a variety of injunctions and restitution orders. This power is to be contrasted with the exercise of its administrative powers, which may then be subject to a referral to the FSMT. The warning notice procedure does not apply to applications to court.

INJUNCTIONS

10.69 Application may be made by the FSA to the High Court for a variety of injunctions (or in Scotland to the Court of Session for an interdict) in cases of market abuse pursuant to the FSMA 2000, s 381. There are three types of order that the court may make pursuant to this section: (a) an order restraining (or in Scotland an interdict prohibiting) the market abuse, (b) an order requiring a person to take such steps as the court may direct to remedy market abuse and (c) an order restraining (or an interdict prohibiting in Scotland) the person concerned from disposing of, or otherwise dealing with, any assets of his which it is satisfied that he is reasonably likely to dispose of or otherwise deal with. These orders could be combined. Those familiar with civil litigation will recognise these orders as types of prohibitory injunction, mandatory injunction and freezing order respectively. The FSA has stated that the broad test it will apply in deciding whether to seek an injunction is whether the application would be the most effective way to deal with the FSA's concerns (EG 10.3).

10.70 An injunction is a powerful sanction, breach of which may result in an application by the FSA for contempt of court. Furthermore, from the perspective of both parties, applications for injunctions may result in a number of compressed court hearings taking place at short notice that are likely to significantly increase costs for all parties. Reflecting this, amongst the non-exhaustive list of factors that the FSA has stated it will take into account in considering whether to apply for an injunction is a cost/benefit analysis (see EG 10.3(6)). Therefore, while all of these powers are apparently extremely broad in principle, practical limitations may restrict their actual use. An example of the use of a similar power pursuant to FSMA, section 380 is *Financial Services Authority v (1) Sean Fradley (t/a Top Bet Placement Services) (2) Gary Woodward* [2004] EWHC 3008 (Ch) in which injunctions were granted in principle.

PROHIBITORY INJUNCTION

10.71 The FSA must satisfy the court that: (a) there is a reasonable likelihood that any person will engage in market abuse, or (b) that any person is or has engaged in market abuse and that there is a reasonable likelihood that the market abuse will continue or be repeated in order to obtain a prohibitory injunction restraining the market abuse.[1]

1 FSMA 2000, s 381(1).

MANDATORY INJUNCTION

10.72　The FSA must satisfy the court that: (a) any person is or has engaged in market abuse, and (b) there are steps which could be taken for remedying the market abuse (which includes mitigating the effect of market abuse) in order to obtain a mandatory injunction.[1] This power must be contrasted with the distinct power of the court to make a restitution order (considered below).

1　FSMA 2000, s 381(2).

FREEZING ORDER

10.73　The court may make an order restraining (or in Scotland an interdict prohibiting) the person concerned from disposing of or otherwise dealing with any assets of his which it is satisfied that he is reasonably likely to dispose of, or otherwise deal with. The court must be satisfied on the application of the FSA if it is satisfied that any person: (a) may be engaged in market abuse, or (b) may have been engaged in market abuse.[1] The FSA has also indicated at EG 10.5 that it may ask the court to exercise its inherent jurisdiction to grant a freezing order. An example of the court recognising the scope to use such power to grant freezing orders beyond the wording of FSMA is *Financial Services Authority v Fitt* [2004] EWHC 1669 (Ch) (a case concerned with an application under section 380(3)). The FSA has indicated that it may use this power in combination with an application for a restitution order for the distribution of such assets (see EG 10.10).

1　FSMA 2000, s 381(3) and (4).

FACTORS THE FSA MAY CONSIDER IN DETERMINING WHETHER TO SEEK INJUNCTIONS

10.74　The non-exhaustive list of factors that the FSA will take into account in determining whether an application for an injunction is appropriate (such policy applying to injunctions in cases of market abuse and for breaches of relevant requirements pursuant to FSMA, section 380) is set out at EG 10.3. Of particular interest in the context of market abuse are: (a) the nature and seriousness of the misconduct or expected misconduct in question as well as the impact or potential impact of the relevant conduct on the financial system in question and the extent and nature of losses or other costs imposed or likely to be imposed on other users of the financial system as a result of the misconduct (see EG 10.3(2)); (b) safeguarding assets from which restitution may be made (EG 10.3(5)); (c) whether the conduct in question can be adequately addressed by other powers such as financial penalties (see EG 10.3(7)).

RESTITUTION ORDERS

10.75　The FSA has power to apply to the High Court (or the Court of Session in Scotland) for a restitution order and also to impose a restitution order administratively in cases of market abuse pursuant to the FSMA 2000, ss 383 and 384. These powers arise where:

(a)　a person has either engaged in market abuse or by taking or refraining from taking any action, required or encouraged another person or persons to engage in behaviour which, if engaged in by the person concerned, would amount to market abuse; and

(b)   profits have accrued to such person as a result or one or more persons having suffered loss or being otherwise adversely affected as a result.[1]

1   FSMA 2000, ss 383(1) and 384(2).

10.76   The court may not make a restitution order nor may the FSA impose such order if they are satisfied that:

(a)   the person concerned believed, on reasonable grounds, that he was not engaging in market abuse or requiring or encouraging another to engage in market abuse as set out in the preceding paragraph; or

(b)   he took all reasonable precautions and exercised all due diligence to avoid engaging in market abuse or requiring or encouraging another to engage in market abuse as set out in the preceding paragraph.[1]

1   FSMA 2000, ss 383(3) and 384(4).

10.77   The figure of restitution is fixed by having regard to the profits appearing to have accrued, the extent of the loss or other adverse effect and, where a profit has been made and a person has suffered loss, to the profits appearing to the court to have accrued and to the extent of the loss or other adverse effect.[1] The court has powers to require a person concerned to supply it with such accounts or other information as it may require in order to consider these factors and may require any accounts or other information so supplied to be verified in such manner as the court may direct.[2] Similarly, the FSA may exercise its powers to appoint investigators or require a firm to provide a report prepared by a skilled person under the FSMA 2000, ss 166, 167 or 168 in considering the factors affecting the amount of the restitution order (EG 11.6 and 11.7).

1   FSMA 2000, ss 383(4) and 384(5).
2   FSMA 2000, s 383(6) and (7).

10.78   Payments made pursuant to a court order are paid in the first instance to the FSA, which must be paid by the FSA to such 'qualifying person' or distributed by the FSA between such 'qualifying persons' as the court may direct.[1] A 'qualifying person' is a person appearing to the court to be someone to whom the profits made by the offender are attributable or who has suffered loss or other adverse effect.[2] The powers of inquiry apply in relation to this exercise.[3] Similarly, when the FSA is exercising its administrative powers to require restitution, it must require such person 'in accordance with such arrangements as the (FSA) considers appropriate' to pay such restitution to 'the appropriate person' (who is defined in the same way as a 'qualifying person').[4]

1   FSMA 2000, s 383(4) and (5).
2   FSMA 2000, s 383(10).
3   FSMA 2000, s 383(6)(c).
4   FSMA 2000, s 384(6).

10.79   Finally, it should be noted that where an application is made by the FSA for a court order, this does not affect the right of any person other than the FSA to bring proceedings in respect of matters to which the section applies.[1]

1   FSMA 2000, s 383(9).

10.80   While in principle appealing, the practicalities of pinpointing the 'qualifying' or 'appropriate' person and the amount of restitution appropriate in any particular case are immediately evident. Perhaps against this background the FSA cautions at the outset of Chapter 11 of the Enforcement Guide (entitled

'Restitution and redress') that 'when deciding whether to exercise these powers, the FSA will consider whether this would be the best use of the FSA's limited resources taking into account, for example, the likely amount of any recovery and the costs of achieving and distributing any sums' (see EG 11.1). This paragraph concludes that the FSA 'expects ... to exercise its formal restitution powers on rare occasions only' (see EG 11.1).

ACTIONS IN DAMAGES ARISING FROM ENFORCEMENT

10.81   Although much of the FSA's market abuse work is concentrated on the intergrity of UK financial markets, certain market abuse behaviours can give rise to investor losses arising from either over or under valued securities. It is therfore important not to overlook that the conclusion of FSA enforcement proceedings may not be the end of liability for an authorised firm and that in ceratin circumstances the FSA's Final Notice can act as an alert of an opportunity to pursue a claim for any losses suffered, by customers of third parties such as market counterparties. In this section of the Chapter, for convenience we refer to potential claimants in the context of an auhorised firm's customers, although claims in damages might arise from other third paries. In many abuse cases, breaches of FSA rules may have given rise also to a breach of a duty owed in law to a customer, which in turn has led to the customer having suffered a financial loss. Whilst customer detriment arising from rule breaches might be dealt with by the FSA as part of its enforcement cases (eg the FSA might make an application to the Courts for a restitution order or it may, as part of any settlement terms reached with an authorised firm, agree that the firm is to investigate potential customer detriment and provide compensation where loss is identified), where enforcement proceedings remain silent on the matter of customer liability, customers might consider it appropriate to pursue other available legal remedies. From a practical standpoint, for firms dealing with retail customers, the likelihood of cases being commenced in the Courts is minimised by the availability of the Financial Ombudsman Service,[1] often being a customer's preferred route for resolution of any claim they may have. Nonetheless, the likelihood of Court proceedings cannot be discounted and for many reasons, customers may choose to pursue their legal remedies through the Courts.[2]

1   For further information on the Financial Ombudsman Service, see Bazley and Haynes, *Financial Services Authority Regulation and Risk-Based Compliance*, 2nd edition, Tottel Publishing, 2006. See also the Financial Ombudsman website www.financial-ombudsman. org.uk

2   For example, during 2007 many customers of UK retail banks issued court proceedings in relation to alleged unfair bank charges. See further BBC analysis 'Slow Progress on bank charges' by Ian Pollock, Personal Finance reporter, BBC News: http://news.bbc.co.uk/1/hi/ business/7365488.stm

10.82   While customers may have a a right of action arising from a number of legal duites owed to them (such as those arising in contract, tort and arising from a fiduciary relationship) in the context of liability arising from proven breaches of the FSA rules, consideration should be given to rights of action that arise under section 150 of the FSMA, which provides at section 150(1) 'A contravention by an authorised person of a rule is actionable at the suit of a private person who suffers loss as a result of the contravention, subject to the defences and other incidents applying to actions for breach of statutory duty'.[1]

1   For a fuller analysis of liability under section 150 see Freshfields Bruckhause Derringer, *Financial Services: Investigations and Enforcement*, 2nd edition, Tottel Publishing, 2005.

10.83   Section 150 provides in essence private persons[1] with an action in damages where an authorised person[2] has contravened an FSA rule. Section 150(1) and (4) does however limit the category of rules for which a section 150 action is available and in particular at section 150(1) does not include rules that specify that contravention does not give rise to a right of action.[3] This specific exclusion places, to some extent, control of the foundation of section 150 liability in the hands of the FSA which may prescribe which rules are covered by section 150 and those which are not. Of particular importance, in the context of FSA enforcement proceedings, is the fact that the FSA's Principles for Business as well as the FSA rules relating to systems and controls in SYSC 2 to 18 are excluded from section 150. Given the increasing grounding of enforcement cases on breaches of high level principles, the usefulness of a final notice supporting a section 150 claim appears limited. Moreover, the extensive use of FSA and industry guidance is designed to support compliance of FSA rules but is not a formal rule and thus is not within the scope of a section 150 claim in damages. Even where an enforcement case identifies a clear contravention of FSA rules, successful claims will not necessarily follow. Section 150 does not create a duty of strict liability and the fact that there has been a breach of FSA rules does not mean that either the breach caused the customer's loss or that the customer will be successful in a claim for damages. Section 150(1) specifically provides a requirement for causation as well as a number of defences. First, it provides that the rule breach is only actionable where the private person has suffered a loss as a result of the contravention. In market abuse cases, in can be difficult to show that it was the identified abusive behaviour that lead to the claimant's loss. While in large scale abusive activity it might be apparent that the abusive behaviour directly led to an arificial valuation in securities, in smaller scale cases, although the person acting in contravention of the market abuse regime may have profited or avoided a loss, it will be extremely difficult to show that any loss was caused to a third party by the abusive behaviour. Secondly, section 150(1) requires that the contravention is subject to defences and other incidents applying to actions for breach of statutory duty. Such defences include the occurance of an intervening act, there being contributory negligence by the customer and that there was a co-existent breach of duty by the firm and the claimant customer.[4]

1   A section 150 action is available only to private persons, and under section 150(3) other non-private persons, that are prescribed by the Financial Services and Markets Act 2000 (Rights of Action) Regulations 2000.
2   An authorised person is a person authorised under section 31 of the Financial Services and Markets Act 2000. A section 150 claim is therefore not available against non-authorised persons who might otherwise be subject to the market abuse regime.
3   Section 150(4) also excludes the Listing Rules and a rule requiring an authorised person to have or maintain financial resources.
4   For further detail on defences to a breach of Statutory Duty see *Clerk and Lindsell on Torts*, 18th edition, Sweet and Maxwell.

10.84   Although section 150 can have some application to customers that have been victims of market abuse, insider trading or other similar market misconduct, its use has to be considered as limited. Its application only to rule breaches by authorised persons excludes from its scope unregulated users of the market who are otherwise subject to the Market Abuse regime. Furthermore, even where a matter relates to an authorised firm, the FSA's increasing reliance on breaches of high level principles, being specifically excluded from the category of rule subject to section 150, can act to restrict the availability of this right of action.

PROSECUTION OF CRIMINAL OFFENCES

10.85 The FSA has acquired power under the FSMA 2000, ss 401 and 402 to prosecute both the criminal offence of misleading statements and practices under the FSMA 2000, s 397 and insider dealing under the Criminal Justice Act 1993, Pt V in England, Wales and Northern Ireland. The FSA has agreed guidelines with the other authorities in England, Wales and Northern Ireland who have an interest in prosecuting criminal offences, as set out at Annex 2 of the Enforcement Guide.

10.86 The FSA will apply the principles set out in the Code of Crown Prosecutors when considering whether to bring criminal proceedings or to refer the matter to another prosecuting authority.[1] Instead of instituting proceedings, the FSA may issue a formal caution, in which case it will follow Home Office Circular 18/1994.[2]

1   See EG 12.2.
2   EG 12.5.

10.87 The factors that the FSA has indicated that it may take into account in considering whether to initiate criminal proceedings for market misconduct rather than impose a sanction for market abuse are set out in a non-exhaustive list at EG 12.8. These include the seriousness of the misconduct, the effect of misconduct on the market and whether dishonesty is involved. The FSA may take civil or regulatory action such as applying for an injunction or seeking restitution where criminal proceedings have been commenced or will be commenced.[1] In determining whether such proceedings should be taken, the FSA may take into account whether the taking of regulatory action might unfairly prejudice the prosecution or proposed prosecution of criminal offences, whether the defendants might be unfairly prejudiced in the conduct of their defence and whether it is appropriate to take such action having regard to the scope of the criminal proceedings and the powers available to the criminal courts.[2]

1   EG 12.4.
2   EG 12.4.

10.88 A person convicted of misleading statements and practices or insider dealing is liable on summary conviction to imprisonment for a term not exceeding six months or a fine not exceeding the statutory maximum or both and on indictment to imprisonment for a term not exceeding seven years or a fine or both.[1]

1   FSMA 2000, s 397(8) and the Criminal Justice Act 1993, s 61.

REFERRALS TO THE SERIOUS FRAUD OFFICE

10.89 In appropriate circumstances, as an alternative to the FSA commencing a criminal investigation into Insider Trading, it may refer the matter to the Serious Fraud Office (SFO). Furthermore, referrals may be made to the SFO from other law enforcement agencies or directly from the public. Indeed in December 2008, the SFO announced an initiative encouraging City professionals to report suspicions of City Fraud directly to the SFO. Although the reporting scheme is directed at all financial fraud, it will cover suspicions regarding the trading on price sensitive information. Seemingly the initiative was in response to growing concern regarding the risk of financial fraud during the economic downturn. In a press release announcing the initiative the SFO stated:[1]

'... In looking for frauds arising from the credit crunch, the SFO is working closely with colleagues in the law enforcement community both in the UK and abroad, with Governments and regulators ...'

Ordinarily the SFO will only accept a referral of a matter that satisfies its referral criteria,[2] the prime criterion being that the suspected fraud appears to be so serious or complex that its investigation should be carried out by those responsible for its prosecution and that the value of the alleged fraud exceeds £1 million. In addition, the SFO apply the following criteria:

(a)   There is a significant international dimension. This might be appropriate where the suspected Insider Trading involves trading activity across markets in more than one jurisdiction.

(b)   Is the case likely to be of widespread public concern?

(c)   The case requires highly specialised knowledge. This might be appropriate where specialist knowledge is required of financial markets and practices within the financial services industry.

(d)   Is there a need to use the SFO's special powers, including section 2 of the Criminal Justice Act 1987?

1   SFO Press release 'City Insiders and Advisors asked to help prevent fraud', 15 December 2008.
2   See SFO website www.sfo.gov.uk/cases/cases/asp

SECTION 2 OF THE CRIMINAL JUSTICE ACT 1987

10.90   SFO staff, authorised by its Director, have power under section 2 of the Criminal Justice Act 1987, for the purposes of an investigation, to require a person to answer questions and provide information or documents. Such notices can have a significant benefit during investigations impacting financial institutions and other professionals who hold information or documents but owe a duty of client confidentiality in regard to such information or documents. A section 2 notice provides them with a lawful obligation to provide information and documents notwithstanding such confidentiality.

Under section 2, although a person may refuse to answer questions or provide information or documents if s/he has a reasonable excuse for not doing so, any answers provided in meeting the notice may not be used in evidence against them other than in relation to an offence of providing misleading information in response to the section 2 notice.

Chapter 11

Issuer disclosure

DISCLOSURE AND THE ISSUER

11.1   Issuer liability for market abuse is an important compliance concern for companies and their advisers. The UK listing rules, which are administered by the FSA, were significantly amended in 2005 to incorporate the extensive disclosure and record keeping requirements imposed upon issuers by the Market Abuse Directive.[1] Most of the ongoing reporting requirements in the listing rules are similar to those required under the Market Abuse Directive. However, the scope of coverage of the listing rules and the disclosure requirements of the Market Abuse Directive are different: the listing rules are administered by the FSA under Part VI of the FSMA and apply only to companies whose shares are admitted to the official list, while the disclosure requirements of the Market Abuse Directive apply to all issuers whose securities are admitted to trading (or for which a request for admission to trading has been made) on a regulated market in an EEA State.[2] Moreover, the Directive extends disclosure requirements to professional third parties, such as lawyers, accountants and investment banks who advise issuers. Disclosure has been determined as the 'sole mechanism to satisfy the directive's requirements'.[3] The chapter will discuss the disclosure requirements as they relate to the market abuse offence and potential liability issues. It will also discuss related areas of issuer disclosure and liability involving takeovers and mergers.

1   The Listing rules only cover issuers whose securities are admitted to the official list, which is a narrower set of issuers than those covered by the Directive. The FSA makes the listing rules under powers in Part VI FSMA. The chapter will primarily focus on those disclosure requirements for issuers and related third parties required by Articles 6 (1) – (4) of the Market Abuse Directive. The Transparency Directive also imposes ongoing issuer disclosure and reporting requirements which are not addressed in this book.
2   See generally J Hansen (2004) 'MAD in a Hurry' 15 (2) *European Business Review* 183–221, 219.
3   Committee of European Securities Regulators (CESR) *Feedback Statement for Level 2 Implementing Measures* CESR/02–287b (CESR Paris)(Dec 2002), 'Comments in relation to Article 1 (insider dealing and market manipulation)'.

DISCLOSURE OBLIGATIONS

11.2   The listing rules contained in Part VI of the FSMA require issuers to disclose via the Regulatory Information Service, information that is not public knowledge that, if known, would lead to substantial movement in the price of their listed securities (ie price-sensitive information).[1] The disclosure requirement applies to all issuers with securities traded on regulated UK markets.[2] This requirement derives from the Market Abuse Directive's disclosure obligations that apply to all issuers who have securities trading, or who are seeking to have securities trading, on a regulated market in a EEA state.[3] This disclosure requirement for UK issuers is wider than the previous UK listing rules, which only applied to securities that were admitted to the Official List. UK issuers are now required to inform the public 'as soon as possible' of inside information that concerns them.[4] This means as soon as the event occurs. The requirement, however, has been criticised on the grounds that the near immediacy of the disclosure obligation would not give the issuer adequate time to assess the relevance of the information and therefore might result in issuers becoming far more reluctant to disclose information.[5] The FSA has authority to make rules governing information disclosure with respect to instruments admitted to trading in regulated markets.[6]

The rules related to instruments admitted to trading on a regulated market are subject to strict disclosure requirements.[7] Issuers are required under the rules to publish and update, if necessary, any inside information. The rules also allow an issuer to delay the publication of insider information in certain circumstances, and require an issuer who discloses information to a third party to publish that information without delay with certain exceptions. It also requires an issuer to draw a list of those persons who have access to inside information that directly relates to the issuer, and requires the issuer's senior management, and those closely connected, to disclose transactions conducted on their own account in the issuer's shares.

1   FSMA 2000, Part VI. Pursuant to Part VI, the FSA makes the Listing, Prospectus and Disclosure and Transparency Rules. The Disclosure and Transparency Rules (DTRs) for listed companies are set out in the FSA's Handbook. The DTR rules require an issuer to publish specified inside information (FSMA, s 96A). DTR 2.2.1 states that: 'An issuer must notify a RIS [Regulatory Information Service] as soon as possible of any inside information which directly concerns the issuer unless DTR 2.5.1R applies.'

2   The Listing Rules set out the Listing Principles which apply to every listed company with a primary listing of equity securities. The purpose of the Listing Principles is to ensure that listed companies have regard to the important role they play in maintaining market confidence and ensuring fair and orderly markets. Listing Principle 4 provides: 'a listed company must communicate information to holders and potential holders of its listed equity securities in such a way as to avoid the creation or continuation of a false market in such listed equity securities.'

3   Article 9, Directive 2003/6/EC.

4   Article 6(1).

5   CESR's 'Advice on Level 2 Implementing Measures for the Market Abuse Directive' CESR/02–89d, (CESR: Paris), p 34. This also complies with the Second Company Law Directive 77/91/EEC. HM Treasury observed that this requirement should allow for a longer period to disclose, but the FSA has implemented CESR's interpretation for immediate disclosure. See DTR 2.2.1.

6   FSMA, s 73A. Rules made under this power and the existing power with respect to listed securities are known as Part VI rules.

7   FSMA, s 96A.

DELAYED DISCLOSURE

11.3   In certain circumstances issuers are permitted to delay disclosure,[1] if it does not mislead the public and they are able to ensure the confidentiality of the information. Based on CESR's advice, the FSA has accepted several examples of when delay is acceptable, such as if disclosure would harm the issuer's interests, or affect the negotiation of a deal.[2] Issuers, however, delay at their own risk and, therefore, if delay is unjustified, they may incur market abuse liability.[3] The FSA has made it clear in several enforcement actions that listed companies must carefully consider what could be inside information and their obligations to disclose. For example, it is unacceptable for a company not to disclose negative news because it believes other matters are likely to offset it. By failing to correct the negative news immediately, an investor's ability is hampered to make informed investment decisions and risks distorting the market.[4]

1   Article 6(2), Directive 2003/6/EC.
2   CESR's Advice (Dec 2002), p 23. See DTR 2.5.1 R and 11.12.
3   Article 6(1), Directive 2003/6/EC.
4   FSA, Final Notice, Wolfson Microelectronics plc (Jan 2009). See also, FSA, Final Notice, Woolworths Group plc (12 June 2008).

SELECTIVE DISCLOSURE

11.4   The sharing of information is key for efficient business transactions in modern financial markets. The internet has facilitated the dissemination of information to market participants. It can also, however, be a source of abusive behaviour. In such an environment, it is important that the distribution of information in the normal course of business is conducted in a way that does not unduly expose the firm or its agents to liability for insider dealing or market manipulation. This concern is reflected in Article 6(3)'s requirement that issuers must make prompt public disclosure when they have disclosed inside information to a third party in the course of their employment, profession or duties.[1] Cross-border disclosures to third parties must be made to the relevant authorities of the jurisdictions in question when such disclosures involve parties in EEA states.[2]

The FSA has put this in practice with Disclosure Rule 9A.7 which allows an issuer to delay disclosure of inside information provided that it does not mislead the public and provided the issuer can ensure confidentiality. The rule states, however, that any decision to delay disclosure is taken at the issuer's own risk. For instance, delayed disclosure could be limited to matters under negotiation, but is unlikely to be extended to other circumstances. When the disclosure is made, it should distinguish between an event giving rise to inside information (ie loss of a big contract) and subsequent events (ie attempting to renegotiate contract).

1   See DTR 2.2. Pursuant to section 157 of FSMA, the FSA has published guidance on DTR obligations in the Handbook.
2   Article 6(3), Directive 2003/6/EC.

MANAGERIAL DISCLOSURES

11.5   The managers of issuers and other senior officers are required to disclose their share dealings in the issuer. All managers privy to inside information are required to disclose to the RNS every time they buy or sell shares in their employers. This has had broad impact on corporate disclosure, as a large number of senior managers below board level are exposed to price-sensitive material. It should be remembered that these rules apply to spread bets and derivatives as well as to shares trading.

SAFE HARBOURS

11.6   Article 8 of the Directive exempts from the insider trading prohibitions an issuer's buy back of shares in an initial public offering and any buying and selling of securities intended to stabilise the market for an issuer's equity or debt securities in a secondary offering by insiders who have complied with the Commission's Regulation containing the stabilisation rules.[1] The Directive states in its commentary that '[t]rading in own shares and stabilisation however must be carried out transparently in order to avoid insider dealing or giving misleading signals to the markets. Trading in own shares could be used to strengthen the equity capital of issuers and so would be in investors' interests'.[2]

1   Article 6, para 5.
2   Commentary to the proposed Directive.

ISSUER DISCLOSURE AND THIRD PARTY LISTS

11.7   The FSA disclosure rules apply to all issuers who have requested or been approved admission of their financial instruments to trading on a regulated market.[1] These disclosure rules require the issuer to publish without delay in the following circumstances: when the issuer has certain price-sensitive information about the issuer's securities; when there has been any significant change concerning inside information in certain circumstances; and when an issuer or any person acting on its behalf discloses inside information to a third party.[2] Moreover, an issuer is required to maintain lists of those persons working for it (as independent advisers or employees) who have access to inside information relating directly or indirectly to the issuer.[3] Individuals discharging managerial responsibilities within the organisational structure of the issuer, and any persons connected to such persons discharging managerial responsibilities (eg family members, close associates or friends), are required to disclose transactions conducted on their own account in shares of the issuer, or derivatives or any other financial instrument relating to those shares.[4]

In addition, issuers must create lists of third parties who are likely to have access to inside information. These lists must be released to the FSA when required or requested by the FSA. This requirement has been criticised because of the significant compliance costs of monitoring information within a business organisation. It has been argued that the cost of maintaining these lists is disproportionate to the regulatory benefit or to the benefit of the market.[5]

1   FSMA, s 96A (1).
2   Section 96A(2)(a)-(d).
3   Section 96A(2)(e).
4   Section 96A(2)(f).
5   CESR (August 2003) 'Feedback Statement for Level 2 Implementing Measures' CESR/03–213b (CESR: Paris), p 12.

ISSUER AND SENIOR OFFICER LIABILITY

11.8   As a general matter, it should also be emphasised that market abuse can be committed by individuals, legal persons (companies, businesses, LLPs, LLCs, and other business entities) where the entity commits the offence. The Directive requires all Member States to impose criminal sanctions for insider dealing on 'any natural or legal person'. This makes all corporations, partnerships and other business entities criminally liable for insider dealing. Article 6 requires that any 'natural person, or entity, professionally arranging transactions in financial instruments shall refrain from entering into transactions, and reject orders on behalf of its clients, if it reasonably suspects that a transaction would be based on inside information'.

The entity may have been deemed to have committed the offence if its senior managers or officers have engaged in behaviour that amounts to market abuse while discharging their official functions for the firm. The attribution of liability to the firm for the market misconduct of its employees was an issue in the FSA's enforcement action against GLG Partners in 2005.[1] GLG Partners was a limited partnership whose managing director, Philippe Jabre, had committed market abuse after trading on the basis of price-sensitive information which he had received from a third party bank. The issue was whether GLG Partners should be subjected to a penalty for Jabre's abuse of the market. The FSA issued a Decision Notice holding that GLG Partners had failed to maintain adequate internal controls to oversee the activities of Jabre, a leading fund manager at the firm, and that the weaknesses in its internal oversight significantly contributed to the environment in which Jabre was able to abuse the market. The FSA imposed a £750,000 penalty on GLG Partners in part to require the firm to disgorge its ill-gotten gains and to deter future poor oversight of its senior fund managers.

Officers, employees, or agents of the company or business organisation may also be held liable personally or individually for the firm's commission of the market abuse offence if certain conditions are satisfied: (a) if the offence was committed with consent or connivance of the officer, or (b) the offence is attributable to neglect on the part of the officer. The FSA would need to show that the individuals in question had in fact participated in some meaningful way – either through action or inaction – in the firm's commission of the offence.

1 See the Financial Service Authority's Decision Notice to Philippe Jabre and to GLG Partners (28 February 2006).

PROFESSIONAL DISCLOSURE REQUIREMENTS

11.9   Civil liability for market abuse arises for any person professionally arranging transactions in financial instruments who reasonably suspects insider dealing or market manipulation if they fail to report the suspected behaviour to the FSA. In other words, professionals must disclose suspicious transactions.[1] For issuers, the determination of indicative factors that identify suspicious transactions is determined by guidelines set forth by the FSA. For third party professionals, indicative factors will be determined in part by professional codes and guidelines approved by the FSA.

Brokers and spread betting firms are obliged to report all transactions to the FSA if they suspect insider dealing or market manipulation. Brokers have complained about these suspicious transaction reports, as they are duplicative of existing requirements to report transactions that might be related to money laundering or terrorist financing. In addition, brokers will have to report the sources of research information and any potential conflicts of interest.

1 This provision mirrors the UK money laundering legislation that requires disclosure of suspicious transactions. Proceeds of Crime Act 2002, s 330.

PROFESSIONALS AND CONFIDENTIALITY

11.10   The emphasis on disclosure in the market abuse regime can arguably be criticised on the grounds that it places an undue burden upon professionals, requiring them to be responsible for policing their firms and professions. Following the corporate governance scandals of the early 2000s and the subsequent weaknesses of financial institutions as demonstrated in the 2007/08 credit crisis, however, the focus on issuer disclosure and third party professional disclosure is now more favourably viewed by investors and other users of financial products.

The market abuse regime's requirements that professionals disclose suspicious transactions has raised confidentiality concerns, as they are obliged to report to the FSA if they suspect insider dealing or market manipulation in respect of a client's account. This action can potentially harm professional-client relationships, possibly undermining investor confidence, and inhibiting issuers from using third party professionals when accessing the capital markets if they fear disclosure to regulatory authorities of confidential information. On the other hand, a strict disclosure regime can reduce the likelihood of market abuse, thus promoting more transparency in the market and enhancing its integrity with the result that more investors will have confidence to invest in the market. It should be recalled that Article 6 of the Directive requires that issuers of financial instruments inform the public as soon as possible of inside information, subject to various confidentiality and other exemptions.[1]

1   Article 6, paras 1–4, contains related restrictions on selective disclosure.

FSA FAVOURS ENHANCED DISCLOSURE

11.11   In light of the recent FSA investigations of volatile share price movements in the shares of UK financial institutions, the UK government has taken a stricter stance on disclosure to enhance the integrity of UK financial markets. Although most of the volatility has arisen from a loss of investor confidence in UK equity markets and a dramatic de-leveraging in asset exposures by institutional investors and hedge funds due to limited access to liquidity, the UK government has blamed much of the market turbulence on short selling by institutional investors and other allegedly abusive practices.[1] The resulting regulatory practice for the next few years will likely require much more strict disclosures by issuers and professional advisers of suspicious transactions that could possibly, but not necessarily, amount to market abuse. In deciding whether to take enforcement action in cases involving issuer disclosure, the FSA will have regard to specific guidance on the identification of inside information set out from DTR 2.2.3G to DTR 2.2.8G.[2]

1   See FSA limitations on short selling in the shares of financial institutions. (Aug 2008).
2   See FSA, Final Notice, Entertainment Rights plc (19 Jan 2009).

ISSUER'S DISCLOSURE DECISION TREE

11.12   To summarise the issuer's obligations in a general context, the following decision tree could be useful. Detailed compliance, however, should always take account of the facts of each situation and the issuer involved and applicable regulatory rules and requirements.

Does the issuer have inside information

Can an issuer legitimately delay disclosure of inside information?

Can and issuer selectively disclose inside information?

Does the issuer have inside information?

To be inside information the information must be:

> ➤ precise
> ➤ not generally available
> ➤ relate to qualifying investments
> ➤ price sensitive (DTR 2.2.1. R)

Can an issuer legitimately delay disclosure of inside information?

It can delay so as not to prejudice it legitimate interests provided:

> ➤ it does not mislead the public
> ➤ selective disclosure is confidential
> ➤ issuer can ensure confidentiality (DTR 2.5.1. R)

> ## Can the issuer selectively disclose inside information?
>
> ➤ **yes as long as there is a confidentialty obligation and**
>
> ➤ **the recipient has a valid reason to receive the information (DTR 2.5.7.7G).**

> *Disclosure must be made as soon as possible if the issuer is not able to ensure confidentiality of the information (DTR 2.6).*

TAKEOVERS

11.13   The Panel on Takeovers and Mergers administers the City Code on Takeovers and Mergers. The City Code (known as the 'Takeover Code') contains general principles and rules governing takeovers and mergers for companies listed on the UK market.

GENERAL PRINCIPLES

11.14   The essential requirements of the Takeover Code's general principles are the following: equality of treatment for shareholders; adequate information and advice for shareholders; the maintenance of fair and orderly markets for shares of the company during periods of the offer; and no board or management action to thwart an offer by a target company during the offer period without shareholder approval. Significantly, General Principle 7 prohibits defensive measures to frustrate bids by target companies (ie poison pills) without shareholder approval. Also important is Rule 21.1, which allows the offeror company to break through certain offeree company restrictions (eg restrictions on share voting rights and transfer of securities) and to tender for a company's shares.

THE TAKEOVER PANEL'S POWERS

11.15   The Takeover Panel has no formal sanctioning power but its decisions are respected and have been given effect by market participants and regulated persons. The Takeover Panel exercises influence in a number of ways including by making critical statements about the conduct of a bid; panel members often influence senior management which can affect a firm's commitment to follow through with a merger. Some Panel decisions may be recognised by professional bodies and by the Financial Services Authority and thereby serve as a basis for sanctions to be imposed against the person in a breach of the Code. For example, the FSA can withdraw authorisation from a person or company for failing to comply with the Code which can result, for instance, in a delisting from the London Stock Exchange.

THE FSA'S ROLE

11.16   The FSA may overrule the Panel in areas such as takeovers where they have overlapping responsibility. The Code of Market Conduct provides a defence for persons who take certain actions to comply with the Takeover Code that come within the safe harbour provisions of the Market Abuse Directive.[1] For instance, if an issuer is engaging in certain acceptable market practices as defined in the Directive and recognised by the FSA in disclosing information according to a timetable recognised by the FSA in the Takeover Code, then that behaviour – ie a disclosure (or not) that is required by Takeover Code – is protected against market abuse liability.

1   See discussion in Chapter 4 at **4.19-4.22**.

MARKET ABUSE

11.17   Certain Code rules if not complied with may result in market abuse liability.

Rule 2 requires that the offeror must announce a possible takeover when, following the approach to the offeree company, unusual movements occur in the offeree's share price, or the offeree is subject to rumour or speculation. Also, the offeror must announce a takeover attempt before an approach is made to the offeree if there is an unusual share price movement and it is reasonable that such movement is attributable to the offeror's actions. The offeror must also announce when negotiations are extended to include more than a restricted group of persons (six or more). Breach of these rules can potentially lead to a FSA enforcement action for market abuse.

ACTUAL OR POTENTIAL OFFERORS

11.18   Rule 2.1 requires third party advisers (eg accountants) who are privy to price-sensitive inside information to keep offer discussions secret and that they should not approach additional third parties without prior approval of the Panel. The FSA can enforce breach of this rule by imposing sanctions. For example, an accountant seeking to avoid market abuse liability under this rule would be required to obtain approval from the Panel before disseminating the information to other parties. This would be an example of acceptable market practices under the safe harbour of the Market Abuse Directive and the FSA would likely recognise the safe harbour by not seeking market abuse sanctions.

Chapter 12

Compliance

INTRODUCTION

12.1

'... Compliance continues, in our view, to play a key role under more principles-based regulation. Compliance should effectively act as the conscience of the firm: make sure that people get strong signals about what is right and what is wrong, and, over time, weed out wrong-doing, and, if necessary, wrong-doers ...' Dr Thomas F Huertas, Director, Wholesale Firms Division and Banking Sector Leader, FSA. Fourth Annual Complinet Compliance Conference, 31 January 2007.

Effective compliance with the Market Abuse regime can only be fully appreciated when considering the overall structure of firms' operating systems of control. To effectively function, firms relay on a complex web of often interdependent processes and policies with both compliance management and senior management being central to the effectiveness of the firm's operation. Importantly, however, it should be recognised that no matter how central these three functions are, their effectiveness will be determined by the strength and soundness of senior management and the firm's overall approach to its organisation.[1]

---

1   This chapter includes material published in *The Regulation of Investment Services in Europe under MiFID: Implementation and Practice*. General Editor Emilios Avgouleas, Chapter 6 by Stuart Bazley, 2008 Tottel Publishing, and in Chapter 4, Bazley and Haynes, *Financial Services Authority Regulation and Risk-Based compliance* 2nd edition 2007, Tottel Publishing.

12.2   Complex and multilateral organisations cannot ensure compliance with sophisticated regulatory obligations through simple procedures and find that they have to consider not only technical steps within their procedures but external factors that might determine the ease at which procedures might be followed, that might threaten compliance with those procedures as well as the propensity of its staff to willingly follow the firm's written procedures and policies. A firm's culture and its values are of equal importance when determining a firm's response to its compliance obligations, as are the technical aspects of the procedures.

12.3   In this Chapter we will consider the legal basis of the regulatory obligations placed on firms to have in place compliance systems and controls and the interrelationship between those obligations and the notion of senior management responsibility. We will then consider some fundamental compliance arrangements necessary to support a firm's compliance with the

Market Abuse regime before we conclude by considering the very essence of the firm's compliance Function and how it serves to support the compliance arrangements established by a firm. The Markets in Financial Instruments Directive (MiFID)[1] and Directive 2006/73,[2] one of MiFID's implementing measures, set out detailed provision for minimum regulatory standards regarding the internal organisation of investment firms. To a large extent these measures have shaped the FSA's rules of systems and controls Thus much of this Chapter's assessment of an authorised firm's compliance arrangements will be directed at the provisions within MiFID.

1   Council Directive 2004/39/EC OJL145/1 on markets in financial instruments. In this chapter I refer to this directive as 'The Directive' and 'MiFID'. The Directive was amended by Council Directive 2006/31/EC OJL114/60 as regards certain deadlines.
2   Council Directive 2006/73/EC OJL241/26, implementing Directive 2004/39/EC as regards organisational requirements and operating conditions for investment firms and defined terms for the purpose of that Directive.

COMPLIANCE ARRANGEMENT SYSTEMS AND CONTROLS

Persons directing the business and senior management responsibility for compliance

12.4   For many years financial services regulators have been concerned that senior management take responsibility for ensuring that the business and affairs of financial services firms are responsibly and effectively organised and controlled. In the event of a firm breaching its regulatory or legal obligations it can often be shown that the matters leading to the firm's failure were either a direct result of a breakdown in the firm's organisational systems or because the activities or practices of individuals were not properly managed and understood by the senior management of the firm. Following the failure of Barings Bank, the Bank of England in the Report of the Board of Banking Supervision Inquiry into the Circumstances of the collapse of Barings 18 July 1995 stated:[1]

'The Chairman of Barings plc, Peter Baring, described the failure of controls with regard to BFS [Barings] as "absolute". We agree. It was this lack of effective control which provided the opportunity for Leeson to undertake his unauthorised trading activities and reduced the likelihood of their detection. We consider that those with direct executive responsibility for establishing effective controls must bear much of the blame.'

1   Bank of England, *Report of the Board of Banking Supervision Inquiry into the Circumstances of the Collapse of Barings*, 18 July 1995, para 13.10.

12.5   The MiFID regime provides a series of measures governing the appropriateness of a firm's senior management and their responsibilities with the firm. Article 9(1) of MiFID provides that Member States shall require the persons who effectively direct the business of an investment firm to be of sufficiently good repute and sufficiently experienced as to ensure the sound and prudent management of the investment firm. Article 9(2) further provides that Member States shall require the investment firm to notify the competent authority of any changes to its management, along with all information needed to assess whether the new staff appointed to manage the firm are of sufficiently good repute and sufficiently experienced. Pursuant to Article 9(3), the competent authority shall refuse authorisation if it is not satisfied that the persons who will effectively direct the business of the investment firm are of sufficiently good repute or sufficiently experienced, or if there are objective and demonstrable grounds for believing that proposed changes to the management of the firm pose a threat to its sound and prudent management.

12.6 MiFID stresses the role that a firm's senior management have in the operation of a firm's business, including their overall role in ensuring that the firm operates in compliance with its requirements. Regulators, including the UK's Financial Services Authority, have sought to ensure that by having a compliance function within the firm, senior management do not abrogate their responsibility for compliance to that department or senior personnel within the compliance team. Article 9(1) of Directive 2006/73/EC provides that Member States should require investment firms to ensure that senior management, and, where appropriate, the supervisory function,[1] have responsibility for ensuring that the firm complies with its obligations under MiFID.

1 For the purpose of Article 9, supervisory function is defined as the persons to whom senior management are responsible, which may mean a governing committee of the firm such as the board of directors.

12.7 In addition, Article 9(1) of Directive 2006/73/EC goes on to support the requirement for senior management's overall responsibility for compliance by introducing the obligation for senior management and, where appropriate, the supervisory function to assess and periodically to review the effectiveness of the firm's policies, arrangements and procedures put in place to comply with the obligations under MiFID and to take appropriate measures to address any deficiencies.

12.8 Overall, the obligations contained in Article 9(1) of Directive 2006/73/EC will result necessarily in a firm's senior management having to work closely with its compliance function to ensure there is a proper understanding of the extent to which the firm is meeting its obligations under the Directive, the risks of it not meeting its regulatory obligations and the measures it puts in place to rectify any risk or threats to its obligation to comply. Senior management's obligations under Article 9 should be assessed in conjunction with the responsibilities of the compliance function under Article 6 of Directive 2006/73/EC, as well as the more general organisation obligations under Article 5.

Systems and controls

12.9 The Directive recognises that a regulatory regime should be able to adapt to the diversity of size, their structure and the nature of investment businesses across Member States. Recital 12 of Directive 2006/73/EC provides that a regulatory regime which entails too much uncertainty for investment firms may reduce efficiency. In light of the efficiency requirement, this Directive expects that competent authorities issue interpretative guidance on provisions on this Directive, with a view in particular to clarifying the practical application of the requirements of the Directive to particular kinds of firms and circumstances.

12.10 The FSA sets out in its Systems and Controls Sourcebook specific rules addressed at obligations for designing and maintaining systems and controls.[1] Many of the rules in SYSC are supported by guidance on how firms might comply with its provisions. The starting point as well as most fundamental requirement in SYSC is the requirement for the establishment and maintenance of appropriate systems and controls across all areas of the firm's business. SYSC 3.1.1R provides:

'A firm must take reasonable care to establish and maintain such systems and controls as are appropriate to its business.'

1   Most firms which conduct business subject to the Capital Requirements Directive (CRD) are also subject to MiFID's regime. In addition, businesses falling outside MiFID's scope, such as insurance firms, may find their business impacted if they are part of a group subject to Directive and the CRD. This development potentially creates a complex set of organisational obligations for multi-function firms and groups of firms. Both the CRD and MiFID have internal organisation and systems and controls requirements. The FSA, recognising that the CRD and MiFID cover broadly the same ground – despite the wording of the Directives not being identical – considered that firms would operate more effectively under one set of regulatory standards as opposed to having to comply with two complimenting, but different, regulatory requirements that potentially apply to the same business of the firm. Consequently, FSA determined to create a unified set of regulatory obligations based on the CRD and MiFID requirements that would apply to both MiFID and CRD businesses. It refers to such businesses as 'Common Platform Firms'. The common platform provision is located in FSA's Senior management arrangements and systems and controls sourcebook in new topic-specific chapters covering matters such as Conflicts of Interest, Outsourcing and Risk Control. Although these changes alter the provisions of FSA's rules on organisational control, the FSA considers there will be minimal impact for firms that already have good practices and procedures supporting management oversight, effective risk management and other internal controls.

12.11   The manner of the drafting of this rule, although imposing a specific obligation on firms, allows a large degree of flexibility in how the firm's systems and controls are to be established and maintained and the extent of the systems and controls required.[1] Firms are required to take reasonable care to establish and maintain their systems. The introduction of reasonableness in one part introduces an objective test when assessing an individual firm's systems arrangements. Secondly, it reconciles with the FSA's principles of good regulation which make clear at FSMA 2000, s 2(3)(c) that in discharging its general functions the FSA is required to have regard to the principle that a burden or restriction which is imposed on a person, or on the carrying on of an activity, should be proportionate to the benefits, considered in general terms, which are expected to result from the imposition of that burden or restriction.

1   See guidance at SYSC 3.1.2G.

12.12   SYSC 3.1.1R also talks in terms of a firm's systems and controls being appropriate to its business. This provides firms with the scope to design and maintain their systems to suit their business. The FSA provide confirmation in SYSC 3.1.2 G of the variety of factors that might be taken into account and will affect the design and maintenance of a firm's internal controls which states:

'(1)   The nature and extent of the systems and controls which a firm will need to maintain under SYSC 3.1.1R will depend upon a variety of factors including:

(a)   the nature, scale and complexity of its business;

(b)   the diversity of its operations, including geographical diversity;

(c)   the volume and size of its transactions; and

(d)   the degree of risk associated with each area of its operation.

(2)   To enable it to comply with its obligation to maintain appropriate systems and controls, a firm should carry out a regular review of them.'

12.13   In the FSA's enforcement action against Citibank Global Markets Limited, FSA observed that the company's systems and controls applicable to the trading desk in question were inadequate in a number of respects, in particular there was concern about the traders' knowledge of what they were required to escalate to senior management and that although eventually the strategy in question was escalated, overall there were inadequate systems and controls in place to ensure that the details of the strategy were escalated adequately and in advance to senior management as well as there being a failure to consult with applicable control functions resulting in the trading strategy not being considered by Compliance, Legal or independent Risk Management before it was executed.[1]

1   FSA Final Notice, 28 June 2005.

12.14   What is clear is that compliance with SYSC3.1.1R entails not only the maintenance of appropriate systems, but by virtue of SYSC 3.1.2 (2) G and SYSC 3.2.6C R, requires that a firm has in place arrangements to regularly review its compliance systems and controls. Regular reviews are an essential mechanism for ensuring that systems continue to be effective and appropriate, partly to assess whether the systems remain fit for the purpose for which they were designed and secondly to establish whether they are been operated in the intended manner. Firms do regularly experience process slippage, finding after time that the application of systems and processes have changed beyond those designed.

12.15   SYSC 3.1.2G goes on to set out that although detailed requirements regarding systems and controls relevant to particular business areas or particular types of firm are specifically covered in the FSA Handbook, there are areas that the FSA would typically expect to see covered by the systems and controls referred to in SYSC 3.1.1R. These matters are set out in SYSC 3.2. SYSC 3.2.6R sets out the general requirement applying to all firms. It states,

'A firm must take reasonable care to establish and maintain effective systems and controls for compliance with applicable requirements and standards under the regulatory system and for countering the risk that the firm might be used to further financial crime.'

12.16   This rule clearly provides firms with the latitude to design compliance systems and controls that are appropriate to their business model and unique business risks rather than providing a one size fits all approach. Further guidance is provided in SYSC 3.2.6A (a) which makes it clear that an individual firm's approach to its compliance arrangements are comprehensive and proportionate to the nature, scale and complexity of the firm's activities.

Systems for financial crime

12.17   Article 13(2) of MIFID applied by the FSA at SYSC 6.1.1R, requires that firms must, in addition to establishing policies and procedures to ensure compliance with obligations under the regulatory system, establish, implement and maintain policies and procedures to counter the risk that the firm might be used to further financial crime. Financial crime is defined by section 6(3) of the Financial Services and Markets Act as any kind of criminal conduct relating to money or to financial services or markets, including Market Abuse, it covers the following:

(a)   fraud or dishonesty;
(b)   misconduct in or misuse of information relating to a financial market; or
(c)   handling the proceeds of crime;

and where the word offence includes an act or omission, which would be an offence if it had taken place in the United Kingdom.

12.18   However, relying on the definition of financial crime, SYSC 6.1.1R draws out from its general compliance systems obligation a requirement that firms pay specific attention to the risk that they may be used to further financial crime. Moreover, the specific reference in the financial crime defamation to misconduct in or misuse of information relating to the financial market will include those market abuse behaviours that also constitute a criminal offence such as trading on price-sensitive information. In highlighting financial crime, both Article 13(2) of MIFID and the financial services authority provide an expectation that firms should put in place special financial crime compliance procedures and policies that supplement their general compliance systems.

12.19   The recognition that both the scale and nature of the complexity of a firm's business should allow for it to determine appropriate policies and procedures applies to the requirement to deal with financial crime risk as much as it does to general compliance arrangements. We have discussed above the flexibility provided by Article 6(1) of the MIFID implementing directive, which has been recognised by the financial services authority within SYSC 6.1.2R.

12.20   The FSA's rules, however, impose upon investment firms an obligation to carry out regular assessments of the adequacy of their financial crime risk procedures for the purpose of ensuring that such procedures continue to comply with the systems and controls obligations in SYSC 6.1.1R. The authority does not provide any minimum expectation of the frequency of regular assessment, and in the same way that it provides scope for firms to determine the appropriateness of overall systems and controls, leaves the question of how regular assessment of money-laundering risk procedures should be determined by complexity of the procedures themselves as well as the extent to which the procedures are subject to change. Investment firms might, therefore, consider that to comply with the regular assessment obligation, that alongside ad hoc reviews they review their businesses impacts upon the risk of Market Abuse each time a change to business is planned.

Personal account dealing

12.21   Of concern to firms with staff who may have access to price-sensitive information, is the extent to which those staff might use that information by trading on it in their own account, whether intentionally or inadvertently. The Market Abuse Directive[1] Article 3 prohibits any person from:

(a)   disclosing inside information to any other person unless such disclosure is made in the normal course of the exercise of his employment, profession or duties;

(b)   recommending or inducing another person, on the basis of inside information, to acquire or dispose of financial instruments to which that information relates.

1   Directive 2003/6/EC on Insider Dealing and Market Manipulation ('The Market Abuse Directive') has been incorporated into United Kingdom law through a series of measures including the Financial Services and Markets Act 2000 (Market Abuse) Regulations 2005 (SI 2005/381).

12.22   Investment firms will typically seek to control personal trading by either pre-approving each individual trade, providing advance approval on certain types of trading activity, and prohibition against trading of certain investments or classes of investments. The control of the firm's staff's personal trading should arguably be an inherent feature of the general systems and controls requirements within SYSC 6.1R, the FSA, however, makes specific provision within for the necessity of controlling personal account trading at COBS 11.7R and again in relation to financial analysts and investment research at COBS 12.2.5R. The primary obligation contained within COBS 11.7.1R is aimed at restricting certain types of activities and applies to firms conducting designated investment business,[1] requiring them to establish, implement and maintain procedures aimed at preventing the three key activities of entering into specified types of personal transactions, advising on, procuring another person to enter into specified transactions and disclosing specified information or opinions to another person. The obligation in COBS 11.7.1R is derived from Article 12(1) of the MIFID implementing Directive and applies only in the case of relevant persons,[2] such as directors, partners, managers and employees, who are involved in activities that may give rise to a conflict of interest, or who have access to inside information relating to clients or with or for clients, which is obtained from an activity carried out by that person on behalf of the firm.

1 Designated Investment Business is defined in Part II of the Regulated Activities Order Order 2001 (SI 2001/544) (Specified Activities), and is an activity carried on by way of business:

    (a) dealing in investments as principal (Article 14), but disregarding the exclusion in Article 15 (Absence of holding out etc);

    (b) dealing in investments as agent (Article 21) but only in relation to designated investments;

    (c) arranging (bringing about) deals in investments (Article 25(1)), but only in relation to designated investments;

    (d) making arrangements with a view to transactions in investments (Article 25(2)), but only in relation to designated investments;

    (da) operating a multilateral trading facility (Article 25D);

    (e) managing investments (Article 37), but only if the assets consist of or include (or may consist of or include) designated investments;

    (ea) assisting in the administration and performance of a contract of insurance, but only if the contract of insurance is a designated investment.

    (f) safeguarding and administering investments (Article 40), but only if the assets consist of or include (or may consist of or include) designated investments; for the purposes of the permission regime, this is sub-divided into:

        (i) safeguarding and administration of assets (without arranging);

        (ii) arranging safeguarding and administration of assets;

    (g) sending dematerialised instructions (Article 45(1));

    (h) causing dematerialised instructions to be sent (Article 45(2));

    (i) establishing, operating or winding up a collective investment scheme (Article 51(1)(a)); for the purposes of the permission regime, this is sub-divided into:

        (i) establishing, operating or winding up a regulated collective investment scheme;

        (ii) establishing, operating or winding up an unregulated collective investment scheme;

    (j) acting as trustee of an authorised unit trust scheme (Article 51(1)(b));

    (k) acting as the depositary or sole director of an open-ended investment company (Article 51(1)(c));

    (l) establishing, operating or winding up a stakeholder pension scheme (Article 52 (a));

    (la) establishing, operating or winding up a personal pension scheme (Article 52(b));

    (m) advising on investments (Article 53), but only in relation to designated investments; for the purposes of the permission regime, this is sub-divided into:

        (i) advising on investments (except pension transfers and pension opt-outs);

        (ii) advising on pension transfers and pension opt-outs;

    (n) agreeing to carry on a regulated activity in (a) to (h) and (m) (Article 64).

    (o) providing basic advice on a stakeholder product (Article 52B).

2 Relevant person is defined in senior management arrangements, systems and controls (markets in financial instruments and capital requirements directives) instrument 2006 and by Article 2(3) Markets in Financial Instrument Implementing Directive.

ENTERING INTO PERSONAL TRANSACTIONS

12.23   Only certain types of personal transactions are prevented under COBS 11.7.1R. In essence these are transactions that would otherwise be derived from the use of price-sensitive information, market manipulative behaviour or where the transaction would be likely to conflict between the firm and one of its customers. COB 11.7.1 cross refers its prohibition to The EU Market Abuse Directive which at Article 2, requires Member States to prohibit persons who possess inside information from using that information to acquire or dispose of a financial instrument to which the information relates. The prohibition is imposed where the instrument is traded for the person's own account as well as for the account of a third party, and where it might be traded either directly or indirectly and where there is only an attempt to transact. Equally, the Directive prohibits at Article 4 any person from engaging in market manipulation.

Suspicious transaction reporting

12.24   Since the Financial Services Authority introduced modifications to its code of market to comply with the Market Abuse Directive, firms have had to pay particular attention to the monitoring and reporting of transactions where there are reasonable suspicions that a market abuse offence has occurred. The FSA rules relating to suspicious transaction reporting relate to Qualifying Investments[1] traded on a prescribed market.[2] The definition, covering a range of common financial instruments such as Transferable Securities, futures and options contracts traded on Markets including all UK recognised exchanges.

1   The Financial Services and Markets Act 2000 (Prescribed Markets and Qualifying Investments) Order 2001 SI 2001/996. The term 'Qualifying Investment' covers; transferable securities; units in a CIS; money market instrument; financial futures contracts; forward interest rate agreements; interest rate, currency and equity swaps; options to acquire or dispose of the above (including currency and interest rate options); derivatives on commodities; any other investment admitted to trading on a regulated market in a Member State for which a request for admission to trading has been made.
2   A prescribed Market includes EDX, IPE, LIFFE, LME, LSE (incl. AIM), Virt-X, Plus (formally OFEX).

12.25   The main FSA rules imposing reporting obligations are contained in SUP. These include SUP 15.10.2 R which sets out the requirement to report:

'A firm which arranges or executes a transaction with or for a client in a qualifying investment admitted to trading on a prescribed market and which has reasonable grounds to suspect that the transaction might constitute market abuse must notify the FSA without delay.'

12.26   Sup 15.10.3R provides:

'a firm that is an investment firm or a credit institution, must decide on a case by case basis whether there are reasonable grounds for suspecting that a transaction involves market abuse, taking into account the elements constituting market abuse.'

12.27   Although the definition of a reasonably suspicious transaction under the Market Abuse regime is a similar test to that under Proceeds of Crime Act 2002 for money laundering reporting, firms impacted by the Market Abuse Directive must consider quite separate obligations for abusive transaction monitoring. Matters to be taken into account: must be sufficient indications to support reasonable grounds; other transactions, behaviour or information known to the firm; or specific elements constituting insider trading or market manipulation. In essence each transaction must be dealt with by way of a case-by-case assessment.

12.28 The FSA rules on systems and controls create an expectation that firms should have in place systems to identify suspicious transactions. The appropriateness of such systems will be determined by the size, complexity and nature of a firm's business, but will ordinarily feature a method to allow for the identification of suspicious transactions. All staff will be required to be vigilant for suspicious activity. However, central to the firm's systems will be compliance monitoring of potential for misuse of price-sensitive information within a firm, through the maintenance of watch and restricted lists. For example, a firm should expect that those individuals given price-sensitive information should disclose that fact to the firm's compliance department who will then monitor for any potential leakage of the information by monitoring the trading activities of staff and its clients as well as restricting the business trading in the securities.

12.29 Having identified a suspicious activity, the matter must be reported to the FSA Market Conduct Team as soon as possible. While the FSA has stressed that it does not expect many reports under the SUP15 regime, it expects quality reports with meaningful information.The report must contain a description of the transaction (type of order and type of trading market), reasons for suspicion that the transaction might constitute market abuse, a means for identifying the persons for whom the transaction was carried out, others involved in a relevant transaction and the capacity in which the firm operates.

General reporting obligations

12.30 In addition to the obligation to report to the FSA detail of suspicions of Market Abuse, the operation of compliance systems and controls creates additional regulatory reporting obligations in the event of a failure in the operation of such systems. Such reporting obligations can arise where there is a breach of procedure or in the event of proceedings by other regulatory agencies. Firms are obliged by Principle for Business 11 to notify the FSA of '… anything relating to the firm of which the FSA would reasonably expect notice.' The FSA provide guidance in SUP 15.3.8G of the types of matters that should be disclosed to ensure compliance with Principle 11. These will include matters such as any significant failure in the firm's systems or controls, including those reported to the firm by the firm's auditor.

12.31 The FSA requires notification under SUP 15.3.1R of matters that will have a serious regulatory impact, in particular relating to the firm's authorisation, its reputation in the market, its ability to service its customers or have financial impact of the financial system or other firms. Each of the specific requirements, although potentially overlapping, must be notified to the FSA immediately the firm becomes aware, or has information which reasonably suggests, that the matters have occurred or may occur in the foreseeable future. The matters are:

(1) the firm failing to satisfy one or more of the threshold conditions; or

(2) any matter which could have a significant adverse impact on the firm's reputation; or

(3) any matter which could affect the firm's ability to continue to provide adequate services to its customers and which could result in serious detriment to a customer of the firm; or

(4)   any matter in respect of the firm which could result in serious financial consequences to the financial system or to other firms.

12.32   Notifications are also required under SYSC 15.3.11R when the firm has identified breaches of FSA rules or provisions of the Act by or against the firm, its directors or employees, approved persons or appointed representatives. The firm is required to make notification under SYSC 15.3.11R immediately it becomes aware, or has information which reasonably suggests, that there are actual or foreseeable matters including any of the following:

(1)   a significant breach of a rule (which includes a Principle) or Statement of Principle;

(2)   a breach of any requirement imposed by the Act or by regulations or an order made under the Act; or

(3)   the bringing of a prosecution for, or a conviction of, any offence under the Act, against the firm or any of its directors, officers, employees, approved persons, or appointed representatives.

12.33   Civil or regulatory proceedings can arise in the context of Market Abuse and can also give rise to an obligation for immediate notification of matters to the FSA under SUP15.3.15R and includes civil proceedings that are brought against the firm where the amount of the claim is significant in relation to the firm's financial resources or its reputation; disciplinary measures or sanctions have been imposed on the firm by any statutory or regulatory authority, professional organisation or trade body; or the firm is prosecuted for, or convicted of, any offence involving fraud or dishonesty.

12.34   Furthermore, the FSA is concerned to receive immediate notification of matters relating to fraud, matters impacting upon honesty and integrity and accounting or record irregularities, including under SUP 15.3.17 R where it becomes aware that an employee may have committed a fraud against one of its customers or the firm.

12.35   SUP 15.3.17R expresses the obligation in terms of events that are significant. In relation to the requirement that the FSA provide guidance and expect firms, when determining whether a matter is significant, to have regard to both size of any monetary loss or potential monetary loss to itself or its customers and the risk of reputational loss to the firm. The FSA is also concerned as to whether the incident or a pattern of incidents reflects weaknesses in the firm's internal controls.

12.36   The question of whether or not to report regulatory issues or rule breaches to the FSA can be a difficult one for a firm. It is certainly the case that not all rule breaches should be reported, but a firm must be able to demonstrate that any identified rule breaches have been managed internally in an appropriate manner, whether or not they have been reported. It may be difficult for senior management of the firm to predict whether an isolated incident or more widespread rule breach should be reported. In determining whether a report is necessary the following questions may be asked:

●   Is the matter sufficiently material that the regulator will want to be notified of the matter? Materiality can be defined as something of great importance or consequence.

●   Is the issue widespread within the organisation? For example, if during the firm's compliance monitoring programme it is identified that the firm has failed to meet its regulatory obligation either universally or for a statistically significant number of customers, then the firm should

consider reporting this matter. However, if the incident is related to no more than one or a few customers, then it may be sufficient not to report.
- Where there is a clear obligation to the regulator to make a report, such as under the approved persons regime where there is an obligation to make a statement in relation to the reasons for the dismissal by the firm of an approved person.

12.37 The question of whether or not to report a matter to a regulator presents many firms and compliance departments with a dilemma. Save those matters provided in the specific guidance, Principle 11 and SUP 15.3.1R and 15.3.11R are not specific about either the type of issues to be notified or the timing of notifications, and thus senior management are often faced with the dilemma of whether to report a matter and if so how quickly to report and how to phrase the report made. Management has to balance between its obligation to notify the FSA quickly and provide an accurate and thorough response demonstrating that the firm has both identified the full extent of the issues and is in control of remedying the problem. The firm's obligations to report and its desire to keep control of the management of the problems become pronounced when the matter is so serious that it might reasonably lead to enforcement. When potential enforcement issues are identified within a firm it is not merely a question of addressing the matter internally. Consideration must then be given to how notification should be provided to the FSA and the consequences of providing that notification.

12.38 A report of rule breaches presented to the FSA should be clear and in writing, containing as much support material as necessary to justify the methodology applied in identifying the breach, the investigation the firm is conducting to identify the extent of the breaches and any corrective work either undertaken or proposed to eliminate the risk of further recurrence. The report should also contain, where necessary, a clear timescale over which corrective action will be completed. It may be that there need to be milestone dates at which certain actions are to be taken and this may very well include further contact with the regulatory authority. In the case of systemic breaches within the firm, the compliance department or senior management may also wish to retain a firm of external advisers or reporting accountants to review periodically the corrective work it will undertake to ensure that it is carried out to the standard deemed acceptable by the regulatory authority. Moreover, the firm may wish to offer external adviser reports to the regulatory authority as a way of providing further comfort.

THE COMPLIANCE FUNCTION

12.39 It is essential for firms to consider whether they need to have a separate compliance function. Once again this decision will be driven by the size, nature and complexity of the firm's business. The inter-relationship between the need to devote adequate resource to compliance and the decision to have a separate compliance function need not be confused. Scenarios are possible where a firm determines that its regulatory obligations can be met with dedicated resources within business units with oversight being undertaken by a small team of specialist compliance resource. The important test is whether the arrangements established by the firm are appropriate for its business. There are circumstances, however, when the oversight of compliance must be allocated to a senior manager or director of the firm. SYSC 3.2.8R provides that,

(1)   a firm which carries on designated investment business with or for customers must allocate to a director or senior manager the function of:

   (a) having responsibility for oversight of the firm's compliance; and

   (b) reporting to the governing body in respect of that responsibility.

12.40   Ultimately, the compliance arrangements established by a firm must be thoroughly documented, moreover SYSC 3.2.7G provides that the organisation and responsibilities of a compliance function should be documented, however, in order to demonstrate that the arrangements are appropriate it also seems imperative that the firm's reasoning and methodology in establishing the arrangements are documented.

12.41   The FSA's enforcement action against Carr Sheppards Crosthwaite Ltd (CSC)[1] addressed matters relating to compliance systems and the involvement of senior management relevant to SYSC 3.2.6R.That case related to inadequate and inappropriate systems and controls to monitor and demonstrate compliance. In particular, the FSA was concerned that CSC did not have in place systems and controls appropriate to its business in relation to the performance of its compliance function. It was reported that FSA found CSC's compliance policies and procedures to be inadequate and incomplete. A major problem for firms can occur when it is found that there are serious defects in their compliance manual or where it is not complete or is inadequate. Indeed such a defect appears to have been the catalyst for the FSA's action against CSC. It was reported that CSC's Compliance manual failed to adequately address matters such as financial promotions, outside business interests, out of hours trading, an authorised signature list containing names of former members of staff and in fact was out of date including copies of documents from the Securities and Futures Authority rules which had been superseded by the FSA rules.

1   FSA final notice, 19 May 2004.

12.42   The FSA's Final Notice reported that CSC had experienced a material failing in its maintenance of senior management arrangements, systems and controls and the involvement of senior management, which the FSA regarded as a key safeguard to ensuring the proper application of FSA rules and principles. This included criticism of the informal arrangements for reporting of compliance matters to CSC management. There was a lack of detailed written reporting such that CSC could not provide evidence that its management had been fully aware of key compliance issues or that management had sufficient tools with which it could measure future progress and monitor compliance issues. CSC had not established and implemented a detailed monitoring programme covering FSA rules and its business.

12.43   Article 6 of Directive 2006/73/EC expands upon Article 13(2) of MiFID listing the arrangements firms are required to have in place to operate in compliance with their obligations under MiFID. The central requirement is articulated in Article 6(1) of Directive 2006/73/EC, which refers to the need to establish, implement, and maintain adequate policies and procedures designed to detect any risk of failure by the firm to comply with its obligations under the directive or any associated risks. A central part of the Article 6 compliance obligation is the requirement of Article 6(3)(b) to appoint a compliance officer with responsibility for the compliance function and of any compliance reporting under Article 9(2).[1]

1   See further **12.44** to **12.50** below.

12.44 Some key points emerge from Article 6 that should inevitably shape a firm's effort to organise their compliance function under MiFID. It is clear that an obligation is established requiring not only the design of policies and procedures to allow the firm to obtain authorisation, but also to ensure that such policies and procedures are put into operation on a continuous basis. The use of the terms 'adequate' and 'designed to detect any risk of failure' in the context of firms' obligations under the Directive, help make it clear that firms' policies and procedures must be designed to meet their individual business model and the risks presented by that model. In the same mode, after initial authorisation, policies and procedures should be kept under review and adjustments to them made whenever the firm's regulatory risks alter.

12.45 Many investment firms have traditionally established a compliance function as an integral part of their arrangements for the oversight of its compliance procedures, sales function and to provide regulatory advice to the firm's senior management and governing body. The need to operate a compliance function has become an inherent part of a firm's arrangements under Article 13 (organisational requirements) of MiFID. Article 6(3) of Directive 2006/73/EC specifies how a firm should ensure that the compliance function can operate properly. The specific wording of that Article might, however, require firms to challenge their existing compliance function arrangements and perhaps make alterations to both the responsibilities of their compliance function and the arrangements for ensuring how the compliance function is able to discharge its responsibilities independently.

12.46 The Directive also describes the compliance function's required responsibilities, breaking them down between monitoring and advising. Article 6(2)(a) provides that the compliance function is to monitor and, on a regular basis, to assess the adequacy and effectiveness of the measures and procedures put in place in accordance with Article 6(1) and the actions taken to address any deficiencies in the firm's compliance with its obligations. The responsibility obligation establishes an oversight role for compliance where it is monitoring and assessing the adequacy and effectiveness of a firm's policies and procedures as opposed to being involved in the day-to-day operation of those procedures. The subtle wording of the Directive at Article 6 creates a role for compliance which can be independent of the firm's business operation, and indeed that requirement of independence is further required from specific requirements of independence contained in Article 6(3). This role of independence is in part confirmed by Article 6(3)(c), which requires that the persons involved in the compliance function must not be involved in the performance of services or activities they monitor.

12.47 In addition, a firm is required to establish a compliance function with responsibility for advising and assisting the relevant persons responsible for carrying out investment services and activities to comply with the firm's obligations under MiFID.

12.48 It is important however, that there is proper and efficient engagement between a firm's senior management and the compliance function. Proper communication of the efficiency of the firm's regulatory procedures in meeting the risk presented by the business as well as the efficacy of steps taken to deal with any identified risks helps to ensure senior management remains appropriately engaged with the firm's regulatory responsibility. This is particularly important given that the Directive makes clear that senior management are responsible for ensuring compliance, although only an independent compliance function may monitor the effectiveness of the firm's compliance arrangements. Article 9(2) provides that Member States shall require investment firms to ensure that their senior management receive on a frequent basis, and at least annually, written reports on the matters covered by Articles 6, 7 and 8, indicating in particular whether the appropriate remedial measures have been taken in the event of any deficiencies.

12.49   The obligations created by Article 6(2) are that the compliance function must be:

- permanent;
- effective; and
- operationally independent.

12.50   The requirement for permanence should be viewed as one of the base requirements for a firm's compliance requirement. However, although the Directive requires the function itself to be permanent, it is not entirely clear whether this is meant to require that the staff engaged in the role of compliance must also be permanent or full-time employees. In this regard, the compliance function might be taken to mean the compliance arrangements themselves, including the permanency of the arrangements for monitoring, overseeing and reporting. In circumstances where technology can be used to provide oversight of the firm's regulatory obligations then an argument might be constructed that the technological arrangements create the functional permanency which is supported by a part-time employee or employees. Indeed, the provision of the 2nd paragraph to Article 5(1) of Directive 2006/73/EC, regarding organisational requirements for firms, provides that investment firms take into account the nature, scale and complexity of the business of the firm, and the nature and range of investment services and activities undertaken in the course of that business. In appropriate circumstances it appears logical that personnel with responsibility for compliance need not be employed or engaged on a full-time basis. Smaller and less complex firms are given scope to operate a compliance function with dual responsibility by the 2nd paragraph to Article 6(3), provided that they are able to demonstrate that in view of the nature, scale and complexity of their business, and the nature and range of investment services and activities, the requirement of Article 6(3)(c) and (d) is not proportionate and that their compliance function continues to be effective. This limited opt-out only partly assist firms, which still have to meet the base requirements for independence, and thus firms should always consider whether compliance staff with dual roles have sufficient independence and ability to operate effectively.

Effective

12.51   Effectiveness of the compliance function partly established by the nature and extent of the arrangements that are put in place to meet the monitoring, review and advisory responsibilities under Article 6(2)(a) and (b) of Directive 2006/73/EC. There is a very clear linkage between the arrangements under these provisions and the general organisational arrangements that a firm must have in place to meet its regulatory obligations. The latter may be designed in the context of the nature and complexity of the firm's business. Thus to allow Article 6(2), the compliance arrangements must also be capable of being designed in the context of the complexity and scale of the firm's business.

12.52 Effectiveness will also be determined by the compliance function's ability to operate and brings into consideration issues such as the compliance function's level of authority within the firm, its resources and whether these are sufficient, its expertise, both in terms of the firm's business as well as the regulatory environment relevant to the business and the access provided to relevant information within the firm.[1]

1 Article 6 (3)(a), Directive 2006/73/EC.

Independent

12.53 The requirement under Article 6(2) for firms to establish and maintain a permanent and effective compliance function which operates independently raises a number of operational sensitivities for investment firms. Although larger investment firms will have the luxury of significant resource that allows them to identify compliance resources separate from the operational function, the criteria for compliance independence in Directive 2006/73/EC will undoubtedly present challenges for many firms. Such independence might be more difficult to achieve for some firms than others. Article 6(3) of Directive 2006/73/EC provides that in the context of independence a compliance function must operate so that the relevant persons involved in the compliance function are not involved in the performance of services or activities they monitor,[1] and the method of determining the remuneration of the relevant persons involved in the compliance function must not compromise their objectivity or must not be likely to do so.[2] These requirements seem to make it clear that a firm will have difficulties where its compliance function operating budget is linked to the firm's financial performance and where compliance remuneration is not determined independently of the business. During consultation on the implementation of the Directive, the FSA considered the question of whether those working in compliance are able to receive bonuses and, if so, whether such bonuses might be based on the performance of the firm as a whole, without calling into question its objectivity. The FSA concluded that it would not compromise the objectivity of those working in and responsible for the compliance function if they received bonuses calculated according to the performance of the firm as a whole. However, it considered that objectivity would be more likely to be compromised where bonuses for compliance staff are calculated according to the performance of specific areas or business lines they monitor.[3]

1 *Ibid* Article 6(3)(c).
2 *Ibid* Article 6(3)(d).
3 Financial Services Authority Policy Statement 06/13, para 4.8, Organisational Systems and Controls, November 2006.

12.54 Creating more complexity, however, would appear to be the implication that compliance function reporting lines would need to be structured so that the compliance function must have direct reporting lines to the firm's board or governing body. The general organisational requirements, set out in Article 5 of Directive 2006/73/EC, in many ways provide the basic structural obligations that underpin a firm's compliance arrangements, and how the compliance function will interact and communicate with the firm's senior management and other parts of the organisation. Although Article 5 is addressed towards the general organisation of a firm, many of its requirements also impact on how the compliance function should operate effectively, these areas include requirements broken down into areas covering procedures, responsibilities, internal control mechanisms, competence, effective internal reporting and communication and record keeping. Furthermore, Article 5 requires that a firm establish, implement and maintain decision-making procedures[1] and that a firm should establish an organisational structure which clearly and in a documented manner specifies reporting lines and allocates functions and responsibilities.[2]

1 Article 5(1)(a), Directive 2006/73/EC.
2 Article 5(1)(a), Directive 2006/73/EC.

12.55 During its consultation about the role of the compliance function under the Directive, the FSA considered the issue of compliance independence in the context of its relationship with other functions and in particular the likely relationship between an independent compliance function and with the internal audit function and whether in particular staff working in the compliance function can carry out internal audit work, where it is not appropriate or proportionate for a firm to have an internal audit function. The FSA's view on such arrangements was understandably based on the complexity of the firms in question and the proportionality of the need to maintain separate functions. Although its view was directed at the relationship between compliance and internal audit, there is no reason why it does not have an application to the relationship between compliance and other governance functions. The FSA expressed the view that where a firm has an internal audit function, it must be separate and independent from the firm's compliance function. The FSA in particular envisage that an internal audit would review the effectiveness of the compliance function within a firm's usual governance arrangements. It went on, however, to express the view that where a firm considers that a separate internal audit function would be disproportionate, it is still required to ensure it has adequate internal control mechanisms and arrangements. The firm's compliance staff may be used to ensure this, provided that the performance of multiple functions does not, and is not likely to, prevent those persons from discharging any particular function soundly, honestly and professionally.[1]

1 FSA Policy Statement PS 06/13, Organisational Systems and Controls, para 4.11, November 2006.

RISK-BASED COMPLIANCE

12.56 A chapter on compliance would not be complete without it giving brief consideration to the concept of risk-based compliance. If there can be one paramount feature of modern financial regulation, it is the role that risk analysis now plays in regulation of the financial sector.

12.57 The concept of risk-based regulation was highlighted in the Report to the Chancellor of the Exchequer on the Reform of the Financial Regulatory System in July 1997 which stated at paragraph 2, Style and process of regulation: Risk-based approach:

> '[FSA] will adopt a flexible and differentiated risk-based approach to setting standards and to supervision, reflecting the nature of the business activities concerned, the extent of risk within particular firms and markets, the quality of firms' management controls and relative sophistication of the consumers involved …'.

12.58 In its publication 'A New Regulator for a New Millennium' the FSA set out its then proposed approach to the supervision of firms conducting investment business in the United Kingdom. The approach was referred to as a risk-based approach to regulation and had been developed around the notion that maintaining market confidence does not aim to prevent all collapses or lapses in conduct in the financial system. Given the nature of financial markets, which are inherently volatile, achieving a no-failure regime is impossible and undesirable. In fact a zero-risk regime would most likely damage the economy as a whole as it would be both uneconomic from a cost benefit point of view as well as stifling market innovations and competition. Moreover, risk is an inherent feature of any financial market. Certain risks should not be eliminated at all. Taking consumer investment as an example, investment performance risk is a necessary feature of a financial market and provided an investment firm has made the investor aware of the nature of the risk involved and not made excessive claims about the investment, the FSA should have no role protecting the consumer from an economic fall in the value of their investment. In fact a zero-failure regime would engender a view by consumers that firms might never be permitted to fail and thus act as a disincentive for customers to assess the risk associated with their investment decisions. The FSA's approach to risk, however, was described as one of seeking ways of minimising the impact of failure in the financial market.

12.59 Issues surrounding the desirability for risk-based regulation and the balance between regulatory intervention and a regime that allowed some risk to materialise were addressed by the FSA's Kari Hale in a speech entitled 'Risk-based compliance for financial services' in which the concept or risk based compliance in the markets. He stated,

> 'After all, most markets have some element of market failure. Often those who favour intervention argue that any market failure justifies intervention. But, the real test goes beyond that: there must be both market failure and the prospect that intervention will provide a net benefit. This involves recognising that regulatory intervention has a cost; and that regulatory intervention, like reliance on market operations, has a non-zero probability of failure ...'[1]

1   Kari Hale Director Finance FSA, 25 November 2004.

12.60 This approach further developed the requirements of the Principles of Good Regulation in the Financial Services and Markets Act 2000, s 2(3) which states in particular:

> '(3)   In discharging its general functions the Authority must have regard to-
>
> (a)   the need to use its resources in the most efficient and economic way
>
> (b)   ...
>
> (c)   the principle that a burden or restriction which is imposed on a person, or on the carrying on of an activity, should be proportionate to the benefits, considered in general terms, which are expected to result from the imposition of that burden or restriction ...'

12.61 The FSA's approach to risk-based regulation has continued to be developed in the seven years since 30 November 2001 and continues to be an approach the FSA strives to develop and improve. It is at the very core of the FSA activities, how it supervises firms and the market as well as being a concept that is closely aligned to the FSA approach to the structure and design of its rules which are now undergoing a simplification process.

12.62 At the root of the FSA's operating risk framework is the issue of cost for the utilisation of its resources, the fact that it has finite resource and how it can best demonstrate that it has met its statutory objectives. A risk-based approach allows the FSA to focus its resources on the areas of greatest risk to its objectives as well as allowing it to develop a bias towards proactively identifying and then reducing those risks before any can cause major damage or failure in the markets.

12.63 The FSA has developed a risk-mapping framework as an operational approach to identifying risk. The framework acts as a bridge between the FSA's regulatory functions and its statutory objectives. The process of risk identification, mitigation and performance evaluation is a central part of how the FSA determines its activities. The process is both thoroughly mapped out and comprehensibly managed. In its second progress report the FSA described its risk mapping system in the following terms:

'... designed to enable [the FSA] to assess risks, whether at the firm specific level or at the consumer, product, market or industry level ...'[1]

1   FSA *Building the New Regulator*, progress report, 2 February 2002.

12.64 The FSA draws on information from external sources asking whether external issues might affect firms, consumers, products, markets or industries in a manner that will impact on the statutory objectives. In addition, other risks are identified throughout the year as part of the FSA's general regulatory activities. These may be risks caused by firms' activities or product developments. Once again as any such risks are identified they are related back to the FSA's statutory objectives.

Risk prioritisation and resource allocation

12.65 In terms of its risk-operating framework, the FSA has to determine whether or not to respond to a particular risk, given its significance to its ability to meet its statutory objectives. To help determine the timing of the FSA's response to identified risk and the resources to be allocated to dealing with them, at the risk assessment and prioritisation stage the FSA assesses and prioritises the identified risks against probability and impact factors. A probability factor considers the likelihood of the risk manifesting itself as an event, and the impact factor indicates the significance of the event if it were to take place. The FSA then use a combination of the probability factor and impact factor to measure the overall risk posed to its statutory objectives and prioritises the risks, enabling it to provide an appropriate regulatory response.

12.66 The use of regulatory themes has increasingly become a major regulatory tool, allowing the FSA to allocate its resources towards assessing the probability and impact of identified risk amongst a sample of regulated businesses. Each year the FSA publishes in its plan and budget the themes for the forthcoming year. In terms of a firm's own responsibility towards identified risk, the FSA states that themes should be sufficiently important to justify the attention of senior management within firms, and provide output which firms can assess to enable them to take steps in order to deal themselves with the identified risks.

12.67 A substantial element of the FSA risk operating framework relates to the time and resource it devotes to the assessment of risk posed by individual firms and the impact that firm's specific risk may have on its success in meeting the statutory objectives. The firm's specific risk assessment framework starts from the point when the FSA assesses new applications for authorisation and continues through their ongoing supervision of firms' activities.[1] The FSA's relationship with firms is risk-based and as part of this approach the FSA aims to give firms a greater incentive to conduct business in a way that reduces their regulatory attention. This can result in well managed firms experiencing a lighter touch of supervision than poorly managed firms. The FSA's publication 'Building the New Regulator, progress report 2' stated the following:

> 'Our relationship with firms will be risk based. This means that there will be a base level of supervisory activity or intensity with each firm ...the base level of supervisory intensity will depend on impact (ie the effect on the statutory objectives of risk crystallising). These will help determine the nature of the relationship that we expect to have with that firm, with a higher proportion of our resources devoted to supervising those firms that pose a higher risk to our objectives.'

1   The FSA firm risk assessment programme is set out in *Financial Services Authority: The firm risk assessment framework*, February 2003.

12.68   To assess the risk that each authorised firm poses to its statutory objectives the FSA has developed a risk assessment programme commonly referred to as 'Advanced Risk Response Operating Framework' (commonly referred to as Arrow). One of the outcomes of the firm's specific programme is to place firms into one of four relationship categories: A high, B medium high, C medium low, and D low. A firm's individual categorisation is determined during risk assessment work by way of the impact (the potential effect the risk will have on the statutory objectives) and probability factors (the likelihood of a particular risk event crystallising). The allocation of a firm to a particular category may change over time if the risk assessment of the firm alters.

12.69   The FSA's first step in its firm risk assessment is to understand the impact of an individual firm. It does this by conducting baseline monitoring of firms in all relationship categories by way of reviews of regulatory returns such as audited accounts, financial returns, complaint returns and notifications. Returns are monitored to identify potential breaches of regulatory requirements. Further preparation is conducted into a firm's legal, business and management structure as a way of deciding what areas within a firm need to be assessed. In most cases the FSA finds that firms' business structures are simple enough for its risk assessment framework to be applied to the entire firm. A number of firms, however, are more complex. They may be a large group where there is a layered legal, management and business structure.

12.70   Once the FSA has completed its impact assessment it will conduct a probability assessment of a firm to assess the likelihood of a risk crystallising and its potential affect on the statutory objectives. The probability assessment is also used to provide the early stages of a risk mitigation programme for an individual firm. The probability assessment comprises desk-based assessment of existing and new information supplied by firms and where the risk category of the firm is A, B or C, the FSA supervisor will conduct a visit at a firm to carry out on-site assessment. An element of the probability assessment is to review the potential for environment risks external to a firm that might directly or indirectly affect a firm's business or control of risk. These will include risks across categories such as political/legal, socio-demographic, technological, economic, competition and market structure.

12.71   Each firm's Risk Mitigation Programme (RMP) will include both an impact score for the firm and a probability score against each of the statutory objectives. The scoring levels are High, Medium High, Medium Low or Low. The report will show against each identified risk the outcome sought by the FSA, together with the date by which it is to be achieved as well as any action to be taken by the FSA or the firm to allow the FSA to achieve the results it desires. The FSA also view the role of senior management within a firm as an important element in the progress of each RMP both in terms of risk identification and the determination of any necessary regulatory actions. The commitment shown by senior management to any risk identified by the FSA can and does have an impact on the regulatory tools the FSA may choose to use to deal with the matter, as well as determining a shift between preventative work and less intrusive monitoring work.

Chapter 13

The impact of other laws: domestic and overseas

INTRODUCTION

13.1   The globalisation of financial markets has resulted in increased interaction among securities firms and investors in different jurisdictions. The securities and derivatives markets underpin economic growth and development and the overall strength of market economies by, for example, supporting corporate initiatives, providing finance for new ideas and facilitating the management of financial risk. Sound and effective regulation can, in turn, enhance market confidence and the integrity and development of securities markets. Increasingly, globalised and integrated securities markets pose significant challenges for regulators. Share transactions are taking on an increasingly international character. In a global and integrated securities market, national regulators must be able to assess the nature of cross-border conduct if they are to ensure the existence of fair, efficient and transparent markets.

13.2   The increasingly global market also brings with it the increasing interdependence of national regulators. Accordingly, there must be strong co-operation and co-ordination between regulators and capability to give effect to those links. Cross-border trading in securities has caused a great deal of overlap in the regulatory responsibilities of national regulators and, in some instances, where economically powerful countries (eg the United States) impose their regulations extra-territorially, it can result in a diminution in sovereignty of affected nation states. Indeed, the world's largest and most liquid securities market is the United States and many non-US companies are subject to extra-territorial jurisdiction under US securities and banking laws because of their contacts with US commerce and financial markets. This chapter discusses some of the issues of institutional coordination in the EU/EEA in applying the Market Abuse Directive and examines the extraterritorial aspects of US anti-fraud law for insider dealing and market manipulation under the US securities laws. This chapter also analyses emerging international standards and principles to control insider dealing and market abuse in an international context. These international standards, principles and rules that relate to market abuse and insider dealing have been promulgated by the world's leading international body of securities regulators, the International Organisation of Securities Commissions ('IOSCO'). IOSCO has adopted international standards and principles to protect investors against market abuse and has set out standards for national regulators to use while investigating and prosecuting those who attempt to use unlawful means to manipulate securities markets.[1]

1 IOSCO Mutilateral Memorandum of Understanding (May 2002), Article 4(a) (describing the MOU's application to national laws and regulations dealing with insider dealing, market abuse and securities fraud). The IOSCO standards are important for understanding how the FSA may interpret the UK market abuse regime and how EEA states may implement these principles in their regulatory practices.

13.3   The barriers to a global securities market are diminishing: financial information has become inexpensive to obtain and advances in technology allow more complicated cross-border share transactions. Ultimately, the forces of liberalisation and technology will link most financial markets with the result that regulators should develop improved regulatory links to improve the effectiveness and efficiency of their financial markets. More efficient cross-border enforcement necessitates bilateral or multilateral agreements between national regulatory authorities that allocate jurisdictional authority amongst regulators so that they would have the jurisdictional authority to investigate and enforce market abuse that has cross-border elements.

IMPACT OF EU LAW ON MARKET ABUSE AND CO-OPERATION IN INVESTIGATIONS AND ENFORCEMENT

13.4   The European Communities have adopted the policy objective of financial integration for EU financial markets. To this end, the EU Council and Parliament approved in June 2001 the Financial Services Action Plan ('FSAP') that contains forty two legislative measures which have been adopted and implemneted by all EEA/EU states.[1] The Market Abuse Directive was one of these legislative measures that required all EEA states to adopt a civil offence for insider dealing and market manipulation.[2] The Market Abuse Directive requires EEA states to create a single regulatory authority for investigations and enforcement which must serve as a point of contact with other EEA regulators for coordinating cross-border investigations and enforcement in cases involving cross-border elements between EEA states. Moreover, the Market Abuse Directive requires all home state authorities to keep records of all transactions, ie the number of instruments bought and sold and the dates, times and transaction prices. The home state is obliged to exchange this information upon request with host state regulators during investigations of financial service firms based in other EU states who are operating in the jurisdiction. Host state's authorities will continue to be responsible for supervising and regulating all firms and persons operating within host state territory.[3]

1 The FSAP sets out a policy agenda to achieve a common European market in financial services. See European Commission, 'Financial Services: Implementing the Framework for Financial Markets: Action Plan' (1999) COM 232 (11 May 1999), p 23.

2 See the Directive on Insider Dealing and Market Manipulation ('Market Abuse Directive') (2003/6/EC). The Criminal Justice Act 1993, Pt V, implemented the requirement of Council Directive 89/552 that all Member States of the EU adopt laws creating a criminal offence of insider dealing for natural persons. See 89/552/EEC (13 November 1989)(OJ L 334, 18.11, 1989, p 30). The Market Abuse Directive replaced the Insider Trading Directive 1989.

3 The Market Abuse Directive provides that the 'competent regulatory authority' may periodically require all investment firms with branches or agency offices in their jurisdictions to report on their activities and to provide all information necessary for monitoring their compliance with the Market Abuse Directive.

13.5   EEA host states are required to facilitate transnational investigations and enforcement of financial regulation in the following way. If a financial firm with a passport from another EEA state is suspected or found to have violated national or EU financial laws, the host state regulator must take the following steps in order to address the breach: (a) approach the firm's home state regulator to seek assistance in conducting an investigation, and then (b) to co-operate with the home state regulator regarding any enforcement action.[1] Generally, the host state must take all appropriate measures at its disposal to end the violation and to adopt measured procedures in seeking co-operation and information before undertaking direct enforcement. Article 25 of the Market Abuse Directive addresses issues of confidentiality which provides that officials of the competent authority are bound by professional secrecy in relation to the information they receive in the course of their duties. These restrictions on disclosure contain exceptions, however, to allow assistance and information to be given to other authorities of EEA states which might have regulatory oversight over particular transactions and parties.

1   European Communities Directive on Insider Dealing and Market Manipulation (Market Abuse), Articles 6–10 (encouraging co-operation in enforcement matters by allowing national regulators to obtain necessary information).

13.6   The Market Abuse Directive also permits Member States to enter into mutual assistance agreements with third countries (eg countries outside the EEA) so long as the information exchanged is covered by guarantees of secrecy equivalent to those provided in Article 25. The UK has entered into many mutual assistance agreements and memoranda of understanding ('MOU') with countries outside the EEA that provide for the exchange of information and evidence to support investigations and enforcement actions by national authorities. For instance, the UK–US 1986 MOU[1] is a non-binding statement of principles and procedures for making requests for information in regard to investigations and enforcement actions in regard to alleged breaches of securities laws. Each national authority retains discretion whether to co-operate in the disclosure of requested information.[2] The UK–US MOU covers insider dealing, misrepresentations in the course of dealing and market manipulation and it applies to securities or futures traded within the territorial jurisdiction of each regulatory authority.[3] The impact of EU law and mutual assistance agreements has been substantial in requiring UK authorities to take account of international developments in financial regulation and to adopt practices that are similar to those taken by other regulatory authorities. Conflicts occur, however, when the laws of some jurisdictions are imposed unilaterally and in an extra-territorial manner without the consent of UK authorities. This has become a major issue in regard to the extra-territorial application of US securities laws as discussed below.

1   The relevant agencies today would be the US Securities and Exchange Commission and the Commodities and Futures Trading Commission and the UK Financial Services Authority.
2   For example, the UK Secretary of State may deny requests for co-operation on the grounds of public interest.
3   Paragraph 11 of the MOU provides for spontaneous provision of information by one agency to another.

13.7   The Market Abuse Directive has established a viable institutional and legal framework to enhance investor confidence and market integrity that has gone beyond enhancing 'co-operation between supervisors' by establishing a more common approach to detection and investigation as well as to enforcement'.[1] Although many EU national regulators agree that there should be some standard for regulating market abuse, difficulties have arisen regarding the implementation and enforcement of an EU-wide scheme. The Committee of European Securities Regulators (CESR)[2] has addressed these issues in a report that called for the establishment of an EU securities regulatory framework. CESR has played a crucial role in devising more harmonised approaches for EEA regulators to implement EU securities legislation and will continue to play an important role in promoting harmonised interpretation and application of the Market Abuse Directive.

1 For instance, the Market Abuse Directive sets 'common disciplines for trading floors to enhance investor confidence in an embryonic single securities market'. See also FESCO, 'Market Abuse: FESCO's Response to the Call for Views from the Securities Regulators Under the EU's Action Plan for Financial Services' (1999) COM 232 (29 June 2000).
2 The Lamfalussy Committee was created by the EU Council of Economic and Finance Ministers to propose a plan to implement the Financial Services Action Plan. See the initial report of the 'Committee of Wise Men' on the regulation of the European securities markets (9 November 2000), pp 26, 35 and Annex 1.

EXTRA-TERRITORIAL APPLICATION OF US SECURITIES LAWS, FOREIGN ISSUERS AND ANTI-FRAUD PROVISIONS

13.8   This section addresses the extra-territoriality of US securities laws in the context of how the anti-fraud provisions apply to foreign issuers and to transactions involving activities that take place, in part, in non-US territories. The extraterritorial dimension of US anti-fraud law merits discussion because of the close links between US and UK securities markets. US securities laws can expose UK persons and other non-US persons to civil and criminal liability for insider dealing and market manipulation. Most US case law addressing the extra-territorial application of US securities laws focuses on the anti-fraud provisions of the Securities and Exchange Act 1934.[1] The courts have developed two tests for determining subject matter jurisdiction in securities fraud cases. One test relies on the 'effects test' that assesses the effects in the United States of conduct that occurs in foreign countries, while the other focuses on the 'conduct' of foreign persons within the United States.

1   15 USCA, s 78a et seq.

Anti-fraud provisions of the US Securities and Exchange Act 1934, section 10(b)

13.9   Section 10(b) of the Securities and Exchange Act 1934 makes it unlawful, *inter alia*, to use or employ any manipulative or deceptive device or contrivance 'in connection with the purchase or sale of any security'. Moreover, section 27 of the Act vests the district courts with jurisdiction of all actions 'to enforce any liability or duty created by this title or the rules and regulations thereunder'. The federal courts, therefore, have jurisdiction to enforce the provisions of section 10(b), while the SEC has authority under Rule 10b-5 to enforce section 10(b) as a regulatory offence. The federal circuit courts have interpreted the anti-fraud provisions to have extra-territorial effect in a number of circumstances. Generally, the courts apply alternative tests: the 'conduct' test or the 'effects' test.[1] Under the conduct test, the court has subject matter jurisdiction 'where conduct material to the completion of the fraud occurred in the United States'.[2] Mere preparatory activities and conduct far removed from the conduct of the fraud will not suffice;[3] rather, '[o]nly where conduct "within the United States directly caused" the loss will a district court have jurisdiction ... '. Essentially, jurisdiction exists when 'substantial acts in furtherance of the fraud were committed in the United States.'[4] The test is met whenever the defendant's activities in the US are more than 'merely preparatory' to a securities fraud committed abroad, and the 'activities or culpable failures to act within the United States 'directly caused' the claimed losses.'[5]

1 *Butte Mining plc v Smith* 76 F 3d 287 (9th Cir, 1996).
2 *SEC v Berger* 322 F. 3d 187, 193 (2nd Cir, 2003); *Psimenos v E F Hutton & Co* 722 F 2d 1041, 1046 (2nd Cir, 1983).
3 *Psimenos v EF Hutton*, 722 F 2d at 1045.
4 *IIT v Vencap Ltd* 519 F.2d 1001, 1018 (2nd Cir 1975).
5 *Itoba Ltd v Lep Group PLC* 54 F.3d 118, 121–122 (2nd Cir 1995).

13.10 Under the 'effects' test, the court has jurisdiction 'whenever a predominantly foreign transaction has substantial effects within the United States'.[1] Thus, remote or indirect effects in the United States do not confer subject matter jurisdiction.

The Second Circuit Court of Appeals held in *Schoenbaum v Firstbrook*[2] that extra-territorial jurisdiction could be imposed on a transaction involving securities issued by a foreign corporation that were listed on a US stock exchange and held by US citizens on the grounds that such a transaction affected US securities markets. The court found that extra-territorial subject matter jurisdiction was justified under the federal securities laws on the basis that the challenged foreign transaction had an 'effect' on domestic US securities markets. Similarly, the Ninth Circuit also found extra-territorial jurisdiction based on the 'effects' test[3] in a case involving a takeover of a Canadian corporation by a US corporation that involved the improper use of the US corporation's securities, which were registered and listed on a US national exchange and had adversely affected both the foreign plaintiffs and the US securities markets. Further, extra-territorial jurisdiction can be imposed on foreign actors who make misrepresentations to US investors in the sale of foreign securities that were only traded in foreign markets.[4] In this case, the Second Circuit premised jurisdiction upon domestic conduct and the direct effect on US investors. Therefore, the US courts will consider two factors in determining whether extraterritorial subject matter jurisdiction will be applied: (1) whether the wrongful conduct substantially occurred in the US; or (2) whether the wrongful conduct had a substantial effect in the US or upon US citizens, wherever they are located.[5] However, extra-territorial jurisdiction will not be conferred on a transaction or occurrence if its only connection to US territory are activities in the United States that are 'merely preparatory' to the actual fraud.[6]

1 *Consolidated Gold Fields plc v Minorco SA* 871 F 2d 252, 261–262 (2nd Cir, 1989).
2 405 F 2d 200 (2nd Cir, 1968); cert denied 395 US 906 (1969).
3 *Des Brisay v Goldfield Corpn* 549 F 2d 133 (9th Cir, 1977).
4 *Leasco Data Processing Equipment v Maxwell* 468 F 2d 1326 (2nd Cir, 1972).
5 *Europe and Overseas Commodity Traders, SA v Banque Paribas London* 147 F.3d 118, 125 (2nd Cir 1998). But effects test will not create extraterritroial subject matter jurisdiction over the federal securities claims of foreign investors against foreign persons if the wrongful conduct in question was predominatnly foreign. See *In re Alstom SA*, 406 F. Supp. 2d 346 (2005).
6 *SEC v Berger* 322 F 3d at 193; *Zoelsch v Arthur Andersen & Co* 824 F 2d 27 (DC Cir, 1987); *Bersch v Drexel Firestone Inc* 519 F 2d 974 (2nd Cir, 1975).

13.11 The extra-territorial scope of the anti-fraud provisions also extends to the acts of a defendant based in the United States who perpetrates fraud upon non-US persons in a foreign country. The Second Circuit observed that the jurisdictional basis was sufficient in this case because Congress could not have intended 'to allow the United States to be used as a base for manufacturing fraudulent security devices for export, even when … peddled only to foreigners'.[1] Moreover, foreign nationals who are resident in the United States are protected to the same extent as US nationals so long as their claims arise at the time they are resident in the United States. This rule applies even though the fraudulent scheme is devised and set into motion abroad,[2] but a foreign corporation whose sole shareholder and chief executive officer was a foreigner residing in the United States was required to prove that losses incurred on account of the fraudulent scheme were directly caused by acts within the United States.[3] However, deception of a foreigner who is a sole shareholder within the United States, while necessary to demonstrate a fraudulent scheme, has thus been held insufficient proof of direct causation of loss.[4]

1   *Consolidated Gold Fields plc v Minorco SA* 871 F 2d 252 (2nd Cir, 1989); see also *IIT v Vencap Ltd* 519 F 2d 1001, 1017 (2nd Cir, 1975); on remand 411 F Supp 1094 (SDNY, 1975).
2   *O'Driscoll v Merrill Lynch, Pierce, Fenner & Smith Inc* Fed Sec L Rep 99, 486 (SDNY, 1983).
3   *O'Driscoll v Merrill Lynch, Pierce, Fenner & Smith Inc* WL 1360, 1361 (1983).
4   *Ibid.*

13.12   The Eighth Circuit imposed extra-territorial subject matter jurisdiction on foreign conduct that involved the use of the US telephone system and US mail to further a fraudulent scheme, even though the only victim of the fraud was a foreign corporation purchasing stock in another foreign company.[1] In this case, the foreign defendant sellers relied, in part, on the US telephone system and US mail fraudulently to induce foreign investors to purchase securities of a foreign company not listed on a US exchange. The court imposed extra-territorial jurisdiction, despite the fact that no transaction occurred in the United States nor involved US securities, by finding that the defendants' conduct (use of the US telephone and mail system) was significant – not 'merely preparatory' – and constituted a fraud devised and completed in the United States.[2]

1   *Continental Grain (Australia) Pty Ltd v Pacific Oilseeds Inc* 592 F 2d 409 (8th Cir, 1979).
2   *Continental Grain (Australia) Pty Ltd v Pacific Oilseeds Inc* at 420.

13.13   The Second and Third Circuits have also upheld extra-territorial subject matter jurisdiction based on conduct in the United States that directly caused a foreign plaintiff's losses, even though the fraud had no direct effect on US securities markets or upon investors in the United States.[1] Therefore, foreigners purchasing securities in the United States are protected by US federal securities laws.[2] Jurisdiction, however, will not extend to conduct that is, at most, 'ancillary' or peripheral and therefore not the direct cause of the plaintiff's losses. The Second Circuit took this position in *Fidenas AG v Compagnie Internationale Pour L'informatique CII Honeywell Bull SA*,[3] when it denied extra-territorial jurisdiction to the claims of foreign investors against a foreign subsidiary that was wholly-owned by a US parent on the grounds that knowledge by the US parent of fraudulent conduct committed by its foreign subsidiary was insufficient US conduct. In a subsequent suit filed against the US parent for the same fraud, the court denied jurisdiction on the basis that mere knowledge of the fraud was insufficient to confer extra-territorial subject matter jurisdiction upon US courts. The court then relied on the Second Circuit's view that the transactions were 'predominantly foreign' and thereby dismissed the suit for failing to satisfy either the 'conduct' or 'effects' test for subject matter jurisdiction.

1   *SEC v Kasser* 548 F 2d 109 (3rd Cir, 1977); cert denied 431 US 938 (1977).
2   *IIT v Cornfeld* 619 F 2d 909, 918 (2nd Cir, 1980). See also *Arthur Lipper Corpn v SEC* 547 F 2d 171 (2nd Cir, 1976); cert denied 434 US 1009 (1978).
3   606 F 2d 5 (2nd Cir, 1979).

13.14   Similarly, the US District Court for the Southern District of New York has applied the transaction test to deny extra-territorial subject matter jurisdiction in a case where the primary fraud and every fact essential to the plaintiff's claim of fraudulent misconduct was committed or occurred in Costa Rica.[1] The transaction was considered not to have had significant enough effects on US securities markets and the fraudulent conduct in question was ancillary to the US and was 'predominantly foreign'.[2] In addition, extra-territorial subject matter jurisdiction will not be conferred where US investors used circuitous means (by setting up an overseas shell corporation) in order to conceal their US nationality so that they could participate in a foreign public offering in which they purchased the non-US securities of a foreign corporation. The court held that the plaintiffs were estopped from bringing a claim under the US securities laws because they had gone to great efforts to avoid and evade the Act's requirements.[3]

1   *Mormels v Girofinance SA* 544 F Supp 815 (SDNY, 1982).
2   *Mormels v Girofinance SA.*
3   *MCG Inc v Great Western SA* 544 F Supp 815 (SDNY, 1982).

13.15   Based on the above cases, the following propositions can be made about the extra-territorial application of the anti-fraud provisions of the US securities laws:

- that jurisdiction will be conferred on acts of material importance that occur in a foreign country if such acts cause losses in the sale of securities to US resident investors in the United States;
- that jurisdiction will be conferred on acts of material importance that occur in the United States if they cause losses in the sale of securities to US residents abroad;
- that extraterritorial jurisdiction can apply to foreign persons so long as the wrongful conduct substantially occurred within the US; and
- that jurisdiction will *not* be conferred on transactions that result in losses in the sale of securities to foreigners outside US territory *unless* acts within the United States directly caused such losses.[1]

1   See *Bersch v Drexel Firestone Inc* 519 F 2d 974 at 993 (2nd Cir, 1975); cert denied 423 US 1018 (1975).

Reporting and disclosure requirements

13.16   The collapse of Enron and WorldCom in 2002 demonstrated the importance of accurate and non-misleading reporting by companies whose securities are listed on US exchanges and/or make public offerings to US investors. The jurisdcitional scope of the US securities laws' disclosure and reporting requirements, however, are more narrowly defined. A foreign issuer's filing of misleading reports to the SEC will not of itself provide a sufficient jurisdictional basis to support a private right of action by foreign investors. This means that there will be no US jurisdiction over claims by foreign investors residing abroad against a foreign corporation for filing misleading reports with the SEC, even though the misrepresentations were contained in documents filed with the SEC and also were circulated in the US press.[1] In contrast, there will be US jurisdiction where a non-US national residing abroad brings an action against a foreign corporation for fraud in connection with the sale of US securities since some of the acts that were apart of the fraud occurred in the United States.[2] Jurisdiction will also extend to misrepresentations in a prospectus delivered outside US territory by a foreign corporation to foreign investors residing abroad if negotiations relating to the prospectus took place in

US territory.[3] The Sarbanes-Oxley Act 2002 creates extraterritorial subject matter jurisdiction over a foreign issuer and its chief executive and chief financial officer for signing annual or quartely reports that are materially incorrect which can lead to civil and criminal liability. Generally, however, the extra-territorial application of US securities law's reporting and disclosure requirements will not permit a foreign shareholder of a US-listed non-US company to bring a private right of action against the foreign company arising out of misrepresentations in a prospectus or other similar documents if the plaintiff cannot provide adequate proof of causation from acts that took place in the United States.

1 *Kaufman v Campeau Corpn* 744 F Supp 808 (SD Ohio, 1990).
2 *Kaufman v Campeau Corpn.*
3 *Alfadda v Fenn* 935 F 2d 475 (2nd Cir, 1991).

Foreign manipulation of US markets

13.17 The US government imposes criminal liability on non-US persons or business entities that are engaged in off-shore manipulations affecting US markets or US issuers.[1] The basis for such jurisdiction is the Securities and Exchange Act 1934, section 9(a) that prohibits 'any person' from using 'any means or instrumentality of interstate commerce' (including e-mails, faxes and telephones) or of the mail, 'or of any facility of a national securities exchange [for a] manipulative or deceptive device or contrivance' in contravention of the SEC rules.[2]

1 *General Foods Corpn v Brannon* 170 F 2d 220, 234 (7th Cir, 1998).
2 *Cargill Inc v Hardin* 452 F 2d 1154 at 1163 (8th Cir, 1971).

13.18 US courts have generally held that, given the principal purpose of US securities laws to protect US investors exposed to fraudulent or manipulative activities that implicate the jurisdictional means of interstate commerce, foreign activities by foreign nationals producing such a result in the United States or affecting US investors will be subject to US jurisdiction, which will displace the foreign law and will, as a matter of conflict of laws, allow US courts to apply US laws to foreign nationals.

Extra-territorial jurisdiction over commodities trading and civil RICO

13.19 Where a cause of action arose from trading on US commodities exchanges, US courts will uphold extra-territorial subject matter jurisdiction, even though the parties to the suit were non-resident US aliens and the fraudulent transactions and conduct occurred in a foreign country.[1] In *Tamari*, the court relied on the 'effects' test to find that 'where the ... transactions involve trading on domestic exchanges, harm can be presumed, because the fraud ... implicates the integrity of the American market'.[2] The court also noted that extra-territorial jurisdiction could attach to a foreign defendant's transmission of orders on behalf of the foreign plaintiffs when such transmissions went from Lebanon to the commodities exchange in Chicago. Such transmissions constituted 'conduct within the United States that was of substantial importance to the success of the fraudulent scheme'.[3]

The Racketeer Influenced Corrupt Organisations Act ('RICO') contains no express provision regarding its extra-territorial application.[4] RICO applies to civil actions and provides an express private right of action for those who were defrauded by individuals who used their controlling influence over a business enterprise to commit a fraud. To determine extra-territorial jurisdiction, the courts seek guidance from precedents 'concerning subject matter jurisdiction for international securities transactions and anti-trust matters'.[5] Therefore, the courts will look to the cases discussed above to determine issues of extra-territoriality under RICO.

1 *Tamari v Bache & Co (Lebanon) SAL* 547 F Supp 309 (ND Ill, 1982); order affd 730 F 2d 1103 (7th Cir, 1984); cert denied 469 US 871 (1984).
2 *Tamari v Bache & Co (Lebanon) SAL* at 313.
3 *Tamari v Bache & Co (Lebanon) SAL* at 315.
4 See *John Doe v UNOCAL Corpn* 110 F Supp 2d 1294, 1310 (CD Cal, 2000).
5 *North South Finance Corpn v Al-Turki* 100 F 3d 1046, 1051 (2nd Cir, 1996).

13.20 In addition, jurisdiction may be imposed on the activities of non-US persons residing abroad when their activities affect the US marketplace. The Ninth Circuit in *Bourassa v Desrochers*[1] held that the jurisdictional link was satisfied by a Canadian broker's telephone call from Canada to an investor in the United States and later the US investor was able to serve the writ on the Canadian defendant while the defendant was on holiday in Florida. Jurisdiction was not satisfied, however, in a case where defrauded US investors brought an action for aiding and abetting liability against a foreign auditor for producing a report that was used by a foreign company without the consent of the auditor.[2] A US court also dismissed a claim based on lack of jurisdiction when it involved US investors who owned American Depository Receipts ('ADRs') and had received a press release announcing a UK company's tender offer for shares in a UK target company whose securities were trading in the United States through the use of ADRs.[3] The determination of whether to impose extra-territorial subject matter jurisdiction will be a highly factual inquiry which must be made on a case-by-case basis.[4]

1 938 F 2d 1056 (9th Cir 1991).
2 *Reingold v Deloitte Haskins & Sells* 599 F Supp 1241 (SDNY, 1984).
3 *Plessey Co v General Electric Co* 628 F Supp 477 (D Del, 1986).
4 *Dept of Economic Development v Arthur Andersen & Co* 683 F Supp 1463 (SDNY, 1988).

IOSCO AND UK EFFORTS AT INTERNATIONAL CO-OPERATION

13.21 IOSCO is the leading international body concerned with the regulation of securities markets.[1] Its membership comprises regulatory bodies from over 100 countries who have responsibility for day-to-day oversight and administration of securities laws. The preamble of IOSCO's byelaws states:

'Securities authorities resolve to co-operate together to ensure a better regulation of the markets, on the domestic as well as on the international level, in order to maintain just, efficient and sound markets'.

To accomplish this, IOSCO encourages its member regulatory bodies to co-ordinate the establishment of standards and mutual assistance with other regulators as follows: (a) to exchange information on their respective experiences in order to promote the development of domestic securities markets, (b) to unite national efforts to establish standards and an effective surveillance of international securities transactions, and (c) to provide mutual assistance to ensure the integrity of the markets by a vigorous application of the standards and effective enforcement against offences.

1 See IOSCO's website: www.iosco.org

13.22 IOSCO seeks to develop international standards to provide advice for national regulators which serves as a yardstick against which national regulatory efforts can be measured. IOSCO also recognises that providing minimum international standards and effective international co-operation in establishing, maintaining and investigating standards will not only result in investor protection, but also reduce systemic risk. IOSCO recognises that the increasing integration and liberalisation of global financial markets poses significant challenges for the regulation of securities markets. Moreover, markets, especially emerging markets, have experienced remarkable growth in recent years, but have also been exposed to the volatility of short-term capital flows which have resulted in some countries experiencing financial instability and the increased risk of contagion. This has been exacerbated by the lack of transparency and disclosure of material information for investors to assess risks in emerging markets. National regulators must now take account of transactions and activities that occur in other countries and IOSCO seeks to establish standards to assess the nature of cross-border conduct with a view to ensuring the fair, efficient and transparent operation of securities markets.

IOSCO and market abuse

13.23 IOSCO recognises that investors should be protected from misleading, manipulative or fraudulent practices. IOSCO adopts a broad definition of 'manipulative or fraudulent' conduct to include insider trading, front running or trading ahead of customers and the misuse of client assets. IOSCO has designated the principle of full disclosure of material information to be the primary principle for ensuring investor protection. Full disclosure reduces information asymmetries in the marketplace and thereby improves the investor's position to assess the potential risks and rewards of their investments.

13.24 IOSCO asserts that a key component of full disclosure requirements is adequate accounting and auditing standards, which should be of a high and sufficiently robust standard to inspire international confidence. Moreover, only duly licensed or authorised persons should be allowed to hold themselves out to the public as providing investment services. This should also apply in the case of market intermediaries and the operators of exchanges. IOSCO also encourages national authorities to require initial and ongoing capital requirements for those licence holders and authorised persons. These standards should be designed to achieve an environment in which a securities firm can meet the current demands of its counterparties and, if necessary, wind down its business without losses to its customers.

13.25 IOSCO also encourages national authorities to adopt strict standards of supervision for market intermediaries for the purpose of achieving investor protection by setting minimum standards for market participants. Investors should be treated in a just and equitable manner by market intermediaries based on standards that should be established in rules of business conduct. An effective system of surveillance is needed which would entail inspection, oversight and internal compliance programmes for investment firms and intermediaries.

13.26 Investors are particularly vulnerable in securities markets to misconduct by intermediaries and others, but the capacity of individual investors to take action may be limited. Further, the complex character of securities transactions and of fraudulent schemes requires strong enforcement of securities laws. In the event a violation occurs, investors should be protected through effective enforcement of the law.

13.27   IOSCO also sets out the principle that investors should have access to neutral fora, such as courts or administrative tribunals, to seek redress for damages and other injuries arising from market abuse and other misconduct. Remedies should include adequate compensation and/or restitution. The network of mutual assistance agreements that IOSCO has encouraged national regulators to adopt should lead to more effective enforcement. Effective cross-border supervision and enforcement will depend on close co-operation and co-ordination by national regulators. The FSMA 2000 contains provisions that implement many of these principles and standards adopted by IOSCO.

13.28   The FSMA 2000 authorises the FSA to co-ordinate their investigations and to subpoena documents and witnesses from foreign jurisdictions and to prosecute parties allegedly committing acts in foreign jurisdictions that breach the market abuse provisions of the FSMA 2000. Part I of the consultation document issued with the Financial Services and Markets Bill emphasised the need for 'extensive co-operation with regulatory bodies in other countries'. Part X provides for more effective information gathering to be collected as part of investigations in foreign jurisdictions and thereby provides mechanisms for co-operation with foreign authorities. It improves upon the Financial Services Act 1986 and its disjointed approach to obtaining information from abroad and co-ordinating investigations with foreign authorities.

13.29   More specifically, the FSMA 2000, s 139 refers to 'assistance to overseas regulators' and is similar in content to the Companies Act 1989, s 82 amendments where it lists a number of matters that the FSA must take into account before deciding whether to exercise its investigative powers or not. Sections 140 and 141 of the FSMA 2000 authorise broad powers for the FSA to gather information and documents from an authorised firm, its employees and even a member firm within the authorised firm's corporate or entity group. These powers build on existing powers contained in the Companies Act 1989, s 83 amendments.

13.30   The FSMA 2000 makes two important changes with respect to international co-operation and enforcement from previous legislation under the Companies Act 1985 and the Financial Services Act 1986. The FSMA 2000, s 139(6) makes provision for the requirements contained in the Investment Services Directive, making it mandatory for the FSA to respond to requests for co-operation and information from other EU Member State authorities. Further, the FSMA 2000 develops safeguards to provisions authorising disclosure to foreign regulators by more narrowly defining and reducing the categories that can be relied on by UK authorities to reject requests for information and to co-ordinate investigations and enforcement actions. For example, the FSMA 2000, s 305(1) tightly restricts the disclosure of all confidential information that arises from fiduciary and privileged relationships. Such information can only be provided with the consent of the person from whom it was sought. The FSMA 2000, s 306(1) provides exceptions to this restriction on disclosure that will be more specifically defined by regulations that are to be adopted by the Treasury. This list of prescribed recipients will be entitled to take, obtain and utilise information that would otherwise be non-disclosable.

13.31   The principle of reciprocity will determine the willingness of the FSA to intervene on behalf of foreign authorities in investigations and enforcement actions.[1] See discussion in FSA Consultation Paper 17 (2001) discussing the

FSA's powers to intervene on behalf of foreign authorities. The FSA will act if there is a corresponding legal obligation in the requesting jurisdiction that would allow them to provide comparable assistance to the FSA, if asked. The principle of reciprocity is a key component of the UK MOU and mutual legal assistance treaties that authorise UK authorities to co-ordinate information collection, investigations and enforcement with foreign jurisdictions if those jurisdictions allow UK authorities to have reciprocal rights in UK investigations and enforcement actions. The FSMA 2000, Pts IV and XII both provide detailed procedures that authorise the FSA, acting on a request from an EU Member State or other jurisdiction with which it has an agreement guaranteeing reciprocal rights, to support an enforcement action of a foreign regulator by allowing the FSA to vary, cancel and intervene in a regulated firm's ability to conduct permitted financial services activities whilst operating in the UK. Part IV addresses disclosure of information from foreign firms which seek to carry on regulated financial activities in the UK. Part XII authorises the FSA to intervene in order to protect the integrity and good governance of UK financial markets by imposing jurisdiction extra-territorially on persons or transactions outside the UK that may affect UK markets.

1   See discussion in FSA Consultation Paper 17 (2001) discussing the FSA's powers to intervene on behalf of foreign authorities.

13.32   The FSMA 2000, ss 42 and 164 are similar to the Companies Act 1989, s 82(4) in allowing the FSA ultimately to exercise discretion as to whether it should exercise its broad powers. It should be noted that such discretion may appear to be an obstacle to enhanced transnational co-operation, yet this discretion is expressly denied if the foreign authority requesting assistance is an EU Member State based on the Investment Services Directive, as implemented by the FSMA 2000, s 139. Outside the EU, this discretion can only be restrained by bilateral or multilateral agreement.

CONCLUSION

13.33   The barriers to a global securities market are diminishing; financial information is becoming available and inexpensive to obtain and it has been become easier to effect share transactions abroad.[1] Ultimately, the forces of liberalisation and technology will link most financial markets with the result that regulators should develop improved regulatory links to improve the effectiveness and efficiency of their financial markets. National regulatory authorities will come under pressure to enter agreements that allocate jurisdictional authority amongst regulators in different jurisdictions in order to forge a more coordinated attack on those who engage in complex and cross-border market manipulation, insider dealing and fraud. The EU Market Abuse Directive has resulted in a more consolidated and efficient European regulatory regime that can address some of the main challenges in cross-border market misconduct.

1   See Merritt B Fox, 'Securities Disclosure in a Globalising Market: Who Should Regulate Whom' (1997) 95 Mich L Rev 2498.

13.34   The impact of foreign laws, especially extraterritorial US anti-fraud securities laws, will pose a major challenge for regulatory compliance by UK companies and other market participants. US courts apply alternative tests: the 'conduct' test or the 'effects' test. Under the 'conduct' test, the court has subject matter jurisdiction where conduct material to the completion of the fraud occurred in the United States. Under the 'effects' test, the court has jurisdiction whenever a predominantly foreign transaction has substantial effects within the United States. The close links between US and UK securities markets require an analysis of how US securities laws can expose UK persons and other non-US persons to civil and criminal liability for insider dealing and market manipulation. Finally, the efforts of IOSCO have been instrumental in developing international standards in the areas of market abuse and insider dealing that have been generally adopted by most IOSCO countries. The IOSCO standards are important for understanding how the FSA will interpret the market abuse regime and for how the UK courts will apply these principles in legal proceedings.

13.35   Overall, the implementation of the Market Abuse Directive into the UK market abuse regime has created more effective cross-border cooperation and coordination between EEA/EU regulators by requiring states to establish a single regulatory agency to coordinate cross-border investigations and enforcement. This has led to more effective regulatory action within Europe for addressing some of the complexities of cross-border market misconduct. The Market Abuse Directive amended the FSMA 2000 to give the FSA express authority to engage in investigations and enforcement actions in market abuse cases that occur partly or solely in the UK so long as it relates to qualifying investments on a prescribed or regulated market in a EEA state. The FSA, however, has confined its enforcement proceedings to cases with a significant link to the UK financial market. HM Treasury's authority to prescribe markets on recognised investment exchanges that could be based outside the UK constitutes a potentially significant extension of the UK Treasury's and the FSA's regulatory authority. UK financial policy might be guided by a principle that allows it to regulate extraterritorial market misconduct – acts or omissions – that take place in foreign jurisdictions, but have a significant or direct effect on UK markets, so long as substantial wrongful conduct occurs in the UK or conduct outside the UK relates to qualifying investments traded on a UK regulated market. Indeed, these legal and regulatory issues will continue to pose complex challenges for regulators, firms and practitioners who will find it increasingly difficult to reconcile different market practices and attitudes across jurisdictions to market practice, while weathering the storm of today's turbulent financial markets.

Index